Mary Loudon was born in November 1966, the youngest of five children. Brought up and educated in Wantage, Oxfordshire, she left school in 1985 and spent the following year working in Cornwall, America and Israel.

She took theatre studies at Warwick University, receiving an award from the university towards her subsequent work in a street clinic in Calcutta; on her return she won the Margaret Rhonnda Award from the Society of Authors for an article she wrote about this experience. She also won a substantial award from the Society of Authors for her work towards her first book, *Unveiled: Nuns Talking*, which also won her a 1992 Achievement Award from *Cosmopolitan* magazine.

She writes for *The Times* and reviews for the *Independent*, the *Sunday Times* and the *Independent on Sunday*. She has also written for the *Observer*, the *Sunday Telegraph*, the *Guardian*, the *New Statesman*, the *Daily Mail*, the *Sydney Morning Herald*, the *British Medical Journal*, the *Tablet* and the *Catholic Herald*. She has broadcast on television and radio and has won two regional prizes for her poetry, which has been published in an anthology of new writing.

Mary Loudon lives in London and writes full-time. She is now working on a novel.

REVELATIONS

THE CLERGY QUESTIONED

Mary Loudon

PENGUIN BOOKS

PENGUIN BOOKS

Published by the Penguin Group
Penguin Books Ltd, 27 Wrights Lane, London W8 5TZ, England
Penguin Books USA Inc., 375 Hudson Street, New York, New York 10014, USA
Penguin Books Australia Ltd, Ringwood, Victoria, Australia
Penguin Books Canada Ltd, 10 Alcorn Avenue, Toronto, Ontario, Canada M4V 3B2
Penguin Books (NZ) Ltd, 182–190 Wairau Road, Auckland 10, New Zealand

Penguin Books Ltd, Registered Offices: Harmondsworth, Middlesex, England

First published by Hamish Hamilton 1994
Published in Penguin Books 1995
1 3 5 7 9 10 8 6 4 2

Printed in England by Clays Ltd, St Ives plc

'I never saw, heard, nor read, that the clergy were beloved
in any nation where Christianity was the religion of the country.
Nothing can render them popular,
but some degree of persecution.'
Jonathan Swift

'To be a loyal churchman is hobbyism or prejudice,
unless it is the way to be a loyal Christian.'
Austin Farrer

'It would be a gain to the country were it vastly more superstitious,
more bigoted, more gloomy, more fierce in its religion
than at present it shows itself to be.'
Cardinal Henry Newman

CONTENTS

ACKNOWLEDGEMENTS

I cannot thank enough the twelve men and women who so generously and willingly agreed to work with me, and for whom being interviewed was time-consuming and not always easy. They devoted a lot of time and energy to the work, not only during the interviews, but afterwards in further meetings, phone calls and correspondence. They were without exception kind, helpful, and endlessly encouraging about the project as a whole. Working so closely with them has been, for me, the best sort of hard work there is: demanding, challenging and tremendous fun, and I have made a lot of good friends in the process. And to all the people close to those I interviewed, who were friendly and hospitable to me, and for whom this book is also an exposure of sorts, thank you.

I could not have stayed sane during the writing of this book without the enthusiasm, encouragement and support of my editor, Kate Jones, at Hamish Hamilton. Quite apart from having a brilliant mind, her dedication to the work, her friendship, her understanding and her calm in the face of several hiccups went way beyond the call of duty. For all this and more I thank her beyond measure.

My agent, Felicity Bryan, was responsible for introducing me to Kate Jones, as well as being a source of ongoing support, advice and enthusiasm. Thanks also to her cheerful assistant, Michèle Topham. The staff at Hamish Hamilton, as well as being very efficient, are the nicest group of people an author could hope to be published by: Karen Geary, Katharina Bielenberg and Keith Taylor were especially involved with this book and have been extremely helpful. Suzanne Dean designed the cover, and I love it.

An enormous number of people within the Church provided encouragement, time, information, perspectives and a lot of lunches. There were numerous people all over the country from whom I sought information or advice, and who responded with unfailing promptness and courtesy, but I would particularly like to thank Eric Shegog, Patrick Forbes, Steve Jenkins and Andrina Barnden at Church House, Westminster, not only for faxing long and tedious documents whenever asked, but for being so witty about it; the staff at Lambeth Palace for being consistently helpful and accessible, but especially Lesley Perry, for her enthusiasm, her sense of humour and her considerable practical help; and her assistant, Jeanne Newman; Colin Buchanan, for talking to me about disestablishment and for taking me to task over my disinclination to religious belief; Ivor Smith-Cameron, for talking to me about racism in the Church and opening my eyes in the process; Philip Crowe for talking to me about clergy training; Anne Dickens at the Church Commissioners for helping to make Church finance almost comprehensible; Timothy Bavin, Helen Begley, Michael Bunker, Michael Hayes, John Polkinghorne and Jenny Welsh, who were also involved in my research for this book, and who gave much of their time and energy towards it; Raymond Barker at Bishopthorpe Palace, York; and Richard Kirker of the Lesbian and Gay Christian Movement.

Julia Denzil, Kym Dyson and Philippa Gibson transcribed most of the interviews from tape, which is a thankless task, and they did it well and quickly. Of the many friends who were so encouraging, and who refused to take me remotely seriously, Sue Smith and Brendan Walsh were fantastic; Tony Parker, Stuart Proffitt, Emma Lindley, Christos Georgiou and Jonathan Lloyd were all wonderful to talk to and share ideas with at various stages. But it was my friend and flatmate, Sian Edwards, who put up with me on a daily basis, and she did so with amazing patience, humour and understanding. She listened when things went well and when they didn't. For the last six months of the work I was preoccupied, anti-social and domestically useless, but she never once complained.

My parents, Jean and Irvine Loudon, were as encouraging, as supportive and as loving to me as they have been all my life; as were the rest of my family, although a special thank you must go to Martha Norman and Rachel Fogg. Kate Murphy came up with by far the best and most unusable title for the book, and Richard Leverington's suggestion prompted the idea for the actual title. Thanks also to Peter Murphy, for remaining my chief source of Australian irony, my love, but, most of all, my friend – even when 11,000 miles away.

INTRODUCTION

To begin with, I was reluctant to write this book. After the publication of my first book, *Unveiled: Nuns Talking*, it was suggested to me that I might interview the Anglican clergy. In fact I had already thought about the idea, but I was concerned that to follow a book about nuns with one about the clergy was, as a writer, just too obvious. Although writing *Unveiled* was one of the most enriching experiences of my life, by the time I'd finished it I was up to my eyes in other people's faiths, but with little or none of my own. As someone who found myself involved with religious matters almost by chance, I was wary of taking on what seemed like more of the same.

I also thought myself in a poor position to be objective, or at least objective enough. Although it's very old history now, my first real experience of the Church was uneasy. I would not mention it at all but for the fact that it had some small bearing on both my initial disinclination, and my final decision, to write this book. Some years ago I went out with an Anglican clergyman whose faith and devotion to the Church I did not share. The relationship was largely conditioned by his faith, the needs of a parish, the demands of the Church calendar and my stubborn refusal to adhere to all three. Such frustrations produced in me not only an excessive defensiveness and lack of emotional commitment, but a general disrespect for things ecclesiastic and a propensity to behave badly, all of which I look back on now with a mixture of embarrassment and amusement.

They also left me with a lot of questions about the value and purpose of life in the Church, and these questions remained at the back of my mind long afterwards. However, once I was away from Church life I was reluctant to tangle with it again. I had met a lot of good and kind people in the Church, but my experience as a very young woman often in the company of older clergy was not always enlivening, for so many of them seemed to me to be profoundly disillusioned and dissatisfied. There were committed and sparkling exceptions, of course, but they did seem to me to be exceptions.

Whether or not this was true I have no real way of knowing. I do know that at that point in my life my own restlessness made me more aware of dissatisfaction than contentedness in others, but again and again I met clergy who seemed to be suffering from a curious malaise. When this manifested itself, as it sometimes did, in defensive or vitriolic behaviour (the like of which I have never witnessed anywhere except within Church circles), I found myself wondering why. Certainly it said more about particular individuals than it did about the clergy as a whole, yet I couldn't help but feel it to be indicative of an underlying unease felt by a lot of them: an unease about their roles, their purpose, their Church and therefore, if only by association, about themselves.

This caused me to consider very seriously how it must feel to live by a faith which very few people want to share with you, and where that faith springs from in the first place. How could a modern man or woman marry the teaching of the Bible with life in a culture and society that are not only increasingly secular but increasingly scientific and technological? I knew that my incomprehension stemmed in part from my own inability to imagine what it feels like to have a strong faith, let alone one sturdy enough upon which to build a life's work. However, if Christianity really isn't at odds with a twentieth-century view of life, then what does it have to offer, and why do the clergy feel it to be so important?

Even after writing *Unveiled*, which gave me a far greater understanding than I previously had about religious vocation, I continued to wonder what sustained the clergy in the face of scepticism, misunderstanding, hostility and, worst of all, indifference. I wondered how they felt about the central tenets of their faith, which so many people dismiss as inconceivable and as grounds for atheism or agnosticism: things like Christ being

God incarnate, the Resurrection, the miracles, the Virgin Birth, and the concepts of judgment, heaven, hell and eternal life. I wondered how they could explain evil, and how their beliefs in a good and righteous God could be reconciled with individual and global suffering, injustice and disaster. I wondered how they felt about other faiths. I wondered how they felt about the Church: about its decline, its in-fighting, its relationship with society and its attitude towards certain members of it. I wondered if the clergy believed that they themselves even had a future. I wondered and wondered and wondered, until finally there was nothing left to do except ask them.

There are three Holy Orders, or ranks, within the Anglican Church: deacon, priest and bishop. All those ordained into the Church are ordained as deacons: then, after a year or two and in almost all cases, as priests. However, until March 1994 women could be ordained only as deacons: now they can be ordained as priests, though not yet consecrated as bishops.

Deacons can officiate at weddings and funerals, and they can administer Holy Communion, although they can't actually celebrate it. Neither can they baptize or pronounce blessings or absolutions. Priests can celebrate Holy Communion (also termed the Eucharist, mass or the Lord's Supper): they can baptize, pronounce blessings and absolutions, and they can anoint the sick or dying. Bishops, in addition to these things, can confirm lay people, ordain deacons and priests, and consecrate buildings and land. Bishops themselves are consecrated rather than or- dained, although when applied to people the terms mean the same thing. Only archbishops can consecrate bishops. If a bishop becomes an archbishop, no further ordination/consecration takes place: an archbishop is simply a bishop with a particular function.

While the terms deacon, priest and bishop describe what a person *is* once he or she is ordained, they do not describe what that person *does*. The term 'vicar' is used very loosely, and often quite inaccurately, to describe all clergymen and women in the

Church of England. A vicar is a person in charge of a parish and is in almost all cases a priest (as opposed to a deacon). A vicar's assistant is called a curate, and is usually a deacon (but can be another priest). A rector is exactly the same as a vicar, the only difference being a historic one, concerning the way in which they were paid in the past. The term parson is generic: it is not a title.

Those priests who are connected with cathedrals rather than parish churches have different titles. Priests in charge of cathedrals are called deans or provosts, and their assistant priests sub-deans or precentors. Other cathedral clergy are called canons or prebendaries.

Bishops are in charge of dioceses, which are areas, rather like counties, into which the Church of England is divided. There are forty-four dioceses in the Church of England, including Canterbury and York. A diocesan bishop has a chaplain (a priest who is attached to a particular household or institution), but a bishop's chief assistant is an archdeacon, who undertakes administrative functions within the diocese. Most dioceses also have suffragan (assistant) bishops, and if a suffragan bishop has special responsibility for a part of the diocese he is known as an area bishop.

Most deacons and priests are officially referred to as Reverend, although deans and provosts are Very Reverend. Bishops are Right Reverend. Archbishops are Most Reverend. Archdeacons, however, are a curious exception to the general rule: they are Venerable.

The majority of clergy are trained at one of the Church's several residential theological colleges. For those with degrees the training lasts for two to three years: those without degrees may be required to train for four. The Church pays for this training and there is no upper age limit for students, although no one under the age of twenty-three can be accepted. An increasing number of clergy are now training at colleges of further education, or on part-time courses, meanwhile living at home and supporting themselves.

Those men and women seeking ordination (ordinands) have to be sponsored by the bishop of the diocese in which they live. This means going through a fairly stringent selection process at the hands of a committee called the Bishops' Selection Conference. If a candidate is recommended for further consideration by the Bishops' Selection Conference, that candidate's diocesan bishop will support his or her application for training. This application is made to a body called ABM (the Advisory Board of Ministry). ABM will interview the candidate over several days. If a man or woman is recommended for training by ABM, only then can he or she finally embark upon training for ordination.

There are just over 11,000 stipendiary (salaried) clergy in the Church of England, of whom approximately 10,500 are men and 750 are women. In addition to this number there are around 900 men and 350 women who are ordained into the Church of England but do not receive a salary from it: they have other jobs and work in the Church part-time and for no pay. These people are called non-stipendiary clergy.

The majority of stipendiary and non-stipendiary clergy work in parishes, although around 1,600 of them exercise other ministries. Most of these clergy are chaplains of some description: in hospitals, in the armed forces, in prisons, in education, in local industries or to the deaf. The remainder are staff in theological colleges or those who live in religious communities.

The clergy are not very well paid. Parish priests (vicars or rectors) earn £12,800 a year, and most curates slightly less. However, taking into account the values of a non-contributory pension, a free house and some working expenses, which all parish priests get, in real terms this amounts to an annual income of around £20,000. Most parish priests no longer live in large old vicarages or rectories: nearly all of these have been sold by the Church and replaced with more modest accommodation.

Suffragan bishops, archdeacons, deans and provosts earn around £19,000 a year plus expenses and live in rather more impressive houses than parish priests. Most diocesan bishops earn £23,160 a year plus expenses, although the Bishops of London, Durham and Winchester (who are the three senior bishops in the Church after the archbishops) earn more than that. In addition, diocesan bishops also receive a car, a chauffeur, a gardener and a huge house. The Archbishops of York and Canterbury earn £38,150 and £43,550 respectively, plus expenses, car, chauffeur, gardeners, office staff, domestic staff and a palace.

It is perhaps not surprising, given its capacity for internal disagreements, that there is some dispute within the Church of England as to when it was actually founded. In 596 Augustine was sent from Rome by the Pope on a mission to convert the English pagans to Christianity. He was to create two archbishoprics: one in the north and one in the south. Augustine was extremely reluctant to carry out the task. He thought the English were barbarians and attempted to turn back when he reached the Channel, but the Pope insisted that he proceed.

Although London was not the capital of England in 596, exactly why Augustine never became Archbishop of London (which was the Pope's original intention), but instead became Archbishop of Canterbury, is not terribly clear. Some say that Augustine simply never got as far as London, which considering he'd already made it from Rome to Kent seems a rather feeble hypothesis. Certainly London was a dangerous place for a Christian to visit, let alone with a mission, and possibly Augustine decided that staying in Canterbury was a safer bet.

At the time, Kent was ruled by King Ethelbert, who was also overlord of all southern England: in other words, he was a man of extensive influence and power. Ethelbert was married to a French Christian woman who was sympathetic to Augustine's mission, and the King and Queen entertained Augustine with lavish hospitality. Not long after Augustine's arrival in Canterbury, Ethelbert was baptized as a Christian, and in 597 Augustine was made Archbishop of the English by the Pope. He stayed in Canterbury, and his title and location became inextricably bound.

In 627 one of Augustine's companions, Paulinus, was consecrated as Archbishop of York, and for the next 900 years Christianity spread across the country and became the dominant religion. The Church in England remained Roman Catholic until 1534, when Henry VIII passed the Act of Royal Supremacy, which made the monarch, rather than the Pope, head of the Church. The ties with Rome were cut and the Church of England as we know it, the established state Church, came into being.

During the sixteenth century the Church reformed itself (hence the term Reformation, which is used to describe the period) in protest against internal financial corruptions (hence the term Protestant). This culminated in Henry VIII's split from Rome. However, the split had less to do with Henry VIII's wish for ecclesiastical reform *per se* than it did with his combined desire for a divorce which the Pope would not grant, and for greater control of the Church's considerable wealth. None the less, even after 1534 the Protestant Church retained its links with the Roman Catholic Church through the Creed (a summary of Christian doctrine) and the scriptures (the Bible).

Whether the Church of England dates its foundation from Augustine's consecration as Archbishop in 597 or from Henry VIII's proclamation of Royal Supremacy in 1534 is a moot point. It was only after 1559, when there was a second Act of Supremacy, that the Church became known as a Church 'by law established', although it was not until a parliamentary Act of 1701, which stated that in future all English monarchs must be Protestant, that the marriage between the Church and the State finally took place.

Prior to this, in 1563, Elizabeth I ordered a set of doctrinal formulae, known as the Thirty-nine Articles (because they contained thirty-nine articles of faith), to be drawn up in an attempt to define the position of the Church of England in relation to the political controversies of the time. Religion was a warring matter, and the Thirty-nine Articles were kept deliberately ambiguous in order to be as inclusive of as many disaffected factions as possible. Sitting on the fence was written into the Anglican Church's constitution early on.

Today the Church of England claims to be both Protestant and Catholic, and there are large numbers of clergy who regard the Creed and the scriptures as the basis of continuing identification with the Roman Catholic Church. These people, while they are in the strictest sense Protestant, refer to themselves as Anglo-Catholic. This is a crude definition, but in terms of externals Anglo-Catholic clergy can be identified – in church at least – by an emphasis upon tradition and a love of historic ritual, in which things like vestments, candles, processions, incense and sung masses play a very large part.

In fact, Anglican clergy can be divided very roughly into three separate categories. At the opposite end of the spectrum to Anglo-Catholics are evangelicals, whose external identifying features of modernity, spontaneity and simplicity reflect the difference in their theology. This even comes down to personal dress. Again, this is a crude illustration, but the majority of Anglo-Catholic clergy are usually clad in dog-collars, cassocks and suits of black or dark grey, while the evangelical is much more likely to wear light grey or blue, with the dog-collar as an optional extra. The popular stereotype casts all evangelicals as tambourine-wielding zealots, but this is as limited a perception of their diversity and beliefs as the idea that all Anglo-Catholics are starchy, gin-drinking conservatives. Certainly evangelicals are more likely than Anglo-Catholics to wear their faith on their sleeves, but both camps encompass an extraordinary breadth of membership and styles.

Sandwiched uncomfortably between the Anglo-Catholics and the evangelicals are the liberals. The Church of England prides itself on embracing difference, and while Anglo-Catholics and evangelicals often let the side down on this one, liberals struggle to uphold the notion. They are tolerance and moderation personified. They exemplify in their dress, their manner, their worship and their theology a desire to be as acceptable and as inoffensive to as many people as possible, attempting all the while not to undermine their Church or their faith with woolly thinking or behaviour. Many of them find this balance somewhat difficult to achieve.

The Church of England is rich. It is commonly supposed to be the second biggest landowner in Britain after the monarchy. In fact, no one is quite sure about this: it is often said that this distinction belongs instead to British Rail.

The Church has assets of £2·5 billion, mainly in property and stocks and shares. These assets are managed by a body called the Church Commissioners, which was founded in 1948, although it has its origins in two bodies dating back to the eighteenth century. Throughout the 1980s the value of the Church's assets rose steadily to a staggering £3 billion, but in 1990 the effects of the recession, and imprudent property speculation on the part of the Church Commissioners, caused a drop in the value of the assets to £2·2 billion. The Church Commissioners, in effect, lost £800 million, and with it a great deal of respect.

The Church Commissioners were hit hard by the recession. Like many businesses, in terms of investment they were over-optimistic during the eighties. Stipends and clergy benefits were increased to meet rising inflation and the costs of the Poll Tax: so was expenditure on pensions, charities and the repair of Church properties. However, the Church Commissioners' most serious mistake (although to be fair to them, there is no greater wisdom than hindsight) was to finance their property developments with millions of pounds of borrowed money. When the market slumped they found themselves lumbered with properties they could not let, and with high interest rates on loans which they could not meet without making cuts in expenditure, borrowing still further and digging into the Church's capital assets (in other words, selling things off or lending money to others at a poor rate of interest).

Today the Church faces a huge financial crisis. If its investments are to increase sufficiently to meet its growing financial needs, it must cut expenditure by £20 million a year, and it must start now. The Church's historic assets provide about 30 per cent of its total annual income, and while the clergy complain continually that churchgoers do not give enough to the Church in the weekly collection (the average is £3 a week per member), donations, covenants and bequests to the Church currently provide 55 per cent of its annual income. The rest comes from dioceses; from bodies like English Heritage; and from fees for weddings and funerals, which cost a minimum of £100 and £113 respectively (baptisms are free). Although the Government provides only 0·5 per cent of the Church's total income, the Church is exempt from paying rates on church buildings, which means an annual saving of millions of pounds.

The Church spends nearly half its annual income on stipends and training for the clergy: on top of that, there are 10,300 clergy pensions currently in payment, about half of them to widows. Church buildings (there are 16,425 parish churches alone to maintain) are the second highest item in its budget, absorbing 30 per cent of its annual income. Educational establishments, charities and central bodies like General Synod and the Church Commissioners soak up the rest.

The Church's annual income currently stands at around £674 million (£1·84 million a day). It is estimated that in 1995 it will need an income of £718 million (nearly £2 million a day) to meet its running costs. It is hoped by the Church Commissioners that most of this money will come out of the pockets of regular churchgoers. Only time will show whether or not it does.

The Church's political life is almost as complex as its financial one. Its national council is called the General Synod, and it is composed of three houses: the House of Bishops, the House of Clergy and the House of Laity. The Houses of Clergy and Laity are composed of elected representatives from all forty-four dioceses: the House of Bishops contains nine elected suffragan bishops, but the forty-four diocesan bishops belong to it automatically during their terms of office. The House of Bishops has fifty-three members, the House of Clergy 259, and the House of Laity 258; of whom 422 are men and 148 women. (General Synod is reflected at parish level by Parochial Church Councils – usually referred to as PCCs.)

The General Synod prides itself on its democratic structure, even though it is still predominantly male and white, and its members have to be able to meet for nearly a week at a time for two weeks of the year: the latter precludes many people in full-time employment from the opportunity to become members. Having said that, although much of what is discussed in General Synod is mind-numbingly dull or obscure, even the most contentious subjects are debated with tact, orderliness and humour. Compared with the loutish House of Commons, the General Synod is a model of decency and decorum.

An enormous number of subjects are discussed in the General Synod, from ordination measures to Third World debt to the question of how to rid parish churches of increasing numbers of bats without harming them. ('Put a stuffed owl on the altar,' said one member. 'That'll get them out in no time.') Measures are voted upon in the General Synod, and a majority of two thirds in each House is required before a measure can be made law. However, the Church cannot make measures into law on its own. The complicated marriage of Church and State means that the Church has to go to Parliament with its measures, and only parliamentary legislation can turn those measures into Church law (known as canon law).

This, combined with the fact that the Church Commissioners are answerable not to General Synod but to Parliament, is one of the main reasons why some people within the Church wish for disestablishment, for freedom from the constraints of being a State-controlled Church. There is no current movement for disestablishment, as there was, say, for the ordination of women: the last one was during the First World War. However, it has a growing number of advocates, who argue that it is ridiculous for a religious body to be shackled to one which in principle is secular and not Christian, and which very often has differing or opposing political interests.

Furthermore, it is the Prime Minister, and not the Church, who chooses the diocesan bishops and the archbishops. While the Church can select the deacons and priests that it wishes for particular jobs, each time a bishop or archbishop is appointed, it has to submit two possible names to the Prime Minister, with a clear indication of its first choice of candidate for the post. It is the Prime Minister who has the final say, and in their time both Margaret Thatcher and John Major have appointed people who were not the Church's first choice for particular posts.

Advocates of disestablishment want self-responsibility: they want the Church to be able to make its own decisions and its own mistakes, and they want to see the devolution of State power to the Church. However, opponents of disestablishment are worried that if the Church is disestablished, the State will walk away with its money. This is highly unlikely, but technically possible, as the Church Commissioners is a parliamentary trust. There is also the powerful argument in favour of preserving the country's heritage, an argument which is dismissed as pure sentiment by the Church's most vocal advocate of disestablishment, Bishop Colin Buchanan. 'Heritage is just a posh word for history,' he says. 'Slavery is history: so is women not being able to own property or vote. Not all history is something we want to hang on to.'

Nevertheless, full disestablishment would remove for good the inalienable right of the Church to operate in every parish across the country, and this is something which few clergy want. At the moment the Church holds the main responsibility for baptisms, weddings and funerals: disestablishment would mean competition with other denominations, greater self-responsibility and, most threatening of all, no more assumptions.

Out of an English population of 46 million, only 1·2 million people, which is less than 2·5 per cent of the population, attend church on an average Sunday. Even during the mid nineteenth century, a period which is regarded as a golden age of church-going, less than 50 per cent of the population went to church on a Sunday. Church attendance does not appear ever to have been terribly popular.

British society as a whole is becoming increasingly multi-cultural and multi-faith. In terms of religious practice (which is not the same thing as nominal or cultural denomination), Roman Catholics outnumber everyone in Britain as a single group: there are 1·95 million of them, compared with 1·84 million Anglicans. There are 2·98 million other practising Christians, composed of several groups, of whom the Baptists and Method-ists make up the largest proportion: there are 900,000 Muslims; 390,000 Sikhs; 140,000 Hindus and 110,000 Jews. Mormons, Jehovah's Witnesses and spiritualists amount to 460,000.

Most people in England, when asked by researchers, say they believe in God. This belief appears to have little or nothing to do with a specific religious faith, although most English people's God appears to be nominally Christian and vaguely Anglican. Surprisingly large numbers of people still classify themselves as 'C of E' and, strictly speaking, many of them are, as they were baptized in the Church of England as babies. Baptism apart, a sense of affiliation with the Church seems bound up with notions about national identity. Being a member of the Church of England, even if you have nothing whatever to do with it, is still regarded by a lot of people as a component part of being English. If this were reflected by church attendance, the Church of England would be bursting at the seams. But bursting at the seams it most certainly is not.

The Church of England's vision is sometimes that of the pro-verbial tunnel. It comprises only 2 per cent of the 70 million worldwide Anglican communion (the international network of Anglican churches led by the Archbishop of Canterbury), which numbers a great many countries, including, amongst others: Australia, Brazil, Canada, Hong Kong, New Zealand, Nigeria, South Africa, the USA and West Africa. Yet, despite this, there is still a deep-rooted assumption that what the Church of England does sets the precedent. Historically, there is some basis for this assumption, but, to take just one example, all of the aforementioned countries, and more, ordain women as priests, and some of them consecrate women as bishops. Times change, and in the eyes of many people the Church of England has betrayed in its general attitudes an unwillingness to move on or to accept that it is part of something much bigger.

Perhaps now that the Church of England ordains women as priests there is a chance that it will turn its attentions to other pressing matters of discrimination. It will have to if it is to convince people that it really does have more than just pretensions to egalitarianism. For despite the integrity, vision and efforts of many very fine and honourable clergy, the Church of England has a bumpy track record where human rights are concerned: over the centuries its disgraceful treatment of slaves, women, black people, homosexuals and divorced people – to name but a few – has only assisted its dramatic decline in credibility and popularity.

Eighty per cent of the worldwide Anglican communion is black, and 15 per cent of the more populous dioceses in England are composed of black members. Yet with the exception of one diocesan bishop, one suffragan bishop (out of sixty-seven), one cathedral canon nearing retirement and one official spokesman in General Synod, no other senior Church of England position is held by a black person. There are no black staff at Lambeth Palace, no black deans or provosts, and not one black chaplain in further education. Church House (the Church's central offices, and the London venue for General Synod) has only one black official, and she is the secretary of the Church's Committee for Black Anglican Concerns.

Only three dioceses have equal opportunities policies as regards race: a few others are 'thinking of it'. But unless the Church makes a point of considering black clergy for senior appointments, it is in danger of being seen by people within and without its ranks as having a hidden racist agenda. One rural diocese, in a survey commissioned by the Committee for Black Anglican Concerns, responded thus to a question about its efforts to combat racism: 'It is impossible to initiate strategies to combat racism when the problem for us simply does not exist.'

Many clergy cite the leadership of Bishop Desmond Tutu in South Africa as evidence of the Church's fundamental lack of racism, and, what's more, they do it with a straight face. But as the Committee for Black Anglican Concerns points out: 'Slavery and colonization have distorted the encounters between people of differing ethnic groups . . . The Church needs to encourage and support indigenous people rather than go for the easy option of looking for the overseas Church to provide leaders. This reinforces the notion that black people are essentially foreign and transitory.'

In 1991 a written statement called *Issues in Human Sexuality* was issued by the House of Bishops, and this is generally considered to be the Church's current party line on homosexual clergy. *Issues in Human Sexuality* appears to have been a genuine attempt on the part of some anxious liberal bishops to address the issue of homosexuality from a theological and practical point of view, but to many people it reads as illogical, outmoded and deeply patronizing. It contains some interesting references to the 'undistorted will of God', and claims that: 'Heterosexuality and homosexuality are not equally congruous with the observed order of Creation or with the insights of revelation as the Church engages with these in the light of her pastoral ministry,' even though, as it hastens to point out: 'Homosexual people are in every way as valuable to and as valued by God as heterosexual people. God loves us all alike.'

What is most striking about such statements is that they reveal an unwillingness to acknowledge that within the Church there are already many homosexual deacons, priests and even bishops. The Church's official stance is that it does not ordain practising homosexuals, but this is not true. It does ordain both practising and celibate homosexuals, and if it did not the numbers of clergy would be significantly diminished. While Richard Kirker of the Lesbian and Gay Christian Movement estimates that as many as 30 to 40 per cent of clergy are gay or lesbian, most other people within the Church estimate that the figure is much lower, between 10 and 20 per cent. However, as no quantitative research has been done either by the Lesbian and Gay Christian Movement or by anyone else, all figures are guesses.

The Church also displays characteristic ambivalence on the subject of divorce and remarriage. This is probably the area where most confusion and conflict arise between parish priests and parishioners. Parish priests are allowed, though not required, to marry couples where one or both of the parties are divorced. Technically, it is the legal right of divorcees to be married in their parish church even if the parish priest exercises his or her right not to officiate at the wedding. However, on the basis that they have the freehold of the parish to which they are licensed and can therefore do as they please, many clergy over the years have refused to undertake Church marriages for divorcees in their parishes.

In all this the clergy have suffered as much as anyone else. Until 1986 no person who had been divorced, or who was married to a divorcee, could be considered for ordination unless very exceptional (discretionary) permission was granted by the Church, and divorced or remarried clergy have often found it very difficult to get jobs in the Church. Being remarried or married to a divorcee remained a bar to ordination until 1993, when an Act was passed giving the Archbishop of Canterbury the right to offer special dispensation to ordinands in just such circumstances.

The misunderstandings which arise over baptisms are not dissimilar from those arising over divorce and remarriage. Every parishioner has an inalienable legal right to baptism in his or her parish church, although the parish priest does have licence to delay it for 'a period of instruction', either for the person concerned or for the parents and godparents of babies. None the less, it is not uncommon for clergy to imply, quite improperly, that their right to delay a baptism for a short period is the same thing as a right to refuse it altogether.

What these issues have exposed much more than hypocrisy or lack of courage on the part of the Church is the anxiety felt by many people about change: for change irrevocably affects the Church's future. The overwhelming majority of people welcomed the ordination of women as priests, but the debate uncovered a much more general fear that when the Church is tampered with, the very fabric of English life and culture is undermined. That fear is centuries old, and has always been irrationally projected on to different component groups within the Church. The Church has reflected the anger, division, fear – and hope – of the country from time immemorial, and probably quite rightly so.

Working with the contributors to this book was a revelation to me. When I first wrote to potential contributors, I did so out of the blue and to people I did not know before. I tried hard to find people who would reflect something of the variety of men and women within the Church's clerical ranks, although it would be foolhardy to claim that twelve people can represent the Church in all its colours, for they can't. Having said that, although there were people who were obvious choices for interview, like the Archbishops, I tried to select contributors in a way that was as arbitrary as possible, and I did so, when I could, before actually meeting them in person. That way, my decisions were less influenced by my own emotional responses, which was at least a small safeguard against working only with the people I liked best. None of the clergy in this book were my friends or acquaintances before I interviewed them. I find interviewing people I know very difficult, because you do not have sufficient distance to ask them the sorts of intimate questions you need to: nor do they have a sufficient distance from you to be able to answer them. When I explain this to people who ask about the interview process, they sometimes say, 'Oh right. The juicy bits.' By which they mean sex. Inquiries about sex couldn't be further from what I mean by intimate questioning.

Two things I am often asked are: Why do people agree to be

interviewed in the first place? and Do they tell the truth? Generosity of spirit apart, people agree to be interviewed for a great many reasons, some of them more conscious than others, although the one constant is that people are usually very happy to talk about themselves. This is not evidence of alarming egocentricity on the part of the clergy: it is an almost universal characteristic amongst humans, and there is nothing wrong with it. Perhaps the clergy came forward as readily as they did because I gave them right of veto over what went into the final chapters. Being able to remove or modify something you have said in private circumstances is very reassuring. Naturally this gives rise, particularly given the reputation of the clergy for pedantry, to questions about editorial interference on a grand scale. But what has never ceased to amaze me is how little is ever removed from a piece when permission to do so is given. Some of the contributors to this book removed nothing at all from their full interview transcripts: others removed one or two things I would have been unlikely to keep in any case. In the end I lost nothing I needed or wanted to use, and I am extremely grateful to the contributors for that.

As for the truth, I believe that the people I interviewed told me the truth about themselves as they saw it. And if that sounds like a crooked answer, it's because I don't think there is a straight answer to the question. Where affairs of the heart and mind are concerned, truth is a matter of perspective. When people talk about themselves it is not only what they say that counts, but what they are capable of articulating in the first place. Verbal adroitness doesn't necessarily mean a greater pre-disposition to self-knowledge.

Truth does not shine from people like a beacon, it fractures like light through a prism, going in all directions, and as an interviewer you cannot follow every single lead. This means making choices about which questions to ask, and when to ask them, and for every question asked there are inevitably some left unanswered. The same goes for writing. The pieces in this book account for approximately one third of the material I could have used. Deciding what to use and what to leave out involved, like the interviewing, some very personal choices. The result is not objective and exhaustive portraits of twelve people, but instead a reflection of the mood and circumstances of interviews where two people were present.

Having said that, questions are the least important part of an interview. If people want to tell you something, they will. If they don't, they won't. I've always thought that interviewing is a bit like watching wildlife: sometimes you have to wait a very long time for something to emerge. That's why I try to spend the best part of a week with interviewees. The danger of turning up for just one day is of missing them altogether.

This book is not about my beliefs or opinions. However, as they obviously have some influence upon my work, it seems only fair to say that I am not a practising Christian, but neither can I put my hand on my heart and declare myself agnostic. I don't believe that people fit into neat categories labelled believer and unbeliever, yet I have been told by several of the contributors that I do protest too much: that the greatest sceptics make for the most ardent believers (a bit like reformed smokers, no doubt). Perhaps there is some truth in this. I'm not sure. But not long before I completed this book I had a phone call from a wise and plain-speaking friend of mine, a Benedictine nun called Felicitas Corrigan. 'How are you?' she asked. 'Are you happy with life?' 'Yes,' I replied. 'Very happy.' 'Ah good,' she said, 'I'm so glad. But tell me, mia Maria: after talking to all these people in the Church, do you feel safe?' 'Safe?' I asked. 'From what?' 'From God, of course,' she replied. 'From God.' And I confess I found myself lost for words.

I hope my work does justice to the twelve men and women who between them rendered me silent, and whose own words make up this book.

JOHN HABGOOD

Age: 66
Age at ordination: 26

ARCHBISHOP OF YORK

Obtaining an interview with John Habgood felt a bit like taking a driving test: absolutely fine if you're prepared and you keep your cool, but fraught with speed limits and No Entry signs. The instructor in question was not John Habgood himself, but his lay assistant, an impeccably courteous man called Raymond Barker.

Raymond phoned me soon after I had written to John Habgood. The Archbishop wanted to thank me for my most interesting letter, and Raymond (who has to deal with umpteen interview requests) wanted to ask me 'just one or two questions'. What exactly did I want to ask the Archbishop? What was the aim of the book? Did I take notes or use a tape-recorder? How many people were being interviewed? Who were they? What was the publication date? Did I have any particular line I wished to pursue? Was I going to show the Archbishop copy? I was a little taken aback as I'd already set out my aims and terms in my letter to John Habgood, but Raymond, naturally, was just checking.

Raymond rang me the following week in a state of barely restrained excitement. The Archbishop had kindly agreed to an hour's interview, three months hence. My heart sank. Two hours, preferably on two consecutive days, was my absolute minimum, and even that was pushing it. I was extremely grateful, but an hour would be pointless. 'Ohhh,' said Raymond, with a deep sigh. 'Oh dear, oh dear. Let me have a think.'

He rang me the following day: 'Two hours, two days running, all yours. Would you prefer January or March?'

I chose January. It was freezing cold and grey, but York looked stunningly beautiful all the same. The Archbishop's palace is not in York itself, but a couple of miles south of the city, in a small village surrounded on all sides by fields. Bishopthorpe Palace sits at the entrance to the village, with the River Ouse running immediately behind it from north to south, and only a few houses, pubs, a post office and village shops for company. It is a beautiful and impressive grey stone building, wide and fairly low, with an oval sweep of gravel drive to the fore, and gardens to the right. There is a clock-tower at the entrance to the drive which is so evocative of times past that to drive beneath its arch in a car rather than a horse-drawn carriage feels a bit like sacrilege.

Naturally, I had had meticulous instructions from Raymond about parking and entering; which buzzers I must press and which I must not; which doors to go through and where to wait for him. I followed my instructions, found Raymond, and after a warm welcome was shown to the Archbishop's study. 'There's just one thing,' said Raymond, as we walked up the stairs. 'I usually sit in on all the Archbishop's interviews.' I'd been dreading such a moment: how to breach protocol, get my own way and not offend anybody. Raymond heroically saved me from this impossible feat. 'But I think you'd rather I didn't, so I won't.'

Although I'd met him once before, I did wonder, after all this anticipation, whether interviewing John Habgood was going to be like the moment in The Wizard of Oz where Dorothy discovers the wizard to be just a small man behind a curtain. Certainly John Habgood looked a little lost in his vast and beautiful study, and I felt almost sorry for him when Raymond disappeared, leaving him at the mercy of me and my tape-recorder. However, John Habgood is a man used to visitors, used to entertaining, and used to tape-recorders, and although I suspect he quite reasonably finds all of these things trying at times, he was charming and amenable from our first firm handshake onwards. I silently thanked him a hundred times over for agreeing to do something he was clearly not going to find as effortless as some: it would have been very easy for him to say no.

John Habgood's reserve and rather patrician manner have been interpreted by a considerable number of people as evidence of chilliness, yet I found him to be straightforward, friendly and, despite his overall sobriety, with a surprisingly dry — if moderate — sense of humour. He is a man of daunting intellectual stature, and, like many very gifted

2

people, he is visibly shy. He smiled at me a lot during the interviews, I think to reassure himself rather than me, and once or twice there was something hesitant about his speech, as if he were unsure, not of what he had said, but of what I might make of it. This was not unreasonable, as brilliant scientific minds scare me to death and John Habgood was probably perceptive enough to sense that. He spoke quietly, clearly and extremely methodically. There was nothing haphazard or sloppy about his thoughts, and although he is a man more given to investigation than introspection John Habgood did not lack openness or spontaneity. Interviewing him was not only the challenge I had anticipated, but much more fun than I had imagined it would be.

JOHN HABGOOD

I come from a rather curious family. My father was a country doctor from Norfolk and he was quite old, forty-five, when I was born. My mother had been married very young, just before the First World War, and had two children, and in 1924 her husband was killed in a shooting accident. When she and my father married they moved to Buckinghamshire and had two children. I was the second of those two, born in 1927, so there were four of us altogether; two belonging to the previous family and the two young ones.

My mother had had a very romantic background. She was the daughter of a stockbroker who was quite impoverished, but had some wealthy cousins with an only daughter. My mother, being rather lively and the youngest of the family, was sent off in the curious way they had in those days to be brought up with this cousin in this wealthy family. She lived in great country houses, had her coming-out ball in Welbeck Abbey, and her first husband was the grandson of an Irish earl, with a castle in Ireland. So that side of the family was quite exotic.

My father was much more straightforward, of a line of doctors extending back three generations. He was a very accepting, quiet, phlegmatic sort of person, whereas my mother was very vivacious. He had tiny writing and she had enormous writing. They were interesting opposites, but they got on very well. The only thing they ever argued about was money, because he was very careful with money and she was very extravagant. My father said my mother always thought that money was delivered with the morning milk. Yet it was astonishing what one could do with it in those days. I went through his accounts some time after his death and discovered that during the war his total earnings were about a thousand a year, and we lived in quite a big house on the outskirts of a country town,

4

and kept a cook and a gardener, and he had two children at boarding school. That's a portrait of my father behind you there, taken by my sister when he was ninety-five. My mother's is over there. She was quite a beauty in her day.

It was a very happy childhood. We all fitted together remarkably well, even though the two children by my mother's first marriage were quite a lot older and had this strong Irish connection. Ours was a very easy household in which to talk about anything, and I was close to my parents, though it became more and more difficult to relate to my mother because she had Alzheimer's or something similar, and her memory began to go when she was still fairly young. She did tremendous work during the war: she was Chairman of the local Women's Voluntary Service. We lived on the road from London to Birmingham where there were military convoys going up and down all the time, and she set up an extremely good WVS canteen, which not only served food but also provided beds for troops on the move, and I think she wore herself out. In the ten years after the war she went progressively downhill, and in the end it was almost impossible for her to communicate, which really was sad for such a vivacious person. But we knew her very well when we were *young*. I've always been close to my sister. The other two moved away, my brother to the estate in Ireland, and they're both dead now. So. There was no one else I was close to at that time.

I think I always had the worst sort of English vice of self-sufficiency. I could be perfectly happy without other people. It didn't mean I disliked other people, but I didn't actually *need* them a tremendous amount. As a child I was fairly solemn, I think, and I've always been quite non-athletic. I've worn spectacles since about the age of six. I was, I think, disgustingly industrious. A bit of a swot, yes. I remember arriving the first day at my first prep school in Eastbourne: in those days Eastbourne was absolutely laden with prep schools. I arrived late, because I'd been in quarantine for measles or something, and I arrived in the middle of a test in which everybody in the school was asked to write down the names of the twelve apostles. I was the only person in the school who got them right, and, having just arrived, this was not a good way to be popular, really. They also had a wretched system whereby the head boy of the school was appointed on the basis of academic work and not on the basis of leadership qualities. And so, being half-way down the school in terms of age, I found myself as head boy; which again was not a good way to be popular. I didn't really notice whether I was unpopular, though. I don't think I would have noticed something like that.

My great love at that stage was carpentry. I adored making things. My father had a workshop at home, and my greatest delight was to go into the workshop and mess about with things. Prep school was good too, because they had a very well-equipped workshop. All rather solitary, though we used to play a lot of card games at home, and at my second prep school one of the curious institutions was that the senior boys played bridge with the headmaster. On Saturday evenings we had *Nicholas Nickleby* read to us by the headmaster's wife, and on Sunday evenings we played bridge. Actually I wasn't bad at it. I continued playing bridge right through to university, and then dropped it for a reason which I'll tell you later.

Shortly after I went to Eastbourne the war began, the school was evacuated to Somerset, and I went to another prep school in Bedfordshire, which was closer to home. It wasn't a very good school, it was quite eccentric. It was in the early years of the war, and in French lessons all I really remember learning was how to dismantle a Bren gun, which was a sort of light machine-gun! The French master was very keen on the Home Guard, you see, which was then the local defence force, so there was a serious purpose behind it because in those days there was a real threat of invasion: we used to listen to the German planes coming over, and spent many nights in air-raid shelters.

I think as a child one doesn't really recognize the seriousness of what's going on, but it was a fairly disrupted sort of life, with this haphazard teaching. The school didn't know much about scholarships either. I think I could have got a scholarship to Eton but I don't think they'd ever sent anybody for an Eton scholarship before and they didn't realize that you have to do Greek. But one of the housemasters of a not very flourishing House at Eton was looking out for bright boys, and there was a distant connection in the House with my mother's side of the family, and I think they must have taken me on more or less free. I don't know what the financial arrangement was, but my father can't have paid much. So the fact that I went to Eton is not to be taken quite at its face value. I was never one of those wealthy children who would automatically go there. It was a choice between Eton or Wolverton Grammar School.

My overall memories of Eton are mixed. I enjoyed the work, and that sounds a terribly dull and pious thing to say, but I've always enjoyed learning, and I don't regret having spent hours and hours at seven-thirty on cold winter mornings writing bad Latin verse, which was what one used to do in those days. I also discovered science. I think I was drawn to science partly because of the practical bent which I've talked about: I like doing things with my hands. I think also that people who are perhaps not terribly good at relating go into science because you are dealing with things which are under your control, which don't answer back! I've often noticed people of my sort of temperament going into science and then perhaps growing through it. But I was interested in it, I was good at it, and I won all the prizes in it during my last year at Eton. I then got a state bursary to go to Cambridge, and that paid all the fees. This was towards the end of the war, and the government was trying to get people to continue research in radar, so physics and maths were very much the skills that they were looking for.

The thing I really hated at Eton was compulsory games. Nowadays they let you do all sorts of other things, like natural history, but in those days you had to do violent exercise. I did quite enjoy rowing, and wasn't as bad at rowing as at games involving balls, which I can never see: I've always said it's

7

eyesight but I suspect it's just general incompetence! They made me captain of the 3rd XI in cricket at my prep school, because as head boy they had to make me something, but I was never any good. Rowing was fun because some of it is done in eights or fours, and it's actually a very good way of being together: the Eton Boating Song – 'Swing, swing together, your body between your knees' – actually represents an experience. You also used to have your own boat, a little thing called an outrigger, a very narrow smooth-skinned boat, and you could row off up the river by yourself, which I enjoyed. I liked to be by myself.

By the time I got to Cambridge the war had ended and I was part of that extraordinarily mixed generation of those who'd come straight from school and those who'd come out of six years in the Army. I never went into the Army. I did research for the Medical Research Council as my National Service, because they were trying to divert people out of the Armed Forces by then. It was a very lean time because the rationing was much worse after the war than during it. Life was very restricted. Travel was difficult, food and other things were in short supply, parties and entertainments were rare, so we were forced to be a rather serious and self-sufficient generation living quite close to actual suffering. My brother who was in the Army had been wounded twice, once in France and a second time in Burma.

This seriousness persisted at Cambridge because school-leavers like myself were working alongside those who were now frantically trying to catch up on five or six lost years. I was helped by the fact that my Director of Studies at King's, Cambridge, didn't like rather dull boys who were just interested in physics, chemistry and maths. They're all fairly arid subjects. So he said to me, 'You must do physiology.' I didn't know what it was, and when he explained I said, 'But I've never even done any biology.' He said, 'Well, you can learn.' So I did physics, chemistry, physiology, and maths as a half-subject, and by the time I'd done the first part of the Cambridge Tripos, which is two years, and got a First in it, I was so fascinated with physiology that I went on to do Part Two, and became a research physiologist.

I began growing into a much greater interest in the human, as opposed to the mechanical or the merely physical. Physiology then was a subject done by all medical students, but there weren't many people who remained pure physiologists. As a result, those who were doing research immediately found themselves teaching, and at the age of twenty-one, having just graduated, I found myself supervising undergraduates. I've been a teacher ever since, really. When you're teaching you have to understand what the difficulties that people are encountering really are. It's also good for developing relationships, and I became more and more interested in people. This began my shift into quite a different sphere of life.

Nobody ever talked about religion at home. We sometimes discussed the vicar, but then I suppose most people discuss the vicar. Religion was there in the background, and nobody would have dreamt of saying, 'We're not good Christians', but I think it's fair to say we were not *keen* churchgoers. We went most Sundays to our local church, which was very high, and my parents would be involved in the usual activities like church fêtes, and my mother was involved in all sorts of good works in the town. But in those days one was very conscious of the social divides. We didn't really know 'chapel' people, for example. As a doctor's son in a small town ... well, you're a doctor's daughter from a small town, you know what it's like. It's socially divided.

I really can't remember anything about religion in my prep schools, but I suppose it's indicative that it didn't make much impact. All prep schools are religious, and when we were in Eastbourne we trotted off to one of the local churches. It was just something one did. But the *words* get into you and I think that's important. At Eton, compulsory religion every day was part of the routine, and I quite enjoyed it. I was confirmed there but then decided fairly soon after confirmation that I didn't believe any of it. In fact, I went through quite a spell at that stage, from about seventeen onwards, of very firmly rejecting anything to do with it. That lasted until the second year at university.

When I arrived in Cambridge I still played bridge. One of the people I frequently played with was Peter Swinnerton-Dyer, who was later the Chairman of the University Grants Committee; at Eton we had been together in a class of two for physics. He was an excellent mathematician, and was frightfully good at bridge, much better than I was. Anyway, I began to get a bit bored at having my mistakes analysed after every hand: one evening he'd invited me to bridge and I felt, I really can't stand any more of this. I'd had an alternative invitation to go to a meeting for Old Etonians, in connection with an evangelistic mission going on in Cambridge. So I went along and found a rather remarkable group of people who showed up my adolescent atheism in quite a poor light. I began going to the mission meetings and was converted, and I stopped the bridge. I've never played since, lost interest in it. From then on I was studying the Bible rather than studying trumps.

My conversion was embarrassingly quick, really. Having been a person who had been sticking my neck out, endeavouring to prove to others what a sensible policy atheism was, I was vulnerable to conversion because I was concerned about religion. I suppose it was all part of the adolescent process of finding oneself. I hadn't come across people before who were either so explicit about their faith or so certain about it or so obviously living it, and this was very impressive. My intellectual objections began to appear less important in the light of this, so in a sense I was converted first and have been working out the intellectual implications ever since.

Looking at it with hindsight, I think the whole thing was about seeing myself as really rather dull and cheap and self-centred, and this made me reach out to something new. Mine was a typical university evangelicalism; I became involved in boys' camps and converting other people and all the other

Christian Union Activities. I think I must have been intolerable! One of the problems was that in your eagerness you could develop a kind of falsity in which you were really only interested in people in order to get their scalps, and I began to realize the artificiality of this. I was also thinking and reading quite widely and didn't stick to the normal evangelical fare which was recommended, and this reading introduced me to a much wider world.

I made contact with the Franciscans who were active in one of the churches in Cambridge, and this was an introduction to a strand of Christian faith which rang bells with my upbringing in a very high church. And I realized then that all those people who'd seemed in retrospect rather dim may actually have been rather good Christians, but I hadn't been seeing it.

So although the process of growing into something else belonged to a different and slightly later stage, I am grateful for the evangelical experience, because it began a change in my relationships with all sorts of other people and the development of some very close friendships, as well as involvement in social activity of a religious kind, which was new for me.

Partly through being involved in evangelical groups where people thought about ministry; partly, and I think probably mainly, through teaching, I began to think about ordination. I taught for Downing, Girton and eventually King's, my own college, and I became very interested in the students as people, usually developing the kind of relationship in which they would talk about themselves; and finding that there was a ministry there, I seemed able to listen to them and communicate with them.

That extended outside too. In the evenings I used to eat in a small restaurant on the outskirts of Cambridge, where I was lodging, and there was an elderly woman who was rather bemused about religion and who used to come and sit at my table, and we'd talk. Eventually she told me she had cancer, and we talked through that, and I saw her through until she died. And this too made me think: why don't you do this more?

I was attracted by communicating with people on a fairly deep level. There was also the sense of actually having something to share, of the evangelistic impulse, talking with other people on a deep level satisfies that impulse, and It's a good thing to do. And I think by the time I was dealing with the students, and with some of the older people I made contact with, I'd gone a long way beyond the kind of artificiality of the undergraduate coffee party to which you invite people in in order to work the conversation round to religion. This time it was a genuine interest in and concern for people, and the beginnings of a recognition of how people suffer and how they get lost, get frightened.

At that time I was not terribly conscious of these things in myself. I've felt ashamed, yes. Puzzled, yes. At times, mostly since ordination, when facing the kind of darkness which comes over people, and the sort of questioning which we all have to go through, I've felt darkness, and I've probably learnt more about myself through ministering to other people. But I never had much cause to doubt myself, which I think was all part of my being this rather self-satisfied child, the youngest of four, who was loved and secure and did well. I've doubted myself since, oh yes, yes, of course. But hypocrisy is the endemic sin of religious people.

However, I think the *trigger* factor in it all was the Korean War. This was the first major conflict after the dropping of the atom bomb, and it was very much on the cards that atomic bombs would be used again. I remember going round as a very pert young demonstrator and asking the people in the laboratory, 'Why do you do research? What interests you?' The answer came back from most of them, 'Curiosity,' and being a bit pious I said to myself, 'Is curiosity enough?' I think now I'd probably say it was, but then I was all for doing good for mankind! Anyway, with reference to the Korean War I thought: if there's a new war and you've got to start rebuilding a world, what ought you to be doing? And I thought, well, I shouldn't be cutting up rats. There are more fundamental things to deal with.

I think this was the fruit of all that dullness and solemnity at an early age, you know, my being so pious: I wanted to press below the surface of things and ask the big and the hard questions. I don't think I had addressed those things when I was younger. I think my adolescent atheism was an attempt to face them, and face them in a rather superficial way; and I think in the job that I'm in now, and indeed in any ordained job, what motivates you is the desire to press questions back to their roots until you see something which transcends them. That is a basic religious imperative. So then ordination became a fairly obvious step. By that time I'd got a fellowship at King's, and I thought, either I stay in Cambridge for the rest of my life as a don or I go and do something else. I'd been in Cambridge from 1945 until the beginning of 1953, nearly eight years. So I left. And I'm sure that was right.

Because I was an evangelical and felt that I had so much to learn about the rest of the Church of England, I deliberately chose to go to a High Church college, Cuddesdon in Oxford. In those days it was very isolated, because it didn't have all the connections with Oxford which it has now, and the teaching was pretty bad, really. In fact, we sent a deputation to the Principal at one stage to say how awful it was. We did New Testament, Old Testament, Church history, liturgy, doctrine, Greek, but it didn't actually make us think very much. It was the sort of boring stuff where you sit down and people lecture at you and you take down notes. The ethos was set by the Principal, Edward Knapp-Fisher, who was new, and had come in after quite a lax regime. Edward Knapp-Fisher was a rather dour bachelor who was determined to tighten up discipline. So we learned doctrine by going through the Thirty-nine Articles, and I'm not aware that we were taught any ethics: I think we must have been but I've forgotten what.

Worship was a great thing at Cuddesdon, and they also taught you to pray. How? By giving you a lot of time in which to do it. There was compulsory meditation every morning, the Daily Offices, the Eucharist. We alternated between the college chapel and the little village parish church, which was rather nice because you got a combination of different styles. What I particularly remember about Cuddesdon was the combination of time, worship and scope to read. You also went out and did practical things in hospitals and this kind of thing, and went off to stay in parishes during the vacations. I learned a lot during one vacation by working in a mental hospital in East London, which was a formative experience if ever there was, because I was just an orderly. That was in the days when if people were mentally ill they were just locked up and that was it, there wasn't any real treatment.

I realize the training sounds a bit dry, but I suspect that some theological training now falls down through being too busy and too fragmented because, poor things, they have to learn so many more disciplines. We were quite innocent of psychology and sociology and management techniques: the presumption was that if you needed these you could pick them up as you went along. I think we went into it knowing that for the rest of our lives we were going to be living very busily, exposed to all sorts of pressures and all sorts of people and all sorts of doubts. So it wasn't cosy. I remember explaining to one of my evangelical friends why I was going to Cuddesdon. I remember saying that it was like a prolonged retreat where you went to discover yourself and your roots, and what you were trying to do was to come to terms with God. That's not cosy. I mean, the training had its cosy aspects, but I think those were less important than the reckoning with what the Church of England was, and what *you* were, before God, which was at the heart of that experience.

However, because I arrived late and left early I was only at theological college for a year and a half. I managed to pass all the necessary exams, but I did pathetically little theology. I've no theological degree, all my DDs are spurious. But I count theological college as an important experience. I met one of my close friends there, a chap called Nick Stacey. He was an

Olympic runner, so we fitted together like hand in glove, with my being so sporty! He received a lot of publicity in his early years and is not so well known in Church circles now; but he was a tremendously entrepreneurial chap, a very powerful character, very disrespectful of everybody. We were total contrasts and rather liked each other and we still meet.

When I left Cuddesdon I did a curacy in London at St Mary Abbot's in Kensington, where I was part of a large staff. That was quite a brief experience, two and a half years, but it was very formative. This was a great London church, which was still recovering from bomb damage. It had a corrugated iron roof, so that when it rained you couldn't hear yourself speak, and it had no loudspeaker system. After my first year I was put in charge of a little daughter church. We worked fantastically hard. The Sunday programme was Communion at seven and eight, Sunday Eucharist at half past nine, Matins at eleven, another Communion service at twelve, children's service in the afternoon followed by baptisms, Evensong and a young people's discussion group, just to fill up the rest of the day. That was a typical Sunday. The congregation was made up of a mixture of old Kensington inhabitants, young people in bedsits, and young people starting up with the BBC, and much of my time was spent preparing individuals of that ilk for confirmation. So we had long discussions with all sorts of fascinating individuals, trying to teach them about the Christian faith, about God.

Being a clergyman is a curiously divided role. There's a certain professionalism based on theology and the ability to translate theology into terms of ordinary life, and those are things which, alas, quite a lot of clergy don't have. A certain amateurism is also required, because it is a role which puts you in contact with a whole range of life in a way which very few other roles do. The astonishing thing is that you are accepted by all sorts of people as having something to offer them in their situation, and therefore you have to learn a little bit about an awful lot of things, so that you can make contact with them.

You have to listen, you have to try to interpret, and theological training splits itself rather uncomfortably between these two things.

There's a lot of dispute as to what the proper background for the clergy is. I would say quite firmly that it's theology, because unless you are relatively secure in the world of theology you are rootless and dependent on secular techniques which anybody else might have. I say relatively because theology is not a secure-making subject. But you need to have a sense of where spiritual insight lies in really quite complex situations, of where God lies.

How did I see God? Well, I can perhaps best explain that through a story. When training at Cuddesdon, we only preached one sermon. This was a sermon to the college, which was then pulled to pieces by one's fellow students and staff, so it was quite an alarming occasion. I had been highly offended by a lecturer who had come to the college, actually a very famous and good theologian whom you will not have heard of, a man called Mascall, who was an Anglican Thomist, i.e., an expositor of the theology of St Thomas Aquinas, and who had very ordered, academic, precise, philosophical ideas about God. I felt totally revolted by this, so I preached my college sermon against him, about how God was the ultimate mystery. I remember one analogy I used. I said that to know God is like seeing the point of a joke; you can't actually explain it, and to try to removes the humour. Actually it was quite a good sermon. I preached it again last year!

But it *offends* me if people think they know too much about God, and this is not because I'm a woolly liberal – which I don't think I am – but because the language about God only makes sense if it refers to that which is actually *beyond* human experience. So all our language is a groping after God; all our images are broken images and so on. There was a book published some years ago, by J. B. Phillips, called *Your God Is Too Small*, and I think lots of people's Gods are too small, in that God's very nicely buttoned-up, thank you, and talks to me every morning, and God's my pal, my friend. Whereas my view of God is rooted in wonder, it's rooted in ignorance. I'm in many ways quite attracted to the Eastern Orthodox view of God as ultimately unknowable, and therefore all that you can say about God are negatives, what God is *not*, which is apophatic theology. For me, the roots of that concept of God lie in science, where you do learn to wonder. I suppose all my adult life I've tried to bring together those two great things in my life, science and faith, and you never do it, because they're both moving objects. Science is always changing and faith is always deepening.

There is a general supposition that the two are incompatible, but I would want to say that God is not part of a scientific story. You don't tell a scientific story and then say, oh, terribly sorry, we've come to a problem here, let's bring in God. Religion is about *meaning*; it arises as you ask, what's this strange thing called life about? What's this strange thing called the universe about? You can trace the story scientifically, or historically, but you are still left with the question – say of the universe – why is there anything at all rather than nothing? Now, you don't answer that by saying, ah yes, well of course it began like *this*. You're looking for a reality which *underlies* the reality of the world in which we live and which we observe. You've asked me about God and time. Augustine very brightly said that time was created by God, that creation didn't occur *in* time, but that against the background of an eternal being there is an outpouring of love for what is *not* God. So one can see creation as something that is at a distance from God, in order that it may reflect back to God something of His own love and glory.

What's the point? Oh, I think it sounds trite, but I think creation was brought about in order to create new possibilities of love: free love, the free self-giving of that which is not God back to God Himself. Yes, of course you can say that that's narcissistic or pointless, but you can only say that when you've gone through a much more lengthy and agonizing process of trying to make sense of the world as we experience it.

If you take the story of the development of faith in the Bible, you can see all sorts of concepts of God's relationship to the world being looked at and rejected, so you get some really horrible views of God in the Bible. Deep within, though, is the sense that there is this fearful and wonderful mystery with which human beings have to wrestle in order to discover themselves. And this is not a solitary thing, it's a communal thing, learning about existence in relation to this reality. The question of what the character of this reality that you're dealing with is becomes more and more pressing, and the final answer given is that its character is self-giving love. Now, it's when you've got to *that* point that you can say, well, why should love want to create anything at all, seeing all the misery that there is in the world? And here you come up against insoluble questions except to say that Love creates for love, out of sheer exuberance of self-giving.

Although my time in London was very happy I left sooner than I should have, because I was invited to become Vice-Principal of Westcott House, the theological college in Cambridge. This was embarrassing because I'd only done eighteen months of theology myself, but it was the sort of offer you don't turn down.

There were only three of us on the staff, a Principal, a Vice-Principal and a Chaplain, and we taught across the board; or at least I did, because the Principal only taught prayer. So I lectured in almost every theological subject, and was there for six years. I learned all my theology teaching it, because I jolly well had to. I don't think they suffered too much through having me as a teacher, but my being appointed was not untypical of the Church of England in those days, which was a good deal less professional than now. In a way my appointment was a fraud.

Whether or not I've been too self-assured in accepting such things I think is for somebody else to answer! I think because I've usually been teaching at the edge of my own knowledge there hasn't been much scope for feeling secure. I've always held to the principle that you can only teach if you are at the same time a learner, and therefore you can't go on churning out the same old stuff. I've always felt that the best teachers are those who see the problems of those they're trying to teach, which means feeling them as problems yourself. I've tried to continue teaching through my ministry and now I do a lot of lecturing. I prepared seventeen lectures last year, and for most of them I was stretching myself, because I'd choose some absurd title two years in advance and then find myself having to write the lecture a month or so beforehand. But I'm quite glad always to have been an amateur teacher of theology and quite an amateur bishop too, because I've always learnt enough to be able to hold my own.

After that I spent four to five years in Scotland, in a small place called Jedburgh, which is a border town. Being an Episcopalian, an Anglican in Scotland, meant that one was a non-conformist, and this was a good experience because it gave me an insight into what it's like to be outside the Church of England looking in. There were about three hundred families we looked after, ranging from nobility to immigrant workers, with not much middle-class, so it was quite an interesting congregation, and a lovely little church. I also used to lecture in Edinburgh Theological College once a week, on ethics, so it was a good, varied place in which to be. We went there primarily because at that time it looked very much as though the whole ecumenical field was opening up in Scotland. The then Bishop of Edinburgh, Kenneth Carey, had been my Principal at Westcott House, and there were conversations going on between Episcopalians and the Church of Scotland, which were subsequently scuppered by the Scottish *Daily Express*, and no doubt by other factors as well, but the Scottish *Daily Express* ran a campaign against any plans for unity. We did a lot ecumenically in Jedburgh, though, a surprising amount for the time.

I was married by this time. I had met my wife in Cambridge, during my last year at Westcott House. I'd worked with women doing physiology, and in the Christian Union at Cambridge I met the first girl I ever seriously went out with. But in those days 'going out' did rather mean going out to look at a historic house or something. I hadn't really thought about marriage very much before meeting my wife, because I'd got a totally absorbing job to do, but by the time we met I was thirty-four and she was in her early thirties too, so we were both people who were old enough to know our minds. She's a musician, and she'd moved to Cambridge to take up a job at King's Choir School and St John's Choir School, and she'd done some concert piano work before that. We met shortly after she arrived in Cambridge, because a friend had brought her along to a party at which I happened to be present, and things took off from there. We met in December and were married by the following June.

The great advantage of this job, of course, is that you work from home. Although you're out an awful lot of evenings, and these days of course I travel a great deal, there is a basic sense of living within the family. I always tried to spend a lot of time with the children, and I think we've done all the normal things that one would do with children. My wife has tried vainly to keep control of my diary and occasionally complains that I'm doing too much. But in the family we've always accepted our different interests and responsibilities, and my wife has never come round with me to endless confirmations and parish occasions, which she would simply hate. She's been concerned to make a secure and happy home for the children, and I think this is shown in the way they've developed.

I think the whole post-modernist tendency towards individualism makes it very difficult to believe or to find where a faith which has universal claims fits into an individualist approach to life. Intellectually that's a problem, but it's not one which worries me emotionally because I think a lot of post-modernism is rubbish anyway. Everybody gets emotionally depressed at times and wonders what they're doing and then picks up again, and I don't think I'm any different in that from anybody else, but it's never occurred to a debilitating degree. Perhaps that's because I've always been in circumstances where things are happening around me. One of the pitfalls for bishops and archbishops is that you're always going to churches which are *full*. I think if you are a country vicar ministering to six people week in, week out and seeing that you're not making very much impact on the rest, it would be easy to get depressed and wonder what you're spending your life on. That's why as an archbishop you have to remind yourself constantly that what you see is not the whole picture.

I've never had a crisis of faith or belief as such, but soon after ordination I went through a fairly hard intellectual time. These were times when, in terms of the philosophical fashions of the day, linguistic analysis was right at the fore, and there was a lot of good thinking being done which actually made it quite hard to see where belief fitted in and how it could make sense. So I had a lot of struggles in those days. I think now I'm less put off my stride by intellectual problems of that kind, because the older you get the more you see problems coming round and round in circles.

I have problems with some things. I have a problem with heaven and hell as they are commonly described. But I think the traditional language of heaven and hell is a vivid way of expressing the seriousness of our choices. I find it difficult to think that God who I believe is eternal love can give up on people; but then one runs into some fairly stern things said in the New Testament! I did write an article some time ago about the only hell being a self-made hell, and got a very cross batch of letters from people who clearly had in mind many whom they would like to consign to a God-made hell!

But I do think that a great many Christians have a very literalistic sort of faith, and you've got to learn when language is meant literally or metaphorically because the Bible uses language on many different levels. Some people faced with the question of the Virgin Birth, for example, would say, well, if it's there in the Creed and you're a real Christian you accept what the Creed says, full stop. What I would want to say is: why is it there and why is it important? I would want to argue backwards, as it were, and say that the fundamental truth which is being safeguarded here is that the life of Jesus is the revelation of God, and is to be understood in terms of the *action* of God.

The *reason* for believing that statement has really nothing to do with the Virgin Birth itself. The Virgin Birth is to be seen as illustrative of it, of the truth, that God acts in and through the life of Jesus. Now, is it illustrative because it draws on concepts of the time and a lot of Old Testament imagery, which the stories certainly do? Or is it illustrative because it actually happened like that? I think one can say with reasonable certainty that the stories, whether they refer to history or not, are written up, and they deliberately draw on Old Testament imagery in order to make their point. Whether there's a historical core to which this relates can be argued either way, and I would hope Christians would be happy to feel agnostic about this because nothing very much hangs on it.

Of course, much hangs on God being incarnate as Christ, and on the Resurrection, but again, in considering the Resurrection, the question to ask is, why are the stories told in this way? Particularly as they don't agree with each other! You can't actually reconcile them, so obviously in the writing of the stories of the empty tomb, say, there's been a good deal of licence. Now the disciples *believed* the Resurrection because they *believed* they had an experience of the risen Christ; and central to their witness was the appearance of Christ after his death, and not the empty tomb; they never referred to the empty tomb in their preaching. The *reality* of the experience is demonstrated by the boldness with which the early Church went out preaching its gospel. After all, if there wasn't something that made them believe, *why* did they believe? So the root evidence for the Resurrection lies in the existence of the Church rather than the other way round. This was expressed in terms of experience of the risen Christ, but part of the vindication of the Resurrection as a historical event is that it actually *works* in terms of changing people's lives.

There are problems about these stories, but they're not incredible. You can ask, why was the Resurrection expressed in terms of stories of an empty tomb, and then you're back where you were with the Virgin Birth. You can see how a story of this kind can be written up in different ways. It is possible, like the Bishop of Durham, to remain open about what actually happened in the tomb while remaining very firmly of the belief that something properly called Resurrection did happen, which I think is roughly his position.

You have to begin with what's real now. And the problem is, we read the stories as if they were the evidence, because that's the way they are presented. Fine. To appreciate what Incarnation is about, you need a vivid image, and you couldn't have anything much more vivid than the Nativity stories. Unfortunately though, it's easier then to get hung up on virginity, and one can see sexual distortions arising out of this as well as all the good things. But what is hard to tolerate in the Church is people who say, 'This couldn't have happened like this,' because that is a direct attack on what many people hold very precious. That's why my question is always: why is this important and why do you believe it and how are you to understand it? I think that's a helpful approach to much of the Bible. It can help you not to slip into the fundamentalists' attitude to it as a sort of inspired encyclopaedia in which you just look up what happened and what you ought to do.

The Christian faith on the whole has practical rather than theoretical answers to problems. Take evil. Why does evil exist? The practical answer takes us to the heart of Christian faith in the redemptive power of the Cross. Also, you've got to work out what kinds of evil you're talking about. Natural evil – earthquakes, hurricanes, floods, and so on – is part of the vulnerability of the environment in which we live, which perhaps could only have produced creatures like us because it *is* vulnerable in that way. Indeed, if you look at the course of evolution it has been the cataclysmic changes which have drawn out new possibilities of living forms, new responses to new environments. Putting it in theological language, I would say that God has taken the risk of creating a universe which is open to accident, to disaster, which can go terribly wrong, because somehow out of this, new possibilities can arise which couldn't arise in something which was from the start created static and perfect.

I would also say that God *allows* evil rather than creates it. And He suffers it. But I believe there is such a thing as evil will in us, and I think it's important not to follow the fashion of always explaining it away. You can say, well, Hitler was so awful because he had an unhappy childhood and was rejected, and so on and so forth. You can see predisposing causes which create the possibilities of evil. But I think people can still make wicked choices or false choices, and can only escape from them by taking responsibility and recognizing evil in themselves. This is why the Christian approach to these things through repentance, forgiveness, death and new life is an assertion of the freedom of the individual. To take responsibility for yourself is to grow as a person. To slough off responsibility on to other people is to lock yourself more firmly into a chain of cause and effect and diminish yourself as a person. So certainly we must analyse the causes of evil. We must try to eliminate them. But not in such a way as to take away that ultimate personal responsibility.

After five years in Scotland we moved to Birmingham, so I could be Principal of a theological college there. Queen's had been an ordinary Church of England theological college, and the initial idea had been to develop it as a staff college for the Church of England. However, the completion of the rebuilding coincided with the bottom dropping out of the ordinands market, because this was the beginning of the sixties, when people no longer thought of the Church as a sensible way to use one's life. There was a marked decrease. I mean, it dropped from something like six hundred a year down to three hundred or so: so colleges were in rather a desperate situation, and this college, which had been built for eighty, had, when I arrived, seven students from the previous generation. One of the main buildings was entirely occupied by Pakistani lodgers, who were lovely people, but something very radical had to be done to build up the college.

We immediately started negotiations to turn it into an ecumenical college. There was a large Methodist college in Birmingham, which was also in difficulties, and the Principal and I began negotiations. It all happened very quickly. After my arrival in the autumn of '67 we were united by 1970. It became Anglican/Methodist, with some United Reformed members, and we had close relations with the local Roman Catholic seminary, but not union with them. It was a fascinating period because it was something which hadn't been done in this country before, and the sixties was a very turbulent time anyway. It was like riding a lot of very frisky horses all at the same time, but it's gone on and flourished from there.

My interest in ecumenism developed at Westcott House, where there was a relationship between the different theological colleges in Cambridge and we occasionally met for united worship. It seemed to me then, as it seemed to many people at that stage, an enormously important rediscovery of something which had been lost. I was conscious of the absurdity of many of our divisions, in particular in line with what I was saying to you about God. It's always seemed to me to be rather offensive towards God that we should shut ourselves up in little separate boxes, all of which are saying they are the right one. So in a sense ecumenism springs directly out of my understanding of God.

How far does it extend? Well, it extends towards Judaism a very long way because we share so much in common with Judaism. Muslims: I mean, I've had dialogue with Muslims, and have got on very well with some individual Muslims, but Islam is culturally enormously different from Christianity and you very soon come up against some blockages which it's difficult to get round. I feel that in many ways Islam finds it difficult to enter into a real conversation, because if you've got an infallible book in which everything is laid down, there's really nothing you can do about it. You just do what you're told. Many perceive Christianity as being like that, yes. But you will generally find that the Christians who are like that are not ecumenical because they think they've already got all the answers. We all do that to a certain extent, it's perfectly true, we all approach faith with cultural presuppositions, and with a history. But we have to learn to identify our own prejudices if we're going to meet people who come at faith from different angles.

I was in Birmingham for six years, and then I was made Bishop of Durham, at the age of forty-five, which was quite a shock, because Durham is one of the five senior bishoprics. I hadn't even been a parish priest in the Church of England, and I very quickly had to learn how the Church of England actually works at top level.

A happy shock? Gosh, you've caught me there. I suppose . . . No. No, I wasn't happy really at first. Queen's had become an ecumenical college in the autumn of 1970. The Bishop of Durham, whom I knew well, and liked very much, died in October 1972. In January of 1973 I had a letter from Ted Heath, saying, would I be Bishop of Durham? I felt that what I'd started at Queen's was still too fragile to leave, so I came and sat in this very room to talk to Archbishop Coggan, and said, 'Look, this is absurd.' But he persuaded me that they were not going mad and that I ought to take it. So I was consecrated on 1 May 1973, and we moved out of a flat into a seventy-eight-room castle.

We had four small children at that stage, because our youngest son had only just been born, and we'd never even seen the house before we agreed to move into it. I saw a picture of it in a biography of a Bishop of Durham, and thought, 'How can anybody live in that sort of house these days?' And in those days there was no training for bishops. You just arrived.

The job needed a lot of work. My predecessor, Ian Ramsey, was a tremendously creative person, but he had started lots and lots of things and left them in the air. And because his system had depended on him keeping all these balls in the air himself, they all fell down when he died. So the whole thing was a mess.

I made lots of mistakes, but not disastrous ones, I think, and of course I learned. Also, the Bishop of Durham, being one of the senior bishops, goes straight into the House of Lords, and I very quickly had a prominent place in the General Synod, so it was a whole new world. It was exciting, and I enjoyed it – I've enjoyed everything I've done, I think – but it was a shock at first.

As the Bishop of Durham I couldn't help but be involved with miners, and very soon after I arrived in Durham there was the 1974 miners' strike. Before it started the Durham miners' leaders came to me as their bishop and said, 'Can we talk?' So we talked, and they spoke very frankly about their inability to get through to the Government, about the fact that the radical Yorkshire miners were making the running and that the moderate miners were willing to settle for something very modest. So only a few months after arriving in Durham I found myself trying to intercede with the Government, and we saw how the whole thing fell to bits, largely through a cock-up at Government level. Some years later, at a conference with Edward Heath and Robin Day, we went through the whole story and it became obvious that the Government either wasn't told, or wasn't able to hear, what was being said to it by people who could fairly easily have avoided the strike which brought the Government down.

The 1984 strike was quite different and a very much trickier issue to deal with. I was not so closely involved in that, because I was Archbishop of York by that time. But the Church of England took a long time to recognize what was happening in the eighties. I think we assumed that you could go on in the rather gentlemanly consultative way that we had followed before, and therefore we were probably fairly ineffectual. I think we underestimated how little the Government listened.

The eighties were a dispiriting time, with Thatcherism and all that. In terms of public life, the most difficult thing about the eighties was the lack of communication with the leading politicians of the day, because we were pilloried as a Church, while saying some quite sensible things, not least about the poll tax. We sensed that values were being commended which were in the long run subversive of the very society which at its best the Conservative Party was trying to create. I had a fascinating evening some years ago with an inner think-tank of the Conservative Party, which had been one of the influences on Mrs Thatcher. I was asked to speak on rendering to Caesar the things that are Caesar's and to God the things that are God's, and it was illuminating but somewhat alarming to explore the gulf of misunderstanding that existed and the way in which my words were taken up and thrown back at me in quite a different sense. That's just a personal illustration of a general difficulty which existed during that period.

I think as a result the Church has learnt some political lessons. But in many ways the Church is not involved enough in the life of the nation, and I see an awful tendency to withdraw still further. All the talk about dis-establishment is a symptom of wanting to diminish this sense of responsibility for the national life. In so far as I've been involved in ecclesiastical politics, I have attempted to keep the Church of England open to the society in which it's set, and for which I believe we have a responsibility.

I was Bishop of Durham for ten years. Then in 1983 I was appointed Archbishop of York, and the first thing I was plunged into was the row over the new Bishop of Durham's consecration. I received an enormous petition against his consecration, and had to make a decision then about what sort of a church the Church of England is. Consecrating him was an expression of belief that the Church of England is an open church. After all, the sort of things he was saying about the Virgin Birth and other matters weren't new, they'd been said roughly every twenty years.

The main difference between being a bishop and an archbishop is that although I have a diocese, the Diocese of York, which is a big one geographically, I have three suffragan bishops, and they take the main responsibility for the day-to-day pastoral care. I make the final decisions on things like appointments and discipline; I'm a court of appeal beyond the suffragan bishops when things have gone wrong, and I share in diocesan and parish occasions when I can; but apart from all that, my job is mostly at national and international level. I was for eight years a member of the Central Committee of the World Council of Churches, and during that time I was Chairman of the Church and Society Sub-Unit of the WCC, which was largely concerned with scientific and environmental policy at a global level.

The Archbishop of Canterbury and I work together very closely, and at national level we really share the work. At the moment, for example, he's away, so if anything urgent needs to be said or done it comes to me, and then there's constant pressure from the press. But usually he takes the brunt of the media, he takes the lead on the major occasions. In terms of the planning and administrative work I'm more fully involved than he is. In fact, I see my role as being a bit of a backroom boy in terms of the administrative load of running a national Church. For example, in the House of Bishops we share the chairmanship between us, but I'm Chairman of the Standing Committee which does the planning for the House; I am also Chairman of the General Synod Policy Committee, which does the background thinking about priorities. And in the Synod itself, the Archbishop of Canterbury would expect, on major issues, to give a magisterial overview, whereas I've always seen my role as coming in with a more particular viewpoint.

When we disagree? Hasn't really arisen. Well, all right, people do disagree in the Church of England, there's nothing new about that, but part of the *art* of being an Anglican is learning how to live with those with whom you disagree! We all give different emphases to things and I think that's healthy. He and I do consult, and I think if there was a serious disagreement on something we would try to thrash it out beforehand, and of course it depends on what it's about.

It could have been difficult if we'd disagreed about the ordination of women. But we didn't. Having said that, I would have preferred it to have happened rather differently. When a decision was made some years ago that in principle there was no objection to the ordination of women, the vote was taken not to go ahead and the matter was left in the hands of the House of Bishops. The idea was that the Bishops would then bring it back to the Synod at the time when they felt it was right. But you can always get hijacked in synodical processes because dioceses and private members have rights, so this piece of legislation came in on a *diocesan* Synod motion, at a time I thought very inexpedient. What I'd envisaged was that we would ordain deacons and get used to them, and then allow the women ordained abroad to minister in this country, so people would get some experience of women priests; and then after that one would move to raise the substantive issue. The aim would have been to try to secure maximum agreement so that the legislation could have gone through without all this trouble.

You can say that that's soft, but I think that a lot of people *are* very worried, both clergy and lay. Many were surprised by the strength of the reaction against it. York is a diocese in which there was a fairly heavy vote in favour. When I invited clergy who were worried by it to come and meet me here, *eighty* came – out of 320. Now the vast majority of those are people who very much want to remain part of the Church of England and I'm pretty sure will accept the proposals that the House of Bishops has put out. But it *is* a serious business.

Homosexual clergy, on the other hand, have been ordained for years, yet what has made the homosexual scene so much more difficult recently is a certain aggressive openness. This is a difficult thing to say to you because the convention in the past was that if people kept quiet about their homosexuality, then nobody would bother. But many are not prepared to keep quiet now, for very good reasons. And I think the Church is going to need a long time to work through this, and would be helped by an understanding on the part of homosexuals that this is not homophobia, but that there are fairly profound theological issues which are raised by the whole thing.

The message the Bishops have tried to put across is this: yes, there is a moral grey area here, and we respect people's choices; but because clergy are public figures, and because they're open therefore to public scrutiny, people do, for good or ill, see them as role models. Therefore we draw the line at allowing clergy to live in quasi-marriages of a homosexual kind. We went as far as we felt we could in trying to be understanding and sympathetic, but it's unsatisfactory, and I don't see things changing quickly.

I am, I hope, a very tolerant person, and I'm not personally offended by the things homosexuals get up to. But I think many of their problems would be solved if there weren't the kind of defensiveness which shows itself in rather *outré* behaviour. I think there's also in many homosexuals quite a revealing kind of self-hatred, and many of the more irresponsible things are done as a way of saying, 'Yes, I know I'm awful and I'm going to prove it to you.' Therefore I would want the Church to provide a supportive attitude; not one which says, 'Homosexuality doesn't make any difference,' because I think it *does* make a difference, but one which recognizes it as a *different* condition which has its own problems but is not a reason for social ostracism. Sexuality is for so many people such an emotive subject.

There was a lot of speculation about me being made Archbishop of Canterbury at the time when Robert Runcie was made Archbishop of Canterbury in 1980, and that would have been absurd. Then when the latest appointment came up I said, and meant it, that at sixty-three I was already too old for it, because it's a hugely demanding job, and I had no wish to start again on something else.

I didn't mind at all about Canterbury, I honestly didn't. I'm not ambitious. I'm a person who's always interested in what he's doing, and obviously I'm motivated by a Christian concern and I am ambitious in that respect, but I've never sought posts. Anyway, this is a much better job in many ways, because you can have all the fun of being an archbishop without all the responsibility of Canterbury, and without such huge pressures. The negative side is that all the worst problems land on your desk, and it's then you say, I wish I wasn't Archbishop; I wish somebody else could decide this. And there are moments when you realize that what you're going to decide is going to be very important for a large number of people, and that can be alarming. There are also very boring aspects of it, one of which is an enormous post. Look at my desk.

But really it's a marvellous job, because I've enough support so that there are lots of things I don't have to worry about. I have an opportunity to meet huge numbers of people, to go to fascinating places. I am forced to think very hard about a lot of very difficult things. And because for most of my life I've been in positions of leadership, it doesn't worry me terribly. But I think there is a danger of becoming self-conscious and saying, I must *do* things, I must make my mark, I must *initiate*. Whereas it's been my experience in the Church that most of the best ideas and creative movements come from people who are at the coalface and not those who sit in palaces.

I think I'm quite a severe self-critic, so I don't *think* I'm dependent on the attention, but you have to be careful. Oh dear, it's difficult to answer that one because it is easy to fool oneself at many different levels. I mean, part of this job is to create *occasions* for people, and there's a lot of emotional satisfaction in that, which you have to be careful not to bask in too much.

I think anybody in a position of leadership would like the power to implement their ideas, but if you believe, as I do, that power is dangerous, then you are thankful for the many checks and balances which exist within the Church of England. If you want to get something done, the Church of England is a maddening instrument, but Churches are necessarily fairly conservative bodies because they are representing something which is eternal, and not something which just belongs to 1994. The Church needs a strongly committed core which expresses its identity, but it also needs very fuzzy edges, so that it can reach out.

It is tempting to do your own thing sometimes. I have my own line to pursue, as everybody has. But the thing which has motivated me most strongly is to help Christianity to be seen to be credible by those who carry intellectual or political responsibilities. That's what archbishops are *for*. Within a hierarchy an archbishop relates to the nation, so it's important that he should know some of the people who operate at national level. I have retained contact with some of the people I was at school with; people like Douglas Hurd and Robin Leigh-Pemberton. That's the great thing about Eton: you can meet a very wide variety of people. But Etonians aren't around as much in the Church as they are in government, so my main use of my intellectual background has been in trying to demonstrate to the scientific and medical and political worlds that Christianity really has something to say in those spheres.

You want to know what really makes me tick. Well, one thing which makes me tick and may surprise you, is poetry. I like a wide variety, although I have certain favourite poets. I suppose I read more of R. S. Thomas than anybody else, his spirituality speaks to me. I love Browning. I'm an avid admirer of Eliot, as I suppose most clergy are. Larkin I enjoy. And I enjoy dipping into new poets, discovering people. I also took up oil painting a few years ago and enjoy that very much. You can make mistakes in oil painting, and then correct them. That's what I love about it.

I think the other thing is that since the age of twenty-one I've been a teacher, and in order to teach I've been concerned to try to understand where people *are*. I do have strong views. I have my own prejudices. Sometimes I get stubborn. Sometimes I get annoyed. I get annoyed when people *lie*, because that makes communication impossible. I get annoyed when they deliberately misunderstand or misrepresent. And I *care* about what people say about me, but I think I've got to the stage at which, instead of saying, 'Poor me,' I say, 'Poor them, I wish they understood a bit better.' Oh, now that sounds awful. No, that sounds really awful! I say this particularly of newspapers. And I think my getting annoyed is a reaction to being hurt.

At the same time I think it's fair to say that as a bishop and archbishop I'm someone who has tried to surround myself with people who are different from me. I think that's due to a consciousness of how easily one can be led from an open attitude into a mere *flabbiness*. So I see them as an important corrective to my predominant line on things, which has its dangers. Because I'm a very conservative person really. I recognize acres of conservatism in myself.

But I love the Church of England – that's a funny thing to say – because I think it represents a truth about what it is to be a rounded human being. And that is always under threat and always capable of being misunderstood. I get accused of being a woolly liberal, but the concern to see different sides of a subject is, I think, innate. It's part of my background, my education, my temperament, and it comes out of a scientific training too, because you don't jump at answers, you question. The critical spirit which has been a major factor in our civilization, but is also at the moment perhaps one of its greatest dangers, is very much a part of me and I don't think it goes with the label liberal or conservative or anything else. I rejoice in it.

DAVID PERRETT

Age: 45
Age at ordination: 36

VICAR OF NEW OLLERTON, NOTTINGHAMSHIRE

'*I must warn you*', *David Perrett wrote to me,* '*that there is no way I could qualify as a "typical" Anglican clergyman. In many ways I am an iconoclast. Still, feel free to get in touch.*'

I got in touch. David Perrett lives in Ollerton, a coal-mining community in Nottinghamshire which was torn apart by the 1984 miners' strike. My brother lives in a village near by, and David Perrett came to his house to pick me up and take me to a pub outside the parish, where he explained the finer details of the miners' strike to me and put the miners, the Government, the Church, my brother, and his beer, to rights. There was nothing especially iconoclastic about this: David Perrett's spirited and opinionated view of the world was no more than I would expect from most people in a pub on a Friday night. Having said that, it was a good deal more intelligent, more interesting and more entertaining than anything I had heard for a while. I wanted to work with him very much indeed. '*Are you game then, Dave?*' *I asked him half-way through his beer.* '*Oh, go on then, why not? Give it a whirl. Don't say I didn't warn you.*'

The warning was unnecessary, for David Perrett's bark is a lot worse than his bite. His bark is certainly loud, and at times quite aggressive, but behind it lies a rock-solid commitment to his faith. '*That*', *he said,* '*is my one redeeming feature.*' *He can be defensive, self-protective, prickly, but he is more often affectionate, enormously understanding and full of plain common sense. Tall, broad and strong, with a round face, greying hair and large hands, his physical message is definitely of the don't-mess-with-me variety. I've seen him in clerical shirts and collars, but when I interviewed him at home in the middle of a sweltering June week he was wearing loose cotton trousers and an open-necked shirt:* '*I would have worn shorts,*

35

but I didn't think I should inflict my legs on you.'

We talked in his study for three days, taking breaks to eat Knicker-bocker Glorys and watch the Wimbledon highlights with his wife, Dorothy, and daughter, Andrea. He smoked throughout the interviews – 'Excuse me while I light a fag, flower' – and, because he was expecting an important call that week, continued to answer the tele-phone. 'Yo! Perrett here!' he would bellow cheerfully into the receiver, which made a refreshing change from the David Attenborough-like tones of quiet concern specially adopted for the phone by the majority of clergy.

David Perrett was an invigorating interviewee. He listened carefully to my questions and usually chewed them over slowly before answering. However, discourse is sport to David Perrett, and sometimes he tackled questions like a rugby player – straight in without fear of bruising; sometimes he tossed them gently back and forth; and sometimes he would turn them back on me at great speed, which was as disconcerting as it was intended to be. Unlike most of the contributors, David Perrett believed that if I could question him about his faith he had every right to question me about my lack of it. I was inclined to agree with him, which was just as well. The challenges came thick and fast and if my performance wasn't up to scratch he was quick to tell me. 'Come on, Mary!' he'd cry, from the theological touchline. 'Call that an argument? You can do better than that.'

I enjoyed every minute of it.

DAVID PERRETT

I'm feeling really laid-back at the moment. I've just had this amazing sabbatical in the States, and I think I'm feeling like this just because I've had time to reflect on my life, which I've never really had before; probably because we started a family so early – we got married at twenty and had three kids under four by the time we were twenty-four. Then I was in business and earning a crust; then I changed careers half-way through and went into the Church; then I moved to a busy parish where I was in charge of three churches and 16,000 people, and did four years there; then I moved here into the midst of a place that was recovering from the 1984 Miners' Strike.

What with the family growing up and all that trauma, well, there was never much time for *me*. I don't mean like going fishing, or on holiday, I mean a substantial period of time where you can allow things to fall into some sort of perspective; the freedom to examine things that you'd been putting off for years and years; silly little personal things, habits, quirks, why do I do things this way? Why do I do them that way? Why am I a very balanced person with a chip on both shoulders? What do these chips consist of and why do I hold on to them? Why do I hold on to things which betray attitudes that are unsatisfactory from a Christian point of view? You don't get the time and space in the hurly-burly of bringing up a family, changing careers and establishing a new one, to look at these things; you don't get that time.

So being in the States for seven weeks: first of all we had two weeks of quality time for Dorothy and I. When you're sat in a car together for two weeks driving across nine states, you know, you really can't avoid each other, and there are some things that come out that you need to do as a couple, things you need to talk about. Secondly, I went on a placement to a church where I didn't have to turn up in the morning if I didn't want to. I didn't have to go to this meeting, that meeting; I could bum about in shorts all day if I wanted to, which gave me time to think, time to pray, time to doze off if I wanted to. All that was lovely, because I could allow things to fall into perspective.

Since I've come back, all sorts of things have resolved within the family. I've found that I've underestimated my kids; that they've had to make quite considerable steps and take very mature views because of being pitched into a clergy family at a very significant time in their lives, at eleven, twelve, thirteen. I mean, the poor little beggars didn't have any preparation: that was what Dad was going to do, and they had to put up with it. Since I've been back they've been able to talk about life, the universe and everything to me. We were out in the garage, me and the two lads, till half past one the night before last, and they really wanted to talk, about their hopes, their fears, their ambitions. I've never had the time to do that. It's been hard enough to keep on top of the job. I never had time to sit out in the garage with the kids for three hours.

I wish to goodness I could have this sort of break every year. I've come to be very thankful as a result of this one. That old Salvation Army song, 'Count your blessings, name them one by one', there's an awful lot of wisdom in that. I began to think, well, I've got the most marvellous woman I've ever met as my wife. My kids are half-decent human beings. And then I realized how much I had to be thankful for, and in the ministry where you're give, give, giving, you get out of touch with your own needs, your own thankfulness, because you're servicing others all the time. When that happens, you're no good to anyone.

The other thing about California is, every day it was just sun, and that affects their theology. Did you know they have no theology of winter over there? Imagine that: no theology of winter and darkness. Anyway, it's all put me in a very good mood. You've caught me at a good time.

I was a baby boomer, 1948. Mum and Dad were married during

the war, on the shortest day, December the 22nd. Dad was in the Army then, in Italy, Montecasino, where the Yanks bombed as many of their own as they did of the enemy – according to him. After that he came out and drove a lorry for British Road Services, and that was a pretty hard job. I've known him to be up at four, and he had to load the lorry himself, drive it to wherever he'd got to take it, and unload it and load it back up before the end of the day, and then he'd stay over somewhere. He was on the Bournemouth run – Northamptonshire to Bournemouth – and the driver did everything. No fork-lifts then. It was back-breaking work.

I was a latch-key kid. Mum worked. I can remember sitting in a shed in the back garden of my granny's house, and inside the shed were two industrial sewing machines, and my granny and my mother worked side by side, with me sat in the corner in a playpen all seasons of the year. They 'closed' boots and shoes: 'closing' is putting the various bits of the shoe together, the front, the sides, the tongue. I remember Granny and I with sacks of completed closed uppers, putting them in an old pram and wheeling them across the village to the shoe factory where they'd be finished, and the soles and insoles put on.

To start with we lived with Granny and four uncles and aunts, which Dad found fairly difficult. Then we moved to our own house, on a council estate in a village in Northamptonshire, and Mum went out to work in the shoe factory, where she would start at eight o'clock in the morning, and we'd have to get our own breakfast and get ourselves off to school. In the summer we spent most of the time out in the fields and woods and rivers, amusing ourselves, playing football until ten o'clock at night.

I never knew my father because he was always at work. If he wasn't on the lorries, then he was working twelve-hour days, or twelve-hour nights, and if he worked twelve-hour nights, I and my brother had to be out of the house because Dad wanted sleep. If he was on twelve-hour days we didn't see him at all.

We saw a bit more of him later on, when he became a foreman at a plastics factory.

Mum was a very strong personality. I think Dad was much more easygoing, and was bullied by my mum, who had all sorts of hang-ups about what people would think of us; she'd do things, or not do them, because of what people would think, and I inherited that. I also inherited her temper; oh dear, the good hidings I had just because she lost her rag. I remember once – those old wooden coat hangers, she broke one of them across me! Another time – I mean, I was a handful as a kid – but another time I had run her ragged, because I was refusing to go back to school in the afternoon, and I was only six, and she actually threw an old wooden scrubbing brush about twelve inches long at me, and it caught me right across here. I've still got the scar. My granny put half a pound of butter on it.

I actually loved school. Mum often used to say, 'If you had a choice you'd live there,' and she was right, I would have done, but I left school at fifteen. No GCSEs, no O-levels, having failed the eleven-plus. I left and swore I would never go into a factory, and got a job in the chemistry laboratory at the local non-ferrous foundry, because I was interested in science. However, because I hadn't got the maths to make it a career, I moved from there to SAATRA, Shoe and Allied Trades Research Association, in the Applied Physics section. That's when I came into my own, really. I worked as a lab technician, and the research scientist would say to me, 'Dave, I need a piece of kip that will do this, this and this: this is how I have to do it, this is how it works. Can you make me a piece of kip?' and that was wonderful, you know. The scientific discipline is something that I've been terribly grateful for, because you test things and test things, and I learned that at SAATRA.

That was an idyllic time in some ways, between fifteen and eighteen, because I got to know my father. We used to play chess every night, and he introduced me to classical music. He was a very remarkable man in lots of ways, a non-drinker, he could mend anything; I've seen him persist with a watch for literally weeks. He used to make aeroplanes too, out of balsa wood, proper ones that would fly, and he loved to be inside engines; he wasn't happy unless he was filthy. I had no patience, I was a flibbertigibbet. My mind was like a butterfly.

While Dad had the most amazing patience, Mother was totally different. We would argue, debate and discuss, Dad and I, but an argument was wrong in my mother's eyes. I suppose she felt that because I wasn't a very nice person, really. I had a reputation for being quick with the mouth and quick with the fists, and that got me into a lot of trouble with my peers and contemporaries as well as with Mum. It was made worse by the fact that I was so tall. I'm six foot two, and I just tower above everybody, and that didn't help as a kid because I threw my weight around. With a mum who was pretty overbearing, and a dad who I couldn't relate to for years, I was a pretty screwed-up kid, and when I was working at SAATRA I was right into drink and drugs and rock and roll. Having said that, I've still got a book on the shelves there, presented to me by a schoolmaster, for outstanding leadership. I always try to live up to that.

I was a very unhappy person then. I was a bit of a thug. It was the drink, really, drink and women, and experimenting with all sorts of substances. Then quite by chance – I could sing a bit in those days – quite by chance my mate and I who knocked about together on motor-scooters, we decided to go round to the Methodist Youth Club where they were putting a folk group together. Well, I loved to perform. At school I took all the leads in the musicals and all the plays that the school put on, and for two years I won a place on the county drama course, which was two weeks away at Grendon Hall in Northampton-shire. There was one point when I very seriously considered going to RADA, and I would have loved to do that.

Anyway, they were putting this group together, and I im-posed myself and started to sing with them. I was a bit of a loner, not many friends, and I took up with these people and found a family that I had always wanted. You see, Mother would give you the shirt off her back, she would give you the last ha'penny out of her purse, but she would never give you any sign of physical affection whatsoever. If I'd come back having been in a fight, then as far as she was concerned it must have been me. If anything went wrong, it must have been me. And it wasn't me most of the time, but I started to live up to the reputation, you see. Why not? It's easier. If you're going to get a belting, you might as well get a belting for something that you've done.

We had a good family life, don't get me wrong. My mum and dad couldn't have done any more, bless their hearts. They stood by me when I said, 'I'm not going to the factory,' and when I got qualifications they were thrilled to bits, but Mum could never give the physical, she could never cuddle, she could never kiss me. I remember the night before I got married, I actually asked her to cuddle me, to give me a hug, and she said no.

Anyway, I took up with these church people and they were nice, good, genuine, thoughtful, truthful people, who treated me with respect, which I felt I'd never been treated with before. They said they were going away on a Methodist Youth weekend at Grendon Hall and did I want to go? Did I! Two months before we were due to go, I came back one evening from my usual pub, which was two villages away, and I missed the bus. I was plastered, out of my tree, and as I wove up the road to this bus stop, who should be standing there but the girl I sang with in the group. So of course I started chatting her up, and I sat on the bus with her and walked her home, but didn't have the courage to ask her out, so I asked her mate to ask her for me, and to my real surprise she said yes. So we started to go out together. She drove a motor-scooter as well, and she was as mad as I was. Now, I've met high and low; I've met bright, I've met thick; I've met all sorts of women in my life – attractive, unattractive, clever, able, the whole lot. I've never met anybody who can hold a candle to Dorothy, I really haven't. I was hook, line and sinker. She's extraordinary.

So we went to Grendon together on this Methodist weekend.

On the Saturday me and some of the other blokes, we decided we were going to inveigle ourselves into the girls' dorms. Now, the guy who was running this obviously knew the score, and while we had supper he gave us this talk, a 'Don't do this, chaps' talk. He quoted the words of Jesus from the New Testament, Matthew 18, and I have to tell you that it was a Damascus Road type of experience. Up until that time it was as if I was stumbling around in the dark, and suddenly the lights went on. He didn't know it, and nor did anybody else. It was just the normal thing that he would say to a group of young people on a Saturday night when hanky-panky was on the cards, but the lights went on like that: bang.

When we went outside, Dorothy and I, to say goodnight, I said to her, 'I've just realized what this is all about, this Christian thing. I've got to do something, haven't I?' I think at that moment I knew I had to make a response. I didn't know how far-reaching that would be, but I knew I had to make a response to a God who knew me absolutely right through, who could see through me. And Dorothy, she was amazing, she just left me to get on with it.

That's how it all began. I then began to learn, because none of my family went to church; church was there for baptisms, weddings and funerals. I began to attend worship regularly. A fortnight after that experience I turned up on the Sunday School Superintendent's doorstep and said, 'Please, I'd like to be a Sunday School teacher.' A *fortnight* later! A week after that I had a class of twelve-year-old boys, about eight of them, and I was learning as I taught. I'd only been to Sunday School twice as a kid; they kicked me out for being disruptive and unruly.

Within two years of that night at Grendon I was Sunday School Superintendent. I started to preach on the Methodist circuit as a local preacher, and I took my lay preacher's exam. I was doing night-school every night, trying to get my academics up, working like stink, as well as doing my job and my church work, really burning the candle at both ends. Then I asked Dorothy if we could be married, and I realized then that I wasn't going to make a career out of science, I hadn't got enough qualifications. Weetabix had just advertised for an assistant computer operator, so I applied for that. I started at Weetabix on May the 1st and we were married on May the 24th, 1969.

Again, I started as the lowest of the low, and within a year I was Operations Manager with about eight people under me, and I just learned on the job – I had to. Soon after that I was promoted and we moved to Leicester, where I was in charge of a big department. It's interesting; when I went to the selection conference for ordinands, the hard man on the committee said to me, 'You don't seem to be able to hold a job down,' because I'd had a few jobs by then. And I was quite a bolshie individual, even more so than I am now, and I said to him, 'Have you got a degree?' and he said, 'Yes.' I said, 'That means nothing to me. I employ people. I hire and fire. Your piece of paper means nothing to me, because I've done the job. I've worked fifteen hours a day. I've been there before anybody else was in the department, and I've been out after everybody else. I learned how to do the job. Your piece of paper doesn't mean anything.' He didn't like that, but it's true. I once employed a bloke with two degrees, and all he was fit for was putting price stickers on books, and that's all he did. I haven't got any degrees, but I can do the jobs, and I won the respect of my people because there was nothing I wouldn't do. So everything I've done, I've done it the hard way. I haven't gone in waving a piece of paper saying: 'Employ me.'

I'd never thought about ministry at all. I carried on preaching in the Methodist Church, holding down a job, bringing up a family, running the youth club. Then I thought to myself, 'It would be lovely to work for the Lord full-time.' I'd also begun to get a bit fed up with the Methodist Church, I felt it had lost its way, lost its *raison d'être*. A friend of mine said, 'Why don't you try St Mark's, Woodthorpe?' and I said, 'The Church of England's next door to Rome. Not on your life.' But he said, 'Go on, give it a whizz,' and I gave it a whizz. I went one night to Prayer Book Evensong, and I tackled the Vicar afterwards, in my usual inimitable way, telling him that this business of set services was terribly bad and awful and wrong – and I found that he was an ex-Methodist. The most wonderful, gentle person I think I've ever met. A lovely man.

He persuaded me to look a bit deeper, and stop being so damn cocky, stop being a pain in the butt. So we started going to St Mark's, and after a year the curate left and the Vicar invited me to take over the youth group. I said no; he said, oh please. So I did. I started with this gang of teenage kids – there were about thirty of them – and within about six months we had a case of spontaneous evangelism that I have never seen before or since. I took a dozen kids away on a house-party for a whole weekend, and at the end of that weekend eleven of the twelve said that they wanted to make a commitment to Christ. They were a mixed bunch. Three of them ended up going to university, some were real thugs – I've always had a soft spot for the crook. We came back and the Vicar rang me up the following Sunday night and said, 'What's going on? These people have come back, and they say they've met with Christ and they've been converted.' So I said, 'Yeah, what about it?' He said. 'They want to be re-confirmed because of you! I'm going to have to get the Bishop in.' Now, of course you can't re-confirm someone once they've already been confirmed, and most of these kids had been confirmed at the age of twelve, but sure enough he got the Bishop of Sherwood in on a Monday night, and the Bishop, bless his heart, invited those young people to come up for the laying on of hands. Then he invited the rest of the congregation for the same thing, and two-thirds of the congregation went up. Finally, at the end of the service, the Vicar said, 'I need this too,' and he asked the Bishop to lay hands on him publicly, in front of the whole church. It was the most amazing evening. Afterwards the Vicar said to me, he said, 'Dave, you've taught me something.' I said, 'I don't know what. I just do what seems natural to me.'

When I left the area, I started to wind down the youth work, but I was still having the school Welfare Officers ringing me up saying, 'Mr Perrett, we've got a young lad, we can't do anything with him. We've heard about your youth group. Will you take this young man on?' And I took two or three on like that; took them away on adventure holidays, and counselled them, and stood up in court for them. Stuff like that. During this time the Vicar said to me, 'Will you come on to the staff as a lay evangelist, if I can swing the finance?' So I said yes. But the Church wouldn't pay, surprise surprise! A year later I said to him, 'What about some other kind of ministry?' and he said, 'Church Army for you, my lad!'

The Church Army is like the Salvation Army, but under the auspices of the Church of England, and it's pretty evangelical on the whole. The training for the Church Army took a year, and at the end of it they said, 'We believe you have a ministry, but not with us.' So the Vicar said, 'Take another six months and think about it,' and I did. Then he sent me to the Bishop and he was the first High Churchman I ever met: Canon Bayes, as high as they come. We had nothing in common except our faith in Christ, but that man became my grandad. A lovely man. He sent me to an ACCM selection conference, which I got through, but ACCM wanted me to go on the Aston Training Scheme. The Aston Training Scheme is a scheme whereby people who have not got a certain level of personal growth or academic achievement are given the opportunity to bring both those things up to scratch. It's a two-year course, using Open University modules, and you hold a job down and study in the evenings, and at the end of it they either recommend that you are suitable for training, or that you are not.

After the two years I did a full-time university training at Durham. I always felt I'd been denied a university training; I always felt that I'd got the intelligence, but the system didn't allow for it. Even by this time it was difficult. I said, 'I want to do a degree,' and they said, 'No, but we will let you do the University Certificate in Theology,' which is fourteen papers, so I did that instead. I couldn't move my family to Durham, because that's when the housing market froze, so I commuted from Nottingham. I used to come back once a fortnight, and Canon Bayes looked after my family. He used to go and sit with my family when I was away, and at other times he'd turn up with cheques and say, 'How's finance?' and we'd say 'eeeerrk' and he'd say, 'Here's a cheque.' Christmas he'd turn up with gifts for the children. He was exemplary as a Christian, and showed me an awful lot.

People like Canon Bayes have been my experience of the real Christian Church. Not the hoo-ha and silliness and childishness that I've often had to deal with in congregations; not the hooligans and idiots who've played politics and games in the Church; but those wonderful, godly people. They're my heroes. They're the people I want to be like, and find it so hard.

Studying opened a whole new world of the arts to me. We did History, Art History, Art, Philosophy, Music, Literature, Poetry. They were closed to me before, and I was like a sponge, I just sucked it all up. I realized that theology is the queen of the sciences because it makes sense of all the other sciences; because if God is Creator, then He's to be found in all of Creation. Theology is a study of God, and if you study God then you begin to find what is behind this wonderful expression of Him. You begin to find that theology is just as much about concrete proof as the basics of science. It is, of course it is! That's the wonderful simplicity of it! That God is there to be found and tested; that He's consistent across the whole of Creation; that there is nothing inconsistent between the God of the Bible and the experience of Creation.

Now, of course it depends on what you mean by proof. When you test a hypothesis, you test it to destruction: you try to disprove the hypothesis, that's the scientific method. But there are hard scientific facts. Acid turns blue litmus red. The speed of light is 186,000 miles an hour. Sunlight on chlorophyll produces a reaction that breaks down sugars into energy. Water boils at 100°C, at sea level. Those are absolute facts.

It's the same with God. If you start out with the premise that God is the centre and Lord of all – and obviously not everybody does – but if you start out with that, then you learn a little humility, you learn that you don't know everything, that you can't do everything. For instance, science cannot create life. It can bend it, it can mould it, it can jiggle it about, but it cannot actually create the spark within a seed that turns that seed into a tree. What you *can* do is learn from the tree, you can learn that there is something bigger than you. If you start from *that* point, then you are in a position where God can disclose Himself. He's not going to disclose Himself to arrogance and pride that says, 'I'm the top of the tree, this is as good as it gets.' So the scientific method in Christian theology starts with the humble admission that God is above and beyond us, and yet imminent and close through Christ and his love on the Cross. That's when you can begin to say, 'Where is the consistency of God in the Creation I'm faced with?' and you can begin to test it out.

I came into an experience of the living God, as clear as me sitting with you here, now. The light went on, I met Christ. *That* was the starting-point, that's what made all the sense, *that's* my proof. All the rest is flumdiddle. All the rest is book learning. You know, someone gave me a Bible and said, 'This is the word of God. Read it.' I found out about Jesus in there, but I found out about him having *known* him.

That's my proof. It's not blind faith. I don't think there's any such thing as blind faith, because faith isn't blind, faith isn't uninformed. Faith is not something that you're either born with or you're not; everybody has faith. I can't think of a bigger demonstration of faith than strapping yourself into a titanium cylinder, full of aviation spirit, hoping that the ground crew have done their job, that the mechanics have done their job, and the pilot's not going to have a heart attack when he lands or takes off. Faith is always informed by the promises that have been made, or it's informed by the character of the person who made the promises. It's not a leap, it's an obvious step. It's about having enough information to make an informed commitment. If you're dealing with a God who is truth and love, who is always just, and is always gracious, and is always forgiving, that's something you can commit yourself to because it's trust-worthy. In the selfsame way, you can examine the New Testa-ment, and whilst you may nit-pick, the New Testament itself is enough, it is trustworthy. It's not sufficient for everything, and that's why we've got brains, but it contains sufficient information about God for us to make that commitment of faith.

If you are looking for proof in the litmus test sense, then you are going to be disappointed, but that isn't the only sort of proof. The sort of proof that I'm talking about is still subject to the scientific analysis: you can still say, 'Given this, this, and this, then the premise, or the hypothesis, is that', and you can demonstrate that time and time again.

However, most people want to argue with me not about proof but about whether they are good enough to be a Christian. But that isn't the issue at all. I know I'm not good enough, but that's the joy of it. That's the thrill of it. I'm not good enough, I don't deserve it, but that's not the issue. The issue is relationship. It's about who you are in relationship with. I am in relationship, through Christ, with God the Father, and that relationship is going to be the thing that matters in the end because it's about who I am; about progressively becoming a human being who reflects more and more truly the nature and attributes of God.

If your primary relationship above all others is with the God who is love and grace and mercy and peace and justice and power and life, then that begins to have the potential to put all the other things right, doesn't it? It means that pride and selfishness come under the jurisdiction of God rather than our jurisdiction. There's a lovely song, a modern one, which goes: 'I choose to be holy'. Well, one chooses to go with the flow of God's love, or one chooses not to. One can always choose.

People don't often choose God, and I think it's because choosing God means hearing what you don't want to hear, facing what you don't want to face. My wife Dorothy is the only person I know about whom I can put my hand on my heart and say, that woman has never told a lie, ever, in the thirty years I've known her. Not once. Now, I don't always like what she tells me. When I ask her opinion and she gives me an honest answer, I don't always like it. But I think that's a godly attribute she's got, because you know where you are. God will always tell you the truth. But lots of people don't want to hear what He has to say because it means facing up to themselves.

Yet to me, that's the adventure. God is the God of surprises. God is the God who says, 'It doesn't have to be this way, Dave: there is room for growth, development, change of heart, change of mind, and change of outlook.' He's the God of change. Whereas what people really want is the God of certainty, and there ain't no certainties. There is only one certainty in life: you are going to die. You can't rely on your health, on your mental capacities, on relationships, on how you feel from moment to moment or day to day. You can't be certain that you're not going to walk under a bus, not be let down, not be hurt or destroyed. So let's get death sorted out. If I'm going to die, what am I going to do about it? What kind of provision should I make? What information have I got? What might there be, if anything, to follow? And let's look at it, examine it, and find out if it's trustworthy enough to base my life on it. Who's made the promises for a start? And what's He like? The issue over and over again is choice.

Now, our choices don't affect God's will, but they do affect us, they do affect the way we are. When somebody gets a terminal illness, you never ask the question 'Should I pray for healing?' Of *course* you should pray for healing – always. It's always right to ask God for things. What it's *wrong* to do is to *expect* that God will do what you want Him to. My father died twenty years ago from a debilitating disease. He was a strong man, a very independent man, an intelligent man, who was struck with a debilitating, wasting disease out of the blue. It was Motor Neurone Disease, and basically the muscles waste and you drown in your own spit, because you can't breathe. It took him two and a half years to die. And what is one to make of this? Well, all of us are going to die some way or another, some pretty and some not so pretty. But I still grieve for my dad. I still grieve for him. And a relationship with God isn't an insurance policy against that sort of pain; it's not an insurance policy to say that I'll never get ill, and I'll die in a pretty and acceptable way. What it *is* is the assurance that no matter what comes my way, God will never let me face it on my own: He will stand with me and He will give me the resources to be able, as far as I can, to deal with the situation.

I was very fortunate in the Methodist Church when I first became a Christian, because I was presented with a very high quality of Christian relationships. My first curacy was great too, because my first Vicar, no matter how many times I fell on my face, he found something good to say about it. Because I came out of college a wreck. I came out broke because we were paid nothing, and I came out having had a lot of my theological thinking altered – which was a good thing, because I was a bit pedantic, and a bit stuck on my Bible. You know, if this is what the Bible says then that's good enough for me, and that was a bit narrow. In fact, I was very narrow as a Christian when I went to college, and college broadened me and introduced me to all kinds of weird and funny people like Anglo-Catholics, which was really wonderful because I found out that these people were Christians too. I couldn't be the same kind of Christian as they were, but there was no doubt that they loved the Lord Jesus, and they were serving Him and that was what mattered, not our differences.

I was ordained in 1982, and was pitched into a marvellous parish, Stapleford, where I was curate for four years. I did all the things that you do as a curate, and I loved it. Being a curate is tremendous. You have all the opportunities and none of the responsibilities. You can do anything you like and the Vicar carries the can. Unless you're really stupid, you can't muck a curacy up.

Then I came here as incumbent in 1986, and it's been pretty difficult. When I was invited to come here, I was green. To come to a place with three churches, in the biggest, most important town around for twenty-five miles in two directions and thirteen and twelve in the other, was a great compliment, and I came full of great hope and full of great joy into what was effectively a different world, a different country. One of the things that is very difficult to come to terms with as a minister is that you know how things could be and should be, but because of the way people are, you are forever presented with things that are quite different. Instead of the Church being a place of love and mercy and grace and, as Jesus said, a giving up your life for others, instead of that you are presented with a mixed bunch. As one bishop said to me, 'Every congregation has its mixture of saints and fatheads!'

So I came in on the crest of a wave, thrilled with the gospel, thrilled with being a pastor, thrilled with being able to serve the people of God, thrilled with the privilege, and grateful for the opportunity, into a place that had very fixed ideas about what its minister was going to be like. I found myself in a place where people had a very narrow sense of the world; whose appreciation of the gospel practically consisted of Holy Communion with chips, and if it wasn't Holy Communion their way it wasn't right. It was a very hierarchical, structured, high-expectation situation; very unforgiving, unwilling, inflexible. Insular and insulated. This place was the hub of the universe as far as these people were concerned.

I came here to a parish that had just experienced perhaps the worst miners' strike ever, where there was a lot of angriness and bitterness and divisiveness around; where controversy in the Church was something that we do not want, thank you very much. We know what we like, and we like what we know. We don't want anything challenged. We're asleep, thank you very much, so please leave quietly and close the door after you. Whereas I saw the Church as the agent of God's love in the world, they saw the Church as a hospital they could retreat to in order to avoid the world, and the contradictions between our two views of the Church just got sharper and sharper and more distinct as the years went on.

I felt that I was doing it all wrong, that my theology was all wrong, that whatever I said was wrong. People misunderstood me, sometimes unintentionally, sometimes deliberately. I found myself in a political minefield, where we had the politics of the playground: 'If you don't do what I want you to do, Vicar, I'm taking my ball home.' As one gentleman said to me, 'My job is to cut the grass: yours is to do the visiting.' Well, if that's the Church I don't want anything to do with it. I once told the PCC here: 'If I was living in this place, I wouldn't come to your church. No chance.'

The first night I was here, the first Sunday evening, my family came to St Birinus for the six o'clock Sunday service, and I had to *run* from the front of the church to the back of it in order to get there before the congregation left. Run! On our first Sunday. They all just left. We then all five of us came back into the vicarage, and we put our arms around each other and we wept. The nastiness, the coldness, the unwillingness, the stiff-neckedness, the pride: everything that was going on in that church was alien to our experience of Christianity.

Pretty soon I discovered that people would say one thing to your face and then another behind your back: they'd go to the press behind your back, go to the Bishop behind your back, go to anybody behind your back. I would hear things on the grapevine that people, to this day, do not have the courage to say to my face. Then we had twenty-one windows put in, people threw rocks and bricks through the front and back windows. My car was vandalized. My kids were beaten up. One churchwarden abused my children, verbally, physically, made their lives hell. The garage was busted into, the kids' bikes were stolen, we were fair game for anyone who wanted to have a go. We were like Christians in the lions' den, and it was Lions 100, Christians nil. That went on for two years. One of my briefs when I was appointed to this place was to bring the parishes together in one PCC, because the three churches here have two PCCs between them. I attended a joint AGM where I stood in front of the three congregations, and was torn to pieces, without any grace, without anybody saying, 'Now hold on, hold on, he's only the same as us.' And one elderly gentleman, dear old Len, whom I buried four years ago, he came out of that meeting and said to me, 'Vicar, that was nothing but a lynching party.' I said, 'Right, Len. Why didn't you stand up and say something?' And he avoided my eyes and walked away. At the end of two years I was so ill, and so angry, that I said three things to myself. I said: 1) They will not get me out until I'm ready to go. 2) If I have to empty the church, I will. 3) I'm going to adhere to what is true against all-comers, no matter what. I'm going to stand and fall by my own decisions.

I decided to look for a new congregation. I went looking and I found them, and I taught them gospel and they responded. We turned over a number of people who left, some quicker than others, and in their place we had a growing number of people who had experienced God in their own lives, and who were willing to be teachable, and were willing to understand gospel and to follow the Lord Jesus, and that took the best part of five years. Out of the seven years, the last five have been finding and teaching and encouraging the new congregation, which is fairly small, but it's made up of quality people who are not two-faced, and who are really learning how to respect one another, love one another, and live the gospel.

About a year ago, I started to look for another job, for a number of reasons. My wife and family up to that time had done what I wanted to do. You know, if Dad wanted to do this, they followed, they didn't have a lot of choice. I suddenly realized that they were people too, and whilst I'm prepared to put up with the garbage that this place throws at me, and maybe I'm robust enough to be able to do that, they may not be. I thought, stuff this. I had seen my children suffer, I had seen my wife suffer, and I had had enough because the bitchiness here has got to be experienced to be believed, the two-facedness. The people I should have been able to trust, I couldn't. My church-wardens went behind my back to the Archdeacon without having the courage or the courtesy to say so to my face. People would much rather mumble among themselves under the street-lamps on the way home from a meeting than have the courage and straightforwardness to stand up in the meeting and say, 'I don't understand this, Vicar. You're driving me potty.' And I thought that if I was open with people they'd be open with me, but it's not true.

So I started to say to myself: actually, my wife and kids deserve better, and I think I deserve better. I've done my apprenticeship, as it were, in a very tough place, and the gospel has worked here, and if it can work in Ollerton, mate, it can work anywhere! I began to look for another post, with very mixed feelings, and decided that really and truly I was an evangelical, and that I belonged in the evangelical wing of the Church, and that I wanted to go to a church that already had on board the things I'd had to fight for here. For instance, I came here and said, 'Right, chaps, we believe in the Bible, don't we?' And they'd say, 'Well . . .' 'Okay, but we believe in prayer, don't we?' 'Yes.' 'Oh good, well, let's pray then.' 'Pray? But we don't do that here.' So I'd say, 'Well, we believe in house groups, don't we? We get together for fellowship and Bible study and praise and worship?' 'Oh, no. We just come to church on a Sunday.' 'All right, but at least we believe in evangelism, don't we? We believe in sharing the gospel?' 'That's your job, Vicar, not ours.' I'd think: what?! I beg your pardon, but that's all our jobs.

But evangelism's the *raison d'être*, isn't it? If you are not doing evangelism, what are you doing? You're just faffing about, basically. Everything else outside of evangelism, everything outside of mission, is flumdiddle. Disciples are made, they're not born. Christians were given a mandate to heal the sick, raise the dead, cast out demons, look after the poor, and preach the gospel: Matthew 10, that's our mandate. That's the whole *point* of the Holy Spirit. But it's not about going out and collaring people, it's going out and loving people like Jesus did, just because they are there.

When I came here I told my congregation that I was an

evangelical. They didn't know what an evangelical was. They wouldn't have known what one was if it had jumped up and hit them in the face! They equated an evangelical with someone who stands in Mansfield Market on a Saturday afternoon, with a Bible in one hand, shouting at everyone. That's not an evangelical at all. An Anglican evangelical is concerned with sharing the good news of God at every point, and showing the relevance of Jesus to modern everyday life in the twentieth century, and doing it on a person-to-person basis. Andrew did that: Andrew found Jesus, and the first thing he did was go and find his brother, Peter, and tell him about it. Someone once described evangelism as one beggar telling another beggar where to get bread. I don't like that description, really, because I'm not a beggar, I'm a son of the Most High, but it serves a purpose.

There's a wonderful story told about George Whitfield. Going home one night from a meeting, Whitfield and his friend saw a guy who'd recently made some sort of Christian commitment weaving down the gutter towards them – drunk as a skunk – and Whitfield's friend turned to him and said, 'George, there's one of your converts.' And Whitfield said, 'Well, he must be one of mine; he's certainly not one of the Lord's.'

So we all do evangelism cack-handedly, but the great thing about it is that God actually takes our silly, stumbling, cack-handed ways, and does something with them. Having said that, it's hard to share the Good News with the indifferent, and it's not only the indifferent, it's the apathetic too. Apathy is an art form here, brother! I mean, they have *worked* at it. It's like I said to someone yesterday, 'I don't have to stand here and be insulted by you, mate. I can go home and be insulted by experts.' So one of the things you have to learn about sharing the Good News is that the secret of evangelism is making friends with people, and people here are friendless.

They're friendless because they're highly competitive with each other, and they're highly competitive because they are insecure. This community is ninety per cent mining, and basically the miners are being screwed by everybody. Maggie Thatcher sold them their houses, very clever move, so now they've got everything to lose. If they take redundancy they may get a lump sum of £30,000, but that has got to last them twenty years. There's no prospect of them selling their houses, because there are no businesses here for people to move in to, so they are stuck. If they take redundancy, then the social services cane them because they have got so much sitting in the bank. There is nowhere for them to go. They are being progressively screwed by British Coal, because now almost everybody employed in pits is employed on a contract basis, and British Coal employ very few people.

On top of that, men are having to rely on their wives' income, and that's very demeaning for such a macho culture. Family life is breaking down. There are no jobs for kids to go to. If you close pits, what do you put in their place? Thirty thousand jobs, they say, thirty pits we'll lose. Well, it's not 30,000 jobs, it's way over 100,000 because of the ancillary things that are dependent on the mines. Businesses here will go down if they close the pit, they'll just shut up shop.

What's happening to the community is that everybody's trying to keep their heads above water. They're garnering their resources, paying off their debts, hoping against hope that they're going to survive, and that makes them competitive with one another. They are also in competition to have a good time. They will cross the road as many times as it takes to get what they want. That's an interesting thing: you know, if I charged £100 for baptism, they'd feel better about it because they'd feel it must be worth it then. I don't charge that, but I do ask for commitment, which they can't give.

Now, although British Coal pay very well, the prosperity among those here who still have work is not going to last. That sort of prosperity is a bubble, and it's going to burst soon. This place is a place of imminent doom: so you get everything you can, while you can, and that's what they're doing. That's why they work back-to-back shifts, take on seven-day contracts, and work fifteen, sixteen hours a day. They're working for the day when there'll be no work here at all.

The women in this community do all the managing, mostly. They have to. They pay the bills, they look after the kids, they run the home. Most miners here are like big sixteen-year-old kids. They have all the fun, they're out boozing, fishing, pigeons, whatever. None of the responsibility. The wife has all the responsibility, bless her heart. As the Vicar, I spend most of my time propping up wives and trying to get men to realize that they have some responsibility apart from five-a-side football.

Having said that, when family life here is good, it's brilliant. When it's bad, it's horrid, really horrid. There's a lot of child abuse here. A friend of mine who is a consultant psychiatrist at King's Mill says she sees half of my parish. Half! So it's a curious, curious place, you know. They might seem open and friendly, but they're as two-faced as they come, and that's to do with competition and insecurity. They hide everything from their neighbours; they hide everything from themselves.

So your job as a minister is to make people your friends. I've got quite a few friends here who don't come to church. We go fishing together, we go boozing together, we fix each other's cars. There's one bloke I've been working on for six years! But I'm not trying to get him as a scalp on my belt, and if he never comes, it doesn't matter. If no one comes to faith, it doesn't matter. I wasn't called to have a success rate, or a sales target, I was called to be faithful. God requires one thing of a man, that he be found faithful. And if they spit in your face, well, they did that to our Lord, so what do you expect? You ain't going to get any better than he got. They put Him on a Cross, and that might happen to you, mentally, emotionally, spiritually, but so what? So what? That's what this costs.

It's not my job to convert anybody. No Christian has the authority to convert anybody. My job is to be a signpost, or as St Paul put it, to be a living epistle upon which may be read the things of God. God does the converting. My job is to bear witness. How shall they hear without a messenger? My priority is to preach and teach the Good News to anybody who wants to listen, anywhere. And always be ready, says Paul to Timothy. Always be ready to give account for the hope that is within you.

So coming here, anywhere I turned I came up against a brick wall. I tried to introduce some modern music, but it was, oh no, it's the Ancient and Modern Hymnbook we like. Ancient and *Modern*! Ancient and prehistoric, more like. Of course, the hymns they liked out of Ancient and Modern had framed their theology, and lots of the hymns in Ancient and Modern are sloppy Victorian sentimentality, not Christian love. We'd got forgiveness in word, but not in deed. We'd got evangelism in word, but not in deed. We'd got lots and lots of things in word, but no cash value.

Now, I would certainly take fifty per cent of the responsibility for the way things are at the moment in this parish, and the way things went in the first two years. I'd put my hand up to fifty per cent of it, simply because I was naïve. I thought the Christian Church believed in certain universal things, and I was immensely frustrated by the unwillingness and the childishness of the people in the church, and I didn't respond well to it. But I would say, in mitigation, that I was told lies at my interview with the churchwardens, and I was also sent here by the Bishop on a brief that latterly demonstrated to me that diocesan people are fairly well out of touch with what happens on the ground. That's not a criticism, that's a fact of how it is. But fifty per cent of it is my bag. Fifty per cent of it I should and could have handled in a more constructive way, in a more helpful way.

But you see, flower, I was *frightened* most of the time. I was *fearful* most of the time. All the people I should have been able to trust I couldn't, because they had betrayed that trust more than once. Love grows out of respect and trust. I had neither in the parish, so I was always off balance. I think that's what made me ill in those first two years, I was quite seriously ill. I look back now and think perhaps I should have had the guts and the grace, and more of the latter than the former, perhaps, to deal with things differently. But I didn't.

The Church establishment was enormously supportive. They couldn't have been more so. The Bishops were extraordinary, and the Archdeacon of the day was kind and understanding. Fellow clergymen were less helpful, because I think they saw in me the things they feared in themselves. The parish was even less understanding. There is an insane and quite, quite ridiculous expectation that people have of clergy families. For instance, not long after we got here, Dorothy got a job. We had one child at college, two at school, and I had a telephone call from an elderly member of the congregation who was disgusted that my wife worked as a domestic assistant at Bishopscourt Old People's Home, and proceeded for the next half-hour to tell me off about that. Being fairly green in the job, and not wanting to be too offensive, I took this on the jaw for quite some considerable time. My patience finally ran out, and I said, 'Look, I'm awfully sorry, but if my wife didn't work, we wouldn't eat!' She then had the effrontery to give me a lecture about my personal finances.

Now, this was the first of many people who seemed to think that I, as Vicar, am fair game for them to tell me what I should be doing, and that clergy pay isn't all that bad, and you get a free house, and you get expenses, and you've got a car, and all the rest of it. People in the church seem to think that they have a right to interfere and comment on my personal and private life. They haven't. I can put my hand on my heart and say that I have never ever volunteered a criticism or a comment about people's personal lives: I never make a comment unless I know they are actually asking what I think. But as a professional clergyman I don't seem to have that choice. They want to dabble in my private life: they think they own me.

People think the clergy have it easy. We don't. The clergy live like amphibians, in air and water. We live with a foot in both camps, and it's difficult, it's damned difficult to live with one foot in this world and one foot in eternity. On a more basic level, I could have been earning three times what I'm earning now if I had stayed in the computer business. I have no house when I retire. We do not have carpets you have to wade through. We do not change our suite every two years and go on foreign holidays. I should like to be able to live like some of my parishioners, even those who are retired. Yet they seem to think that because I'm their Vicar they have a right to poke and prod in my private life, and I don't wish to be crude, but there have been times when I have said, 'Bugger off, will you. Keep your nose out of my affairs.'

Now, this comes back to something I remember you saying: that you don't think the clergy should have vicarages, that they should have the responsibility of managing their own houses like everyone else. I can see your point of view, but in the provision of a house, at least you get some sort of uniformity across all the parishes, and it cuts out what used to happen where different benefices attracted people of different incomes. Now everybody gets more or less the same income and more or less the same sort of house. There is a standard clergy house now: the Church Commissioners say it shall be so many square feet of area, and that's good because it cuts out the people who have got marvellous houses and the ones who've got rubbish ones.

As well as that, you do actually need a wall to hide behind. We've been so grateful for this brick wall that runs round the property and separates us, not because we want to be separated, but because if you're in a semi and you do happen to have a row and raise your voices and throw the china and stuff, that's a bit embarrassing for those next door if you're the Vicar. So you do need a safe haven. You do need to be able to shut the door and lock the gates.

What I would really like to see is clergy having a decent wage, being able to support a mortgage, and every church providing office space, so that the clergy could travel to work. I would like to be able to live in Wellow, or Walesby, and travel in to the office at the church and work my day and do my visits and be available, and have a multi-purpose room where you could hold meetings and stuff, and not have to use the vicarage. But I can't. What I have done is teach my parishioners that the vicarage is not church property available for them to book meetings at, because it's my home. I invite people here for meals or for a cup of coffee, or to hang out, or to watch a video, or to mend the car, but very little church business is done in my home – in the study, yes, but not in the home.

Wives are in a cleft-stick in all of this. My wife gets invitations to various clergy meetings, but she doesn't want to meet clergy wives, because she only ends up either being totally over-whelmed by the super-efficient, wonderful all-singing, all-dancing unpaid curates who involve themselves in the work left, right and centre, or she gets to hear all the same moans that she's got, with no resolution. So we have friends in the parish. I was told when we came here that you shouldn't have friends in the parish. I think that's nonsense. I couldn't care less where my friends are as long as they're my friends.

But the congregation has treated my wife abysmally. For instance: if the plumber comes and does a job at your house and makes a cock-up, you get on to the plumber. You don't get on to the plumber's wife and moan about what he's done, do you? Well, they do with clergy. She's been used as an avenue to get at me. So she's said, 'I'm going to exercise my Christian ministry in a secular setting in an old people's home, doing what I think I can do best, and stuff the Church.' And she's been quite right. But her faith has suffered incredibly. Like most clergy wives, she's a very tough person, and she's always been content to make me available, but there's no doubt she's suffered, and there have been times when I've had to say that my marriage is a darn sight more important than the Church, and it comes first. I was called to be a husband first, a father next and a minister last. That's how it happened in my life, and that's how I try to keep it.

No Christian was ever given any guarantees. I think Christians ought to sit down and say, 'What was I promised?' Tribulation, hard work, being treated like dirt, being told to pick up your cross and get on with it. Nothing else – at least not on earth.

And yet it's worth it. On Good Friday morning my curate turned up half an hour before the United March for Witness through the village, and it was raining. I don't think he'd had a very good night – he'd got a new baby – and he wasn't in the best of humours. And he intimated that he really wished we didn't have to do this. So I said to him, 'If my Lord can hang on the Cross on a stinking Palestinian summer day, amongst all the filth and the rubbish, out of love for me, I can spend half an hour out in the rain for him,' and that sobered him up somewhat. I think the Lord's worth it. I think the gospel's worth it.

That is why you do the job. And anyway, you're called and you can't escape the call. It niggles and niggles and niggles away until you give in. I mean, who really wants to stand in silly clothes at the front of a church and be associated with all the stereotyped ideas that you are not quite bright enough to make it, or you can't do anything else; that you're effeminate and ineffectual, so you'll be a vicar? Who wants to do that? Who would be stupid enough to want to do this job? Because it's a thankless task and it's twenty-four hours a day, seven days a week, fifty-two weeks a year. You're begrudged your holidays, your days off are invaded, your family life is ruined and you're the target for every idiot who thinks he can do better. You're over-trained and over-prepared in lots of senses, yet you're not recognized by other professions – except the more perceptive among them, and there aren't a lot of those about.

I would change, mind you. If I had known then what I know now, I wouldn't have been ordained. There are things I think are good about the Church, don't get me wrong. I think the Church of England's the best boat to fish from, and I think it's got right so many things that the other Churches haven't a clue about. I think the support and training of the clergy are exemplary. I think the way we've got a paid employee in every patch in the land, where the Methodists, the Baptists, the Pentecostals and the Roman Catholics have moved out into leafy suburbia, is exemplary. The parochial system's good; the establishment is good, though I blow hot and cold about it; it does mean that with my collar I can walk into any house anywhere. It gives the Church constant opportunity. And if the Church is moribund or unresponsive, you can still have a marvellous ministry in the community. I don't mean propping up a bar, I mean actually working for the benefit of the community, and without recourse to a board who don't like the way you preach or what you're doing with your time. I don't have to account to anybody, except to the good Lord Himself. As I've often said to my PCC, 'The reason I tell you the truth is I'm more afraid of Him than I am of you. I have to account to Him, not to you.'

In fact, there are only three ways that I can be removed from this living. 1) If I am convicted of a criminal offence. 2) If I keep a bawdy house – but I haven't got the energy for that; I've reached the age when I'm built for comfort, not for speed. 3) If they put an Act of Parliament through. Now, that has tremendous advantages and disadvantages. The disadvantage is, you can't get rid of a bloke who is screwing up. On the other hand, nobody can shift me, which leaves me free to preach the gospel where and how is necessary without hindrance.

Having said all that, I wouldn't become ordained again, because I'm less effective in Christian ministry as a Christian minister than I was as a layman. As a layman I didn't have the constraints and expectations, or the paperwork; the paperwork is appalling. And the facilities and the *buildings*. If I had my way, I'd pull the lot down! All of them, from York Minster downwards. Yes, I would. I'd flatten every single church. Oh, they're beautiful, yes, but if the people of England want their heritage, then let the people of England *pay* for it! And if they don't, pull them down, and put in their places multi-purpose halls and offices, and let's do it properly. Let's recognize that a Church is not buildings, not the cathedrals. Even Durham Cathedral, which I love, I'd pull the thing down, I really would.

Why? As a stand. As a way of saying, 'This is not the Church. The Church is the body of Christian believers committed to the work of the Gospel.' When choral Evensong and tourists become the sole justification for keeping a thundering great building open and a millstone round our necks, then we're playing at being a Church. I said that to a Roman Catholic, who was on the same clinical theology course as me. We stood at the window having a cup of coffee, looking at Durham Cathedral, upon which they were spending two million pounds, which was offensive to me, a disgrace. The Church is spending two million quid on a building which, while it is glorious and wonderful, is going to flounder and decay. What the hell are we doing, spending two million on a building, when for want of fifty or sixty thousand quid here, the gospel could be set forward in an amazing way? That's a betrayal of our priorities, and that is just one reason why the Church has been set aside by people, and can you really blame them?

On top of that, the Church is full of people using Christianity as an excuse to witter on about their own thing: and while you've got the Selwyn Gummer idiots and the cuddly bunny brigade – animal rights people – and the gay and lesbian activists; while you've got that sort of ill-informed, tactless wally in the Church, who hasn't got two brain cells to rub together, using the Church as an excuse; while you've got people who witter on about the traditions of the Church, even though those traditions are pretty well negotiable anyway; while you've got all that, you are faffing about with things that are *irrelevant*! Far be it from me to say who should and shouldn't be in the Church – okay, I just did – but we're faffing about while the country is going to hell on horseback! While families and communities are falling apart for want of good Christian education, love and support, we're wittering about buildings and the ordination of women as if it mattered a damn! They don't! These are tertiary issues. The primary issues we're too afraid to get hold of, because it means letting go of the props that come with the job: the house and a position in the community and some kind of automatic respect. Lots of clergy are scared shitless about what would happen if you took the props away. That's why I *would* take the props away. *Then* we'd sort out the men from the boys. *Then* we'd separate the committed from the career-minded.

That's why I say to those clergy who are leaving the Church now, all those hooligans going off to Rome, I say: off you go then! And I wouldn't make any financial provision for them either, they wouldn't get a brass farthing from me. If you go into a job, and you decide to leave – you leave. I wrote to a fellow clergyman, in this deanery a kind, thoughtful and generous letter – I can be tactful when I try – asking him to explain what the problem was with the ordination of women, because he's acting the fool at deanery synods and bringing the professional caring ministry into disrepute by his stupidity. I asked him openly to write to me and tell me, please, his point of view. I got a three-line letter back. 'Thank you for your letter. It was most interesting. Yours sincerely.' Now, whilst those Anglo's – and they're not all the same – cling to man-made traditions, and whilst they hide behind 'The universal Church has never done this, therefore we shouldn't do this now', and don't give well thought-out arguments that will stand up, then they deserve what they get. Let them go, we are better off without them. Much better. We can get on with the gospel then.

Have a biscuit. Now, did I tell you I've had the Archbishop of York here, to consecrate St Paulinus' Church? Great bloke. Good fun. I thought he would be useless as a preacher, he was damned good. Damned good. I mean, he's a liberal, and I would probably disagree with ninety per cent of his theology but he's a good bloke. D'you know, I often wonder what it would be like to be a bishop or an archbishop. I think they're the worst jobs in the Church, I really do, because they're all responsibility and no fun. On the other hand, I'd like the chance to really make a mark; change something for the good of the Church.

It's very difficult to know how to handle ambition as a Christian. On the one hand, I don't think there is any point in joining a company unless you want to be managing director.

On the other hand, the way the world measures success and ambition ain't necessarily the way the Kingdom of God does it. But that's no reason to opt out of doing things properly and well. It does matter to be good and gentle and compassionate; but it also matters having a cutting edge, and being a prophet, and doing all sorts of things that stir up the people. I used not to approve of the Bishop of Durham. I thought he was a complete wally. But at least he got the ordinary person talking about the Resurrection in the pub. I wouldn't mind the opportunity to rock the boat like that. I rock my own particular boat already, but I'd like to rock a bigger boat, really.

I suspect the reason that the diocese hasn't found me something else here is that I'm a little too hot to handle. That's why I'm moving to Basingstoke. And I don't resent that. I understand it. I do understand that I'm very untypical, because when I came into the Anglican ministry I already had a theology, I had spent twenty years hammering one out in experience. College didn't teach me anything, it just helped my theology to hang together more coherently. I also came into the Church without any hang-ups of having been brought up in the Church; so I don't get turned on by choirs or choral Evensong and all that stuff, even though I appreciate it.

It's the cucumber sandwiches on the vicarage lawn mentality I really dislike. I mean, the Church is still very frightfully-frightfully, old chap. And there are some people who want me to be the frightfully-frightfully stuffed shirt, so I play the game. And there are some people who want me to put my feet up on the kitchen table and have a cup of tea and a fag, and I do that. So you play the game. But if I thought for one minute that choral Evensong and tea on the vicarage lawn was the be-all and end-all, I think I'd go out and become a monk. After all, the Church couldn't organize a bonking in a brothel, so why do we go around behaving as if we're so different? We're not. Any minister who tells you that he doesn't hide behind the frock and the collar is a liar, because we do. And we should remember that the Church is made up of sinners. Look at the disciples: a bunch of deceitful, weak, argumentative, ambitious, self-centred hooligans. They were. I wouldn't choose them. They were a bunch of drop-outs. Peter had a great chip on his shoulder; so did Judas. John and James's mother tried to get them the top jobs. They were just as bad as we are. But Jesus trusted them, and gave them responsibility, and that's how he treats us. He says, 'I call you my friends.'

We, the Church, have a duty to carry out our responsibility, and I'm glad we're going through a refining process at the moment. Call it a crisis if you like, but the Church has been in crisis for 2,000 years, so that's hardly news. It's having to change and grow and move with the times — as much as anything because it's running out of money — and that's very good for it. It's also set against a society that in biblical terms is growing darker and darker, and as a result the Church is beginning to shine more and more. Because it is a very dark place out there, and it's getting darker. Society; it's going mad. It's going mad and there's no hope. I don't believe in the gradual betterment of mankind, because I can see no indication of it. There is only one place where society is getting better and that is in the Church, for all its silliness. The only place where I have found that people really fundamentally change for the better is in the Church. Why? Because, stumbling and grappling as we are, we have God, and God has the answers. Once you begin to trust God your life changes, and society changes. I know, I see it happen all the time. There's a lot in the Book of Job about all that. Read the Book of Job, flower. Good book, that. Especially the end bit, when God says to Job, 'Where were you when I planned the universe? Did I have to consult you? Am I accountable to you, Job?' You know. God isn't accountable to us; we're accountable to God, and the sooner we realize that the better.

There are still many things that I cannot grasp, but nor can anybody else, and they're kidding you and me and themselves if they think they can. The Bible says that some things are the hidden things of God, and they are nothing to do with us. You might say that that's a get-out clause, and I would robustly say to you that it is not, because the one thing I do know is that God is all good, and sometimes He has to keep us in the dark and sometimes He has to be cruel to be kind. As it says in the scriptures, 'Those whom He loveth, He chasteneth.' He's not a milk-and-honey God. He's a God of judgment.

There's no getting away from judgment. Some people like the idea of purgatory, because they think it lets them off the hook, but you can't find purgatory in the Bible so I don't believe in it. And if there's no scriptural basis for it, then as far as God's concerned it ain't a good idea, so it ain't on the agenda. End of discussion. That's why Jesus spent so much time talking about hell – or at least, more than he did about heaven. And hell to me is being on the outside looking in – knowing what could have been. That's where the weeping and the gnashing of teeth comes in. It's that realization that you could have been in there strutting your stuff and doing your thing, but you were stupid so you ain't, because you get one chance at life and that's it. I don't believe in second chances. Neither did Jesus.

Yes, he believed in forgiveness, but we're not talking about forgiveness, flower, are we? We're talking about relationship. I made that clear yesterday. We're talking about relationship and destination now, and I don't think forgiveness has any bearing on your ultimate destination, because Jesus didn't apply it to destination. I'm stuck with what he said, you see, that's my problem as a biblical evangelical, that I don't speculate on what he didn't say. He said, 'Strait is the way, and narrow is the gate that leads to salvation. Few there be that find it.' He made it fairly clear that repentance is open to everybody and anybody, and to repent doesn't mean that you are sorry: it means to change your mind, to turn around, to go a different way. But not everybody's going to take it, and those who don't take it are going to be on the outside looking in. Awesome, isn't it? People spend their whole lives denying God, but it doesn't stop God coming back and knocking on the door time and time again. So ignore Him if you want to, but do it at your peril. Doesn't make any difference to God, only to you.

Let me ask you a question. Do you sin because you're a sinner, or are you a sinner because you sin? That's right. You sin because you're a sinner, because you have a predilection and a fascination with sin, and you cannot do what is right. Once you accept that, you're getting somewhere, because you begin to admit that fundamentally you're upside-down. It says in John 1, chapter 4, 'He who loves God will not sin.' That's the English translation. If you look at the Greek, the thrust of it is, 'He who loves God will not *persist* in sin'; in other words, it will not become an habitual way of life. Because you've admitted that you're fundamentally flawed, that you're a terrorist in God's world, and once people do that, that's when they change. Don't ask me how, but I just know that they do; sometimes instantaneously, sometimes over a long, long period of time. And they change because God made a promise to us. He promised sin would be forgiven if we repented. So it's up to us. We do have a choice.

The biggest lie the devil's ever spread, and people believe, is that we have got time. The truth of the matter is that there isn't time. Now is the day of salvation. Do it now. Don't put it off. Turn to God today, now. People think, 'When I'm older.' But when you're older you are fixed. The first time you say no to God, the first time is hard; the second time is not quite so hard; the third time it's getting easier. By the time you get to the fiftieth time, you've had it. That's the only reason I do this job, the only reason. I want everybody at some point or another to have heard God's message and understood the basics. People need to know that there is a heaven and there is a hell, and there are consequences for what they do in life. We need to tell them.

So think about it. Think about God today. Because tomorrow may be too late. Don't wait until Judgment Day and say, oh, sorry, God, I didn't realize. Because if you do, He'll only say, oh yes you did, flower; because Perrett told you.

FRANCES WARD

Age: 34
Age at ordination (to the Diaconate): 30

TUTOR IN PRACTICAL THEOLOGY, NORTHERN URC
COLLEGE, MANCHESTER

In the autumn of 1992, when I began work on this book, I took out a year's subscription to the Church Times. *Naturally, this was for research purposes only but it gave my flatmate – whose idea of a good journal is* Vanity Fair *– much cause for mirth and derision. She had a point. The General Synod's vote on the ordination of women loomed large, and the* Church Times *devoted more and more column space to long, impassioned letters about why women should or should not be ordained. As November 11th neared, the paper grew bloated with anger, expanding in the middle by at least two pages to accommodate the wrath, pain and sense of injustice felt by so many within the Church. Occasionally a letter stood out for its brevity, integrity and calm. Frances Ward's letter was one of them.*

I wrote to her asking whether she would be interested in being interviewed for this book and she replied promptly in the affirmative. She told me that she was married to a paediatrician; with three children, and she was anticipating career blocks in the Church, 'because of the problem the Church – laity and hierarchy – has around the issue of women holding authority'.

'I feel very motivated', she wrote, 'to create more space for women in the public realm of the Church. I'm also committed to changing the archetypal world which lies behind religious faith by ensuring that the feminine has a real and healthy presence within it. Where better to start than the holiest of holies – the priesthood!'

Frances Ward and her husband, Peter Powell, both work under their own names, but they've also taken the unusual and imaginative step of combining their names to make a family name, Poward. This made for slightly confusing answerphone messages. Sometimes it was Frances

Ward and Peter Powell who were out but would get back to you as soon as they could, and sometimes it was the Poward family. It took me a while to grasp this concept.

I went to meet Frances Ward and her family while she was still a curate in a suburb of Bolton, Lancashire. A petite and pretty woman, with short hair and a sensible but snappy dress sense, Frances Ward is cheerful, friendly and practical, with a capable and outdoors-ish air about her. On the evening of my arrival she managed to make supper for her three children, answer the phone, and cope with complicated arrangements for a funeral at one and the same time. Soon afterwards her husband, Peter, came home and put the children to bed while Frances Ward and I made considerable headway with a bottle of wine. Peter joined us for a second one, and we talked into the small hours – I don't remember what about, but certainly not this book.

I returned some months later, by which time the Powards had moved to Bury, where Frances Ward was due to take up a post as a tutor in a theological college. She and I talked for almost two days solid. I was rather surprised, given her gregariousness and wicked sense of humour, at how quietly and earnestly she spoke to me: she was purposeful, calm, and quite intense at times. She has a beautiful, rather limpid voice, with the traces of a childhood Australian accent still hovering around the vowels. It is a clear voice with no hiding places, and Frances Ward's faith and commitment to her work shine through it.

FRANCES WARD

I was born in Australia. My father had gone out there to teach, and he met my mother there, who's Australian. I was there until I was seven, and my brother, who is two and a half years younger than me, was born there as well. My sister was born on a visit home – I call England home now, which is interesting, because I haven't always done that. We came over to England three times altogether, backwards and forwards on a ship, before coming back for good. They're my first memories, really. I learned to swim on that ship.

When we got to England we went to live in Essex, near Dedham, and my father commuted down to London where he was teaching at Westminster School. He then got a job as the headmaster of the King's School in Ely, so we moved there when I was ten. I was always quite a tomboy, and I remember having a very wild country childhood for two and a half years in Essex, where I played outside and climbed trees and it was lovely, and then seeing our enormous great medieval house in Ely in the Cathedral close and my heart just sinking because it was so built up and towny and oh, I hated it to begin with. They weren't very happy years at all, in Ely. I went through school as one of the first girls in a boys' public school. There were nineteen girls to start with, and I always felt a bit on show, being the headmaster's daughter, and I didn't quite have the personality to cope with it. My parents weren't always very happy during that time, either. I mean, they've got a very solid marriage now but it went through some very rocky times during my teenage years, and they could so easily have broken up. I'm glad they didn't.

My childhood was such a mixture. There was plenty of affection because my parents are affectionate people, but I don't think my mother was ever very happy. She and my father didn't communicate then nearly as well as they do now, either emotionally or intellectually, and she had a breakdown when I was fifteen. She came through it, and she did an Open University degree and began teaching full-time and she completely changed. She was much healthier as a person. I think that had a very profound influence on me: it left me feeling that staying at home looking after children is not good for women. Well, it wouldn't have been for me, anyway. I always vowed I'd never just be a mother.

We went to church because my father was a lay reader. We went to Ely Cathedral to begin with, which was really boring – *oh*, I was bored – then we went to the parish church in Ely, which was a bit better, and obviously the seeds of my faith were sown during that time. That's why I think it's really valuable that children go to church up to about the age of ten or whenever they want to stop going, because it gives them a value-system that they can pick up on later if they want to. In fact I went to church in a very disciplined way until I left home, but with all sorts of questions. I read a lot of existential literature when I was a teenager, Jean-Paul Sartre and Camus and all sorts of twenties and thirties novels, and they raised all sorts of questions in my mind which didn't really sit very well with the Christian faith that I grew up with; so I dropped out for a bit when I left school. I went out to Australia and was there for seven months, and I remember one night sitting with my boyfriend right out in the bush, having a long conversation about faith and things like that, and I remember feeling quite certain that there was something I would call faith in me, but at that point it didn't have any specific content, it was just an intimation of something.

I came back to England and went up to university at St Andrews in Scotland. There I did my best to explore what I had realized in Australia and I attended Quaker meetings, which felt very much the right place to be, with their silence and their lack of credal statements. Then, after a year of doing Fine Arts and History and English and Theology, I changed into the

Faculty of Theology to do Theology alone, in order to continue that exploration. I thought to myself, if I'm here studying, I might as well study something I'm actually very interested in as an agnostic. I enjoyed Theology very much, and actually worked hard for the first time. I hadn't really worked at school, very much as a rebellion against being the headmaster's daughter.

I've never been a very sociable person. I've learnt to be extrovert and sociable, but it's something I've acquired, not something I already had. One of the problems at school was that I never could get on top of the social scene. I was always agonized by what people might be thinking about me. I was quite sensitive, with this added role of being the headmaster's daughter, which really oppressed me, and until I went out to Australia I couldn't start to define who I was for myself. Then I began to feel, hey, I'm beginning to know who I am.

I think that's something that's always been important to me, that people should be allowed to find who they are for themselves; especially women. Perhaps that's something we can talk a bit more about later on, because that's part of what being a priest and a woman is for me. My mum is always berating herself for not being a very good mother, but I don't think that's the case at all. I think that we always do the best job that we can at the time, and it's very easy to blame your parents. Now I've got kids of my own I realize that she had her own things to contend with when we were growing up, and it was a good childhood compared with a lot of others. It was fine. And all three of us, Nick and Vanessa, my brother and sister, we've all come through with very exciting things to do with our lives. And that's to my parents' credit as much as anyone else's, that they've turned out some really creative people.

I think a lot of people today have quite sort of relativistic value-systems, you know, the kind in which no value can be held out as better than another. I've believed that too in the past and feel that it's not enough for me, that it's too nihilistic, because I think we all recognize when things are unfair. I think we all have an innate sense of justice, and I think it's tied up

75

with an innate faith in God, however vulnerable and fragile that is today. How you locate God objectively I've no idea, but I think that belief in God has been too persistent just to be a human projection. I still have very profound agnostic feelings that God is just what I want God to be, but then I also feel defined by God. And I feel that God defines us by allowing us to grow and be the wonderful people that we're created to be. That's not something I can do to myself, so there *has* to be a different reality, a personal God who does that for me. I suspect that deep-down I've always believed that.

When my mother had her breakdown she became so depressed that her identity semed to be imploding. Imploding sounds too dramatic, perhaps, but she used to curl up in bed in depths of misery. I remember talking with her for hours and hours just trying to persuade her . . . well, I don't know what I was trying to persuade her, that life was all right, I suppose; and it was very hard because one minute you'd think you'd convinced her and the next she'd be depressed again. That was quite a lesson to learn, that you couldn't just put things right. I learned that the motivation had to come from her, and that's something I've had to hold on to in pastoral situations. People have to want to change. You can't force them. However, for a long time after that I didn't cope with things very well. Dad was very preoccupied with the school and Mum was very preoccupied with her problems and I think I could have done with a lot more listening to and just straightforward guidance. But that's all right. You come through these things.

I think I've modelled myself on my father more than anyone. Difficult to say, isn't it, because I really feel my own person now and I never idolized him, but there are things about him that I really respect. He put a lot of work into King's. He was there twenty-odd years, and he made that his work of creation. It turned from being a school which actually would have collapsed if there hadn't been someone like him there into a really good school. Seeing him doing that and taking the flak that introducing changes inevitably entailed has given me a lot of determination and a lot of vision which I prize quite highly.

A lot of my teenage energy went into wondering whether boys fancied me. Far too much time, really. The first real relationship I had was just as I was leaving school, with an Australian who came across to the school for a year. He was a very good cricketer, a lovely man, and we struck up a friendship. It didn't come to much. Then I met someone in Australia who was the person I mentioned before. We had a relationship in Australia for seven months, then wrote and spoke on the phone and had something going all through my four years at St Andrews. It was entirely sustained on letters and then he finally came across and it . . . it just didn't work. But these things happen. He was a very good person and still is.

While I was at St Andrews I had two other serious relationships, though having that Australian relationship in the background meant that I didn't have to commit myself particularly to anything. However, one of those relationships was extremely important, because we talked a lot, and I think that's when I discovered who I was. In fact it was that latter relationship, and doing my finals, and really having to study hard and be committed, that began building foundations for things that were to come later. The first building-block was just recognizing that God is love and is as nebulous as love and as abstract as love, and needs to be sought and found and worked at. I think that recognizing love in that relationship was a way in to God for me, as well as the fact that the man I was involved with was more into Christianity than I was. We used to talk long and loud and he made me think through things in a way which was good for me.

I did my theology alongside people who were training for the ministry, and I remember one or two people saying to me, you should think about this, but then they always say that to Theology students. And I remember thinking, 'Well, maybe when I'm about forty. I've got some living to do first and I'm certainly not ready for all this yet.' I'd felt that I'd had a very privileged upbringing and one that was actually quite irresponsible in some ways. I mean, I'd gone through a public school and I'd gone to St Andrews, which is very beautiful and middle-class, and I just felt, what can I do that's actually going to broaden me a bit? So I went and did a nursing training at the London Hospital in Whitechapel. That was hard. I was twenty-three and I'd come with all these ideas and was still brimming over with all this theological stuff and I went in with a class of eighteen-year-olds.

I was miserable. Having to work hard in a different discipline was really difficult. Being dressed as a Victorian under-housemaid, which was what the uniform was modelled on, with the caps and the starched aprons, just felt like, oh well, goodbye free spirit. Also, being a feminist, which I consider myself to be, and going into a profession of women who were not at all feminist, was really challenging. I thought, well, if my faith's going to mean anything to me then I'd better start here. So what does it mean to be nursing people who are very sick? What does it mean working in an environment which isn't at all sympathetic to who I am? It was interesting what that did to me because in some ways it gave me a real sense of discipline. When you need to be at a shift at quarter to eight in the morning, you're there, even if you've worked until ten o'clock the night before. And you do ten shifts on the trot or seven nights on the trot. I'm very glad not to be doing it any more, but I learned to be patient. I learned to cope with my own feelings of tiredness and put them aside because someone else had greater needs than myself. And I learned to smile when I didn't feel like it. All sorts of things like that have given me a sense of self-control which I didn't have before and it was very character-forming.

Throughout my time at Whitechapel I went to Quaker meetings. Then I started going to St Dunstan's, Stepney, which is a wonderful little church with a city farm next door. It's a lovely, idyllic place. Anyway, I started going there, and I'm probably going to get quite upset talking now because Norry McCurry was the priest there and he died very recently. I remember bouncing up to him after a service one time and saying, 'I think I want to be ordained,' and he just said, 'Well, you've got to be coming to church *regularly* in order to do that.' You know, he was very sort of upper-crust and very . . . ah, it's difficult to describe Norry, but he really helped me. He nurtured me through the beginnings of a more pressing sense of vocation than I thought I had. He became my spiritual director and guided me through all my questions in a solid way. He could be terribly strict. 'If you're serious about this, then you must stop going to the Quakers and start coming to church regularly. You must show that this Anglican Church is where you belong.' He was of the old school. But you know, it was interesting listening to the address at his funeral. It was given by his oldest friend, whom he met at Oxford fifty-two years ago. And this person Gerard Irvine was saying how Norry had come out of a very Anglo-Catholic background and had grown through that and was now very much in favour of women being ordained, and very alive to the changes in liturgy and the freshness that the Anglican Church can represent when it's really in touch with God and in touch with what the people are saying and wanting. And that's very true.

I met my husband, Peter, at St Dunstan's He was completing his medical training and doing house jobs at the London Hospital. I knew him for about two or three years as a friend, and then on the basis of that friendship we got together and got married within six or nine months, and Norry married us.

I was ready to get married. I felt I'd reached the point where I'd had quite a few relationships, but I also felt I could be single for the rest of my life if that was what was right for me. I mean, it would have been at great cost, but I could have been happy, and I think feeling like that is important before you commit yourself to another person. And then in Peter someone came along who could speak to me in so many ways, and he was different. Yet we share a lot of the same ideas about child-rearing, the same values, and our faith; things which are really good and solid. We communicate very well together. It's a very good relationship.

During that time I had moved into a Quaker community off the corner of Brick Lane, and I lived there for three years. It was where Peter and I started our married life, and Matilda was born there. The community was quite an established one: I think they've got their twentieth anniversary coming up soon. While I was there there were sixteen of us in one building with our own rooms, but we had shared kitchens. I went there because I wanted to explore what love meant in practice in a community, and we had 'relationships meetings' and that sort of thing, and it was fascinating. There were Sufis and Buddhists and Quakers, and Peter and I were almost the only ones who actually attended Anglican Churches, but we were a minority; buying into institutional religion! The community was called 'Some Friends', and friends of mine used to call us 'Some Veggies' because we were all vegetarian and very earnest and quite middle-class, but that was okay because they were good people, and it was a good place to be, it really was.

It was a very interesting way to start out married life. It felt good that we weren't just becoming a couple. We were two individuals in the community, and our marriage was extended into the community. After we married I'd still say prayers with another woman every morning, and Peter would sometimes join us. The bonds that I had made as an individual were still strong, so I didn't feel as if I was cutting off everything. I think Peter and I would do it again in some way if we could. We've always wanted to have quite an open house or be part of a community again one day, because it's a very good way of living. It brings you up against who you are in a very different way from just living as a couple or a family. It's hard work, because you can't run away from problems, but I think that's a good thing.

After living in the community we moved to Cambridge. I had been accepted by Westcott House, the theological college in

Cambridge, and Peter got a job at Addenbrookes, working with premature babies and doing a research job too. After doing nursing I was so glad to be studying again. I loved theology, and during my last year there I did a postgraduate diploma in theology on top of my training, which was very well-taught. There was only one battle I remember before theological college. When I wanted to be considered for training I had to see the Diocesan Director of Lay Ministry, and going to see someone who was a director of *lay* ministry really annoyed me. I had to do that because I was a woman and I wrote a stroppy letter to the Archdeacon and said, 'I am already a lay minister. I want to be ordained as a priest. I want to be considered on those grounds from now on.'

When women are priests and bishops the lay/clerical divide will be transformed, I hope. It needs to be. It stinks in a lot of ways. You know: priests are men; lay people are women. But we're all people of God. We're all disciples and we all follow Christ, and what it is about a vocation to priesthood which separates people out from other people I don't know and I'm very suspicious of. But I have to say, for me, that being a priest is about who I am in some sort of essential way, and that's been confirmed since I was ordained a deacon; that this is *me*. It's something that's very difficult to explain because I'm also aware of so many other ways in which I might be conning myself, but it feels to me as if ordination is a life-long commitment to a way of being which is a way of *service*. I don't want to say it's about being separated out or singled out or anything like that, because I don't think it is; but it is about serving. When I think back to nursing I think of all the ways in which I've cared for people who are in need, while obviously giving them the responsibility of caring for themselves too, and my work now is so similar. When I'm counselling people who are bereaved I'm being a servant to them in their needs.

There's also the other side of being a priest, which is helping the people of God to develop a vision of what's possible for them, and sharing my own vision of what's possible for them so that together we develop strategies for moving towards that goal. So there's a leadership element in there, but it's a leadership which is exercised as a servant, because you're there for others, not for yourself. It's incredibly paradoxical, but that's where the gospel calls us to account, because if leadership becomes something that we seek for its own sake, then it's a power trip and that's not Christlike. Leadership so often becomes something which is just an ego trip, and that's when dog-collars and the persona of the role become more important than who the priest actually is. You see that happening again and again. And you can see it happening to yourself as well if you're not careful, because the structures of the Church militate towards that, they push you into unhealthy ways of being. But then the Church is a fallible institution and it's built its structures up over the centuries and they're extremely difficult structures to change, mainly because there's an in-built antipathy to change in the Church of England. The fact that the vote to ordain women went through last year is *astounding*, given the resistance to change and the reluctance to rock the boat.

Although I really enjoyed Westcott, the training wasn't very integrated. At Westcott we had Pastoral Studies but it was a bit like armchair psychology: you do a funeral and a visit to the undertaker's and the crem; you do a bit of community analysis, a bit of counselling. It was as if your academic theology was paramount and everything else – like Pastoral Studies – was a bit of a soft option, and ne'er the twain should meet, which I think is a very bad attitude. What's exciting about the post I'm going to in the United Reformed Church is that we will work hard to integrate theological reflections and the skills, knowledge and attitude needed for ministry. They have a different pattern of training. There's a four-year training and during that four years the ordinand has three places of being and doing: the Church, the community and the college, and the three work in a dynamic together. What happens as a result is a formation which is much more integrated in theory and practice than mine was, where you do your intellectual stuff and then you go and apply it to the parish from your ivory tower.

The other thing about training in the Church of England that needs looking at is what happens at the end of it. The ordinand is ordained to a parish where people don't know her or him, and yes, there are advantages in that, because as an agent of change it can actually be quite a powerful thing if people don't know what to expect. The disadvantage is that you're imposed on people whether they like you or not, and they are deprived of a proper chance to be full participants in the decision. *Because* of the way clergy are appointed the structures militate against collaboration between parish and priest, unless the priest initiates it, and that oppresses the people of God, because it infantilizes them by not giving them the responsibility of developing their own Christian roles.

That's why I'm so excited about working in the URC because accountability is written into the way the Church is structured: people are accountable from grass-roots upwards. The authority is given by the people of God to the Minister in order that she or he serves the congregation, and I think that's got a lot of integrity, although it's obviously fallible too. There are benefits about the Anglican way, but sometimes they're difficult to find. I mean, it's like disestablishment. I think in many ways the connection between Church and State is a very positive thing, but if it ever happened, I think the Church of England would realize what a wonderful wicket they had been on for so long, having it so easy.

It sounds bad, I know, but I worry about people who are eclectic in their religious beliefs. There is a real rootlessness in society and one of the ways people express that is through religion by saying one day, oh yeah, Buddhism, great, and then it's Sufism the next. Going to the URC isn't an abandonment of my Anglican roots, because Anglican is what I am. But the URC's motto is *semper reformanda*, always reforming, always moving onwards rather than looking backwards. And that, to me, is extremely exciting.

However, I was brought up as an Anglican, and Anglicanism is my roots – and therefore my identity to a certain extent. When I think about Anglican distinctiveness the first word that comes to my mind is worship, and within Anglicanism there is a tremendous variety of ways in which you can worship. I mean, Norry's funeral was just the most beautiful offering to God, and it was so Anglican. There was incense and there were candles and there were wonderful hymns, and it was a celebration and a festival, and it enabled emotion rather than repressing it. It was challenging and it was lively and it was corporate; it was the body of Christ celebrating Norry's life, celebrating his life as an offering to God. And I think if I were to say what my Anglican identity was, I would say that something about Norry's funeral sums it up for me: the corporate celebration of life as an offering to God.

Just before I left Westhoughton, where I was a curate, the churchwarden stood up in a meeting and said, 'It's been wonderful having a woman priest in our midst.' And I felt recognized for something that I feel I am already. By the time your book is published I'll almost certainly be ordained as a priest, and that will be a public recognition of who I am, but inside it won't make much difference to me. It's a bit like living together before getting married: the relationship changes when you're married, but not fundamentally. It's already there and operating. I feel the same about waiting for my ordination to the priesthood. I feel I'm a priest now and I regard myself as such, but when I'm ordained I will be able finally to celebrate the Eucharist, and that will remove some of the pastoral and liturgical frustrations I have now. At the moment I'm a priest throughout the week in terms of my pastoral work, in terms of the contacts I have, in terms of who I am; yet on Sunday I can't offer that one service on behalf of the people, which is the celebration and remembrance of the body of Christ. When I was in charge of a small part of the parish at Hart Common they took to me as their priest, but there always had to be a man coming in to do the Eucharist and that felt very disabling.

It makes me angry – if I let it. But I'm a very determined person, and anger motivates me. Adrienne Rich has a wonderful collection of poetry called *A Wild Patience Has Taken Me This Far*, and that 'wild patience' seems to me to be about anger; that it keeps you at it, keeps you moving forward. It's a brilliant line because it's wild and it's passionate, and yet it's strategic to be patient: being patient means knowing where you want to get to, and perhaps suffering too. There's nothing wrong with being angry. Self-control's about keeping quiet when it's necessary: it's also about speaking out when you need to. Quakers have a wonderful phrase, 'speaking truth to power', and I like that because it's about oppressed people speaking out against oppressive people. Sometimes it's easier just to collude, and that's the big danger, especially when it's comfortable. But there are women in the past who have stuck at it, people like Una Kroll and lots of women all through the centuries who have had this sort of treatment, and if they've stuck with it, why shouldn't I?

I've always thought it much better to fight from within an oppressive institution than marginalize yourself by leaving. It's no good doing that. It's much better to be there and to be articulate than it is to not be there, and instead to be an invisible priest or an angry lay person. The problem is that if you *don't* get angry, you are seen by some as colluding with oppressive structures, and if you *do* get angry, you are dismissed as strident. It's so difficult for women, that one of the commonest ways we are put down is by being labelled strident or angry. It happens time and time again and it's *such* a put-down and such an easy way of trivializing what we have to say. It also means that as a woman you have to be a strategist with your anger, and I think humour's the best tool to use there, because you can be angry and humorous and people listen because you made them laugh, rather than thinking, 'Oh God, here she goes again.' I'm not actually very good at that but I try to be. I try to fight it with symbol as much as action. Being a full-time working mother, being pregnant behind the altar, as I was with the two boys, are both ways of having a presence and of saying things about priesthood in a way that is different. That feels very important to me, because it means using a bit of imagination about who I am.

I know that if I am labelled a feminist it gives people a good excuse to marginalize me and not listen to me. I remember preaching a sermon once and coming down and shaking people's hands at the end of the service and someone came up to me and said, 'You're not one of those feminists, are you?' and I was caught on the hop and said, 'No,' which I've *always* regretted because it felt like a loss of integrity. I felt I betrayed something of myself. But it made me realize that it's my responsibility to put my feminism over in a way which does not completely alienate, and to do so through who I am as much as through what I say or do.

Throughout my curacy it was always my priority to affirm women and to encourage them to take on leadership roles, to become churchwardens or lay readers, or to go back to work if that was right for them. That sort of encouragement has always been a priority of mine. I've wanted to express preferential options for women. I've also done that through my preaching, through trying to offer insights. One of the ways I've tried to show the visibility of women is by changing the language of the liturgy, so that I say 'neighbour' and drop the 'men' in the Creed. People soon get used to it.

One of the most difficult things for women can be self-definition. I know when I was nursing that I lost confidence and I lost the ability to articulate things that were important to me. I became less than myself through wearing that uniform and through being part of those structures. It's a very invidious process, and yet you can stand by watching it happen to yourself and be quite powerless to say, 'This is who I am. Listen to me. I'm here.' I think this happens to a hell of a lot of people in society today. It happens through unemployment. You get labelled 'unemployed' and that shrinks you, however much you might fight against it. It happens through poverty, through lack of education opportunities. It happens to women all the time. I mean, I've heard other male clergy say, 'Oh, the Mothers'

Union, the old dears,' and it *shrinks* those women and it's really debilitating and it makes me very angry. At least feminism is making women more visible. I look forward to the day, too, when gay people can enjoy a more public presence than they do now.

I've felt for some time that there's not nearly enough consultancy work done between incumbent and curate. The URC put the 'curacy' during the college years, so a person has a church placement for those four years, and then they go straight on to their own congregation after the training. That seems a much better scheme to me, because during those four years they are well supported by different groups and are always analysing what they're doing back in college, whereas with the Anglican structure the curate has only the incumbent to relate to, and if the incumbent is set in his ways, that can be very difficult for both parties. Not only that, but all too often curates turn into the sort of incumbent who repeats those patterns. So I've got a lot of questions about the way formation of priests happens in the Anglican Church. I've been very lucky myself. I fell into a relationship which I gained a lot from. But others of my friends have had awful times, so awful that I'm surprised they haven't left.

The other thing that's happening at the moment is that people are getting a very biased impression of the reaction of those within the Church to the influx of female incumbents. You know, some priests are standing up and causing a great rumpus and saying, 'Well, of course my parish is with me on the issue,' when in fact many are not at all. Some congregations might be in favour of having a woman priest, but of course the priest has the voice, and that voice is heard, and congregations are often quietly but firmly told they don't really understand the issue. When that happens, it's deeply patronizing, and that makes me very angry because there are a lot of very mature congregations out there whose lives are their own, and they sustain themselves regardless of who the priest is. Westhoughton is very like that, and that was a wonderful training for me. I learned more from the congregation and the parish than I did from anyone else.

While I was there I was the only woman among twelve other male clergy in the Area Deanery and I sometimes found it difficult to find a voice. But that was again part of the process I was talking about earlier, where you are de-voiced, or you collude with the structures and by doing so de-voice yourself. I remember the first meeting when the Area Dean said, 'Right, brothers –' and I said, 'Um, I'm not a brother, I'm a sister,' and he said, 'Oh, here we go.' One of the other priests said, 'Listen, we have to take it seriously that there are women in our midst nowadays,' and from then on the Area Dean called us 'friends' or made a joke about it, and I actually ended up getting on really well with him.

I didn't actively seek to be working with the United Reformed Church. I was on the lookout for a teaching job, knowing my curacy was coming to an end, and this job came up. Because the URC has some exciting ideas about the training of ministers as an integrated process, I thought, why not apply? I was also very resistant to the idea of taking another curate's post until I am ordained as a priest. I do think to be an assistant has long-term effects on people, that bits of them close down and shrink. A lot of women have to battle against an acquired assistant's mentality.

Teaching really excites me. I felt for a number of years, and especially when I was at Westcott, that I would really enjoy being part of the process of formation from a teaching point of view, and I felt that I had something to contribute to that. I also welcome the way in which teaching in another Church will force me to grow in gaining different perceptions and different perspectives, and I hope that'll deepen my ecumenical sensibilities.

Ecumenism means a lot to me. A good way of looking at it is to look at the body of Christ, and to remember that it's a very broken body. I think our calling from God is to make it a whole body. I think that's what we should be really striving towards, and much more passionately than we do. Having said that, I do think diversity is to be valued, and to lose that would be a real shame. I think we need to be growing towards deeper understanding of each other and respect for each other. Our unity should be in our mutual recognition that baptism is the sacrament we all start with. Baptism binds us together, and the Eucharist should hold us together. It's when Christians of different denominations start thinking theologically about their differences that they start getting irate and things start falling apart, so we need to strive towards the ability to transcend our differences in a vision of greater unity.

This of course can be done to a fault, and it's something the Anglican Church is very good at. It prides itself on its liberalism, but the problem with liberalism is that ideologically it can lose any idea of transformation and become very regressive and reactionary. So although I'm a liberal in some respects, I do have misgivings about liberalism. Liberals talk very much more about a God of Love than they do about a God of Judgment and a God of Justice, and that God is there too. I do think we need to be saying sometimes, 'This gay bashing is wrong,' or 'This sexism is evil,' or 'This greed is sinful,' which are very unpopular words to use. I think we need to have the courage of our convictions. We need not to care that those sorts of view are very unpopular and sometimes very controversial.

One of the most invidious things about liberalism is the idea that it's all about even-handedness when it isn't at all. I mean, I do feel that those 'liberal' priests who are against the ordination of women, and who claim to be terribly fair and just and egalitarian, haven't honestly and with insight and self-knowledge put themselves in the imaginary situation of having their own vocation to the priesthood denied them on the grounds of their sex. I don't think they've ever thought through what that would feel like. In the end it comes down to misogyny; sometimes that misogyny is vicious and sometimes that misogyny is very courteous, and both are difficult to cope with. We all, men and women, suffer from ingrained sexism that goes back a long way.

I don't think that's what the gospel calls us to. What I think we're called to, and what I feel driven by, is a vision of the Realm of God. For me that is a vision of people living in community on the basis of justice, of good relationships, of peace. It's more than a vision, it's an overriding desire, it's a passionate quest, and it engages all of me. It engages my intellect and my emotions. It's something I just feel pulled towards. And part of being an ordained person is saying, as Luther did, 'This is where I stand and I can do no other.' It's a statement of intent and purpose and life.

If people think the clergy are finished, then maybe that's because the Realm of God is a marginalized concept in today's society; but Jesus lived in a society where it was a marginalized concept too. Not only that, but he lived among marginalized people, and we need to be with marginalized people the world over because they're the people who go into the Realm of God first. Therefore, being 'relevant' in terms of our message is irrelevant: being 'relevant' in terms of the way we *proclaim* our message is another matter. Clergy need to be much more skilful about presentation and about ways of proclaiming, and that's something that I'll be wanting to say as a tutor. I'll be saying, 'Right, what can we do about gaining communication skills, using the media, using the press?' Because this is the world we live in today, and perhaps a sermon isn't the best way to put information over didactically any more.

One of the things I enjoyed in my curacy more than anything else was doing school assemblies and getting 150 kids engaged and acting and talking. There are so many exciting ways to put the gospel over, and of course in a way it's easy with children, but it *is* a desperately exciting thing to be doing, to be proclaiming a message which isn't fashionable but is real. So I'd never see the Church or the clergy's purpose as finished, because the Realm of God isn't finished; but we are living in a society where relativism has the ideological sway, because it's easy, and to my mind that is an ideological way of undermining any corporate move towards something that is good. That's why I believe that if I have a vision of the future, and of the body of Christ, then one of the best places to move towards that vision is by trying to influence for the greater good those who are training for the Church of the future.

It's very easy to knock the Church. And to be honest, I don't blame people who do. Okay, some of it's just the press, some of it's people not wanting to believe the best, but perhaps we don't talk enough about what we are doing and what we are for. We don't talk enough about the evils of violence, the evils of homelessness, the evils of racism, the evils of homophobia. There are plenty of things I can think of which are crying out to be addressed by the Church in a very public and outspoken way, and I think that most people would agree. We need to be shouting a lot more and saying, 'This is wrong, and it's for us and everyone to take responsibility for making this right.' I can understand why it doesn't happen, because voices get fragmented, and that's part of the brokenness of the Church. It's very difficult for us to speak with one clear voice because we don't have one clear voice.

That's perhaps why we have to be content to work on a very small agenda, while seeing that agenda as part of something greater. That is why focusing and strategy and being economical with energy are important, although having said that, I think there's something absolutely glorious about the real generosity of love in Christ on the Cross, which isn't strategic or economical with energy at all: it's totally unstinting. I think sometimes we in the Church should look harder at that and say, yes, let's *go* for it. I mean, I get quite bored by the smallness of the debate about the ordination of women, not because it's not important – it is – but because I think Jesus Christ is waiting patiently for us to catch up with some of the *really* important things that we should be addressing now. The environment and the whole survival of this planet are the biggest thing we face. As God's Creation, what are we *doing* to it? It's the incredibly big things which we prevent ourselves from looking at properly, because looking at them means that we have to change, and we don't want to.

When I think about the issues facing us, and when I think about the fragmentation of voices, I'm reminded of the diversity of voices in the Bible. The Bible doesn't have a common voice, but the Gospels describe a common vision, and if you look at the Bible you'll find what you need to know right there. I'm not saying I take everything the Bible has to say literally, but I do see the Bible as a description of normative Christian experience. When I use the Bible I look to it with imagination, with an eye to the subtexts, to the different layers of narrative and meaning that are there. What I love most about it is the fact that it's a story, and like any story there are main characters and less important characters: I love looking to where God might be speaking to us through other biblical characters, through those who are voiceless in the Bible or marginalized. It's a very alive series of stories which we hear as people of the twentieth century with our own perspectives, but which still speak to us. There's judgment, too. We can't forget that. I know I tend to gloss over the passages I don't like, but I try to remind myself, well, no, hold on a minute, go back on that, because okay, it *might* not be fashionable to castigate fornicators and homosexuals as Paul does, but at least you need to look at why he was doing it. Or then again, perhaps you don't! So when women are told to be subject to their husbands, I'll say, okay, in Palestine of that day maybe I'd have taken that on board, but I'm also going to say, hold on a minute, we have to continue to re-interpret scripture in today's light.

Each of us selects what suits us depending on what our perspective is, and I think perhaps we shouldn't be frightened of that: perhaps diversity of thought is something which is God-given. And okay, if I read the Bible differently from Tony Higton or Graham Leonard, how are we still going to communicate? We're all Christians, so what is our basis of unity? And how do we listen to each other? This is one thing that I'm going to be coming across when I'm tutoring, trying to help ordinands gain insight into their own ways of thinking, and the attitudes that they have: you know, why is it that they're picking out particular texts? That is a fascinating process, but clergy are actually very resistant to self-exploration at that depth. So are we all. But when people can do that, that's when they make really good ministers, because they can take the risk of being vulnerable to that extent. And that's exactly what should be happening with ministers, so that you don't get bigots turning out the other end of college with great big egos to defend. And don't we know them!

I don't have any particular goals for the future. Ambition's a word that most churchpeople feel quite awkward about, and it makes me squirm, because what I feel called to is growth in Christ's presence. Of course I want opportunities to come my way, and this is perhaps why the word 'ambition' makes me wriggle, because demand and vision are implicit in the word 'ambition': I want opportunities to come my way for me to develop in ways which I believe are God-given. That means that I've got to be very responsible for ensuring that where I go and what I do is always responding to the will of God, and that if I seek authority or power I don't seek it for its own sake. If what I do furthers the Realm of God, then I'm not going to say no to power or authority, because I think that's almost as sinful as saying yes to the wrong sort of power.

I said I don't have any particular goals, but teaching was a goal. I wanted to teach and I'm glad that's been recognized. But after this teaching job, which is going to last for five years or so, I've no sense of direction at all. I mean, I might find myself returning to a parish as an incumbent, or I might find myself carrying on teaching. It will just depend on what comes up and what feels right to go for at the time. But wherever anyone finds themselves there's always work to be done. So you start where you are. You start with the people around you, and it doesn't matter where you are – it *really* doesn't matter where you are. If as a priest you are frustrated where you are, then that's because you're not looking deeply enough at why you're frustrated. I take a big degree of responsibility for who I am and where I am and what I should be doing in a situation, and I think it's dangerous to allow myself to imagine that the Bishop's going to look after me, or that God's going to look after me, when in fact I should be looking after myself. If you accept self-responsibility you have a recipe to avoid frustration, wherever you are placed and whatever you have to do.

For myself, I wouldn't mind where I was or what I was asked to do, but because I'm married with three small children, that's where the cutting edge starts to come in. I mean, I don't feel my children should sacrifice, say, their education because of my vision of where I should be. On the other hand, we go places as a family, and if other families are living in housing estates in the middle of Birmingham or the middle of Manchester, then why shouldn't we as well? Just because we're middle-class, why shouldn't we be there with the marginalized? So far we've not had to resolve that contradiction – and there is a contradiction there. I think a lot of clergy are faced with that much more sharply than we are at the moment. So I think you have to say to yourself, 'Okay, if other people are enduring violence, perhaps we, as a clergy family, might be able to do a little bit towards countering that.' When you've got three small children it's a very very hard question, but if we have to face it we will.

The other thing that comes to my mind when talking about this is the importance and centrality of a prayer life that opens you up to God, and strengthens your faith when things are hard and choices are really difficult to make, or there isn't really an option at all. I think you can sustain anything with a sense of the presence of God. Having just moved house, I'm looking for a new pattern of prayer at the moment, and I'm using the Anglican Daily Office. A habit of daily prayer is a real strength. I seek the presence of God in my life, and I think I reflect theologically a lot. To my mind it's a form of prayer to be thinking, 'Where is God in this place?' or 'Where is God in this situation?' or 'What are the imperatives of the Realm of God in this situation?' Prayer is also something more contemplative. Una Kroll once said to me that when you're a busy person there's nothing wrong with 'plummeting prayers', which take you deep down into stillness, even if only for a few minutes. Those sorts of prayer take me back to my Quaker days, where I used to centre myself in greeny-black depths – they're always dark green, which is odd, isn't it? Dark, dark green, like the green at the heart of a forest, is a place where God has always been for me. It's like being in a very deep, cool, gentle, refreshing place. So perhaps two or three times a day I try to stop and centre down into that green place. I find God in silence more than anywhere else, and I don't create enough silence for myself, but every so often Peter and I say Compline together, which is a lovely end to the day.

There are some essentials which just don't change, and parish life is one of them. When I think about life in the local church congregation I think it is pretty constant, especially in the ways that people are good neighbours to each other, and have been through the centuries. That's the real apostolic succession: grand-mother to grandchild! You know, whether they're in or out of the Church there is a very special and ordinary discipleship which goes on all the time, and I think that's something we all should strive for. Maybe I'm being idealistic because I had such a good curacy, but the fact is that the Church is supposed to be experiencing real upheaval at the moment, and yet I think we might well look back in thirty years' time, fifty years' time, and say, 'What was all the fuss about? What has actually changed, really?' My bet is that the essentials won't have changed. Parish life won't have changed. God won't have changed.

I think we in the Church have always to be open to being surprised. I don't know where the Church of England's going, but I know it doesn't look enough for the surprises in life, and when it does see one it calls it a crisis. Well, crisis is the Greek word for judgment, and that's always going to be there. The present crisis, which the media keep discussing at such length, I don't see at all. I see a lot of adapting to the modern world that has to happen, and I see a lot of change, but that's not exactly crisis, and as long as we root and locate our faith in God, then change isn't something to be frightened of. It becomes an opportunity.

As human beings we're very good at reducing mystery to human boundaries of thought, and I think we need to be careful not to do that. There are some things which we just can't know, but we're very acquisitive about knowledge. We want to own it. I remember the Resurrection first came alive to me when reading the story of the disciples on the road to Emmaeus, with their grief clouding their vision, with their eyes closed to seeing the surprise of what life had to offer, and then how their hearts warmed within them when Jesus met them on the way and started talking about the scriptures. There was a gradual illumination as they walked, and that's what I mean about our tendency to reduce things. As I journey through life I can cloud my vision by restricting my idea of what is possible. God is much more immense than my parameters of thought or comprehension, and I don't need to understand everything. I don't need to know where I'm going, whether in this life or the next, but I do know that God is drawing us onwards all the time, onwards and onwards and onwards, until the Realm of God is realized here on earth. I know we're going somewhere. There is something ahead of us. We've not arrived yet, and perhaps that's what we try to express when we talk about the Second Coming.

If the body of Christ is broken and fragmented, I want to hold on to that as a symbol which embodies the truth of our existence. That's very close to how I see the Realm of God. I think the fact that the Resurrection has remained in our Creeds through the centuries means that we do see ourselves as constantly broken and renewing, constantly striving towards wholeness, and that's a very wonderful and awe-inspiring vision. I find it utterly captivating as a purpose and a vision by which to live my life.

I've staked my all on my faith. And it could turn out to be a terrible waste, but I think holding on to a sense of waste in the face of the preciousness of life is very important. I often think how strange it is that Anglo-Catholics get so caught up with consuming the elements after a Eucharist. I know it's because we must show real respect for the body of Christ that has been consecrated on the altar, and so we should consume all that is remaining because we don't know quite what might happen to it if we didn't consume it. It would just be poured down the drain or whatever. And I often think to myself, well, yes, but Jesus poured out his life for us in a gesture of enormous waste. There was so much waste in his death, and I think we have to hold on to that waste as a lesson and a reminder of his very real sacrifice for us.

I see my priesthood as lifelong, just as I made my marriage vows wholeheartedly for life. Ordination vows aren't oppressive things, they're there because they're a public recognition of a change of state, of a change of being, and they're made in the eyes of God. When I married Peter, I was no longer single, I became married, and that was part of who I was then and part of who I will continue to be, God willing. Ordination is the same.

I don't see priesthood as confined to the priestly dog-collared 'role'. If somebody leaves the Church to do another job, then I would say that he or she is still a priest, dog-collar or not, parish or not. It's not only what you do, but it's who you are. It is not an impermanent thing, and I would really want to resist the idea that you can be a priest one day and not a priest the next day, that you can drift in and out of it, because I don't think you can. I think people who do think that are just buying into a sense of impermanence and lack of commitment. It *is* very difficult to make commitments that are lifelong, but we've got to carry on trying, even though so often the odds are stacked against us to sustain marriages and families and vocations and communities.

I feel good about being a priest. I feel good about who I am, and I enjoy being a woman. I don't want to cast myself as a victim in any way. But the fact is that women in the Church are finding a voice now which they've not had before, and that's exciting because it means that we can start saying new things, different things. What I think we also need to remember is that we're fallible and we're just as liable and open to corruption as men. It's quite easy to get carried away by a sort of feminist utopia and forget that we have so much to offer precisely because we come with an experience of being victims. We need to hold on to that experience and bring it with us, because that way, hopefully, we can help other people who are still victims the world over. That's really important, otherwise we'll end up perpetuating the same oppressive ways of being.

I want to take all the experiences I have with me into my ministry of priesthood, because being a priest will fulfil what I know and what I have and what I am. Being a priest is about commitment to a life of service, and commitment to God. Being a priest is about who I am and who I will be for the rest of my life. It's who I am in the eyes of God and I hope it's the best of me.

(*Frances Ward is now ordained as a priest.*)

GRAHAM LEONARD

Age: 72
Age at ordination: 27

(RETIRED) BISHOP OF LONDON

I did not expect to like Graham Leonard. Thoroughly outspoken on many issues, but perhaps best known for his fierce opposition to the ordination of women to the priesthood, his conservative image had never attracted me. His reputation is mixed. There are many people in whom he arouses feelings of colossal hostility, and there are those who will not hear a word against him. In fact, when writing to potential contributors I very nearly dismissed Graham Leonard as someone with whom I felt sure I could not work. But I did so, and for three reasons. You usually learn the most from interviewing those with whom you disagree. Because his views had driven me up the wall for years I genuinely wanted to find out what made him tick. Also – and I am embarrassed to admit it – a part of me believed that if he spent a week in my company he couldn't fail to change his mind.

If come-uppance was what I deserved for such motives, I certainly got it. When I wrote to ask Graham Leonard whether he would be prepared to be interviewed, he replied promptly and courteously in the affirmative. When I spoke to him on the phone the following week, he was disarmingly friendly and talked about trees and pubs and good beer. He also expressed a certain amount of surprise and pleasure that I wanted to meet him. 'I am humbled,' he said, and I believed him. He didn't patronize me on the grounds of my age, my sex or my opinions. I felt rather ashamed that I had imagined he might.

Quite what I had expected Graham Leonard to be like I don't know, but the real man was a good deal more attractive; polite and kind, with polished manners. I spent the better part of a week with him, driving daily to Oxfordshire where he lives with his wife, Priscilla. Given that they have lived in more than one episcopal

99

palace, I had rather expected the Leonards of my imagination to be living in a house to match my notions of their retired life; something substantial and Edwardian perhaps. Wrong again. They live on a tidy 1970s housing estate in Witney. 'We wanted to live somewhere manageable,' Priscilla Leonard told me over her delicious homemade bread and soup. 'We've lived in big houses all our life. And besides,' she added, 'they leak.'

Graham Leonard is a disconcerting mixture of stiffness and informality. Tall, square-faced, with grey hair and very bushy eyebrows, his sense of protocol, his dress (he wore episcopal purple throughout the week) and his gait (he walks, stands and sits ramrod straight) seem tailor-made to keep people at a distance. Yet he was not only charming to me throughout our time together, but also rather affectionate. We got on very well indeed, but he didn't seem to find being interviewed terribly easy, I think because he is more vulnerable than he would ever admit. The fact that he remained committed to our work together, and at some cost to himself, only increased my respect for him. He sat very still throughout our conversations, as if he were waiting for something, puffing on his pipe and occasionally getting up to find a book or a paper he wanted me to read. He sometimes took a while to get to the point, interrupting himself with anecdotes, but get there he always did. However, if I caught him unawares with a question he could be badly thrown, which gave the impression that the unexpected is regarded by him as less of a challenge than a disturbance.

I've met people who are easier to tease, but Graham Leonard always appreciated a good joke and, like all clergy, he had a fund of amusing stories about his fellow clerics which he was more than willing to share. Not only that, but he and his wife went out of their way to provide me with as much time and as many lunches as I wanted. They have been doing such things for years, albeit on a grander scale, and there was little real reason for them to do it for me, except out of kindness and generosity.

GRAHAM LEONARD

No, I don't mind a bit having a chat first, don't mind me. Could I just ask you a question, which is: have you read my biography? I mean, do you want to look at it or do you not want to look at it? No, well, that's all I wanted to know.

Tell me a bit more about yourself. I mean, I read your blurb in there and so on. Where do you actually come from originally? Ah, Wantage, I see. And you're the youngest of five. So what does your father do? Oh, that's interesting, because my elder son's a doctor, and so's his wife. Of course my wife and I both read botany, and that involved quite a lot of biochemistry and physiology, and things like that. Are you a botanist or a gardener or anything like that? Your great-great-grandfather was? Oh well, that's very fine.

Yes, I'm fine to start. Is that thing switched on?

My parents were relatively old when I was born, and I was in a sense the apple of their eye. I was an only child, and my mother was told she couldn't have any more. Whether that's true or not I don't know, but I regard being an only child as a great deprivation. I do think that because you do not have to rub up against brothers and sisters you can become very self-centred.

My father was a priest, and so was one of his brothers. He came from a large family, there were nine of them altogether, and they either died fairly young or went on to great age. He was the youngest and he was a very good mathematician, a genuine mathematician, he read Maths at Cambridge and got a First. The one thing he taught me was that I wasn't a mathematician. He'd have an equation and he'd say, now, if we do such-and-such to this equation, then this follows. And I would say to him, yes, I can see that, but *why* do you do that to that equation? And he would say, well, it's the obvious thing to do, isn't it? And I could never make that jump.

My father was methodical, organized and utterly reliable. He was a contented man, and not at all gregarious: he thought it was a really slightly extravagant display of emotion to send his brother a Christmas card. He was an evangelical, ordained when he left university and theological college, and he met and married my mother in his first parish. My mother came from a much simpler background. She hadn't got my father's intellect but she was a woman of immense determination who went at everything, it didn't matter what it was. I remember during the war when you couldn't get clothes, my father's overcoat was getting very shabby and she said, 'I will turn it.' She'd never turned an overcoat in her life before but she just took it to pieces and turned it and put it together again and it wasn't bad.

My mother wasn't given to ruminative thought. She made up her mind about things quickly and that was that. She also had some very strange characteristics. One was that she had a totally fixed idea that if somebody wasn't looking at you, they wouldn't hear what you said. So I can remember some marvellous occasions when, having talked to somebody, she'd turn away and then make a comment about them: '*He's* a bit of a wag, isn't he?'

I was fond of her. She died when she was seventy-six, relatively young compared with my father who went on to ninety. I heard about her death during my first staff meeting as Archdeacon of Hampstead on a Monday morning; they called me out and told me she'd died the day before. But she lived long enough to know that I was going to become an archdeacon: when I told her she said, 'What! You an archdeacon? Don't be ridiculous!'

Nothing daunted my mother at all. She went about everything at great speed, unlike my father, who went slowly. He was one of the least athletic men I've ever known. Her constant cry was: 'Come along, Douglas, come along! Hurry up! Come along!' The only time he ever became physically animated was when he got on the shores of what to his dying day he *insisted* on calling the German Ocean, which is the North Sea. And you know how the East Coast is quite dangerous in places, it shelves quickly and there are undertows and so on. Well, get him in there, in one of those old-fashioned bathing costumes, and he *hurled* himself into the waters! He used to pull me in with him and I was absolutely petrified, and I really never enjoyed it. I love being *on* the water but I've never enjoyed being *in* it, and I think it goes back to that.

It's very difficult to say how close I was to my father as a child. Certainly I was in the last years of his life. And although I would unhesitatingly have said that my mother was the more memorable, other people remember my father. They remember his kindness and his gentleness. They remember his utter reliability. This surprises me, because he didn't give the impression of being a very inspiring person, but he obviously had an impact which I was really not aware of as a child. But then you see, I was terribly self-contained: I usually had my nose in a book.

If you were to ask me where I come from, I would almost certainly say Norfolk, even though I was born and brought up in London, simply because I had a Great-Aunt Matilda there who was a tremendous character. Matilda was looked after by a Cousin Nancy – these were the days when you called your relations 'Cousin' so-and-so – and we went to see them every year. It was a great performance. Up to Liverpool Street with a huge portmanteau with a curved top. And you wouldn't remember it, but you used to get Peters' milk chocolate, and it came in round tubes and each piece was wrapped up in paper; the tubes were chocolate-coloured with gold lettering on. And when we went up to Great-Aunt Matilda's my mother always bought a tube of these for us to have on the journey, it was the only time in the year we had them. Then we changed on the Midland and Great Northern line, and went on to Holt. Matilda lived just by the station, but the railway track is now a ring-road, and they've built an estate just south of that. It's very sad. I feel I've lost part of my history because the house has gone.

However, the first home I can really remember was in Battersea, which we moved to when I was small. I went to a little dame school there and then an all-age school which had boys of seven or eight, and went right up to eighteen. Actually they taught very well, it was probably the best teaching I ever had. Then I went away to Monkton Combe school, near Bath. My godfather was the headmaster, and I think he helped to make it financially possible for me to go there. Academically it wasn't good. On the other hand it did mean that I had to rub up against people. My wife always says that I have all the marks of being an only child. All I can say is they'd be a lot more evident than they are if I hadn't been away to school.

Despite the fact that my father was evangelical, there was not as much religion at home as you'd think, although I was expected to go to Crusaders and things like that: Crusaders was a club for young Christian middle-class children. Later on, at Monkton, there was the Christian Union, and if you weren't a committed evangelical at Monkton you could have a pretty painful time. But at this stage I'd never been in contact with anything other than the evangelical tradition – except once, and that was very interesting.

I must have been about ten or eleven, and there was this great mission in Battersea. A lot of churches and bodies took part, including the Salvation Army, and there was a great rally in the Town Hall in Lavender Hill. During the course of the evening a party came in from a very high church of great tradition: in they came with banners, swinging incense, which I'd never smelt before, and the vicar gave a marvellous address. And to my astonishment, having been told that anything Romish was very wicked, the Salvation Army people next to me started singing Hallelujah and clapping their hands and generally approving! And when I went back and asked my mother about this I was told not to ask questions. But I remember seeing that procession and smelling the incense, and I just knew that this was right for me. It was a totally different sort of feel and outlook from anything at home or at school.

Monkton was very conservative and evangelical, even more evangelical than my father, and it was rather assumed by every-body that I would be ordained. I always thought I might be called to be ordained but I wasn't prepared to drift into it. Two things, really, caused me to change my allegiance from the evangelical position of my father and the school. The first was that when I read 1 Corinthians with all that St Paul was saying to the very peculiar lot who were in the Church of Corinth, I thought to myself how this was totally unlike the Christian Union at Monkton which was all the respectable people, all the good people, all the people who were toeing the line. I suddenly became aware of the fact that the Church was for sinners, and the Christians at Corinth didn't become holy overnight just because they had become Christians. The second thing was that although it was always being drummed into me that I was justified by grace and by faith and that it was all God's work, nevertheless it seemed at Monkton to depend upon whether I'd had a particular experience of conversion, which I couldn't say I'd had because I'd been brought up as a Christian.

I remember once when we were saying the Prayer of Humble Access, 'We do not presume to come to this thy table, O merciful Lord, trusting in our own righteousness, but in thy manifold and great mercies . . .' and I suddenly saw that the sacraments were there as something which I could *do*. They were an expression of my willingness to love and serve God, and they didn't depend upon how I *felt*. This is why sacramental life has been so fundamental for me, not only personally but in my pastoral dealings. To the muddled, to the doubting, one can say: I know you're muddled, I know you're doubting, but you can come with total confidence, and without presumption, to God in the sacraments and receive His grace. This deliverance, this sense of assurance, was a great liberation to me.

I went up to Balliol, Oxford, and read botany. Because of the war I did the whole thing in a very short time and I have what is a very convenient thing to have, an Honours Unclassified Degree, because I wasn't up long enough to be classified. (Unlike my wife who did the full course and has a very good First.) I think one can say that it was on the whole only the odd bods from my school who went to Oxford; those who were conforming went to Cambridge. Certainly I was a bit of an odd bod. In fact, by the time I went up to Oxford I was in a pretty muddled state, frankly.

War had broken out in September '39 when I was still at school. There was an arrangement called the Reception Unit Scheme by which, if you were in the Officer Training Corps at school – and I think you had to be a sergeant or something – you could join up and then you were released until you were old enough to be called up. So a friend of mine and I went across to Bristol and joined up before going to university. I always like to think I was a volunteer and not a conscript in the war.

After my six months in the ranks I went to the Officer Cadet Training Unit, and at the end of that I joined a regiment. Three, four, possibly even five times, I was meant to go abroad and it was always cancelled, so I only served in this country. Then, at the beginning of '44 the War Office suddenly discovered that I had a science degree and I was seconded to the Ministry of Supply to do research. The Ministry of Supply was the body which was responsible for providing all the equipment for the Army and the Services, and I worked in the Army Operational Research Group until I came out of the Army at the end of '45 and went to theological college.

There were various factors that led me to a theological training. When I left school, all my instincts were to do something else for a period, which was one reason why I decided to go to Oxford to read Science, until I could see how things worked out. However, I'd already discovered early on that theology and philosophy made enormously good sense to me. Yet when I finally accepted that I was going for ordination, it didn't seem to be all of a piece with the earlier assumption of my father and the school. It was something new.

I'd also met a number of priests during the war, chaplains, who helped my development in various ways. There was one in particular, when I was stationed in Worcester. I met him in Smith's, I remember, and he said, 'Where do you go when you're off-duty?' I said, 'Well, you can go to the YMCA, but that's about it.' You never knew what to do when you were off-duty, you see. He said, 'Well, we've got plenty of room in the vicarage. You'd better have a room there.' So he gave me a room there, with a key, and said, 'Use it as you like, bring any friends you want.' I was able to go down there and relax and read and listen to music and so on, and that was super. After V E day, there wasn't much to do because our research had all been ended, so I also spent a lot of time in the library in Warminster where I was stationed, preparing for my theological training at Westcott House.

I was married fairly young, and being married made a difference to my choice of theological college. Priscilla and I had met at Oxford, in the labs, and there was never any doubt about it, none at all. *She* maintains I never actually proposed to her, that we took it for granted. I know I *did* propose, because I remember her saying I hadn't, so I remember doing it specially. But it was never in question, and we were married on 2 January 1943. And that's fifty years ago last January.

Because we had to live on a small grant while I was training we couldn't afford to move away from Cambridge where Priscilla's home was, so Priscilla worked in the genetics lab there while I was at Westcott. But I was very unhappy. What really made me unhappy about Westcott was its attitude. I mean, I'd come out of the Army, I'd been used to having a pattern which you either accepted or you didn't, but you worked within it. Yet the attitude at Westcott when I was there was: 'We don't have any rules but this is what we all do.' And I found that really morally offensive. I mean, it's blackmail. You either have rules and then you let people free within them, or you don't have any rules. What you don't do is to pretend you haven't got any rules when you've got lots of pressure to accept unspoken and undefined conventions.

I don't remember very much about the academic side of the training. I remember doing Old Testament, New Testament, Ethics, but I don't remember being taught much doctrine. As far as I remember, doctrine was geared to the Thirty-nine Articles and we went through them one by one. We spent quite a lot of time on the development of Christian worship. It was generally very scholarly, as you'd probably expect in Cambridge. And I may be wrong, but I don't remember any real help about things like pastoral visiting, or how you actually went about arranging worship in a parish. As students we didn't get much practical work at all. We went and taught in a school for a bit, and we used to go and visit in the hospitals. We visited the workhouse too – oh yes, they still had workhouses. I used to go to the workhouse regularly when I became a curate in Cambridge, it was part of my ordinary visiting, and they were really pretty awful.

I think the real trouble was that we had no experience to hang anything on to. You must realize that when I was at Westcott in '46, '47, it was very much in the spirit of Gentlemen in Holy Orders. The great majority of men there had been at public school; most of them had never been in an ordinary primary school or hospital, and they didn't know how it operated. The only piece of pastoral advice I can remember was the Principal telling us that when you went into a sickroom you shouldn't stand between the sick person and the fireplace because of the danger of infection!

In those days they didn't take all the care that we took later over placing people for their first curacy, and when I left Westcott nobody wanted me. I thought I'd better go to the north, because everybody said this is where the *need* is, so I offered myself to about five dioceses, but none of them wanted me at all, mostly because I was married and they hadn't got anywhere for me to live. Then one day I was in Cambridge, riding my bicycle down Drummer Street, and I pulled up by the traffic lights, and the Vicar of the parish where we worshipped in Cambridge, John Wallace, drew up beside me on a bicycle, and said, 'Have you got your title fixed up yet, Graham?' And I said, 'No, I'm really getting desperate. Nobody seems to want me.' 'Oh,' he said. 'Well, you'd better come to me then. That all right?' And the lights changed and he rode off. And that's how my first curacy was fixed up.

So we stayed on in Cambridge. John Wallace then left when I was a deacon, which didn't make life easy, and it was obviously not right for me to stay with the next man, so we left the diocese in '49 and I went down to Stansted where the airport is.

Stansted was wonderful, because they actually provided a curate's house, and we were a lot more comfortably off then than we had been. Before that I'd had to provide my own housing. I mean, the clergy today have no *idea* what the circumstances were like then, they just don't realize: no house was provided, no car, no expenses. Vicarages were provided, but curates' houses were not.

When I went to my first parish, three years later, I had to pay for the repair of the house and it was deducted under what they called 'dilapidations'. They assessed you over a period and if work had to be done, for which there wasn't enough money, then the Church Commissioners took a mortgage out on your house, to raise the money for paying for it, and the cost of that was deducted from your stipend. If you left before it was paid off, your successor inherited the debt. If your predecessor had retired and was still alive, part of his pension was deducted from *your* stipend, and paid quarterly in arrears.

This all goes back to the old concept of the Church of England benefice. A benefice (that is, a living in a parish) was a piece of property which you acquired and it had attached to it an endowment income which was yours by right as a freehold owner for as long as you were there. Out of that you were expected to pay for everything. You paid for the upkeep of the house; you paid the rates; you paid for any staff you had; you paid the curate, if you wanted a curate, or you persuaded the parish to pay. Now, the endowment income of each benefice varied enormously, depending how it had been endowed by various people over the years. For example, in Cornwall in 1904, the value of the benefices varied from £38 a year to over £2,000. And that's why people moved, or, if they got in on one that was fairly well off, they didn't move. It was as simple as that. This is why in the last century you had these clergy who were very comfortably off, and who didn't do much work; they hired a curate to do it, and they paid him a lot less than they had themselves. It's only since the war that there's been a central fund in a diocese for paying clergy. Even in 1964, when I was made a bishop, I wasn't provided with a car, although that was essential for the work, and the annual expense allowance was sufficient only for three months.

So the circumstances in which the clergy operate now are totally different, and the extent to which the Church of England was subsidized in the last century by the clergy has never been appreciated. When I was involved in Education for the Church of England I used to look up the accounts of the schools in the last century. Again and again you'd see the outgoing head-mistress's or headmaster's salary: on the other side you'd see perhaps something like a few pounds from the squire, local collections and so on, but the balance from the vicar.

In my first parish, Ardleigh, for instance, the church tower had been rebuilt largely at the personal expense of the vicar, Canon Perry, in 1877. If you look up there, you can see the photograph. There, that's my first parish church, and do you see the house behind it? It was the most lovely house, very cold, I mean we perished in it, but it was the nicest house we've ever lived in. And there, do you see the church tower? It's a lovely tower, that. It has a wonderful fifteenth-century tenor bell in it. Oh, I loved it there.

*

I never thought of being anything else other than a parish priest. I was very conscious of what I was trying to do. I was trying to 'enable people to become holy', or, 'enable people to become *themselves*', in the proper sense of that word. When I first went to Ardleigh, there was hardly anybody going to church at all, so the policy I adopted, because it was a very big parish, was to concentrate as much as I needed to on the people with whom I came in pastoral contact: the bereaved, the dying, those who came for baptisms, marriages and so on. I would be prepared to spend a great deal of time with one person or one family, and then I would say to them, 'Now, look, I've given you an enormous amount of time over these last few months. I'm here if you want me but I shan't be calling again for some time because I'll be doing the same thing with other people.'

This worked. I went through my first parish like a dose of salts, and by the time I left there was a very good congregation in the church, and some of the people who came to our Golden Wedding in January were the very people whom I brought into or back to the church when I was there all that time ago in the fifties.

I wonder if you should put this in, because it sounds very bigheaded, but when I was Bishop of London, a couple wrote to me and said, 'We're celebrating the fortieth anniversary of our wedding. Can we come and see you as part of our celebrations?' They were living in some place like Redditch, and I assumed they'd come up to London to see a show or something like that, but when they came in, charming couple, and I said, 'What else are you doing to celebrate?' they said, 'Oh, nothing. Seeing you is the way we're celebrating.'

I said, 'Really?!'

'Yes,' they said. 'You see, it hasn't always been easy over these forty years, but it was what you taught us when you prepared us for marriage that has kept us going. We just wanted to come and say thank you because we wouldn't have celebrated our fortieth wedding anniversary if it hadn't been for you.'

And it was lovely, it really was, but you see, the Lord is very good: most of the time you go on blindly, hoping you're doing something, and then suddenly the curtain comes up and you see a little bit of what's going on behind. This happened to me when that couple visited. And it's very often the things you're not conscious of that make a difference to people, quite simple things like how you actually speak to somebody. A shop assistant, for example: if you actually treat them as a person that will very often have a very profound effect upon them. And I'm not just talking about priests. I'm talking about anybody. The way you greet somebody, or the way you respond to their problems, are the ways that I believe the Christian gospel is communicated, or is hindered.

But things are very different for priests these days. One of the greatest differences between the time when I was ordained and the present time is this: when I was first ordained, I thought my job was ultimately to enable people to live with God in eternity; and therefore eternity was very important. I can remember taking it as a matter of fact that if I came across a street accident I would do what had to be done in terms of physical things, but I would then ask the person if there was anything on their conscience that worried them, and try to get some sign of repentance and give them absolution. This was absolutely vital to me, and I remember doing it on many occasions. Then I suddenly realized some years ago how one just didn't do that now!

I had some amusing experiences even then. I can remember when I was a curate in Cambridge, I got a message saying would I please go and visit Mr So-and-so who was at the point of death. I went straight round to his house, and there, in the living-room, were a couple of young men, who were the sons, and the old man, looking, I must say, jolly ill, lying in his trousers and vest on the sofa. I tried to have a word with one of the sons. I asked, 'Does he know how ill he is?' and the son seemed slightly embarrassed. So I started preparing the old man to die, whereupon he suddenly sat bolt upright and said, 'And where the hell do you think I'm going?' I said, 'Well, that depends on you, doesn't it?'

Of course he was nowhere near death. There had been a mix-up. The man did have cancer, but he was enjoying a remission. Several months earlier, when the man had been very ill, the younger son, who was a lapsed Catholic in fact, thought that a priest should visit him, and had asked a server at the church to ask me to go, but the server had forgotten to do so for some months. By the time I did turn up, the father had recovered temporarily. But the point I'm making is that in those days people took eternal destiny seriously in a way they don't now.

When I went to Ardleigh as vicar in 1952, I thought I was there for life, but after three years I was asked if I would go and be Director of Education for the diocese of St Albans. It seemed the right thing to do, so I went, again thinking that I would be some considerable time there, because there was a lot of reorganization to do in the light of the 1944 Education Act. Then three years after that, the Secretary of the National Society and the Church of England Schools Council died suddenly, and they said, 'We want you to go up to London to do the job.'

My interest in education really started in Stansted, at the local church school. I was in the school every morning of the week, and I loved it. I like young children. I've always loved just sitting down and talking to them and making plasticine elephants and things. That was quite a thing: they all knew I could make a plasticine elephant, so I always used to have to do this for them.

I don't know if you know the difference between aided and controlled schools, but after the 1944 Education Act a school could be aided or controlled. Aided meant that it was financially aided by the local authority, but it was basically a church school. Controlled meant that it was financed and run by the local authority, with the Church having limited rights. Well, my interest really started when the vicar in Stansted wanted to let the local school go controlled and I didn't. I fought a campaign in the parish, and we won – and the school's still going today, flourishing. That was really how I got into the nuts and bolts of education. And one of the interesting things about the Church of England and education is that the Church has always seen itself as a *partner* in the national system, having pioneered it initially, and has seen religious education not as an isolated part of the life of a school, but as the *background* to it.

When I left Ardleigh to become Archdeacon of Hampstead, the then Bishop of London said he thought I needed a break from education, and he put me on to the Social Responsibility side in the diocese. It was through that that I was appointed as a member of the General Synod's Board for Social Responsibility in 1967. In 1976 I was appointed Chairman of the Board, which meant being responsible for debates in Synod on such contentious issues as nuclear disarmament, race relations and South Africa. I also served as Chairman of the Church of England Board of Education from 1983 until 1988, and this meant taking a very active part in the debate in the House of Lords leading to the 1988 Education Reform Act.

I was Archdeacon of Hampstead for two and a half years. That was interesting because I had a parish church in the city, and I was doing pastoral work again after all that education. Then I became Bishop of Willesden. I was still very concerned with parish relations and after a few years I decided that the only way to be able to relate to the parishes properly, and, I might add, for the proper use of time, was to develop this system of pastoral visits to parishes. So when I was Bishop of Willesden I would go and spend a day in different parishes visiting people in their homes, visiting factories, visiting schools, and then it would all come to an end in the evening with a Parish Eucharist when I might baptize, confirm, or consecrate an altar. I never went to a parish to do those things alone, because I saw my job as a pastoral one.

When I became Bishop of Truro I developed the same system. Between us my suffragan bishop and I were able to make pastoral visits to all the parishes in eighteen months, and I got to the point in Cornwall where I knew lots of lay people in their homes, because I'd been and stayed the day in the parish and gone round visiting them. So in a sense I was able to go back and be a parish priest as well; not in the same depth, I agree, but I was nevertheless able to establish a continuing relationship with people, and it's surprising how they remember that.

I was Bishop of Truro from 1973 to '81. People have said that they were sending me off down there to be out of the way, because of my attitude to the Anglican Methodist Scheme, which I was against, and which had just been rejected. Well, whether they were or not, it actually didn't work out like that at all, because due to my chairmanship of the Board for Social Responsibility I was having to travel up to London really every week. It was killing, very arduous, but it did mean that I was still very much in the centre of things. I was in on other things as well, like the Anglican–Orthodox Doctrinal Discussions, which actually met in Truro on one occasion. So although I loved it down in Cornwall, and I really did love it there, it was a problem keeping the central demands in balance with the demands of the diocese.

I was still able to go on working on a pastoral basis to some extent as Bishop of London, though to nothing like the same degree. I still went to see all sorts of people. But I was concerned not simply to make a visit to a parish to do something ecclesiastical, but to see the community as a whole. Yes, you were in danger of becoming a bit of a royal visitor, and that was very unsatisfying sometimes; but you see, when you become Bishop of London, you are faced with something like 170 fixed dates in your diary before you do anything else, and a lot of them you can't avoid. There's Church Commissioners. There's General Synod. There's bishops' meetings. There's the Churches' Main Committee. There's the House of Lords. Dinners I cut as much as I could. I did try to distinguish between invitations where it was quite clear they simply wanted somebody to come and adorn the situation, as it were, and those where I really felt they were interested in what contribution the Church could make to what they were doing. But even when I did go to a dinner or a banquet in Guildhall or the Mansion House, I found it was very rare for nobody to come up and say, 'Can I have a word with you?' and talk to you about their own personal situation or problems. So in that sense being the Bishop of London was no different from being a parish priest.

When I look back at the way I neglected the family, particularly during my three years in Ardleigh, I really feel ashamed. I mean, it was partly out of sheer pastoral care for the parish, but it was also, I must admit, partly out of a desire to be thought of as a good parish priest. I can remember thinking, 'Oh, if I go and help my wife in the garden, people will think I'm neglecting my job.' Well, that was a totally wrong thing to think, but I did and do feel that I neglected the family in those years.

James was born when I was still in the Army. Mark was born when I was at Westcott House, and I didn't spend as much time with either of them as I should have. They went away to prep school really very young, and then to Rugby, thanks to the local education authority. We tried hard to visit them regularly, and we did a lot of things with them in the holidays, so I think they felt they had a fair crack of the whip then. The one thing I was always insistent on, whatever I was doing, was that we really did have a proper summer holiday, a month, so one really got away. We've remained on very good terms with our children.

When it came to Truro, the children were grown up and I look back and think how it must have been very difficult for Priscilla, the amount of time I had to be away, living in an isolated place as it was, and on her own. I don't think I was nearly sensitive enough to the demands it was making upon her, but she was very good about it. You'd better ask *her* about it all, I think, but being my wife and being a mother and a hostess – she's superb at that – she saw as her job, for which I was very appreciative. She has always been extraordinarily good at just welcoming people to the house and making them feel at home. I hope you feel that. She never sort of tried to be a bishopess, that wasn't her job. I still get letters about the hospitality she gave, and the friendship she offered even years ago.

She's had her other interests like the garden. She's a very good gardener and she was able to do things for the garden in Cornwall, which was enormous. It was a great sadness that we had no garden in London, but she's done the garden here. Gardening and her embroidery, which you've seen. I mean, she regards actually making a home as an extremely important job and she's done it wonderfully well.

I don't think she ever wanted to pursue an academic career. But I do think she would have liked to have applied her botany in some way; landscape gardening, or design, something like that. And although she is, as you say, of considerable intellectual ability, she's also very very practical, very good with her hands and so on and she likes applying things rather than thinking about things in the abstract. She finds it very difficult to think in the abstract, think philosophically. She can't be bothered with philosophy at all. I love philosophy, it's something I really enjoy. And in our reactions to people she's usually right, I must say. I can think of certain appointments I've made and so on where she's said to me, 'I don't know why, but you're not right,' and I've gone against her advice and I've almost always been proved wrong. Her instinctive reaction was the right one. So I would say that we have been complementary in our approach to things. Very complementary.

People have very often said that my sermons are rather intellectual. Well, that may be so. And people certainly have said that one thing I do is preach with conviction. That may also be so, but I'm very suspicious of mass evangelism. I have always, and this is partly due to my very conservative evangelical upbringing, had a great fear and abhorrence of attempts to manipulate people. Something I've said again and again and again is that one of the *essential* points of the gospel is that God has chosen to redeem us in a way which leaves us free to choose. There is no manipulation about the Cross, Christ simply dies on it and leaves it to us to respond or not. That is why I've always been very worried about using personality or emotion to try to convince people about something to which they are not committed in mind or attitude.

What I've always wanted to do is bring people to Christian discipleship which they embrace because they believe it to be true and relevant. Therefore doctrine has a very important part to play because I believe that Christian doctrine is rational: I believe it surpasses reason, but it doesn't go *against* it. It matches human nature. So for me, teaching is absolutely cardinal. But I'm not going to ask somebody simply to accept Christianity because they like me or because they think it'd be a nice idea. I want them to try to live as Christians because they are convinced of its truth with their minds, their bodies and their spirits, even though they may have many doubts.

I therefore find it very difficult when I'm criticized by people like the Archbishop of York for being an absolutist, because he assumes that if you believe that there are absolute truths which have their origin in the nature of God, you will try to force your views on others. In my experience, it is those who don't accept absolutes who are the very people who try to manipulate you. I think that when you don't believe in absolutes you come under the tyranny of subjective emotions or stances; and because they have no logical basis, it means that you can't argue about things, and the only way you can make somebody do what you want is by force or manipulation. I find that abhorrent, and yet I have always been criticized for talking about absolutes. Well, I believe that absolutes come from the *reality* of God, and if you accept that there are God-given absolutes then you always know that you're living under judgment, under obedience to God.

Now this also relates to the question of the sacramental life. It is the sacramental life of the Church which gives people the freedom to express their obedience to God while remaining free. You can come to the sacraments and accept your dependence upon God. You can have lots of ideas or confusions in your mind and so on, but they don't matter. What you *can't* do is to come to the sacraments making what God does for you dependent on the way you think or the way you feel. Do I make myself clear?

And just as the sacramental life of the Church is part of the way in which God gives us freedom, He also gives us freedom by giving us a world on which we can rely. Oh yes, it's unjust. It's certainly unjust. There's a very interesting passage in the Gospels: the episode of the tower which fell down and killed eighteen people, and the disciples said, 'Were they more wicked than anybody else?' And Jesus's reply was, 'Of course not, but if you don't behave yourselves something like that might happen to you.' It's very significant, that, because he was saying that accidents happen because people are careless or ignorant, and not as a direct result of their sins. But he was also saying that *if* you sin, if you are careless, that kind of thing can happen. This I think is very important. Yes, the world is unjust, but it is the other side of us being able to rely upon its character.

You use the death of a child as an example of absolute injustice. But why? It's injustice if you believe that that child's life is limited to this life only, I agree with you. And it's terrible for the parents, yes, but it's not necessarily *unjust*. No one has the right to expect a long and pain-free life. What matters is how the experience is used and what effect it has on them. I can think of cases where by some experience such as that, people's lives have been utterly transformed. It hasn't made the pain any better, but I don't think one can talk about a situation like that as altogether bad or altogether good. I mean, we are in a position where we have a responsibility as human beings to bring what is good out of what happens to us. And we don't do that by denying the potential for good in terrible situations.

I would also say that I believe one *has* to take the dimension of eternity. I mean, if everybody really believed that we're extinguished at death, that would have a very profound effect upon the way the world lived in all sorts of ways. But people don't live as if they believe they were just going to snuff out when they die. They don't behave in the logical way which would follow from that belief. Given the conditions that some people live in, I'm often surprised that more people don't commit suicide than do. And this isn't a purely biological hanging on to life; you can't explain it away in that kind of way.

I don't know what happens to us when we do eventually die. I've often been asked whether I believe in hell. I do. I think hell's a question of the kind of people we *become*. It's rather like trying to look at the sun: if you do, you ultimately become blind. I believe it's a possibility we all have to have before us, that there comes a point for some people when they have become so self-centred that they have to exist alone in every sense of the word, isolated from everybody and everything else; and that would be hell. In other words, hell is the possibility of becoming incapable of relating to anybody else. Whether or not there would be an 'I' to continue, I don't know, and I wouldn't want to pronounce on that. But the possibility is there, I'm sure. And it's a terrifying prospect, it really is, it's appalling.

I find the thought of being in the presence of God and facing Him almost as terrifying. As Gerontius says, in *The Dream of Gerontius*, pain and pleasure are intermingled when you face God. There is the joy of seeing God and the pain of seeing what you actually are yourself. That is why I think purgatory is one of the most consoling of beliefs, and although the Church of England does say some rather rude things about the doctrine of purgatory in the Thirty-nine Articles, it doesn't actually deny it. In fact, there's a marvellous prayer for someone at the point of their departure which I think explains it:

> We humbly commend the soul of this thy servant our dear brother into thy hands as into the hands of a faithful Creator and most merciful Saviour, most humbly beseeching that it may be precious in thy sight. Wash it, we pray, in the blood of that immaculate Lamb that was slain to take away the sins of the world, that whatsoever defilements it may have contracted in the midst of this miserable and naughty world through the lusts of

the flesh or the wiles of Satan, being purged and done away it may be presented pure and without spot before thee.

Now, if that isn't the doctrine of purgatory I don't know what is! And that's in the Book of Common Prayer. So purgatory for me is about facing the pain of being, and it seems to me to be a most comfortable doctrine not only because it recognizes what we are, but also what we can become.

When people talk about heaven, they use picture language, but I think one's got to think of it in terms of a personal relationship to God, in which the goodness of this life is transformed and fulfilled. I see heaven as the created world re-created in Christ so that it is transparent to the glory of God. It is a world in which the self will be fulfilled, and yet it is not an individualistic world, it is an essentially communal one. There are all sorts of ways of trying to put that into picture language, and whether or not harps and things help is another matter, but they're not essential. They don't help me. I must say music helps me a great deal. Have you ever heard Michael Haydn's setting of *Vespers for the Eve of the Feast of Holy Innocents*? It has such a wonderful sense of timelessness, I could listen to it for ever.

For me the best book that drew all this out is C. S. Lewis's *The Great Divorce*. I think it's the finest of his books. The story is of people who go out from the grey town, which if you don't stay there for ever is purgatory, and if you *do* stay there for ever is hell. You are allowed to go on a bus excursion to heaven where you're met by bright spirits who come and see whether you can accept the reality of heaven. Anyhow, there's a woman who goes on this excursion, who has never got over the fact that her child had died, and when she arrives she wants to see him; why can't she see him? 'If God were good, he'd let me see him.' But the spirits say to her, 'You can't see him yet, because you're only wanting God for the sake of seeing Michael and you've got to want God first and then you'll be able to see Michael.' I think that's a wonderful picture of the potential for transformation, rather than destruction, of natural instincts into holiness. And that's how I see heaven. I do not believe that in heaven anything of God which we have experienced on this earth, whether in beauty, in love, or in holiness, will be destroyed. It will all be fulfilled. And what is not of God will be purged away.

That is not to say that I believe in dualism, where you've got God and evil set against each other, because I don't. Dualism is quite incompatible with Christianity, which sees God as the Creator, responsible for all things. What I do believe is that evil is always a possibility, because love involves the freedom to reject. But if you ask me, 'Where does evil come from, then?' the answer is, I don't know, but I do know that you can't talk about love without the freedom to reject. And in so far as that freedom to reject is destructive, it is evil.

I don't see evil as a separate opposing force, although one cannot deny that evil often manifests itself in very mysterious ways. I've had a good deal of dealings with evil influences, evil phenomena, for example, and in my experience they are usually the result of troubled spirits. The physical manifestations are usually very specific, like smells and lights and noise and so on.

Obviously one doesn't publicize these things, but I've often exercised the ministry of deliverance. In fact, I can remember a case which was particularly interesting, when I was Bishop of Willesden. There was an elderly lady, blind, who lived alone in a bungalow. She managed for herself wonderfully well, but there were the most appalling smells in this house and a real sense of evil. We couldn't think what it was. Her social worker was quite convinced that she'd left food about and it had gone mouldy, or there were dead mice around. But in the end the smells were so bad that the social worker, who was a very hardbitten typical sixties sort, said she was going to come and spend the night there. And to cut a long story short, she ran out screaming. So in I went and said a simple form of exorcism and a requiem as well, and we discovered later on that the house had been built on a place where there had been a peculiarly unpleasant murder. Now, this sort of thing is not uncommon, and it doesn't surprise me because we are all mind, body *and* spirit.

Much the same thing applies to sin as applies to evil. Sin is a negative force, rather than the result of an opposing force. How can I put it? Sin comes from rebellion, whether against God or against other people. Sin is never creative; it is always destructive. In the gospel we see God who is Love and knows that in the end love will win, even though there will be pain on the way, and there may even be those who cease to be able to love at all.

But in the end, yes, God is overally responsible for everything. One can't avoid that conclusion. And yet love does prevail. One sees this all the time in human life. I mean, you can destroy somebody physically, you can destroy them mentally, but you cannot, if that person goes on loving you, destroy him spiritually. That doesn't mean I deny the problems of sin and evil and suffering at all but I do believe that they are the cost of man being made in the image of God.

Now: I know you want me to talk about the miracles. Let's take the Virgin Birth first of all. I don't think the Virgin Birth is a miracle. The Christian gospel is clear that no new person came into being at the time when Our Lord was born. He was the second Person of the Blessed Trinity, God himself, who took a human nature and a human body and came to share our human life. If his birth was *not* a Virgin Birth, a miracle would have been necessary to prevent the normal consequence of sexual intercourse actually coming into effect: namely, the creation of a new human being. Because I believe truly that God came to share our life, it seems to me perfectly logical, and what I would *expect*, that he would have been born by the taking of a body and soul from Mary and not as a product of ordinary human intercourse. So to my mind the Virgin Birth is really a question not about miracles, but about who you believe Jesus is. Do you see what I mean?

Now, you can't say that anybody who doesn't believe in the Virgin Birth doesn't believe that Jesus is God. Nevertheless, the fact is that throughout the history of the Church, belief in the Virgin Birth has always been a kind of touchstone; so that if somebody believes in the Virgin Birth it implies they know the meaning of the Incarnation. You can't, however, imply the reverse, because it doesn't necessarily follow.

The Virgin Birth is the beginning. Let's look at the Resurrection, the end. For me the Resurrection is absolutely cardinal. The Lord rose again in body, mind and spirit. For the first time ever human nature was taken through death in total obedience to the Father, and was therefore liberated. Death, which signifies corruption, the end, was not allowed to have its way.

I think that the Resurrection appearances are quite remarkable in this: you'll find that where signs of immortality are given in legends and myths and so on, they're always either manifest in great clouds of glory or they're ghost-like apparitions. The stories of the Resurrection appearances are nothing like that at all. Christ appears: he eats, he drinks, and yet he is not bound by space and time. That to me is a clear demonstration that human nature is actually liberated, and I see this as entirely congruous with the way we're made as human beings. As St Paul said: 'If Christ be not raised then is our faith in vain.' Because if Christ be not raised, what in fact happened? What is the result? Merely the declaration that he didn't die, and in some mysterious way continued to survive?

And the story of the Ascension, which you can't separate from the resurrection, is also very important, because what Our Lord is doing at that point is saying, 'I've appeared with you here to make it clear that I am alive in the totality of my humanity. But I'm not going to do this any more. I'm now going to leave you.' And he does, in what would be the most natural way for a Jew, for whom the cloud was the great symbol of the abiding presence of God: he disappears into the clouds.

I also think it's remarkable the way in which the Gospel narratives are not dramatic. They use simple ways of making these truths clear. As for the miracles, I love the phrase of Austin Farrer's, 'There were moments when Our Lord's divinity slipped from him into the world which he created.' There's a very interesting book on divine revelation which the present Professor of the Philosophy of the Christian Religion at Oxford has written. He says that if God did reveal Himself, in order to make it clear that it was divine revelation you were experiencing you'd *need* miracles. And if you can't accept the miracles as they are, then what do you believe actually happened? On the other hand, the Incarnation was not so dramatic that we could not help but follow Christ. It wasn't something which overwhelmed everybody.

The miracles undoubtedly raise questions, not least historical ones, but the thing about the miracles is that they do have a narrative purpose. Take the feeding of the five thousand. You do know, don't you, that there's the story of the feeding of the five thousand and the story of the feeding of the seven thousand? Some scholars say that these are the same story being told in a slightly different way, but that's missing the point. Later on, when the Lord is talking to the disciples about the bread of life, he says to them, 'When I fed the five thousand how many baskets were there left over?' And they said, 'Twelve.' 'And when I fed the seven thousand how many were there then?' It's as if he were saying: 'How many *more* times have I got to do it to convince you?' And that's the point. But some people don't seem to see this.

Still, there are some things about the Gospel narratives that are more difficult to accept than others. I mean, I always find the cursing of the fig tree a bit odd. That's the one which took place as they were going in and out of Jerusalem towards the end of Christ's life. Christ saw a fig tree which hadn't borne its fruit and he said, 'Cursed be the fig tree,' and the next day it was withered up. I don't understand that one. But then, you see, you've got to be quite realistic about the fact that the Gospels were written by fallible human beings like ourselves, and you can't take every single thing as read. They would have seen things differently to us.

So I accept that there are problems and inconsistencies in the Gospels, but what impresses upon me more and more is the fact that the record of God's revelation is given to us in such simple ways; not in great books of theology, not in great tomes of philosophy and so on, but in these simple events which continue to speak to successive generations and people of every kind of ability and temperament.

As far as I am concerned, the priesthood is not about performing priestly functions. It is about *being* a priest, like being a father. I think the biological analogy that I have made in the past is actually a very sound one. I mean, whether one likes it or not, one is because of what one's parents did. I didn't bring myself into being, and though I did offer myself for the priesthood, my ordination was at the hand of the Bishop, it wasn't anything I *did*. But talking about the nature of being as opposed to the nature of doing is simply not understood these days. We are in a profoundly *functional* society now, and the argument is that everybody ought to be able to do everything.

Now: I don't believe it was an accident that God became incarnate in a patriarchal society. I don't think it's a trivial argument to say that Our Lord only chose twelve male apostles. And I do not believe that the choice and place and time of the incarnation were a matter of indifference. I believe, as the scripture says, that they were in the fullness of time, by the deliberate choice of God after a very long period of preparation. For me therefore they are not negotiable.

What worries me about the Church of England is that this decision to ordain women implies that all those events *are* negotiable. What worries me is that nobody, not even the most ardent advocates I've ever read, can say that you can conclude and prove the ordination of women from scripture. They will argue about it and they will bring in other things to support their view, such as the fact that the culture of today demands that we should alter our views. Yet what the Church of England is really saying at the moment is, 'It doesn't matter very much what you believe about the creeds, it doesn't matter very much what you believe about the resurrection and so on. The one thing you've really got to believe in, if you're going to be a Christian, is the ordination of women.' They've now made this a new canon of orthodoxy, a new requirement of belief, because you cannot *escape* it: it's something done or not done, it's not just an idea that people hold. So for me the decision is an undermining of scripture, and scripture is the record of the events of our redemption.

As I see it, the ordination of women involves a rejection of the way in which God chose to redeem us, a way which reflected the way He made us. I do not believe that it was an accident that God chose to redeem us by being incarnate as a male. That for me is part of God's deliberate choice. I also do not believe it to be an accident that God gave the highest vocation of any created being to a woman, namely to Mary. And this represents for me the complementarity between the sexes.

God made us male and female, and male and female were our image of God. Now I'm prepared to argue about this. For me the sexes are equal but different, and I believe that difference reflects the very nature of love. So I naturally get very worried when people suggest that God made a great mistake in making man male and female, and that it would have been much better if He had made us sort of androgynous. Which is what people have said. They have. I've read a lot of it.

On top of all this, the Church of England has always claimed to be the Catholic Church in this country: always. It has also always claimed that it can't do anything by itself, that it has got to be obedient to the overall Christian Church. And that means the thousand million traditionally orthodox Christians in the form of both the Roman Catholic Church and the Eastern Orthodox Church. That's a lot. There are only sixty-five million Anglicans worldwide. So I cannot see how the Church of England can go on claiming that its ministry is identical and in accordance with the beliefs and values of a thousand million, which it has always claimed up to now, and also say, 'We've got the authority to make a decision like this on our own.' And what I believe the Church of England has done by making this decision is to make itself into a sect. If the Church of England wants to do that, let it do it. But it cannot say, 'Our ministry is the same as the apostolic ministry which is shared by the Roman Catholics and Eastern Orthodox and which goes back to the institution of Our Lord himself.' It cannot continue to make the claims which it has made in the past.

One of the most popular arguments in favour of the ordination of women is that the job of a priest is to represent humanity and that as long as it's only done by a male, it's partial. Well, now, my answer to that is twofold. First of all, nowhere in the ordination service do you find it suggested that the job of a priest is to represent humanity. His job is to represent Christ as the head of the Church, and continually to call the Church to obedience. But if you take the argument that the advocates use, and assume that it *is* the job of a priest to represent humanity, then you are in fact saying that the Incarnation itself is inadequate, because God only shared half of humanity by becoming incarnate as a male person.

Now, of course there has to be a choice, God couldn't be incarnate as both man and woman; and it's not a question of better or worse. But I'm quite certain God didn't just toss up a coin and say, shall I be man or woman? It was a deliberate choice. Why? Well, we can only speculate, but for me the fact is this, and you may not like what I'm going to say now, but in human terms, psychologically and symbolically there's a reason. We're all both part man and part woman, but psychologically and symbolically it is the man who represents the initiative and the woman who represents the response. This is the case in human reproduction. The incarnation reflects the fact that the initiative is masculine and the response – of being human and dependent on God – is feminine.

For me, it all comes back to the nature of loving, which is both giving and receiving, and I don't think the two should be confused. I think being a woman is a positive quality. But the fact is that I believe that maleness in human thought does represent initiative, and I don't mean that in a moral sense, I mean it biologically, psychologically and symbolically. Femaleness, or femininity, represents reception and response, and that is true of an act of sexual intercourse, whether one likes it or not. Therefore I find it very difficult to see how the person who is representing the divine initiative can appropriately be somebody who, in human terms, represents the receiver. Yes, there are plenty of initiating women, but I still maintain that the basic symbol remains the same, and I see the symbol as articulating something.

I accept your point that there are plenty of not very masculine clergy already, but I can think equally of some very masculine women. I hesitate to say this but I think one must: the kind of men you're talking about and the kind of women I'm talking about are regarded as exceptions to the norm in ordinary human thinking. The fact that we are talking about it represents an acceptance of the differences.

What you really come back to here is the restriction of priesthood to males, which has been uniform in the Church for nearly 2,000 years. Now, has this been something which has simply developed because of culture or is it in fact from divine authority? If it's a purely human tradition, you are perfectly entitled to change it. But I don't believe it is, I believe it's of divine institution. There have been cases where they've attempted to have women priests, like the Collyridian sect in the fourth century, but these are exceptions and were declared to be heretical.

Having said all that, my personal response to the vote was one of relief. People were surprised, I think, but it was. At least it's over now. But I do feel that the Church of England has lost its bearings: this is why I'm talking about those of us who can't accept it trying to establish some sort of relationship to the Roman Catholic Church, and I'm therefore prepared to accept the *magisterium* of Rome. By *magisterium* I mean the authority which decides what interpretations and expositions of doctrine are consonant with the Catholic faith. Now, I'm not prepared to go to Rome if it means being regarded as a layman. However, to avoid being a solitary Christian, which you can't be, I would far prefer to accept the infallibility of the Pope than I would the infallibility of the General Synod.

What also hasn't helped is the nature of the provisions for those who can't accept it. I cannot see how the Archbishop of Canterbury can call for us to play a full part in the life of the Church when the provisions of the legislation provide for our extinction. No new bishop will now have the right to oppose women priests. Present bishops are able to as long as they're in office, but once they go, that right disappears. So it's hardly surprising that those who are opposed do feel that the temporary easements are of no permanent value.

You asked me why I didn't object when women were ordained to the diaconate. Now, I've ordained lots of women deacons – I did seventy-one in one afternoon, once – and the reason I didn't object to it is because it's a different sort of ministry. In the early Middle Ages, for reasons which we needn't go into now, the diaconate became the sort of stepping-stone to the priesthood from a lot of lower orders below that. There were acolytes and exorcists and readers and doorkeepers; seven orders altogether, and you worked your way up this ladder. But this medieval ladder concept was a change from the original concept, where the bishop was the essential minister, and the deacon and priest assisted him in equal measure but in different ways. That is why I was pleading, oh, years ago, that we should get the permanent diaconate right, and see it not simply as a stepping-stone to priesthood.

So I'm sorry about any confusion I may have caused by my willingness to ordain women as deacons. I could not have refused to do so and retained my theological integrity; whereas the same integrity prevents me from accepting the ordination of women as priests. I see the latter as a very regrettable decision, and whatever the Archbishop may say, the changes *are* fundamental. But I don't rejoice in having to oppose it all. I mean, life would be a lot simpler if I didn't, but it's something that I cannot see as right.

Change my mind? No. I've changed my mind on other things but on this I've never thought of it. Not on this.

I think perhaps you're right when you say I am very concerned with logic. And perhaps I don't deviate much. I've certainly been affected by the writings of Charles Williams and Gerard Manley Hopkins, because they are always concerned with the *is-ness* of things, what things actually *are*. So you're right about that, but it isn't only a question of logic, it's also a question of a belief in cause and effect, based in the physical and spiritual realms. I mean, if I hate, I am destroying myself to some extent, and that is as much for me a cause and effect as if by drinking cyanide I cause my own death.

Therefore, on some moral issues my arguments are in favour of what you might call traditional Christian morals; because traditional Christian morals do reflect the unity of the human person. They demand that I shouldn't do something with my body which doesn't match what I'm doing with my soul. Do you see what I mean? I feel very strongly, for example, about the whole question of adultery and fornication and so on, because I believe that what I do with my body has got to be matched by what I do with my self, my soul, my spirit. I can't commit a kind of schizophrenia and use my body as a convenient tool for something I want, irrespective of my relationships, because this would represent an unhappy divorce between my emotions and my will, and the two should be united.

You asked me earlier about homosexuality, and I think I can say that my feelings on homosexuality have always been quite consistent. If somebody were to come to me and say, 'I am a practising homosexual indulging in genital relations,' I would say I could not ordain them because I believe that to be sinful. On the other hand I do not believe it is my job to inquire of people whether they are practising homosexuals. Nor have I any reason whatever to suppose that if two people of the same sex are living together they are living in a homosexual relationship. And frankly, the homosexual clergy in London knew this and appreciated it, because they told me so. On the one hand they knew perfectly well that I couldn't accept that it was right. On the other hand they knew I would never act on hearsay. Sometimes people wrote to me and said, 'Do you know that X and Y are living together?' And I would write back and say, 'Will you please give me your evidence?' And that was usually the last I heard of it.

What I have also said, and said publicly, is that I've known some particular priests who are of homosexual disposition, but I know that they see that as consecrated in the service of God: for that reason some of them are some of the best priests I've ever known. For them, celibacy is a calling of God by which they make themselves available in a way they couldn't if they were married, and very often they do some of the hardest jobs that there are, and do them supremely well. I find the thought that they would come under the same condemnation as those who are merely promiscuous very offensive.

Having said that, I don't think homosexuality is what human beings are made *for*. The sexual relationship is meant to be between the sexes, and I do think that scripture is quite clear that homosexuality is not in accordance with the will of God – which is a phrase I prefer to the word 'sinful', though they mean exactly the same thing. Don't misunderstand me. I don't think of God punishing people for their sins, as an angry father might punish his child. I think of sins as having their own consequences. I think God gives us freedom and if we choose to ignore the maker's instructions then certain consequences will follow, which God, I believe, profoundly regrets. He will forgive us, and restore us, but He doesn't remove those consequences. But to use the word 'punishment' about God has all sorts of overtones which I wouldn't want to imply; namely, that God is deliberately vengeful. I don't think of God in that way, I think of Him as giving us freedom in a predictable world in which certain things have certain consequences, not least the fact that what is not in accordance with the will of God is destructive, both of persons and of society.

Yet I find today people imagine that they can do exactly what they want without having to suffer the consequences, and this seems to me to be a quite untenable position. Take marriage, for example. It's not merely a commitment of will, it's a total unity of person, and traditional Christian morals reflect the unity of the human person. The scriptures talk about 'the one flesh', and Our Lord endorsed this phrase himself.

When I used to have to prepare people for marriage, one of the things I used to say was that if you recognize that your marriage is lifelong, when difficulties come along, your reaction is, 'Well, this won't do, will it? How are we going to get over this?' And very often as a result of some tension within marriage you are closer together afterwards than you were before. But if you are thinking in even remotest terms of the possibility of divorce, then the little crack becomes wider, and there's no healing.

The Church has never said it would compel people to live together, come what may. It has recognized for centuries the need for what was called *divortium a mensa et thoro* – 'separation from bed and board' – which is the equivalent these days of a judicial separation. And there's never been any problem with the Church in a situation like marital violence, for example. You are always going to have marital failures of one kind or another in society. The problems arise when you say, well, how does the Church cope with the failures? What is the meaning of forgiveness? What about frustrated vows?

The *real* problem, from the Christian point of view, is re-marriage. I believe the Church of England's position on this is really quite illogical. It won't allow the remarriage of divorced persons in church, and that, I believe, is right. Yet on the other hand it will bless a remarriage. Well, how you can bless something which at the same time you're saying is not in accordance with the will of God, I do not understand. And I find it quite inconceivable that priests divorce or marry divorcees. I mean,

apart from anything else, how on earth do you prepare somebody for marriage if you or your partner have remarried after
divorce? How can a priest use the marriage service – which
makes no bones about what marriage really is – in those
situations?

This is why I get worried about all the fuss over divorce
when the real problem is remarriage. Divorce is a single act
which can be forgiven: remarriage doesn't make sense because
it's a continuing state. However, the attitude to marriage in this
country is really destructive of it. There is no longer the frame-
work in society which actually enables marriages to succeed.
And I'm being frank with you here: I've sometimes felt it is
more *honest* for people simply to live together. Now, that gets
very complicated when people have children: having a baby is
actually a very responsible thing to do. And I don't think living
together's the ideal answer. But I don't pretend there is *any*
answer at the moment except a massive change of heart on the
part of society with a recognition of the responsibilities which
marriage brings. Because you do have to work at marriage, and
it's not easy, very often. We've been married fifty years and it's
not always been easy, not least because living and working as a
priest and a bishop is not easily compatible with a family life,
but we've survived. It never entered our heads that we wouldn't
be able to solve any problems that arose, you see.

Of course, lying behind this whole discussion is a commonly
accepted assumption that sexual experience is absolutely vital for
a full human life. Well, I just don't believe that to be true. And
please don't think I'm just talking a sort of moral ABC, but if
your marriage is dependent upon your emotions, you spend
your time trying to keep your emotions up to scratch, which for
a human being is a very unrealistic thing to do. Because when
they fail, as they will, you have nothing.

I look back over my life with great . . . I can't think what the
word I want is: to say 'satisfaction' looks as if I'm looking at it
from what it's given me. I look back on my times in a parish,

my dealings with people, with individuals, and that's been wonderful, it's been glorious. But I can't say that I've enjoyed the political infighting, which I've – not from choice – been involved in so much.

It's an interesting question, this. I mean I've been involved in so many battles and negotiations and so on, and yet it's the infighting in the Church that I've found really difficult to take. Fighting over things like the Anglican Methodist Scheme, the Covenanting, marriage and divorce, and now women priests. I haven't enjoyed that a bit. People always seem to think I do enjoy it. I don't. Life would have been infinitely easier if I'd just been able to go along with things. Yes, I'm prepared to stick my neck out if I think it's necessary, and I enjoy an argument, it's true. Quite true. But, and I think I can say this quite honestly, I've always done what I felt I had to do without any thought of the consequences. I think I can honestly say that I can't think of any action which I have not taken for fear of the consequences it might have had for me personally.

I don't think I'm someone who has been very interested in power. No. I think on the whole I've almost always erred in being too soft rather than too hard. It was always said by Brother Michael Fisher, the head of the Franciscans, who was my suffragan bishop in Cornwall, that I was hard as nuts on principle and soft on people. And I think there's quite a lot of truth in that. I know people were often disappointed when I said, 'You have got to make up your mind about this. I will put the case, but it's your decision, not mine.' And I know there are those who said, 'Why didn't he give us a stronger lead when he was in London?' You can't win.

I do think there have been times when perhaps I should have been stronger than I was because I was fearful of manipulating. I've said to you how I abhor manipulation. But, you see, I have no doubt whatever that Our Lord is the one Saviour of Mankind: how you go about sharing this without any attempts at what one might call forcible conversion is not easy. I believe the chief way in which we are called upon to witness to the Christian gospel is by being the best kind of Christian people we can be, and I really hope I've done that.

I don't know what the future holds. It's too uncertain. I would actually very much like some time before I die, both for my sake and for Priscilla's, when we really could have a more peaceful existence together, without all this pressure. Perhaps it'll never come. People so bombard me with requests for advice and guidance and this sort of thing that it really is very demanding. But it would be nice for me and Priscilla to be able to go out and have relaxed days. We hoped we'd be able to do it with our retirement, but almost every day seems fully occupied with one thing or another.

I would also really like to have some time in which to think more deeply about what God wants me to be without having the complications of ecclesiastical battles. That is one thing I would hope for: to concentrate upon trying to become a little holier in my remaining years.

(Prior to the decision of the Church of England to ordain woman as priests, the House of Bishops stated that, in the event of women's ordination, 'those who could not continue in communion with the see of Canterbury would need to find other ways of continuing their existence in the Universal Church and would be entitled to explore such ways'. Graham Leonard is one of the Anglican clergy who, since the decision to ordain women was taken, has become a Roman Catholic priest.

HUGH MONTEFIORE

Age: 73

Age at ordination: 30

(RETIRED) BISHOP OF BIRMINGHAM

Hugh Montefiore's most striking feature is his voice. Oscillating between a cheerful bark and a rich drawl, it is strong, colourful, varied, steeped in privilege, and would doubtless have been described in bygone days as 'pukka'. He is one of the few people I know who can make a vowel sound as if it has two or three syllables, and a consonant sound like a starting pistol.

Very tall and sturdy, with a benevolent, good-natured face and white hair, Hugh Montefiore is an extremely fine and distinguished-looking man. When still, he looks elegant, but he is seldom still. He is bouncy and energetic, and he leaps about rooms, armchairs and conversations with an indiscriminate and palpable enthusiasm. When he gets really carried away he fails to notice objects in his immediate surroundings: watching him assemble lunch or rummage through papers on his desk can be worrying.

Hugh Montefiore lives in an attractive Victorian house in south London with his wife, Elisabeth. Elisabeth Montefiore is in poor health and cannot be left unattended, and Hugh Montefiore cares for her with unfailing devotion. I spent four days with him, talking every morning in his book- and paper-crammed study, and staying on afterwards for long lunches cooked either by Hugh Montefiore himself or by Elisabeth's daytime companions, Louise and Joan.

Hugh Montefiore is a man of tremendous conviction and an irrepressible passion for the truth, which combination has caused him a great deal of trouble in his life. He has never been afraid to express openly and fervently what he thinks, regardless of whether or not such thoughts are fashionable or even generally acceptable. This unguardedness has earnt him the labels 'controversial' and 'outspoken', although it would be practically impossible to argue that anything Hugh

Montefiore has to say does not have a moral and intellectual consistency. He has never been afraid to take theological risks when writing or preaching, and while logic, clarity and reason are important to him, abstract ideas seem to excite him the most. I got the impression he welcomed them as a terrier might welcome a bigger dog; as something to be wrestled with, but not necessarily overcome — humility being the better part of true endeavour.

For all his ebullience, Hugh Montefiore is a sweet and affectionate man, who was exceptionally easy to work with. Conversations with him were always amusing, vigorous, and rarely confined to one day: it was not unusual for notes or faxes penned in his swooping and slightly spiky hand to arrive twenty-four hours later with an afterthought or anecdote. And while he was occasionally thrown by my questions or shaken by his own answers, he was never once evasive or defensive. If anything, he appeared to seek a certain amount of approval throughout our conversations, giving the lie to the supposition that strong views go hand in hand with a blustering self-confidence. In Hugh Montefiore's case they don't. He is one of the kindest and most highly sensitive people I have ever met, imbued not only with concern for others but with a grave and profound self-doubt.

I belong to a Jewish family, and a well-heeled Jewish family, too. At one stage we lived in 2 Palace Green, which is now the Israeli Embassy, and heaven knows, life was *unbelievable*! I had a very nice but rather illiterate Norfolk nanny, and I think there were eight servants altogether, including her. I saw my parents very little, because that's how people were brought up in those circles: it was the sort of household in which you were brought down to your parents at five p.m. for an hour, and you'd see your father perhaps for a quarter of an hour before he went to the office in the morning. My mother was rather rum: she was a manic-depressive, used to retire to her room a lot, so we didn't see much of her.

I was born in 1920, and my brothers, Oliver and Denzil, were already in school when I was in the nursery, so they belonged to different worlds, though I saw them in the holidays. My parents had a holiday house in Scotland, which was enormous fun. There were lots of picnic dances – they did things like that then – Scottish reels, tennis, lots of people. I had twenty-two first cousins on my father's side, a lot of them near by in Kensington Gardens, although who you saw really depended which nannies were friendly with each other. So I had a rather lonely childhood. Very lonely, really.

My family was a religious family – a .*really* religious family; not particularly orthodox, though my father was President of the synagogue, but we always had family prayers, and there was a real love of God. There was also a great family tradition passed down from old Sir Moses Montefiore. He was a great world figure, was Sir Moses Montefiore. He was frightfully patriotic and a friend of Queen Victoria's, but he did actually start the first Jewish settlements outside the walls of the city of Jerusalem. In fact, there's still a windmill which dominates Jerusalem, which he gave to the Jews because he didn't think they were doing enough to bake their own bread.

He died about 105 years ago, but I mention him because he has dominated the family. You lived up to the standards of Sir Moses. That's a picture of the old boy over there, have a look at him, do. He went into business with his brother-in-law, Rothschild, and they floated the loan for the emancipation of the West Indian slaves, and he made a pile in the City and retired at the age of forty to help his fellow Jews for the next sixty years. He even went with coach and four to see the Tsar in St Petersburg to tell him, 'Stop the pogroms!' – which he did for a bit, but of course only for a bit. So he was a bit of a saint, was Moses.

The extended Montefiore family is huge, and we were the Sebag-Montefiores. Strange name. Lends itself to all kinds of oddities. But I dropped the Sebag, because I didn't think anyone would ever want to see a clergyman with so many letters to his name; and also, it embarrassed the family somewhat, to have a clergyman called Sebag-Montefiore. Such a Jewish name.

After prep school I got a scholarship to Rugby. It was quite a liberation for me, school. We worked terribly hard at Rugby: school before breakfast in the summer, and some slave-drivers of masters whom I'm very grateful to. But I think I lived a fairly normal life. I got my colours in the rugger Fifteen, and was Head of House and all the proper things. I used to spend a lot of my time with the two art masters, Watkins Pitchford and Talbot Kelly. Fine chaps. They were kind to me, and I spent a lot of spare time in the art school doing water-colours, etchings and oils.

I enjoyed having friends at school. You see, I told you I was a bit lonely at home. Home was a bit of a male society, and I had great difficulty not being shy with girls afterwards.. If you're brought up with two brothers at home, and the only female influence in the home apart from your nanny was your mother, and she was *hors de combat* a lot of the time, it wasn't an easy start. I had to start from scratch later on, really.

It was at Rugby that I became a Christian. I had a visionary experience. I don't think religious experience is ever very communicable, nor do I relish talking about it, strangely enough. I suppose it's too holy for me. But I will. I saw a vision of someone in white whom I knew instinctively – and God knows why – to be Jesus. And I heard the words – although they weren't spoken words, they wouldn't have been caught by your machine there – to follow him. Extraordinary.

It was all very strange, because I'd never been allowed to read the New Testament, or go to chapel. A nice old man used to come down on Sunday mornings to teach me Jewish studies instead. Anyway, I had to tell my family about it, didn't I, so I told them within the week. I can remember to this day holding the letter before I dropped it in the letterbox; it's the sort of thing that impinges itself on your memory. I was upset at the thought of telling them. I became a Christian straight away, and I knew they would be upset.

I remember it was the most exciting time of my life, reading the Gospels for the first time. Wonderful. The school was scared stiff of being accused of proselytism, so they sent me down to the Vicar of Rugby. I didn't know whether to become an Anglican or a Roman Catholic, but the Vicar of Rugby said, 'I think you'd better join the Church of England,' so I did. There was a Roman Catholic seminary up the road, but I was put off Roman Catholicism by its blasted *bells*, which seemed to ring all day and all night, and I thought this was a very un-English practice. I know it sounds very trivial, but I was only a teenager.

Actually, I'll tell you why I *really* became an Anglican: I didn't want to be *different* from other people. Of course I still *felt* different. Always have, because the C of E's such a Gentile Church and they go on about the Jews in sermons. They haven't a clue about it either, they're not really interested in the Jews: anti-Semitism has never been far below the surface of English life. But I never felt that I stopped being Jewish. I thought of myself – I still think of myself – as Jewish. I *am* Jewish. For me this experience of Christ was a fulfilment: it's the only way I can understand Christianity, as a fulfilment of Judaism. Jesus was a Jew; the New Testament doesn't make any sense without the Old Testament; and the Old Testament was Jesus's Bible. In fact I felt rather proud of being Jewish. I was a member of the chosen people! I still am proud of being Jewish. After all, it's the race Jesus belonged to, and there's something very rum about that race: the way they have persisted down the centuries amidst *unbelievable* persecution is amazing.

However, although I never felt alienated from being Jewish, I've been alienated from the Jewish community. I was regarded as very dangerous. When I was at Cambridge, the Chief Rabbi warned people against me. And on one occasion after I had been invited to speak to the Jewish Society there, the President came up to me and said, 'This is very awkward, but the Wolfson Foundation will cut off our money if you speak.' Which illustrates what I mean.

But that was later. My family, it alienated me from them right from the beginning, it really did. I hardly saw them for years. I see them now. I don't think I'm regarded as so dangerous now I'm retired, and they're very kind to me, some of them. But I had a very difficult time with my brothers, and that seemed a bit tough. When I preached at Eton, where my elder brother's son was, he wouldn't speak to me for a year. As his son wasn't allowed *near* the chapel, I couldn't think that he was religiously very endangered by my preaching in it, but none the less this caused a great rupture. Now it's all right. Thank goodness.

I didn't go straight to university. I stayed on an extra term at Rugby to get a scholarship to Oxford, and then I taught at the Dragon School in Oxford for a term: Latin verse and spelling. Didn't think much of that. Then I went abroad to the University of Geneva, as an auditeur. An auditeur goes to lectures, hangs around, learns French. I never learned German, because the

Germans were not very popular in the family, for obvious reasons, and I've always regretted this, because there's so much theology in German.

My family weren't particularly politically-minded, but I discovered the other day that my father gave enormously generously to help Jewish refugees. They were well aware of what was happening in Germany at the time. Jewish persecution was reported in the *Jewish Chronicle*, and we used to have refugees to stay, those who got out in time. They'd stay with us for a bit before they went out to the Argentine or somewhere like that.

When I came home from Geneva, war started. I remember agonizing whether to bring myself to fight and kill people, and I remember thinking that I didn't feel I could look myself in the face if I allowed people to bring food in to me through the submarine bases and did nothing. It seemed to me that if I was prepared for people to die to enable me to eat, really I had no moral justification for not fighting myself. And there were a few of my brothers and sisters after the flesh in Germany of whom one thought: my God, what's happened to them? I also felt that Nazism was so evil in itself, not only in its anti-Jewishness, but generally. So I don't regret having fought in the war, though when it came to it I didn't fight the Germans, I fought the Japanese.

My time at Oxford was cut short by the war. I read Classics, and that was a bit of a disaster because my tutor went round the bend. Locked himself up in his garden shed. It's true! Then he started supervising us in the shed, so I did less well than I should have done, and it hurt me very much, but it was too difficult because he went bonkers.

Everything in Oxford was rather closed up for the war, everything was a bit at half-cock. In the vacations I went and hewed wood in the college woods as part of the war effort, and I also joined the Student Christian Movement, which was a big show in those days. In fact I met my wife there, Elisabeth. She was at Lady Margaret Hall at the time.

I was determined not to join the Officer Training Corps

when I arrived at Oxford. It was something one did but I thought, 'If I've got to join the Army anyway, why the hell should I join the OTC? To hell with it. I'm probably going to be in the Army for the rest of my life.' We didn't really expect to come through it all, you see. We had the record of the First World War behind us.

After a year I did join up, and I went to train at Blubberhouses Moor, near Harrogate. There was an enormous yellow-faced Colonel in charge of us — what's the name of the mustard? — Coleman's, that's right. That was his name. And who should be called up in the same barrack-room but a chap from Balliol, called Healey, with these big eyebrows, but not quite so big as they are now, and we made friends. We used to fall out for a smoke and play dominoes together, Denis and I.

When I started on Blubberhouses Moor I was just an ordinary gunner, because I hadn't done my OTC. Then I got my come-uppance and was sent to Ilkley to train as an officer. My uncle was in the Army, and unfortunately I was sent to his Officers Cadet Training Unit. He was a great character. He had a car, and when he drove up a hill he used to urge it on like a horse. And he said, 'Hugh,' he said, 'there's going to be no favouritism here. I've given orders that you can have all the worst jobs.' Which I did.

Then my uncle said, 'Well, my boy, I've got a posting for you in the Royal Bucks Yeomanry.' So off I went to the Bucks Yeomanry, which was a rather la-di-da gunner regiment, though my Captain was a very interesting man: always said he'd make a mint out of seaweed after the war, and blimey, he did! Anyway, we didn't know where we were going to be sent to fight. We were issued with thick clothes, and so we imagined we were going to Persia. We actually went to Bombay, and from there we were taken up to just beyond Poona, where Nehru had been incarcerated. We were put there to guard him.

We stayed there for a bit and trained on the beaches of Juhu at Bombay, assault-landing by sea, and so on. Then we went down to the Arakan to support the Indian Army, who hadn't been taught to fight in the jungle, and were hopeless, just *hopeless*. It was absolute chaos. The battle was being run from Delhi, over 1,000 miles away, and in the end the Japs came round the jungle and circled us, and we were very lucky to get back again to the other side of India.

By that time I was a bit bored. We did some jungle training and then we were suddenly rushed across India to Kohima, to take part in this very savage battle against the Japanese, which we won. It was one of the most savage battles in the whole of the war, and in the most impossible terrain – you wouldn't credit the terrain. Steep jungle sides, which you couldn't climb without ropes; deep nullahs on the side of the road, and filthy rain, pouring monsoon.

I'm a bit ashamed of myself when I look back at it all. I used to get a certain amount of pleasure out of a good shoot, you know. War coarsens one. But I learned quite a lot about the Holy Spirit from being in the Army, strangely enough. There was a tremendous camaraderie amongst people, a very strong feeling of togetherness, and I learned my pastoring in the Army. You see, we had a hell of a Colonel when I first went there, a great stickler. You'd never, never be able to sit down to your own food until all the vehicles were washed, and you watched your men have their food. And woe betide you if you didn't know the names of your men's children. I thought this was about the best training you could possibly have for pastoral care.

I made up my mind when I was in the Army that I had to be ordained, but only because I couldn't look myself in the face if I didn't. I was a very reluctant ordinand. Does that strike you as odd? I rather enjoyed my life with other people, and I didn't want to have a dog-collar because that would make me different and odd and peculiar. I also thought that if I lived to the end of the war it would be fun to be successful in something: my father had made a great success of his broking firm. So I didn't much want to be ordained, and I applied for theological college with great trepidation. After all, it seems a bit stuffy, doesn't it, to become a clergyman. It was the joke of the Mess when they discovered I was going to be ordained. They never let up!

I came back in the middle of November '45, and I was married in a fortnight. I hadn't had any real girlfriends before I met Elisabeth, I was very awkward in the presence of girls, I told you that. But Elisabeth and I had got engaged when I was twenty-three, before I'd gone away to fight. I'd known her for about a year then and I was absolutely certain. Does that seem young to you? You people get married later now, don't you? That's my impression. Though my brothers certainly married very young. Good heavens, they married out of nursery, practically. My brother Denzil got married and didn't finish his degree, and my brother Oliver got the most bogus degree Peterhouse said anyone ever had before leaving and marrying. One year's work and he went down.

But good heavens, it was the *war*! You didn't very much expect to come back, so you seized your opportunities - though I didn't want to marry before I went away in case I didn't come back. People do get married very quickly in war-time. I suppose it's nature determining that there will be progeny.

After we got married, we went back to Oxford. Elisabeth fortunately had a godmother with an empty house there, so we took it over. By that time I couldn't bring myself to read Greats because it would have taken so long. I was twenty-six by then and I wanted to get on, so I read Theology. Elisabeth got pregnant quite soon and Teresa was born, during the great cold, I remember. The warmest place in Oxford was in the waiting-room at the hospital.

Oxford *after* the war was even dimmer than Oxford *during* the war, because the shortages were greater. Even potatoes were rationed. Although we had been lent this house, we were rather badly off and had a couple of people as lodgers. I couldn't ask my father for money to train as an Anglican priest, could I? Even though I got a £100 scholarship, they wouldn't give it to me because my father was well off, so we were a bit pushed, really. I did have some money of my own, thank goodness, and we got by on that.

After Oxford, I got into Westcott House, Cambridge, and the Principal advised me not to bring my wife, because it would be distracting for me, and of course I took no notice. Honestly! Where on earth was she supposed to live? With the little money I was living on I bought a house, and then we were even poorer, but I still had to live in college most of the time. Our house was the last house in Cambridge, and Elisabeth was very lonely. She always said it was a great event when the postman came. I was miserable, I thought it was cruel. Those whom God has joined together, theological colleges put asunder! They did!

In the second year we students were allowed to sleep at home, but that first year was awful for Elisabeth, on her own with two small children. Poor Elisabeth. I used to bike back in the afternoon if I could, but not for the night, only for the afternoon, because you had to come back for supervision at five p.m. It was so cruel. I was appointed to the staff there eventually, and I resigned because of it. I felt that the college was ruining my marriage. The Principal never forgave me. But I had to get into chapel by seven-thirty a.m. and I wouldn't get home until eleven p.m., and I thought this was totally unreasonable. The other thing was – you wouldn't *believe* this – when I was on the staff Elisabeth and family would come to the chapel for the service on Sunday, and when I went into the college for breakfast they would be sent two and a half miles home for theirs. I thought it was appalling. *Appalling!*

I don't think the Church understood marriage. The basis of the theological college was monasticism. I remember Elisabeth and I were once invited back there to talk to the students about marriage and the Principal said, 'You won't mind if Elisabeth has dinner with the housekeeper, will you?' so I said it wasn't convenient for me to dine there after all. They were appalling institutions for marriage, and they didn't seem to realize that it's the sanctification of the family that matters, not the sanctification of the ordinand. And as for small children! I had small children when I was at Westcott and they used to come to chapel and make small noises, and this wasn't popular but I absolutely insisted on it.

Westcott House believed in having people of different sorts of churchmanship, which was why I went there, but I wasn't happy. The Principal, Ken Carey, was a man who liked being friends with his students, but I was never one of Ken's boys. He used to rather like ruling their lives, I thought: they made their confession to him and so on, and it didn't appeal to me, that kind of set-up. I think he had rather an inferiority complex. The other awful thing about the place was that there were no rules, and that created a lot of guilt. The ethos of the place was not to my liking either: there was an element of nervous laughter about the place, and heartiness, and I didn't warm to that.

We weren't taught about parish ministry. The clergyman's role seemed to be quite clear then, that you should care for the souls and welfare of the people in your community, but we were nevertheless taught nothing about these things! All I can remember was a doll when it came to infant baptism. For most people, the training was slogging through exams: 'tell me ten facts about the Holy Spirit before breakfast' sort of thing. But because I had a First in Theology I was excused half the papers, which meant I was able to read at some depth, and I enjoyed theology very much. I remember being very liberated by literary criticism of the Bible, which had always struck me as rather a rum book: *finally* I was allowed to take it to pieces!

I didn't yet know what I was doing it all for. I told you I didn't much want to be ordained, I just felt I must be. I had never lived in a parish, and although I was sparked by scholarship I knew I wanted to be a parish priest. It's always seemed to me that there's no point in being ordained if you're just a scholar. In fact, it was when I became too good at footnotes in New Testament scholarship that I decided to stop being a don. But that was later on.

I didn't know where to go to after Westcott, though we were

all determined that we had to go north. If we didn't go north, we were considered *soft*. So I went up to Jesmond, in Newcastle upon Tyne, to be a curate in a parish which was recommended to me by Father Dennis Marsh, a Franciscan friar who was a friend of the famous Father Algy who used to go round with a hot water bottle under his habit. But it was a bit of a disaster. My Vicar only stayed six weeks. Nobody told me he was leaving to be a bishop, because they thought I might not go there if I knew, and when I heard on the grapevine instead, I thought, 'What kind of a set-up am I joining in the Church of England?' They put all this emphasis on the Vicar you are going to be training with, and then the Bishop doesn't bother to tell you he's not going to be there!

Six weeks later I was in charge. We had a poky little house, but we weren't allowed to move into the vicarage – good Lord, no! – because I was just the curate. It wasn't a frightfully well-attended church, and the tower was falling down, and as it was a copy of the Campanile at St Mark's, Venice, it was quite a big thing to put right, so the first thing I had to do was organize a thermometer outside the church and get the money raised. I can't *tell* you how different things were then. D'you know, I got in a row simply because I agreed that the Mothers' Union could go to the theatre in Lent! It's true! I also used to take the youth club on a Hike and Bike across the moors, and the first year the rain was coming down in lumps, so I took them into a pub. Got into a hell of a row for that too.

Still, I enjoyed it enormously there. They were very warm-hearted, and once you had gained their affection you never lost it. Until you'd done that, however, they could be very blunt: when I went visiting, some of them would be quite clear that I couldn't come in. I was only there eighteen months, because Ken Carey asked me back on his staff at Westcott, so back I went. I'd been unhappy there, particularly, as I say, because of the way our wives were treated, but I thought it might be rather different on the staff. I was also young and inexperienced and I think I accepted the job without too much question.

I was there nearly three years, and then I packed it in. I told you I was grossly over-worked – forty-five people to do all the New Testament and doctrine with, in groups of five and six – it was a terrible sweat. And then there was Elisabeth and the family, three daughters, and we were paid a pittance there too, an absolute pittance.

Westcott House was always a place of great unhappiness for me. When I was later asked whether I would consider being Principal I said it was out of the question. I said how it nearly ruined my family life and that I felt some frustration over its attitude to women generally. Also, I was very shy, and when my friend Bob Runcie, who was very extrovert, came on the staff, I felt rather inadequate. I felt *stifled* within the Church there. I never have been a churchy person: I was converted to Christianity by Jesus, not the Church, and I was interested in the world, not the Church. I wanted a larger environment than this forcing-house for producing priests.

There was a man called Charles Raven, who was Regius Professor of Divinity and Master of Christ's College, Cambridge, and he was a most extraordinary man. I had known him slightly when he lectured at Westcott, and he got me the job as Dean at Caius College. The Master of Caius was a great scientist who discovered the neutron, and he hadn't a clue about people. He suffered from accidie – lethargy. He had smelling-salts on his desk, and when you came to tell him unpleasant news he would shut his eyes, hoping that when he opened them you would be away. Anyway, I went to see him about the job, and having said, 'How many candles do you like on the altar, Mr Montefiore?' he sank back exhausted and that was the end of the conversation. Nothing much happened for some time after that until the Precentor, who was usually drunk but wasn't on this occasion, discovered I had been in the Army, and we had an Army conversation, and that was my interview. Ludicrous!

I had an *enormous* sense of release when I went to Caius. I was meeting ordinary people, all nice, and I adored the undergraduates, they were lovely, lovely people. We also had a fascinating Senior Common Room, there were thirteen Fellows of the Royal Society in it, and that's where my science interest started. So I had a marvellous time there, and Elisabeth met more people too.

Then I got made a university lecturer, a don, and I was tremendously busy. In fact I had a breakdown once! I had to prepare my lectures in the vacation, and didn't have a single spare day in the whole vacation, and when term came I was unable to do anything. I just couldn't lecture. Came to a standstill. The doctor said, 'You've got to get away,' so I took the term off and went off with Elisabeth to the old vicarage that we'd bought in Wales.

That wasn't my only breakdown. Later, when I was Vicar of Great St Mary's in Cambridge, I worked myself to a standstill. My back was playing me up like hell, and I found myself supervising from the floor. In the end my curate stepped over my body at a staff meeting, and rang up the Bishop and said, 'Will you order this man to go away?' Which he did. But I did always have a tendency to depression. The children of manic-depressives often suffer from it. I certainly did, though oddly enough, ever since I left Cambridge I haven't suffered from depression. I had certain stress illnesses when I was Bishop of Birmingham. My heart went irregular, which I thought was an obvious harbinger of death, but they said, 'You mustn't eat Stilton, or drink caffeinated coffee. We'll give you some Beta Blockers and you'll be all right.' But the day I retired I threw away all my medicines, and I haven't used any since, and now I'm fit as a fiddle. Sleep used to be difficult. I could make do on very little sleep, but in Birmingham I was so busy I'd have to make do with four or five hours sometimes and I don't think that was very good for me.

I feel frightfully guilty about the effect of all this overwork on my family. When I became a don, I had 450 students, and the only way to get to know the freshmen was by feeding them, because they were so shy. At least if they had a knife and fork in their hands they could talk with me. I also had a duty of reading grace in the evening, so I used to eat in college, and I neglected my family terribly. I . . . oh, I wish I had spent more time with them. I had three months' vacation in the summer, and that was lovely, but during the year I fear I did neglect them. I got into the habit, I suppose, from Westcott. Though we used to have fun. Of course they were all girls, so their interests were slightly different from mine, but being a don I was a little better off and, as I said, I'd bought an old vicarage in the wilds of Wales, and we had wonderful holidays together, very happy times. But I wasn't at home as much as I should have been or would have liked to have been. It seemed at the time so very important that I should be pastor to all the college, and looking back it seems to me more important that I should have spent time with my family. I think it's a very difficult one for a clergyman.

I don't think many people have intellectual doubts about God, not genuine intellectual doubts. Some do. I think what most atheists are justifiably complaining about is a false vision of God, which has been either set before them, or which they've picked up, and heavens above it's easy enough to pick up.

I've been through periods of doubt myself, but in a sense they were somewhat superficial. I've certainly been through periods of intellectual doubt about the existence of God, when life has seemed absolutely bloody, but I had a certain experience behind me, which meant a great deal to me, and I would look back and say, 'Well, what happened to me when I became a Christian? Was this self-delusion, hallucination?' And I felt impelled to keep on. I wasn't like William Temple, who never ceased to have the sun's rays shining brightly upon him, it wasn't that sort of faith: but there wasn't a time when I felt, 'I've been had for a mug, and the sooner I get out of this show the better.' I never felt like that.

For me, intellectual difficulties about God mainly focus on the problem of evil, which is impossible to solve, and on the two natures of Christ, human and divine, which I don't accept. I think Christ was a human being who was set apart by God; who was guided, called, chosen, inspired, and responded totally so that he was a mirror of God, and God worked through Him. What I just *cannot* understand, however, is how the passible could be joined to the impassible. How can the contingent be a part of the eternal? If God emptied Himself to become man, so that He lost all His divine attributes, what continuity is there between the two?

I'm not trying to diminish Christ. I'm just saying that I don't think humanity and divinity are compatible. I think that God took the only action He could take to save the world through Christ, and I'm happy to call Christ 'God incarnate', because for me he is a mirror of God; he is the icon of God; he is the person through whom God functioned. But I cannot square one person having two natures. It doesn't seem to me to add up. I mean, how can God be bereft of God? To say, 'My God, my God – why hast thou forsaken me?' simply doesn't make sense if Christ *is* God.

I think one of the problems is that the orthodox Christian faith has been formulated in terms of Greek metaphysics, and although I believe in the truths for which they stand, I don't think that it's credible today. I think many people have grave difficulties with these Greek terms on which our beliefs about God are founded. The ideas are important, but because they're expressed in the categories of a past age they have become distorted and confused. For example, take the concept of the Trinity, three persons in one God. The very word *persona* in Latin meant something completely different from what we think: it was the mask which an actor wore, whereas we think of it as personality. Hence, we have very strange ideas of the Trinity as three people communing, which is not what was meant at all, it was a much more metaphysical idea of three permanent aspects of the one being.

Therefore I've always found it very difficult to explain what I think God is, because I've never had an image of God, except in terms of human personality in Jesus. God is larger and bigger than I can imagine, and I mustn't make an idol of Him by producing some kind of human image. I've always been *aware* of God, and I thought I had experienced God, or rather His effects in me, His grace. I believe that after my early experience I had a pattern of life, and a person to follow, in Jesus Christ, and that was enough for me, really. But God Himself: we only see His footprints. His inner nature is hidden from us.

Certainly God's omnipotence needs considering, because He appears powerless to prevent certain things happening, but I believe very much in providence. I don't mean that I think everything's all mapped out already, because we do have real freedom, and if I didn't believe that I don't think I could believe the Christian faith, because I couldn't really account for the bloodiness of everything. Freedom is absolutely essential to the Christian faith, and God allows far more of it than we do. If it weren't there, we'd love to order, which is no good to anybody.

This is where prayer comes in, because I see prayer as basically being with God. At Westcott House we were taught the various modes of meditation, where you might picture a scene, immerse yourself in it, and ask yourself what it means to you and what you have to do as a result. But I far prefer the contemplative to the meditative sort of prayer, which is to be found in all the mainstream faiths, where you still your own wandering thoughts, desires and feelings, and just wait passively upon God in the stillness of His fathomless being.

My ideas about prayer have changed quite a lot. I do think we tend to tell God more about our needs than thank Him for what He has given us, and I think prayer should be thanksgiving because we are surrounded by His providence on all sides, and we take so much for granted. Having said that, I think it's absolutely right that we tell Him of the innermost desires and needs of our hearts, but I don't expect them to be met. If He met all our desires, life would be chaos. You'd desire this, I'd desire that, and they'd clash. It'd be rather like both sides praying for victory.

*

I don't think God interferes in the natural order of things. But I do think that spiritual things can override material things. If you look at the Virgin Birth, for example, I'd say that although there are important, abiding and permanent truths that are illustrated in the story, it's nevertheless improbable. Virginal conceptions do take place in some species, in various forms of aphids, for example, by the female chromosomes splitting so that you get a clone of the mother; but you don't have a *male* child from a female, virginal conception, and in any case, the human reproductive system isn't made that way. In human beings, it's necessary to have twenty-three male chromosomes, and twenty-three female chromosomes. If in Christ twenty-three were supernaturally provided, at least one had to be a specifically male chromosome. Also, those twenty-three chromosomes must have had an inheritance, otherwise Jesus wouldn't have been a human being, so *I* think Christ's father could only have been Joseph. After all, according to Jewish law, betrothal was much more serious than it is today, and it was not forbidden for couples to have intercourse before marriage.

What I'm saying here is that in terms of modern genetics, the virginal conception of Christ has no *bearing* whatsoever upon his divinity. Theologically it seems to be unnecessary and improbable. I also think that there is a lot of evidence against the Virgin Birth. How on earth could Jesus's mother have thought that he was out of his mind as she did, according to St Mark's Gospel, at the beginning of his ministry? After all, if she'd known that she was pregnant without a man, she would know that there was something very *strange* about Jesus. I think that rather than being myths, the Virgin Birth and the Resurrection are more likely to be what the Jews call *haggadah*: that is, moral stories with a spiritual point to them.

When it comes to the Resurrection, my feeling is that it definitely took place. I can't see any other explanation of the phenomenon, frankly. After all, Christianity wouldn't have started with a lot of downcast, depressed people thinking that they'd backed a loser. How *could* the Church have started without an enormous turnaround and spiritual experience of some kind?

If you look at the Resurrection narratives, they aren't in mythical form at all, they're in very sparse, short stories, describing what happened, and usually giving marching orders for people after recognition of the risen Christ had taken place. I think it is very difficult to reconcile the stories of the simultaneous Resurrection appearances in Galilee and Jerusalem, but that doesn't worry me very much, because the differences in the stories are mostly theologically motivated. According to St Mark, Jesus had brought the end of days upon mankind, and Mark's Gospel ends on a note of terror, as though the end of the world had begun.

Yet I do think that the evidence points clearly to Jesus's Resurrection. It certainly seems to be the only reasonable explanation for the empty tomb. You could say that Jesus's body was stolen by the Jews; but why didn't they produce it? You could say that it was stolen by the Christians; but what on earth for? If they had stolen it, there would have been a martyrs' pilgrimage to it. And there's no hint of that.

The *Romans* could have nicked it?! What an *extraordinary* idea. They couldn't have! What's the motive for the Romans nicking the body anyway? If they'd nicked it in order to prove that Christ hadn't risen from the dead, they'd have produced it, wouldn't they – even if it was a bit decomposed. No, my dear, it couldn't have been the Romans. There would have been no reason for them to do it.

Some people think that the Resurrection is a myth made up, in order to show that good prevails over evil. I think that's very improbable. St Paul was converted within four years of the Resurrection. He was quite clear that Jesus had risen from the dead, and appeared to him, so there wasn't much time for that story to be made up during the lifetime of the people who knew Jesus. People forget that: that there was very little time for people to create this myth. The other thing is, I don't know whether you know this, but women's evidence in those days wasn't legal testimony, not in Judaism. Therefore Jesus's Resurrection appearances to the women weren't to *prove* anything.

Perhaps the closest analogy for the Resurrection appearances is veridical hallucination, which sometimes happens when people die, when you think you see people. I'm not saying that's what happened, but it's the closest analogy I can make. But the mode of his Resurrection isn't as important as the *fact* of his Resurrection. If God did it, then He must have done it for a very good reason, and I think He wanted to show everyone that death to resurrection is the way in which we must all go.

I am, however, somewhat ambivalent about some of the miracles. Some I find credible, and others I don't. I don't think Jesus turned water into wine. That was an old story, pagan, Hellenistic. And the multiplication of loaves puzzles me. I can't believe it, it strains my credulity too much: yet without doubt, something very rum happened that day in the wilderness. So I'm selective in what I believe, and I'm happy to be selective. Why shouldn't I use my mind to evaluate? I find it quite credible that Jesus walked on the water. That kind of thing has been known elsewhere, like Tibet, and the effect of the spirit on the human body can produce results which are not expected by people who are concerned simply with physics. But as I said, I do think that a lot of it is *haggadah*, stories. The way he is supposed to have calmed the storm seems to me to be precisely what he does to the storm of the human heart.

I don't think that Jesus ever undertook miracles in order to prove that he was the son of God, although the most astonishing things happened in a very short time. The public ministry of Jesus was only about two and a half years long, yet just think how he could stir up thousands of people. His movement spread very quickly during his lifetime, and I don't believe that would just happen by preaching – after all, there were no modern media. It must have happened because of these marvellous miracles.

It certainly isn't necessary to believe any miracles of Jesus in order to hold that he was the Messiah: this is a theological red herring. Jesus understood his mission as Messiah in terms of Old Testament prophecy, and although this wasn't always straight-forward it does seem as though he regarded his healing miracles as signs of the coming Kingdom; giving sight to the blind, making the bent upright, and so on. These are the miracles that really got him known. You must remember that he lived in a time when there were no doctors, so they must have been very impressive. They're not so to us, because we know a bit more about psychosomatic medicine and the effect of spirit on matter, but I think one always has to ask oneself whether the physical occurrence in a story measures up to the profundity of its spiritual meaning. I think that the miracles contain significant spiritual truths. When Jesus turned the water into wine it was the underlining meaning of transformation which was impor-tant, not saving a hostess from looking a fool at a wedding party!

Yet because of these things, many people hold that the Bible is inerrant. I think that's very strange because it took over 300 years for them to decide which books should be in it, and if the books are inerrant, it's strange that it didn't strike anyone earlier, really. The Bible does contain some inconsistencies within it, and this leaves you asking, which bits are wrong? How am I going to decide what is true and what not? The answer is, I have no means of deciding but my own spiritual intuition and reason-ing, combined of course with other people's, because it's unlikely that Hugh Montefiore is the only person in possession of the truth. But I do think that the Bible comes out of theological inquisition amazingly well.

When I was a don in Cambridge, I became a parish priest for the first time. I was made Vicar of Great St Mary's, which was not only the university church, but the civic church as well, and I had sixty square miles of visiting.

In many ways I wasn't frightfully good. I was slightly donnish and didn't always recognize people in the street, and gave offence and so on. It wasn't easy to know people well. We had these immense student services – 1,500 people or so – and I had inherited a tradition from Mervyn Stockwood and Joe Fison, who'd been there before, of getting in this marvellous mixture of people to preach. The Archbishop would come down quite frequently. Politicians would speak. People like Auden would come down and read us poetry. Cliff Richard came for a pop service.

At the end of seven years I was *exhausted*. I told you I had a breakdown at one stage, and couldn't keep it up. I had forty-two courses of sermons to arrange over that time, and every Sunday we had services at eight, at ten, at eleven, at twelve; the university sermon at two-thirty; Evensong at six-thirty; an undergraduate service at eight p.m. It was the largest congregation of lay people in Cambridge, so there were funerals and weddings and baptisms and problems and parish dos. The parish was so big I had to buy mopeds for my curates, and a little red Mini for myself. And of course by the end of my time there I was not only exhausted, but I was infamous for having made a remark about Jesus's homosexual orientation. And that was terrible. Terrible.

The whole thing was a chapter of accidents. I went over to Somerville College, Oxford, in my Mini, to give a paper on Jesus as the revelation of God to the Modern Churchmen's Union 100th anniversary. Firstly, I didn't realize there was no water in my Mini, and I was only a few miles out of Cambridge when the whole thing blew up! So I had to crawl back and get another car, and arrived in Oxford just before the lecture began, which meant I didn't have time to ask whether the press were there – it never occurred to me they would be. I gave the lecture, and all I said was that as Jesus usually identified with the under-privileged, it might have been because he had homosexual tendencies – because in Jewish culture if you're not married and producing children by your twenties, something's *up*! And he had very close friendships with men, and so on. But I didn't say he *was* a homosexual, I said he might have had homosexual tendencies.

Anyway, I was woken up at twelve o'clock that night by the *Daily Express*, and then when I got back to Cambridge the telephone was ringing as I got in, and it was the *Express* again, saying, 'What comment have you got to make on the Archbishop's statement about you?' That was the first I'd heard of it, and I realized that the balloon was going up, and it was *awful*. The press! The letters! I had 2,000 letters of complaint. And the *fuss*! Just like the Bishop of Durham and the Virgin Birth.

Homosexuality was regarded by the Jews as wrong, and that's where the fear started. After all, the Greeks were very much in favour of it. But the Jews had a horror of it, and it never occurred to them that two people of the same sex could actually love one another; they always put it down to lust, and those are the grounds upon which it is condemned in the New Testament. They regarded it as unnatural, because obviously our sexual instincts have been bred in us in order to produce children, and they saw it as contrary to nature. I have somewhat modified my views on homosexuality being unnatural, which I used to feel, since they've discovered recently a gene that they think predisposes people to homosexuality. That gene *must* have some contribution to make to the well-being of the species or it would not keep turning up, because, for heaven's sake, homosexuals don't reproduce themselves!

As for those people who are born homosexual, my own theory is that if they're not born to be celibates, it's very unfair to say to them, 'You may never have any sexual experience because you've been born that way.' Especially when they love one another. I mean, I've met some of these gays and lesbians, and they're very *lovely* people. They're not perverted, lustful maniacs in the way St Paul regards them, d'you know? Many of them are very loving and tender towards their partners.

So although I take seriously what the Bible says about homosexuality, I don't think it's dealing with a lot of homosexuality that's about today, and I do feel that the Church is unkind to them. Even the last statement of the Bishops was odd: it said you mustn't condemn lay people who practise homosexuality, but clergy shouldn't do it. I don't believe in a double standard for clergy and lay people. I thought that was what the Reformation was partly about – that we are all under the same command of God, and it's wrong to put upon ordained clergy things you don't put upon lay people. Of course clergy must be examples of Christ, but so must every lay person.

The trouble is, the Church operates on three criteria: the Bible, tradition and reason. The Bible and tradition look, on the surface, as though they're against homosexuality, and this is why the Church finds it difficult to approve it. But I look at it in terms of justice, and homosexuals are unjustly – unreasonably – treated. It used not to bother me as a bishop very much. I used to say, 'I'm not going to look through your bedroom keyhole: what you do there is between you and God.' After all, if a chap can't have a partner, those instincts are going to come out in places like public lavatories, and they do. This is one of the tragedies; that the Church forces some of its people into adopting a way of life that they despise, because it won't recognize them in their own right. And there are quite a lot of gay clergymen who have partners living in their houses. London was full of them. So I think there's a lot of unfinished business on this issue.

I became very desperate at Great St Mary's. I was ready to move, but no one had offered me a job because I was in the doghouse over Jesus and homosexuality, and I thought I'd never get away from Cambridge. But I'm a great believer in thinking that things will arrive for you, even though they don't always arrive when you want them to arrive, and they're very seldom what you expect.

One day I went out to lunch with John Robinson, who was Dean of Trinity College, and after a bit he said, 'What would you think about being Bishop of Kingston?' And I said, 'Never thought about it.' So he said, 'Well, Mervyn wondered if you'd like to consider it.' Mervyn Stockwood was the Bishop of Southwark, and Kingston was one of his suffragan bishoprics.

I was knocked over by this suggestion, but I'd always liked

Mervyn very much, so I gladly came here. The Kingston area is very varied because it includes Clapham, Streatham and Battersea, Wimbledon, Kew, Richmond, and goes right the way down to Reigate, to all those commuter areas and delectable little village parish churches. It was a great culture shock. I'd only seen the odd black in Cambridge, and he was usually a brilliant research student, but the Brixton and Streatham areas are largely black, so I had a lot to learn, actually.

There were two suffragan bishops under Mervyn; myself and the Bishop of Woolwich, David Sheppard at that time. We all got on extremely well and Mervyn kept me on a very, very loose rein. I was able to chair the Independent Commission on Transport, and pursue my environmental concerns, which had begun when I was a curate in Newcastle, and for which I'd been considered an eco-freak! When I first went to Kingston I was President of the Heathrow Association of the Control of Aircraft Noise, because Richmond was in my area, and that awful Concorde was just coming in. The noise of Concorde was appalling, far above what was permitted, and I spoke up very volubly about it, as I have on many other environmental issues: because I do think Christianity has things to say about the environment; that technology shouldn't give people nervous breakdowns and so on.

The first thing I noticed about becoming a bishop was being bereft. You don't realize what a wonderful support a parish is until you leave it. When you're a bishop, you're on your own. When you're a vicar, you're very much not on your own. When I became Bishop of Birmingham I was very much on my own. That's why I think bishops should always have chaplains, someone they can talk to. Chaplains also like to leak things to you, which is vital!

I was in Kingston for seven years. My predecessor was a single man, who had a kitchen about ten by three, so Mervyn told me to find a proper place, and that's how I found this house. The only competitor was someone who wanted to make it into a cat home. But the Church Commissioners said it wasn't big enough. They wanted us to live in an enormity just down the way, one of these places where you have to have shutters everywhere, and I said, 'No. This is where I'm going to live, and if you won't buy it for me, I'll get it myself.' And they wouldn't, so I did. My mother lent me the money, and I let it out when I moved on to Birmingham. Best investment I ever made in my life. It is a fairly modest house for a bishop, this, but it's quite reasonable. I had all those people living downtown in Lambeth and Brixton, and I couldn't have faced them if I'd lived in some great big huge house. I really couldn't.

I learned everything about being a bishop from Mervyn Stockwood. He was an impossible chap in many ways, but a marvellous pastor, and always great fun. One of the things I learned from him were visitations; when you went and visited a parish for thirty-six hours, and stayed in the vicarage. It was a bit lonely for Elisabeth. I did take her once, but the bed wasn't big enough, and we never went together again. There's no way of getting to know a parish like a visitation. You go and visit the sick; you take Communion; you go and look at the commerce and industry in the parish; you visit the schools; you have a question-and-answer session with the congregation; you have a meeting with the PCC, and by then you really know what's making them tick. That's what I learned from Mervyn, and when I went to Birmingham I did the same thing.

One of the things you *must* realize is that throughout my ministry I've never been a very *churchy* person. I'm concerned with God's work in His world because that's where His people are. The Church consists of 98 per cent lay people, and if a bishop's not careful he spends most of his time with the clergy. Because Christianity's about people, isn't it, it's not about running institutions – don't you think? So it's absolutely crucial that a bishop should also be known by lay people. It's too easy to fall into the trap of only meeting clergy and their wives.

My move to Birmingham was a tricky one. A terrible row broke out when it was announced that I was going there. There was an article against me every day for a month in the local paper! It's true! They thought I'd be bad for motor-cars because of my environmental interests. I must say I didn't particularly *want* to go to Birmingham after that, but I knew if I was offered it I should take it.

I remember old Archbishop Coggan, he rang me up during all the fuss and said, 'Hugh, I'm very worried about you. I'm just off to Moscow, I'll give you my telephone number, so if you've any trouble, ring me up.' But by the time I got there they were all so ashamed of themselves they were rather decent to me. Very kind, in fact. And I've never been so happy *anywhere* as when I was in Birmingham.

Birmingham is the place that no one wants to go to, but no one wants to leave. It's a very happy, friendly place. They're very warmhearted, without being blunt as they are in the north: and it's an enormous city, far and away the second biggest city in England, and it has such a wonderful mix of people. When I got there I determined that I would spend a third of my time on the parishes, a third of my time on the city, and a third of my time nationally, because by that time I was Chairman of the Board for Social Responsibility, and there is nothing that isn't the social responsibility of the Church, so I used to have to do a lot of reading around when things blew up, whatever they might be; homelessness, crime, abortion, gene therapy, or whatever.

I got very involved in the local community, especially as British Leyland at that time was on a death-wish course. I also befriended the blacks in Birmingham, and saw a lot of their top people, because they needed supporting and affirming, and we were very concerned that we hadn't got enough black ordinands, so we made sure we got some. We also began an inter-faith council, and that was one of the most important things that happened while I was there. It arose partly because the Muslim imams used to ring me up and say, 'Bishop, can you help us? It's the nurses. They're trying to take the girls out of their traditional clothes and put them into uniforms, and it's against our faith.' I was rather touched that they'd ring up the Anglican bishop to try to get his support. I'd also visit the gurdvaras and the Sikh Temples, and the Hindu Temples, and I'd go to the Mosque.

There's a great fear of Islam at the moment, but it's an ignorant fear. Most people in Britain don't know what Islam thinks. Islam has a view that religion is the concern of the society in which you live. Protestants have a very individualist view of religion, so they don't appreciate that if you're a Muslim you must see God in all aspects of life, including public life. I think Muslims produce a challenge for Christians, actually. The other thing many people don't realize is that there are very positive things said about Jesus in the Koran, and very positive things said about the Virgin Mary. There are differences, of course, but I think there's got to be more religious dialogue between Christians and Muslims, because you can't know your own faith until you're brought up against somebody else's.

There are four different views about other religions. One is that they're the invention of the devil, put there to mislead you; one is that Christ is a fulfilment of other faiths; one is that all faiths are different ways up the same mountain; and one is that God is unknowable, and that the various faiths are the various ways in which we try to apprehend the unknowable. But whatever view you hold, it really doesn't cut any ice saying, 'I'm a Christian, I know that the rest are rubbish.' You can't do that until you've heard what they have to say, and to do that you have to listen.

Therefore, I find it unbelievable when people say that Christianity is the only route to salvation. What kind of a view of God is it that thinks He condemns the majority of his Creation to hell? God wills *all* men to be saved. I believe that Jesus fulfils all that other faiths have, but I also think that the word of God which was incarnate in Jesus is present in other faiths. Many, many people have a very real experience of God: the word 'Islam', for example, means 'obedience to God'. The Jews, the Muslims and the Christians belong to the same family of faith, and the Sikhs are quite close to Christianity in their vision of

God, and I have a lot of respect for them. I hope I don't lack any commitment to my own faith, but God has placed these people in other faiths, and He must disclose himself to them in other ways. My whole being *revolts* at the thought that they won't enjoy eternal life.

What is *really* interesting is that English liberal-minded people cannot understand that people actually take their faith seriously. I think it's very unfortunate that the fatwah was issued against Salman Rushdie, which as far as I can see is quite contrary to the Koran, but what the British can't understand is that people should be deeply hurt when their religion is held up to ridicule, and I think nothing showed up the insensibility of liberalism so much as the Rushdie affair.

The Christian ecumenical movement is also in a very strange position. The Christian Churches have grown further apart, and individuals have grown unbelievably closer together. Yet I can't see reunion with Rome in the foreseeable future, mainly because we have a different view of authority. In the Anglican Communion we have a view of disseminated authority. In the Roman Church they have a view of pyramidal authority, and I see *no* justification for thinking that the Pope is infallible. Jesus never claimed he was infallible, and if Jesus didn't say he was infallible, why the heck should the Pope?! I also think some things about the Roman Catholic Church are awful, really. I'm not saying that the Church of England's perfect: I love it and I hate it. But I am saying there are fundamental problems between us. If I were to become a Roman Catholic, I'd have to be re-ordained, and that strikes me as ridiculous. I couldn't possibly agree that my Anglican Holy Orders are absolutely null and utterly void. This doesn't mean that Anglicans and Roman Catholics don't have a very large area of agreement. We believe in common much more than we disagree about, and what might happen in a few hundred years I don't know. After all, we've only had 2,000 years of Christianity.

Our purpose in life is quite simple: to love God, and to love our neighbour as ourselves. Those are the two great Commandments, and, as I see it, the purpose in life is to become more and more Christ-like. I see that as a great preparation for being with God forever. Yet we're not fit for that as we are, and that's why I believe in purgatory, though I don't like to call it purgatory because it sounds negative. I'd rather call purgatory a getting ready for the party: not just washing, cleansing, but putting on new clothes, and a new body, and so on. And we have to do this in order to be ready to share with God forever in His ineffable blessedness. That's the vision I have of our purpose.

You may well ask why God created this testing part in between. Well, I think He created life as we know it because He didn't want to produce automata, who would inevitably respond to His love: He wanted us to be free to respond to it. Our purpose during this life is to integrate our conscious souls with our unconscious souls, and this is a process which takes the whole of life to do. But I still sometimes think that God's a bastard. I do. If He lets all these terrible things happen to us on the way to eternal life, I sometimes feel He must be an old so-and-so: unless He has something which I can't grasp in view, which I believe and hope He has.

Evil sticks out like a sore thumb in all of this. Isaiah says: 'I create darkness and I create light.' There is no possibility of progress in good, unless there is also the possibility of increasing evil, and whether we do evil or not is down to us, absolutely. Yet we have inherited characteristics and traditions which include evil within them. We are shaped by our heredity and our environment. So avoiding evil is not quite so simple a matter as free choice: in order to do so we have to free ourselves from social structures and traditions which are inherently evil.

Yet the fact remains that there are still hurricanes, there are droughts, there are earthquakes, there are sun spots; meteorites can hit the earth, all sorts of things can happen. These are all part of what God permits. He has given His universe a degree of freedom, He doesn't interfere with its function. He permits it all. And why? Well, we don't know the options open to Him, but if He is going to produce a universe in such a way that eventually, on some obscure planet, in some obscure solar system, in some of the billions of galaxies, there will emerge intelligent beings who are capable of free choice, then that universe has to have some freedom within it to evolve as it wants to, and therefore these natural calamities are bound to happen. It seems to me that we are not in a position to criticize the method of evolution by which you and I exist unless we know the options open to God in Creation.

You say: what was there before Creation as we know it? But you can't ask that because there was no 'before'. Time is part of our own being, not something outside us. We live in a four-dimensional universe; three dimensions, plus time, and before the world was created there was no time. I know we find it very difficult to think of God living in eternity, but He does. In God we live and move and have our being, but we have a different kind of being from His eternal being, in what the Thomists call our 'participating in the divine being'. Neither are we going *back* to eternity when we die, because there is no going back. We'll just cease to be beings of time and space.

I'm not one of these people who think that we are merely held within the memory of God when we die. Yes, we lose our bodies with death, but I think we have a new form of body, and a new kind of being about which we know pretty much damn all! My feeling is that we must have some sort of body, because without a body you are entirely passive, you can't express yourself and you are incapable of any creative activity – but I don't know. Mercifully, we are not told anything about our future life, because we are meant to get *on* with this life. Our job is in this world.

I have always thought that I've never been career-oriented, in the sense that I've just expected things to happen, and they have. I resigned from Westcott House, and something *happened*. I was feeling that I'd got to the end of being a don, and something *happened*. I was desperate at Great St Mary's in Cambridge, and

Mervyn had me here; and then I was feeling a bit desperate here after seven years, and Birmingham *happened*. So I haven't planned out a career.

That doesn't mean I haven't wanted things. I didn't want to be the Bishop of London, no. My idea of hell. But Archbishop of Canterbury? The question is not really relevant, because I'm sure Mrs Thatcher would never have chosen me even if I had been one of the two names selected. When Robert Runcie was made Archbishop of Canterbury I believe half of me wanted it, and half of me knew I couldn't have done it. I knew I hadn't got a tough enough hide. I was passionately interested in truth, and that was incompatible with being – sounds an awful thing to say – but it was incompatible with being Archbishop of Canterbury. I don't mean by that that Runcie was *agin* truth, because he isn't; but he is by nature a sitter on the fence. Given his nature, I think that he did the job superbly.

I haven't got a thick enough skin for a job like that. I told you I was very shy when I was young. I'm also preternaturally sensitive, I'm well aware of that. I've been very deeply upset by things that have been said about me. As well as a passionate desire for truth, I've also a desire to be liked, and they're not very compatible. The desire for truth takes precedence on the whole, thank goodness, but I do have a need to be liked, and I do find criticism – especially criticism which I think is unfair – I find it very hurtful.

It may sound funny, but sometimes I put off reading the letters I get. When people wrote to me in Birmingham I had to have a harder skin, because sometimes I was actually threatened with violence for some of the things I said about racism: you know, I said how wicked and wrong it was, and when people threatened me with violence, it made me rather angry. That didn't worry me so much. It's the personal things. Personal things get under my skin very much. Then I have to say to myself, 'Hugh, you're taking yourself very seriously,' and I tell myself that I'm probably not wholly in touch with myself, therefore I must listen to what people are saying.

I do actually think that I'm not a terribly attractive person. It doesn't stop me jolly well going on being myself, but I am bound to think that I can't be wholly in touch with myself, or people wouldn't say such nasty things; because they have, and I am aware that there may be aspects of myself which are undesirable. But it still hurts quite a bit, and when I say that I mustn't take myself so seriously, what I mean is that you have to accept yourself, don't you? Christianity is about acceptance, and if God accepts me as I am, then I had better do the same.

I feel accepted much more than I did, I think. I tell myself that that comes with old age, that my edges have got rubbed off. I told you how I wanted to fit in, how that was one of my reluctances about being ordained, and I think that stems from a desire not to be different, although I *am* different. And I used to feel it, rather. At bishops' meetings I felt different because they didn't naturally gossip with me, and I used to feel that terribly. But then perhaps I wasn't a very gregarious person in some ways. The only place I didn't feel this was in Birmingham. They were so friendly, and although I was in a position of power and influence, I felt very accepted.

Although my relationship with my brothers eventually got better, my relationship with my mother never improved. I've always felt a bit guilty that I didn't get to know her better, and didn't see her more. She always said, 'I don't want to bother you,' and there's no doubt that it *was* a bother when she was around, too. When she was ill it was hell! Even though I always felt that my parents wished me very well, and loved me, I always felt I had a slightly deprived childhood: I remember my father bribing us all with tuppenny bars, 'so as not to make a noise in the house, because your mother is resting', and one always knew she was in one of her queer moods.

I never spoke very openly to my mother. I felt she was . . . she was a strong personality. Great waves of disapproval would come over her and communicate themselves to me. I was her little one, and I suppose she had quite a soft spot for me. But when I became a priest I was the little boy who was naughty, as it were, and I was bloody well going to go on being naughty, because I thought she was so wrong. So there were always these emotional complications, and so much of the time she was bonkers. But there were rather fine things about her too. She had a remarkable intuition of getting at the truth of people and things. She was quite shrewd, despite her battiness. And she was kind. She bought this house for me when I first came here, as I said. She gave a lot of her money away, though it always had strings attached. She usually made things into trusts, so that they'd revert back in the end!

My father I was very, very fond of; he was a wonderful man. He used to care for all his extended family, and he ran an East End Jewish Boys' Club, and he used to preach to them. He and my mother were very ill-assorted really, because he was a go-getter who made his firm into an enormous success and always did everything at the double. I know my mother very nearly packed up the marriage before it even began. Rather glad she didn't, or I wouldn't be here! But my father couldn't cope with it. He would have been Lord Mayor of London if my mother hadn't been a manic-depressive but he couldn't accept it because there was entertaining to be done, and she was never very good at running the huge household. She was even certified at one stage. Lithium hadn't come on the market for manic-depressives then.

I was frightened of her, of her disapproval. Classic, really. She exerted a great influence over me, well aware of that. But I was always frightened of her disapproval, because you'd never know whether she'd blow hot or blow cold. My poor eldest brother, who was so conscientious, used to have absolute *hell* at times, and was right out of favour and wouldn't be spoken to. She was never like that with me, but still there was always an element of this . . . this fearfulness in me, of her. I said to you over lunch that I didn't feel free until she died, and that's true.

Good heavens, this is interesting. I'm very interested in myself, in all this, the way I seize up, don't I? Do you notice that? I mean, I'm very well aware of this. I seize up when you ask me about my family. My roots. Hard to talk about, d'you know?

When I look back at my life, I'm always conscious of failure; of how much better and more I could have done. On the other hand, I've been very greatly blessed, and I am very grateful to God for the jobs He's enabled me to be in. They have enabled me to be a little less immature than I was, because I think I was very impetuous and immature when I was young.

But my goodness, there's so much more that I could have done, and there's some mistakes that I made. For instance, I don't withdraw what I said about Jesus's possible homosexual orientation, but I wish I hadn't caused such offence. And I wish it as much for Elisabeth as for myself, because she had hell over it all in Cambridge.

I look at my life in positive and negative terms. There are still lots of things I want to do. That's the trouble, really, isn't it? It's not so easy with Elisabeth being ill, although I'm rather pleased that things are as they are at the moment, oddly enough. I always told the Lord that I thought that He treated me too . . . well, I've always felt slightly guilty for being well-heeled. I've never been able to give away any of my capital, because my father had a mad fear that I'd go and build churches with it, so everything was tied up in trusts. In the end I went to law to break them, because I said they were not beneficial for my children. Still, I can understand it, as it's Jewish money. And I couldn't give it away, because this was given to me as family money and I think it would be a breach of trust, d'you know what I mean?

My children are always urging me to spend money on myself, but I always feel guilty if I spend money on myself. Anyhow, I've been keeping some in case of these nursing homes, for when Elisabeth goes into one. But I *am* rather appalled at how well-heeled I am, and I don't want to live at a higher standard than I do. I'm always well aware I haven't known the insecurity which comes from not knowing where you are financially.

Now that Elisabeth is ill ... I've always told the Lord that I've had things rather easy, and it would be rather good for me to have things not so easy. It never occurred to me that it would be this way. But I don't regret it, strangely enough. It would be stupid to, because she's reasonably happy. She mercifully hasn't had one of these character changes you can get with Alzheimer's, and she's not in distress or in pain. And I'm ... well, it's jolly good for me to have these problems, I think. Oddly enough, I don't feel bitter about it at all, I feel rather glad that it's happened. Not for *her* sake! For God's sake, not for her sake! But *having* happened, I feel it's only appropriate and right that I should have to cope with this problem. Anyhow, I feel it's rather a challenge not to give in. I do. dislike self-pity, and I try not to succumb to it in any way, d'you know?

I think we had a happy marriage. I *think* we did. There were times when we were a little more distant with each other, when I was absorbed in other things, I think I told you that. And she suffered a bit from depression, did I mention that too? But she was a lovely, lovely person, and her quietness and tranquillity and constant support were marvellous for me. She was also a very intelligent person and we did love each other. We *do* love each other. You've seen how she is: she doesn't know who I am, doesn't know I'm Hugh, but she knows she loves me, because she says so. She says so.

I don't get lonely. I'm always too busy to be lonely. If I lived here on my own I would be, and I will have to live here on my own some day, but then I feel that's not a bad preparation for death, really. I haven't got a large number of close friends, strangely enough, so I don't have people I talk to, no. I have friends, don't misunderstand me, but there are friends and friends, and these aren't bosom friends. It's not by choice, it just happened. One of the things I greatly regret is that I was so engulfed in my job that I didn't keep as many friendships in repair as I would have liked, but I haven't been conscious of standing alone. How interesting you should say that. But I think

I have always stood *apart*. Yes, I've always stood apart. I rather regret it, but that's the way it is.

I was thinking about what I said when I bared my soul to you. I don't think I told you the whole truth (who does?). My feeling different is all connected with my Jewishness. By becoming a Christian, I have been alienated from the Jewish community, and as a Jewish Christian I will always be an odd fish in a predominantly Gentile Church. This lies at the root of my sensitivity. But it was Elisabeth's love and support that managed to unloose my shyness and awkwardness, and I should have said that better than I did. I couldn't have done it on my own.

I hate to be introspective, but I thought I had better fill in the blanks.

DAVID RANDALL

Age: 46
Age at ordination: 25

PASTORAL DIRECTOR OF CARA, LONDON

I first met David Randall at a friend's post-ordination party in a flat in London. The flat was small and packed and full of clamorous, inebriated clerics and a couple of slightly bewildered-looking lay people. David Randall was squashed against a wall with three or four others, clutching a very large glass of wine. I noticed that he bore an uncanny resemblance to the late Freddie Mercury, except for the white satin flares. 'Hello, darling, and who are you? Oh, Maaaary . . . Well, honey, why haven't we met before? Are you with him, you lucky thing? Ooh, now listen, I know a lot about you.' Well, I knew a lot about David Randall too, as it happened: we have one or two friends in common. He gave me his card and told me to call him. So I did.

We met for the second time in rather more sober circumstances. David Randall works at CARA, a support group set up by and for those who are living with HIV or AIDS. CARA is a registered charity, and the basement from which it operates has been donated by a local priest who lives above it. Until fairly recently CARA had never received official approbation from the Church establishment, but following a visit and financial donation from the Archbishop of Canterbury, that situation has altered. The CARA office is tiny and impossibly crowded. It is about fourteen feet square, and when I was there there were about seven people in it, all on the telephone or working at computers.

David Randall and I had lunch across the road from CARA, at the London Lighthouse, and as we had both been held up that day it was snatched, brief, and punctuated by his leaping up from the table to speak to people. We failed to have more than five minutes' proper conversation with each other, and I left with little sense of what he was like, except for the impression that he was a very angry man. In the short time we did have together he was extremely open with me, but I wondered if that was just a complex form of self-defence. Frankness can be very successfully employed to throw other people off your trail, and the notably 'honest' often manage to hide a lot more than people who are visibly reserved. Subterfuge of this kind is an art form, and David Randall struck me as a consummate artist.

Not long afterwards, we spent several mornings together at the West London house which he shared with his boyfriend, Charles. The house is attached on one side to the local vicarage, and when we met for the interviews the entire place was being rewired, and was full of builders and dust-sheets. The garden is absolutely beautiful and still very Victorian in style: there is a big yew tree, a white wrought-iron table and chairs, lots of dark green shrubbery and large drooping roses, peonies and daisies. David Randall is a keen gardener, and it shows.

We talked in his study, with his black Labrador Ben for company. The room was decorated with large abstract pictures painted by Charles in striking blocks of orange, blue and black. All my fears that David Randall might attempt to lead me up the garden path with his slightly blasé artlessness, thereby forcing me to employ heavier interviewing tactics than I like to, were soon allayed. He talked quietly, thoughtfully, and though he was often very funny, without recourse to excess wit. Though he clearly found it difficult to do so, he was less afraid than most to reveal weakness or vulnerability, and I liked and respected him a lot for that — just as I like and respect him for his outrageous theatricality, his sense of humour, his energy and his passionate hatred of hypocrisy.

DAVID RANDALL

My problem in answering all these questions is that I'm in psychotherapy twice a week at the moment, fairly intensive, and we're working on all this stuff, so whether these are my memories or my psychotherapeutic bits I'm not sure. Anyhow.

I grew up feeling very guilty.

I grew up feeling very guilty about my mother, and I had a very bad relationship with my father, for which I feel guilty. He was a very lonely, friendless man, inadequate in many ways, and he treated my mother badly, although she would never admit it. He was very bad-tempered, usually had a row with her on a Saturday, which ended in virtual violence. He was absent from me emotionally, and seemed even more so from my sister. I resented it and treated him badly.

I was born in Surrey in January 1947. Post-war bulge, peak month, peak year. My older sister was a pre-bulge baby. My father was a railwayman and my mother was what we used to call a housewife and mother, and an activist in the local church. And saying that's actually saying something to you about my anger, because she was far more busy with Mothers' Union and all that stuff than she ever was with us.

Up until the age of about ten, I was taken over by my father's mother. She had a companion who really dominated my life, and there was a power struggle between this woman, Anne, and my mother. Anne was an unmarried, lost sort of person who had latched herself on to the family and become my sort of surrogate mother. They used to vie for my affection, and that power struggle lasted right through to when I left home at eighteen. I've got a lot of anger about that still, having to please them both all the time.

I do have some memories of sitting on my father's lap and of him making me laugh, and memories of before he died, when I was an adult; taking him to the pub and trying to resume a relationship. But my sister had none of that whatsoever from him, she never really knew him, and as a result she's suffered, and she and I aren't very close.

My mother's still alive and very much part of my life. She lived here until two years ago, lives round the corner now. She's a sweet and holy old lady, but she doesn't really understand why I feel like this about the past. She'd be absolutely horrified if she could hear this conversation. I'm not sure if my father was weak, or just quiet and silent, but my mother was very much a victim of the suburban Surrey snobbery syndrome. I grew up feeling we were second-rate because I didn't go to private school and we didn't have money and we didn't have a car and a telly and all that. And my mother used to say things like, 'Oh, that's a nice person, she comes from a good home,' and what she meant is that they'd got money and all that stuff, and that makes me really angry still. As a result I loathe the place I grew up in. I never go back there if I can possibly help it. Awful place.

I was a bit of a schizophrenic child, I guess. I was very creative, I was a born leader, but I was very naughty at school. I went to the local primary school, where there were fifty-eight people in our class, about eleven of whom were called David, and about nine of whom had birthdays on the same day as me, and I felt very lost in all that as a child. So I sat at the back of the class getting a reputation.

When I got to secondary school, I blossomed. I failed the eleven-plus miserably, and was put in the bottom of the second-ary modern school, and that's when I began to discover life. I began to flourish. I discovered I was intelligent, which I hadn't realized, so I began to achieve and went in three years from the bottom level to the top level, and then into what they called the Grammar stream. There I became the head of the drama class and the leader of the choir, oh, very much a responsible person, but always a bit naughty still.

Outside school, I led a very active and, now I think about it,

probably very unhealthy, do-goody life. I was terribly involved
with other people's lives. I sang in the choir, I taught in the
Sunday school, I ran the Cubs, I produced the shows, I worked
in a mentally handicapped unit in Epsom on Saturdays and
sometimes Sundays, I played the piano. I was never at home. I
loved entertaining people, and it was good, I don't want to feel
bad about it. But it was very compensatory for what was going
on at home, of which I was slightly ashamed really. I don't
think I was precocious, but I always mixed with older people: a
lot of middle-aged women adopted me. I was a very odd child,
I should imagine; don't you think? I was very popular at school
and in certain quarters, but I didn't fit anywhere really. I
certainly felt different, but nobody talked to me about it.
Nobody ever talked to me about anything that mattered.

Going to church was part of life. The church we went to was
very Low Church evangelical and I couldn't bear it. It was so
dreary and class-ridden. I think I was the only working-class
boy that went to it. Then one day I was taken by my adopted
'godmother', who lived round the corner, to a church in Epsom
on Holy Saturday. There were only about ten people there and
it was the old-fashioned Easter vigil, all this light and colour and
incense and the priest with the biretta who they called 'Father',
and it was like, wow! There was also a couple I knew who
started carting me off to St John the Divine, Kennington, in
London, which was very exotic. The thing that was most
incredible to me was that you had all this exotic religion and
ordinary people going there, people who were smoking and
going to the pub after church.

Something attracted me. I can still feel the sense of real
excitement and thrill of when I first discovered it, and I think that
a part of the excitement was a discovery of a much broader
view of God than I was fed by the evangelical stuff that I was
used to. It was foreign, I suppose. The colour, the light, the
appeal to the senses. There's something deeply sensuous about
Anglo-Catholicism. The theatre, the drama, the mystery, all

that. The link with the world seemed real too. I mean, now it gives me the willies, these poncy priests walking around in birettas being paternalistic, but *then* it seemed real. Where I grew up there was no link between the church and the community; there the church lived for itself.

So from the age of fourteen I longed to run a parish. My dream was to be the actor–manager in a parish, and it was to do with looking for my father by being a father to everybody else, I know all that. In many ways that's what's still going on, I suppose. My childhood was about people not believing in me, and yet there was a terrific ambition and drive going on inside, which I suppose was being worked out in all this do-gooding and charging around organizing other people. I thought an Anglo-Catholic parish combined with a political ministry meant I could be involved in the lives of the community and really bring the two together.

No one had ever mentioned anything to me about the future. Then one day, this priest from Canada whom I knew and used to go round to see all the time – Colin and his wife were like alternative parents – one day he said to me, 'Have you ever thought about ordination?' And it was like, wham! He's taking me seriously as a human being! And I said, yeah, I'd like to think about that.

So Colin set the ball rolling, and suggested I went to Kelham. Kelham was a college run by a religious community, the Society of the Sacred Mission, and in those days it was 200 strong. It trained priests, but it also took boys of fifteen or sixteen from working-class backgrounds to train as monks.

I applied to go there, but was turned down because I hadn't got any O- or A-levels. The Director of Ordinands for the Diocese of Guildford said he wasn't surprised. I remember the selection conference Secretary saying, 'We don't want rabbits in the Church of England.' I don't know what he meant by that, probably something second-rate, and he said that in *front* of me. This snobby Church! Anyway, a year later I got in to do a one-year course in O-levels and pre-theological training. I loved the place but I was *so* unhappy. There was a wonderful aura about the place, but it was very strict, very hierarchical. Cold showers at five o'clock in the morning, and the junior members treated like shit by the senior ones.

I didn't finish my course there. I felt very small and unloved in that setting, very insecure. Then, through someone whom I knew, I was introduced to a priest in Stepney, and I left Kelham and went to live with him. There I did my A-levels. I worked on them for two hours every day, and I earned my living by getting a job in a youth club and a job in an old people's club. I did that for just under a year, and then the mental health unit that I'd worked at in Epsom wanted someone to run it, so I went and did that for a bit too. That was quite fun. I had a job far beyond my age and qualifications, and I did it very well, I think. In Kelham I felt like nobody, and here I was being brought in by these doctors who were pioneering mental health.

Straight after that I offered myself formally to the Church for ordination. I was selected, and suddenly it all took off. The Bishop of Guildford rang me up and said they wanted me to go to the Bernard Gilpin Society in Durham for a one-year pre-ordination training, and I was there within a week. And that was *fab*. From being the rabbit that nobody took seriously, I'd earned my way into the Church, and was second top of the class at Bernard Gilpin and offered a place at Durham University. I often regret now that I didn't take it, because I've got a thing about not having a degree. My father had that as well. He was very opposed to me going into the Church, and very angry about the way the Church treated me. So he must have had some belief in me.

Emotionally I was in a terrible mess. My first important relationship had been with someone called Clive when I was at school. We used to hug and hold hands. We never dreamed that it was a homosexual relationship, but of course I can see now that I was in love with him, and I think he was in love with me. We were very close and intimate for a year, and then one day on the way to school he was killed on his motorbike, and that was absolutely devastating for me. We were both eighteen, and he's been part of my life ever since. I can still remember his smell.

I didn't have sex with girls much. When I was about seventeen I had a go, tried it with a couple of girls from the youth club, but it never really worked. I did have a girlfriend at school for a bit, and when she ended it I was pretty devastated. Rachel. It was never a great success, I have to say. I can do it physically with women, but I can't do it emotionally, and that's always been true: I've had a number of sexual relationships with women over the years and they've always been a mistake.

After Durham I went to Salisbury Theological College for three years, and emotionally and sexually I became more confused. I was there at the end of the sixties, and it was the arch-bastion of liberalism. I deliberately chose it because it was a radical college. I didn't reject Anglo-Catholicism in the sense of the drama and the mystery, but I became aware that I wasn't a hard-line Anglo-Catholic, that I'm more concerned with integration, and at that stage the theology which I tuned into was liberal theology. I became a very socially and politically active left-winger. Honey, I was outrageous; into trendy rock masses, and I looked like a hippie when I was ordained. Jeans, long hair, beads, all that stuff. But that, I suspect, was a smokescreen for deep agony and pain. I was outrageous in everything *except* sexuality.

I suffered a lot at Salisbury. There were homosexuals there, and the Principal was homosexual, but the word gay I never heard of until later. A lot of the guys there were engaged, and my childhood friends were beginning to get married and have girlfriends, and I was never getting it together. I'd always felt very guilty about seeing girls; I felt I would be betraying my mother by making a relationship with another woman. By the time I went to Salisbury the confusion that had always been there was not going to go away. I was falling in love with people.

*

From the word go I saw myself wanting to be a priest on the edge of the Church. When it came to ordination time I was looking for a parish in the East End of London, so some of the old fantasy stuff was obviously still there, and I ended up in a team ministry in Poplar. There were about ten of us, at the end of an era when you had huge teams like that. There was a very wise, rather traditional rector, who was very lovely to me, I could tell he really liked me; then there was this posh deacon from Westcott House, and the others were brilliant too.

I loved it there. I was paid to do what the hell I liked, and I did. I worked jolly hard. It was a real fringe ministry I had: the house was always open, and kids used to pile in. I never went to bed at night. Mind you, I didn't always get up in the mornings either, but I was good pastorally. I think I've got away with the rather lunatic-fringe ministry by being quite good at the other as well.

Two months after I was ordained priest, a young guy who had served at my first mass said he wanted to talk to me. I said, yeah, great, come round. So he said, I think I need to tell you I'm a homosexual. So I said, I think I need to tell you that so am I. And that was – it was like a bird flying, an eagle launching. That was the moment of liberation for me, and I'm eternally grateful to him.

I was twenty-five when I first admitted what I'd probably known all along. And it was so exciting. It was wonderful. I started going to gay pubs. I started to talk to people who I thought were gay about being gay. I went back to my old college and found there was a gay group, and I met Malcolm Johnson, who founded the Gay Clergy Consultation, which I joined. My relationships came to fruition with everybody as a result of coming to peace with being gay. But I didn't tell my mother.

A year later I fell in love properly for the first time. It was General Election night, 1974. Ted Heath was defeated and we got a Labour Government, so I had a party. I was very politically active, and anyway I was always having parties. A friend of mine brought a friend of his, John, and we fell in love. I'd had the odd boyfriend before that, just a few, but nothing like this.

When John moved in, about a month or two later, I rang Bishop Trevor Huddleston, who'd ordained me, and said, 'I've met the man of my dreams, and he's going to come and live with me in Poplar. I thought you'd like to know.' And he said, 'Thank you for letting me know, dear, I'm very pleased, but do be careful.' That's all he said. He was so sweet.

The Rector of Poplar moved on, and for about a year afterwards we ran the parish on our own. Then the new Rector came, and that's when it started to go wrong. He couldn't handle the fact that I was gay and living with John, and he wanted me out. To cut a long story short, we had six months of hell and in the end I resigned. I was then asked to apply for a job as Diocesan Youth Officer, but when it came to the crunch it transpired that they didn't like my situation with John. I then discovered the weight of the establishment against anyone it wanted to thwack for any reason.

Malcolm Johnson, who was by this time the Rector of St Botolph's in Aldgate, rang up and said he would like to create a post for me as Youth Chaplain in the East End, so that I could continue my work with young people. By then the diocesan mafia, this group of right-wing clergy and lay people, turned their attention to Malcolm. They weren't after him or me particularly, they were after Bishop Trevor Huddleston because he was so radical: they were using anything to discredit Trevor and we got used as part of that. They even got one of the papers to print an article about him being a paedophile, which was absolute rubbish and nonsense. He had a breakdown as a result of it all. Oh, they were cruel!

Then they turned to me. They blocked the grant that the Diocesan Committee was meant to be paying me and they persuaded the Bishop of London not to license me. I was homeless and jobless until we were given a home by a Roman Catholic priest I knew. Meanwhile, Malcolm was working to get me a post – it took him six months – and finally he said, 'We've got no money, no licence, no nothing, but the Bishop of London has agreed that you can come here.' So I started doing this ministry among the detached youth of the East End. During my time there I was involved in starting the first gay teenage group in London, and in creating the Kipper Project, which is one of the biggest homeless young people's projects in the East End now, a bit like Centrepoint, but more local. I worked with drug-users, homeless kids, and the embryonic music culture which grew into rock groups like Iron Maiden.

We still had nowhere to live. The Archdeacon of Hackney told us about a flat in Holloway that was vacant, but nothing happened, so in the end we just moved in. 'Oh, my God!' said the Archdeacon, 'they're *squatting* now.' So the Bishop of London, Gerald Ellison, had me over, and actually we got on rather well. He said he was very worried about the whole gay thing, and about Malcolm getting a reputation for developing a gay ministry; the Establishment was very jittery about it. He was *terribly* Establishment, dignified sort of bloke. But a nice man, and good to me in the end. When I told him all about my ministry, he said, 'I'd love to come and see it. I'll come and visit, but I'll come incognito.'

I said, 'Well, I think you'd be better wearing a collar, Father. It'd make more sense really.'

But he wouldn't have it. 'Oh no, I want to come incognito.'

So then of course he arrived at St Botolph's in a chauffeur-driven car in a *fabulous* grey suit and great big purple tie with a silk handkerchief hanging out the pocket, and I thought, well, that's *really* incognito. I mean, he looked like some elderly pimp! At least if he'd had a collar on I could have said, 'This is my vicar mate, Gerald,' because he'd said, 'Introduce me as Gerald, I don't want people to know I'm the Bishop.' But no.

Anyway, we had a *fab* evening. We started in the local pub at Aldgate, and I think we had about six brandies on the house. He subsequently confirmed the landlady in St Paul's Cathedral, and as she was about the only resident in the St Botolph's parish in those days, we used to claim a 100 per cent conversion rate!

I took him round various youth projects, and then we started on the clubs and the pubs. He met prostitutes and gay people, we went to a really shitty gay dive, and we were out till about one o'clock in the morning, and he was absolutely charming and fascinated. I think that did a lot of good. I said, 'This is the ministry that the Church will not support.' He said, 'I had absolutely no idea.' I also talked to him a little bit about being gay, and how difficult it is for priests being gay, and he said, 'Thank you for telling me about that. No one ever talks to me about that. I didn't realize.'

After that, someone from the diocesan mafia I mentioned before went to the Bishop's house, saying that if he didn't disown me by that night they would go to Fleet Street with a dossier of documents that would expose Trevor Huddleston 'and all the mincing Marxists of the East End'. Awful. But the Bishop of London said to him, 'Get off my doorstep. I never want to see you again,' and he rang me up and said, 'I will license you at the earliest possible opportunity.'

Six months later I had a phone call from the Bishop of Kensington saying that he had a very difficult job in Notting Hill, and that the Bishop of London had said I was the man for the job. Would I consider joining a team ministry as Vicar of St Clement's, Notting Dale?

Well, this was my childhood ambition. St Clement's, Notting Dale, is one of the famous back-street churches of the Anglo-Catholic revival, but never well-endowed, never fashionable. Notting Dale is at the bottom of Notting Hill, but it's not a registered geographical area in the sense that Notting Hill is. At the top of Notting Hill in the early nineteenth century was a racecourse, the Hippodrome Racecourse. Around the racecourse lived all the tinkers and the gypsies and the totters. Then when they built the grand houses for the ladies-in-waiting at Kensington Palace, the tinkers and gypsies and totters were moved down the hill into Notting Dale, and that's how the parish was born. It was described by Dickens as the worst hovel in London.

The Bishop of Kensington had warned me that the future of the church was very much under threat, except for the fact that this huge estate was just opening and they felt that there might be some potential there for renewal of community life. The congregation was very small. There were forty people at my induction on the Friday night, and the churchwarden's boyfriend read the Epistle. On the Saturday afternoon I found him dead in the gutter outside my house: alcohol. Then on my first Sunday there were eleven people. That was my beginning.

Meanwhile, there were endless clergy meetings. That's why I think team ministry's a waste of bloody time: you spend all your time talking to other clergy and, in a place like Notting Hill, to one or two articulate lay people about the poor people down the hill. Terrible classism. And the team ministry, for all its good intentions, was promoting and propagating something that was paternalistic and disempowering of the people who worshipped at St Clement's.

Apart from the meetings I didn't know what to do in the parish, in this small congregation. I thought, where do I start? The school was the biggest resource. There was this wonderful headteacher, Judith Roberts, and she and I worked together. She had no music teacher in the school, so because I had nothing to do to start with, I taught music in the school. The first time that a Sunday morning really took off was a Mothering Sunday, because we sent a note through the school saying there was going to be a special service for kids, so please come along. And they flooded in. Many people who arrived on that day are still there.

After that it took off within weeks. The community was really thirsting for renewal. People were longing, not particularly for the church community, but for something. So whenever I got an opportunity to visit people at home, I would. It was very simple, basic stuff; caring for people, but believing passionately in the parish. You know, everyone had written the parish off, but ten years on, when I left, it was one of the most significant parishes in West London.

When I first went there, the upper storey of the school hall was being used for some youth project meeting, and they wouldn't let us use it. However, technically it belonged to the church, and I wanted to get it back for the parish to use as a community resource. There was lots of politics involved and it was all very heated, until one night one of the local youths set fire to it and gutted it.

That was the best thing that ever happened to that parish. I said, well, that solves that one. I called a public meeting and asked people what they wanted, and out of that came the idea for a Community Development Project. We applied for an Urban Aid grant, which we got, and two years later we launched the Community Project. We converted the church's vestries into a community centre. We had a bar and a weekly programme for everyone, from old people to youth, and we employed two Community Workers. We then got another grant, and created a separate Youth Centre in the old hall that had been burnt. By 1982 we had a full-scale Youth Centre and a Community Centre too. When we first opened the Youth Centre it attracted thirty or forty kids sometimes, and they were in there smoking their pot and doing their stuff, and some church people were offended by that, but I mean, what the hell is the Church about? And not everybody involved in the Community Project came to church, but that didn't matter. Church life grew and was stimulated by it, and it was very exciting.

We also began to get involved in the Notting Hill Carnival. Both the Roman Catholic and the Anglican Church broke new ground by having carnival masses, which would be totally unheard of in the West Indies, where carnival is seen as totally separate from the Church. In Notting Hill it was a celebration of Afro-Caribbean, white, Spanish and Moroccan communities too, and I loved that. It was lovely. Great era.

The other really exciting thing about Notting Dale was the

ecumenical stuff. A priest called Michael Hollings moved into a parish near by; a wonderful man, got a great vision. There were some very lively Methodists around too, and some evangelicals, and I said that we should do a walk together through the streets one Holy Week. Well, we did it five times while I was there, with a cast of hundreds, and that brought all the churches and races together in a very dramatic way. Cardinal Hume led it the first year, and the second year Robert Runcie came and we had a black Christ. Caiaphas and Annas were played by the Roman Catholic and Anglican bishops, and all the High Priests were played by the local clergy.

It took three hours mostly. We'd start at one end of Notting Hill and weave through the estates, using natural theatres like middles of blocks of flats for the trial scenes, and an adventure playground for the Garden of Gethsemane. The crucifixion took place in the middle of three blocks of flats, and all the Afro-Caribbeans came out on to their balconies, playing hymns on their record-players. It was absolutely terrific, and out of that we formed the Notting Hill Council of Churches.

I remember feeling very much on the crest of a wave then. I remember feeling that I knew it, I knew the answers. I do have a very clear vision about the Church. For me personally, my vision has always been about my bridging role. The priest's role is to empower the Christian community to be a bridge; for itself, for individuals, and for the wider community. Instead of a sermon at my first mass we played Simon and Garfunkel's *Bridge Over Troubled Water*, oh so sixties, but actually, that's what it's about. And when I think about what I'm doing now, CARA's about building bridges between worlds and communities and individuals. So it's a big image in my life, a bridge.

Yet what I thought the Church *could* do and achieve when I was ordained in 1971 I naïvely assumed it *would* be doing. I thought the Church should be about building a community of people who'd support and serve each other unconditionally, and that's what I tried to do. In many ways that's what I still believe, but in those days I was naïve. I hadn't taken on board why people were so alienated and angry with the Church. I thought all I had to do was be nice and they'd change their attitude towards it. I now know differently.

Take now, for example. All the bitter arguments about women and their ordination. That's the painful bit of the Church at the moment, the fighting about the roles of gays and women, and the fighting's symbolic of fear. Yet it could all be so simple. Maybe I'm naïve, but we're terrified of talking about sexuality, aren't we, and that's what the ordination of women is about. It's about sexuality, about power, and about the nature of the Church. I think when we first met I said to you that ten years ago I totally believed in the ordination of women, but could not vote for it until Rome was for it. Well, that's bollocks. I no longer feel that's what the Church should be about.

I think the reason I came into my own in Notting Dale was because I began to learn what it should be about. I had a very strong and varied community behind me. It was very extreme, very Anglo-Catholic, but also very folksy and very rooted, very difficult to define, really. We transformed the church not by raising hundreds of thousands of pounds to put in priceless works of art, but by getting the local members of the congregation to make banners or decorate it for a different theme. It was wonderfully exotic, it wasn't institutionalized. That's the mistake the Church makes; to institutionalize. I'm not into churchiness myself. I find churchiness paternalistic and patronizing and not terribly intellectual. 'My dear people, the Church teaches this . . .' They never got that crap from me, I can tell you.

Let's face it, most churches are horrendously dull. It's all very good theology and very good music, and dreary as hell. I want to scream sometimes when I go. It's so bloody respectable, and I suppose that's one thing St Clement's wasn't. There used to be a piece of graffiti up on one of the great corrugated iron walls in Notting Dale, and it said: Is there a life before death? There was a lot of hopelessness there, a lot of hopelessness. But then

Christ's model was never about giving answers, and once you remove the threat of hell, which I don't believe in, and the emphasis on sin, which I think is unhealthy and un-Christian; once you reduce the necessity for an emphasis on the after-life, you're not left with much else that's hopeful.

That's why a vision of *this* world is so important, and that's what I tried to teach. I think it helps people to be able to say, well, it is all a bit bigger than us. I think there's also a link between politics and theology, so that if you're praying for peace then you are actually praying for a reduction in your standard of living. If you're praying for justice in the world, you're actually praying that the white suburban Church stops sending millions to the Christian Missionary Society in Uganda for its theological college, and instead starts talking to its black neighbour in Streatham, and voting politically on that issue.

Did you know that in Leviticus there is this concept that every fifty years all debts will be wiped out, all leadership will be re-elected, and the land will be returned to the people? It's a symbol of early utopia, but it's got a serious point. Christianity is about justice. Therefore the struggle for justice must be the most spiritual thing that we do, and worship is about celebrating that. And as I read the Gospels, Christ was not obsessed with sin and judgment at all. He was much more concerned with raising people up from where they were at, not coming back tomorrow when they'd improved.

And all that stuff about 'Unless you are like little children, you cannot enter the Kingdom of God': I don't think it's about making people infantile, it's about reminding us that it's in our simplicity, our innocence, our smallness, that transformation begins. Which is why I think St Clement's in the seventies and eighties was as important as Taizé or Lourdes or Canterbury Cathedral as an incarnation of the Kingdom of God.

Now when I pass by the church it's locked, all day and every day. Okay, people steal things, but so what? What's the point of a locked church? That's my biggest question. What is the *point* of a locked church? What sort of sign is that? What is it saying about our vision of God, our vision of the world, our vision of the community? I actually think it's a scandal. The Church needs to be incarnational, and bricks and mortar are as much a part of the incarnation as anything else. A closed church is the incarnation of a dead God.

John and I split up in 1977. Don't really know why now, but he was devastated. I think it must have been me that did it. I then got together with someone called Patrick. He was a friend of a friend, and I used to know him when I was at college and I couldn't stand him, he was a real traumy little queen.

Anyway honey, Patrick and I lived together for ten years. We didn't ever fall in love, we just got together. He'd been a very lost person, never settled anywhere, very insecure in many ways. But he was very talented. He took over my domestic life. He decorated, made all the curtains, made the house beautiful. He was responsible really for my change of image from being the hippie to creating a home and all that stuff.

Patrick and I . . . He was a very controlling person. It's difficult to talk because it was . . . it was a very, very painful break-up. I was very much in love with him in the early days. Did I say I wasn't? Well, I don't think he was ever in love with me. But looking back, I gave him security and friendship, and many of the friends he made through me are his friends still. So I think it was a very good experience for him although the break-up was horrendous for both of us.

I was quite frightened of him. He could be terribly vitriolic, and I used to go out and drink and socialize without him. In the end I used to go to the West Indies every year, just to escape. I don't think he really wanted to end it, but he couldn't bring himself to love me either. I mean, if he could have changed his attitude to me, then we could have negotiated, but he wasn't the kind of person to negotiate. I remember saying to him once, 'Let's go and get some couple counselling.' 'Bloody nonsense!' And he'd never go on holiday with me. He hated holidays.

It really felt like he didn't like me. He scorned the very things

I held most dear, and would say everything I did was an ego trip. Well, it was probably true, but I was doing my best. So I used to work hard in the parish just to escape, and in the end I was leading a double life. Patrick never came to church, though he was very controlling of the people we had at the vicarage; if he didn't like someone then they didn't come. Yet people adored him. My grandmother adored him, and my mother still does. And people in the parish were very shocked when we split up. It was never a hidden relationship, and I think they thought we would be together for ever, even though it was stormy. I worked a lot longer at that relationship than I should have done.

In 1985 I went for my trip to the West Indies and when I came back I was very ill. I was taken into St Mary's Hospital with suspected tropical disease. Looking back on it, I think that was when I developed the HIV virus. But I didn't get tested. I don't think I could really face it.

AIDS was beginning to emerge as an issue in London by that time. I got involved in an AIDS conference, and a friend of mine, Nick, was there and said could I give his brother a home, he was coming back from New York and he wasn't very well. I said yes. And that was when Richard came to live in the parish.

Richard was amazing. He was very open and honest about being gay and about having AIDS and got really involved in the community life of the parish. But inevitably people started asking questions, and I had a choice of telling him to shut up and go away, or actually using it as an opportunity to face the issues with people. And we chose the latter. He was such a great teacher. We had public meetings in the school and in the church and the community centre and the youth club, and it was great, it really opened up the issues in the parish.

That was the year when I finally felt, I can't handle Patrick treating me like this. I went off as usual to stay with my friend Steven in the West Indies that summer, and when I got to the airport there was a letter in my bag, and he'd never written me a letter in his life, but there it was, this twenty-page letter from him, which I read and tore up. It was so bitter and twisted I can't actually get my head round it now. Basically he said he was leaving. And when I came back he had gone, moved out. He took all the furniture, all the lovely bits that we'd collected, because we had a lovely house. And he'd stripped it, taken everything, and I came back into this house with no settee, and the place more or less stripped bare.

That was an awful period. The break was right but it was so vitriolic, and I don't understand that at all. I was very lonely and lost and sad for a long time after that. Then Richard died on the cusp of the year, on New Year's Eve, 1987. It was a pretty grim period of my life.

Not long after that the Bishop of Kensington, Mark Santer, who was always very loving and supportive of me, said, 'Why don't you take a year out and go and look at AIDS?' Because I didn't know what to do. I'd done over ten years in the parish, and I think I'd had enough, I was beginning to get bored with all the bloody committees. And Mark Santer was the first Churchman I ever heard saying, 'This is a big issue that will challenge this generation and the Church must take it very seriously.' He was very committed to it, and I think he encouraged me not just for my own sake but for the Church's sake.

So I went to San Francisco. Just before I went I had my fortieth birthday, and I had a wild party. Five hundred people came: the whole parish was invited, all my gay friends, all my black friends, the steel band, some of the cast of *La Cage aux Folles*, and my Bishop, and it was *fab*, we had *such* a night. I did 'Nobody loves a fairy when she's forty'. I've got some nice pikkies of it somewhere.

In San Francisco I worked as the Chaplain in a hospital. It was part of a training programme for AIDS ministry, and although I still wasn't diagnosed I'd been up to my eyes in the issues, what with Richard living in my house and the preparations and plans for the London Lighthouse going on at the same time, which I'd been involved in.

San Francisco changed my life. I was a foreigner in a strange land, and you don't think of America as being a strange land, but it felt like that. The hospital had a prison unit and a psychiatric unit and a casualty department that I've never seen the likes of, and then this huge HIV unit with a very wide cross-section of people, the real underbelly of America. I was part of a team of twenty-six chaplains, some of whom were priests, some nuns, some not even Christian. I went from being the parish priest of Notting Dale, the actor–manager, to being exposed to this horrendous suffering, and everything was turned upside-down.

I discovered a lot in San Francisco. I discovered gay community life in a way that I've never done before. Do you know about the Castro area? Well, they have gay policemen there, and all the businesses are gay and the churches are gay. Everything's gay. Even the beggars are gay. San Francisco was in great crisis then. Whole church congregations had been halved by people's deaths from AIDS. The business life of the community had been affected in a way that I don't suppose we'll ever know here. Here in Britain it's just as real and just as dangerous and just as frightening, but it's much slower. There was a tremendous sense of solidarity, but also a tremendous sense of desolation and devastation, and that was ghastly. Everyone in San Francisco was involved in the gay community in some way, and when AIDS came along there was no question about doing things, they just got on and did them. Over there I saw parents marching in the Gay Parade, with banners saying, 'I'm proud of my gay son,' and gay and lesbian pensioners on floats. Whereas over here, they're still writing reports about it and holding conferences and doing fuck-all, to be perfectly honest.

I worked very, very hard on that unit, and I went on a deep personal journey which was very painful. A lot of assumptions about myself were challenged; mainly my assumption that somehow I was a good priest and the way I operated meant that I was good. I actually learned that my whole style of ministry was an ego trip that was paternalistic, that was more to do with propping up my own stuff and not other people's. My ministry suddenly seemed so insignificant. My image of God was untenable. And as a gay man I thought I was way out of the closet and in fact I wasn't. So I had to ask, who the hell am I, if I haven't got this front any more, this bag of tricks?

I suddenly didn't know who I was, and that's what I had to discover. I had to go through this transition of becoming just a person rather than a priest or a religious person with goods to offer. And that, although I didn't realize it at the time, was a preparation for what was to come later, both in my personal life and in my ministry. I had to learn that it was all right not doing anything except being the loving presence of God in a situation which is about sharing the pain as much as it is about offering cheap comfort. So much spirituality is cheap and meaningless, because it's about making people feel better, and the reality is that people *don't* get better from AIDS. When you're dying, you're dying.

Still, I had one hell of a good time as well. I tell you what I did enjoy discovering was that men liked me, fancied me. I was cruised rotten for three months! Every time I went out men were cruising me. That's never happened in England. But then, you see, American men like older ageing English queens. So that was great fun.

I also discovered something about being able to make people laugh. On the whole, Californians are very serious and earnest and hardworking. And I was the clown in the training group. There were six of us in the group: a Jesuit from Los Angeles; a very charismatic, flamboyant woman from San Francisco; a very tiresome Baptist minister, older guy, who thought all Englishmen loved cricket and the Queen. In the end I had to just tell him, 'Your image of what an Englishman is is deeply insulting.' He hadn't got a clue. And he kept speaking for me: 'As you English would say.' In the end I had to tell him, look, fuck off. Bless him.

So I made people laugh. I think I was also very good at challenging the American crap. I mean, they're as obsessive in their recovery programmes as they are in their debauchery, they had recovery programmes for *everything*. If you farted too much you had to go in recovery. People kept trying to encourage me to join a self-help group. I'd say, 'But I quite enjoy being a drunkard, I quite enjoy having sex.'

Yet although I found that I couldn't take that side of it too seriously, I was very open to the whole concept of spirituality as being who we *are*. I mean, the Anglo-Catholic baggages will all be dead on the carpet at hearing that expression, but I had been spending all my time with churchy people, and in the Church, and it was a very rude awakening to discover that there was a wealth of sprituality outside it. It was very liberating. But very confusing as well, because it was like ditching everything I'd come from. Shedding the armour.

When I got back to St Stephen's Hospital from the rather isolated San Francisco with all that profound experience, I felt like a spare prick at a wedding. I didn't want to be just a priest any more, so I asked if I could come and work as an auxiliary nurse instead. They said yes, and went to a lot of effort to make it possible, so I learned how to empty bedpans and make beds and take temperatures. But I felt terribly lacking in competence, thinking I didn't ought to be there. I think the hospital staff were very perplexed by what I was doing there. You know, I was really a vicar.

Because I'd been around the gay community so long in London I knew loads of the patients and I quickly established a role on the ward. Now, don't ask me what as: one minute I was emptying the bedpans and the next minute I was being asked just to be there for people. So I became an unofficial counsellor, and sometimes I got involved as a priest, they'd ask me to take their funerals and all that. And do you know, I discovered that people actually wanted me for who I was, not because I was a priest or a nurse, but for myself. I'd always thought any gifts I had were inexorably bound up with being a clergyman, but they weren't, they were authentic to me as a human being. That was a very good thing to learn, and I was as happy there as I was unhappy in the unit in San Francisco.

During Richard's time in the vicarage the seeds of the London Lighthouse were sown. It was through my experience with Richard that I got involved with the Lighthouse: I led the delegation to the Town Hall for its planning permission, and when he died, Lighthouse offered me support. The Lighthouse then was in the basement where CARA is now, and was just a series of support groups. Christopher Spence, the Director, suggested that I might join the gay men's support group which was being run by two guys. So I went to this group and there I learned co-counselling. I don't know if you've ever heard of it, and I wouldn't treat it as a panacea for the whole world, but the principle of co-counselling is that we all have within ourselves the ability to care properly for who we are, and for others. You learn to do it in a non-abusive situation by giving people equal time to talk, and it taught me a lot. Now when I go into Church groups I get really furious because I realize no one's listening to each other.

It was the first time I was ever exposed to that sort of support. Through that group I met a whole new world of young people infected by the virus. They were among the first wave of gay men dying from the virus in London, and they were our friends, my friends. Now most of them are dead. They mostly died within the first two or three years of the crisis in London. And it's got worse. Now when I hear people saying, 'We're going to San Francisco to see what we can do,' I think, 'Fuck it, what do they think we're doing here?' You know? So that's a bit of an issue.

By this time I knew I couldn't ever go back to parish work, so I went to see the Archdeacon of Middlesex, who lived in my parish and was a very supportive man, and I said to him. 'How about the Church paying me just to do this full-time? What do you think?' He said, 'You haven't got a hope in hell of the Church giving you a penny.' So I wrote to the new Bishop of Kensington, and he wrote back and said, 'Yes, I'd be very pleased to have your resignation from your parish, but no, we don't have any money.' I knew he wanted me out. He didn't like my reputation.

Still, I thought, I've got to do this. I spoke to a few people and said, 'Look, I want to do this. Will you help me?' They said yes, and Bill Kirkpatrick – another priest in this field – raised me a salary from Laing's the builders. They agreed to pay me some money for three years, and in order to be able to receive it we had to form a limited company and charitable trust, and it had to have a name. So that's when the idea of actually identifying CARA – which is Gaelic for 'friendship' – came about.

Then I called a few other people together, friends of mine, and they acted as a support group, as administration, to enable me to do full-time work. We found a basement in Fulham to work from, and the Archdeacon found me this house, for me and my mother and two dogs, because my mother had come to live with me six months before.

So that's how CARA began, as a support group. I started full-time as a pastor for CARA on 1 June 1988, and my God, was I desolate! I thought, what the hell have I done? It's very different, you know, not being part of anything, having been part of the parish and St Stephen's Hospital and all that. Now I was just working on my own. I remember thinking: I've made the biggest mistake in my life. I was drinking and I was lonely, I was very lonely. And then things started to happen. People started phoning in and I was getting funerals and people volunteering to help. We then got some money from another trust to pay an administrator, and I started a volunteer training course in the autumn.

However, I still wasn't happy. I was on the edge of the Church, with no base, and I was on the edge of the HIV world, and not belonging to either. That's when I got really sick. I still hadn't been tested for HIV. The other thing to bear in mind is that for all these years I've been suffering from clinical depression, on and off. Oh God, this sounds so depressing! You can see why I need a good party every now and again. But it is probably the most horrendous period of my life I'm telling you about. That and the break-up with Patrick.

I don't know what drove me to it in the end, but I went and had the HIV test, at St Stephen's Hospital. Two weeks later, on the Tuesday, I went to the hospital en route to run the CARA training course, can you believe, to get the results of my test. The person who gave me the results was a friend. And when I walked in she wouldn't . . . I sat there . . . and she walked past looking the other way so I knew exactly what the result was before she could tell me. And I went into her room and she couldn't look at me. And then she got out of her chair and she said, 'I'm sorry, love, you're positive,' and burst into tears. And I said, 'Oh, there there, don't worry.' And I said – and it's a cliché and a joke now – I said, 'Oh well, I suppose I'd better see it as a gift then, hadn't I?' and sort of blaséd out. Strange, wasn't it, really? I mean, we talk about gifts, albeit wrapped in crowns of thorns. All that crap.

Then I . . . I'll tell you what I did. I went upstairs to one of the offices where some friends of mine were working. I went up, and they were all sitting round in their office, and I just sat there. I can't remember what I said. I just sat there. And then I rang up my very good friend Steven and all he said was – and it was good advice, very wise – he said, 'You don't need to tell anybody yet.' In other words, take your time. I then went off and ran this volunteer training course. The next night I went to the opera. And then gradually it dawned on me. I was going to die. I went through everything that I'd been told you go through, and I talked to other people about going through it, and I knew that the reality was that although HIV-positive does not equal death, nevertheless that was it. It was absolutely terrible.

I bore it all on my own for days. I think the biggest fear was what I was going to say to my mother. I know I went back to the consultant, which is standard routine, and I went to a doctor who put me on anti-depressants, which was dreadful. They nearly blew my head off. I had two months of feeling physically vile, not because of AIDS or HIV but because of these bloody anti-depressants. I couldn't speak, my mouth dried up, I was dizzy. I was on them quite a long time on and off.

Then, oh dear, oh dear. I got a phone call here one day. 'Hello, it's Patrick.' My ex-lover. 'Somebody's told me you're positive. Is this true?' I said, 'Yes, it's true.' And he said, 'Well, I've been crying all night.' 'Oh,' I said, 'I didn't think you'd be that bothered.' He said, 'Nor did I. Can I see you?' So I said yes. And I went to see him that night. I told you the pain I'd gone through before: well, when I went to see him, he said he realized he was in love with me and perhaps what we should do is resume a relationship. He didn't want me to tell my mother, but he said he'd look after me and we needn't tell anybody. And of course I responded. This was like a gift out of nowhere, to receive this.

Having said that, he wouldn't let me touch him or anything like that. So we had this period of intense reconnection which was very confusing. He kept saying, 'Don't you ever tell your mother. It'll kill her,' which is probably the worst thing anyone's ever said to me, because I believed him. This went on for about a month, I suppose, and then one night I took him out to the opera, which he wasn't really into, and afterwards over dinner he said, 'I've got something to tell you. I must apologize. I've over-reacted. I don't love you and I don't want a relationship with you.' Well, that was . . . oh, that was worse than before. I felt really shattered by that. I didn't need it, really, did I?

I hit rock-bottom depression-wise. I remember my 1989 birthday, I was in tears, I felt so isolated and lost and lonely and that nobody loved me and in the end I cried with my mother. It's the first time I'd ever cried with my mother in my life. And she rang up Steven and Judith and said, 'Would you come out to dinner with David tonight for his birthday?' And they both came and we all went out for dinner. She must have been heartbroken, my mother.

By then I realized I'd got to do something about this depression, but months after my birthday I was still feeling really low, and my mother sat down and said. 'What's the matter?' And I started to cry and she said, 'You're trying to tell me you're HIV-positive, aren't you?' So she told *me* in the end. *Wow*! Oh, wow, another liberation. And that did it. We sat up in here until three o'clock in the morning. I told her everything about being gay, about every person that she knows who's gay, about all the relationships I'd had, the whole lot. There wasn't a stone left unturned. And she was marvellous, and of course far from killing her it gave us both a new life. Amazing. Absolutely amazing.

That summer there was this gorgeous man I kept seeing at the Lighthouse, gorgeous-looking man. I couldn't work out what nationality he was, but I thought he might have been Portuguese or West Indian. He would smile across and I'd smile back. Then the Administrator at CARA said to me one day, 'Oh, that's Charles. He wants to meet you.' I said, 'Oh, don't be so silly.' He said, 'Yes, he does, he's read something that you've written, and he really wants to meet you.' Well, this went on for weeks, like schoolgirls we were, silly, giggly girls. Then one day when I was sitting with a friend in the Lighthouse, this person came and sat next to us, and it was Charles. I thought, my God, this man's crazy, because he was talking about radios. He was having quite disturbing mental images at that time, because he'd just been very ill with toxoplasmosis. Still, I was all jelly; and then about a week after that I was just sitting in the CARA office on my own and the door opened and in he walked. And that was it. That was the beginning of our relationship.

Charles turned out to be of Greek-Cypriot parents though he was born in Soho. His parents have been here for years, though you wouldn't think so to meet them. He's ten years younger than me, thirty-five. He was a construction engineer, quite a high-powered one, for Higgs and Hill, but he has AIDS so he's retired now. But if you asked him what he did he would tell you he's an artist, because that's what he does now. Those are his paintings there; we've got some up at CARA too. He'll talk to you about them if you want, he's got loads upstairs. He's a bit frustrated at the moment because he's been too ill to do any for a while, but he's going to start again soon. He's a great man, lovely, unconditionally beautiful and loving. It's the best relationship I've ever had in my life. He's a character, too. Crazy as hell. Anyway, we've virtually lived together ever since meeting. Three years and one month. And we've been through a lifetime together in that time. We've lost so many friends, been through so much suffering, and yet we've had such fun. Wonderful holidays and travel and parties and we create a lovely home for people, people enjoy our home. It's been such a big transforming experience for me; he's given me so much.

I still get the depression. Funnily enough, at the same time we met I'd arranged for myself to go into psychotherapy, and I've had psychotherapy twice a week for the whole three years we've been together. It's been wonderful because it helps me to go deeper into the pain, but the pain is still there. I sometimes wish it wasn't, but at least the heights are there as well. Still, it's a long, deep journey, trying to look at and heal the dark side of my life. And I think that's one of the deepest theological nonsenses of the Church; that we feel we've always got to comfort people, we've always got to make it nice, it's always got to be about light. I think that the shadows and the dark areas must be addressed too, because it's when we bring Satan and the Archangel Michael together again, the dark and the light, that we are healed. The Fallen Angel should be raised up with the rest of us, not trampled down and vanquished. I suppose I'm a heretic saying it, but if there isn't hope for the devil, then there's no hope for me.

I don't believe in a God who excludes people. My theology is of a God whose love is absolutely unconditional and eternal. And in many ways I've learnt that through Charles, because my relationship with him is the only relationship in my life which is unconditional. He doesn't care about who I am in the sense of what I do. I haven't got to behave in a particular way. He's tremendously affirming, and I've never experienced love like that before, so it's a tremendous gift. These two dying old queens find each other, but why does it take a virus to enable that to happen?

I'm conscious that my life must sound like a horror story, but the pain doesn't actually detract from the joy and the tremendous love for life that I feel. My greatest fear is not death. In fact, sometimes I long for it, especially in emotional pain. Deep internal pain is such hard work. And I think one of the great weaknesses of some spirituality is that it doesn't deal with pain, beyond saying it's something we have to endure in order to reach a higher plane. But it gets in the fucking *way*. It's a torment. If you have first-hand experience of depression then you'll know what I'm talking about. There's that emptiness and that nothingness and I don't want to die in that state.

Apart from emotional pain, I fear that my dying will involve a physical pain that will get in the way of being able to enjoy dying. I've been hospitalized twice, and I've never experienced pain like it. Dear Charles was having to nurse me. Terrible pain. And indignity. I can't recall it now, it was so terrible, but I would have been quite happy to close down and die.

And you know, the trouble with a lot of Christianity is that it presents Jesus as a prescription, as a pill that you swallow and it'll all be all right. Well, it's clearly not like that. Suffering goes on. Pain goes on. You can sing as many happy-clappy choruses as you like: it doesn't change the situation. *But* if you see Christ's life as a description of what we all go through – we live and we suffer and we make relationships and we die – then he's a model. And the Resurrection is actually saying that somehow there is a hope, there is something eternal, something purposeful; and while we may not be able to articulate it, we call that thing God's love. The pain and suffering remain a mystery, and the Hindus and others who think of it as a sort of preparation for eternal life may be right. I'm not sure, but it's certainly a jolly sight more hopeful than a lot of the Christian stuff of the Victorian era: you know, suffer now, but it'll all be all right when you're dead. Whereas if you see this part of our life as being a part of something bigger, then who we are matters *now*.

I think that's one of the reasons I did finally get tested for HIV. In order not to pretend. The worst pastoral situations I have to deal with are the ones where the truth is not told and people are living in the shadows of dishonesty. And you can't take care of yourself, you can't live healthily, if you're living lies. But it's easier said than done. I know clergy who are absolutely terrified about coming out of the closet. I also know that living with the fear is as undermining spiritually, and one of the hardest lessons I'm learning is that I can't take responsibility for where other people are at. The hardest person I had to learn that around was my own mother. But letting go of all that is part of dying. And the trouble is that sometimes the soul's so afraid of dying it never learns to live.

I don't have great guilt hang-ups about the sort of lifestyle I've led, because I've had such fun, I've had really good times. And I've done lots of things in the last three years since I stopped being a parish priest. I've actually gone and done things that I've always wanted to do, because you stop thinking, 'I'll do them one day,' and then life slips away. I've actually done more or less everything I've ever wanted to do in my life, so the fear isn't that I'm going to miss out on something. Although there are times. Times when there is so much I still want to do.

At the moment I'm going through a difficult patch, because every bedside I get called to, I think that could be Charles. I live with the fear of his getting sick and dying before me all the time. I fear Charles's death much more than mine. Life without him. Life without him. And I hope the world knows that and the Church hears that. Because it would have been wonderful to have the most precious relationship in my life blessed and honoured by the Church and not treated as second-best or second-rate or handicapped.

I also feel very, very angry and hurt that the Church still doesn't see that the work we're doing at CARA deserves their official support in some form or another. I know they've got financial problems but they can find money to do the things they want to do: the Church is always setting up boards of this and boards of that, endlessly using money. Just one salary, that's all we ask. And they make every excuse in the world not to do it.

Having said that, I get lovely support from individuals. Westminster Abbey gives us terrific support. Some bishops give us support and lots of individual religious communities give us support. But I suppose, really, we frighten the shits out of a lot of people, and I can understand that. I remember how scared I was when *my* barriers were taken down. I only hope that the Church – and it's what I try to do as part of that Church – I hope it will find ways of giving people life without making them feel guilty or sinful or whatever. The Church should be a life-giving body, a community empowering people to live *and* to die.

Yet in the end HIV has made me look at my life and live it in a way that no Church has ever done for me. Sure, there are whole bits of my life – like my relationship with Patrick – that I can't celebrate. I can't do too much about that. You know, I want to heal everything, in order to die in peace; Jim'll fix it, that's me. But I can't. So I suspect that I'm going to go to my grave with my pain intact, but I hope not ruining my life.

And faith? Faith doesn't help much. These days my faith's very frail. Having said all that, I don't want to die outside the Church. I think I need to be sustained by the community of faith in order to survive. But it's the community that's important, not the institution. Though I think we have so little faith in the Church as a community that we try to preserve it as an institution. We don't need to preserve it, if we really believe in it, because it's there; it is us. Yet I don't think many people really believe that, especially all these old baggages against the ordination of women. I mean, of *course* the Church can change, for God's sake! It's changed for centuries. It's never stood still, and that's part of its glory, isn't it? Part of its mystery.

I've always thought that the Church is all about stones and bread, and we're into stones at the moment. All that fucking stuff about *sin* and *guilt*. And there you have it. The reason we've forgotten how to feed people is because we in the Church have forgotten how to feed each other. I need to be nourished by the Church and on the whole it doesn't nourish me. I want to be in a community that can contain my pain and anger and the dark as well as the light, and not just a community that looks at me when I behave. Because Christ wasn't like that. But the Church: it is like that, isn't it, especially if you're a priest. You've spent all these years building up the body of Christ and organizing the festivals and then, God, you're not allowed to feel bad. Not allowed to be real. Not allowed to be honest. Not allowed to be free.

And is it better for me to face my virus and my pain as openly and as lovingly as possible to myself, or would it be better for me to shut up and go away and let someone else take all the responsibility? Well, I know the answer to that. And the miracle of it all is that in some extraordinary way I'm being used as I've never been used before as a priest. My ministry's more blessed than it ever was when I was in the mainstream conventional Church. I'm full of ambivalence, but I know it's what I was born to do.

And yet my heart's still afraid of breaking. Being broken again.

The Psalms are very good on all that, I think. It's Psalm 42 I'm really into at the moment.

So longs my soul for you, oh God, my soul is thirsty, thirsting for the living God, when shall I come to see His face? My tears have been my food day and night while they ask me all day long, where now is your God?

As I pour out my soul by myself I remember this. How I went to the house of the mighty one, into the temple of God. To the shouts and songs of thanksgiving, a multitude keeping higher festival.

Why are you so full of heaviness, my soul, and why so

unquiet within me? Put your trust in God for I will praise Him yet who is my deliverer and my God.

I will say to my God, why have you forgotten me? Why must I go like a mourner because the enemy oppresses me? Like a sword through my bones my enemies have mocked me, while they ask me all day long, where now is your God?

(Five months after this interview, Charles died in the London Lighthouse. David was with him.)

SUSAN COLE-KING

Age: 59
Age at ordination: 53

VICAR, DRAYTON, OXFORDSHIRE

Susan Cole-King surprised me. Although she is deeply admired by many fellow clergy, she is also regarded by some people in the Church as radical and subversive. All the adjectives that are usually used to patronize strong women – like 'strident', 'stroppy' and 'pushy' (as opposed to 'courageous' and 'determined') – have been used in my hearing about Susan Cole-King. It was precisely this sort of paranoid description that made me want to meet the woman on her own terms.

When I did meet Susan Cole-King I found her quiet, I found her defensive and I found her twitchy. I found her anything but confident, and I could hardly blame her. Ever since she returned to England from her training and ordination to the priesthood in America she has been the focus of much unwanted press attention. Partly because of the absence of many other women priests in the UK, and partly because of her active involvement with the Movement for the Ordination of Women, Susan Cole-King became an obvious target for detractors of the cause. When the Movement for the Ordination of Women ran an advertising campaign prior to the General Synod vote, they used Susan Cole-King's photograph and history with which to make their point. One advertisement featured a full-length photograph of Susan Cole-King with the caption: 'It isn't being a woman that stops her becoming a priest. It's being a woman in England.' In the weeks leading up to the vote, Susan Cole-King and the Movement for the Ordination of Women became synonymous in the minds of many people, and earned her both praise and derision.

After our initial meeting, I went to interview Susan Cole-King at her pretty Oxfordshire vicarage. While her looks suggest capability and robust good health, she still seemed nervous and ill at ease, and nothing about her manner betrayed the confidence for which she is renowned. After a while she began to relax. She cooked me some marvellous lunches, showed me around her house and garden, and in these rather less formal times together the reasons for her unease became more apparent. As many clergy do, she was going through a period of feeling very isolated in her parish, running it alone and without support at home. She was feeling exposed by all the media attention focused upon her during MOW's campaign and both excited and alarmed by the prospect of at last being able to exercise her priestly ministry in England. Above all, she clearly didn't – and doesn't – find it easy to talk to people about such things.

Susan Cole-King is a good and kind woman, with a fine mind, high standards and a great sense of independence. I liked and respected her very much, although I really only felt I got to know her once our interviews were over. She is, however, a curious mixture of determination and reticence, and while this has clearly helped to get her where she is today (against considerable odds within the Church) I suspect it has also worked against her. Such a combination appears to have set up a tug-of-war within and left Susan Cole-King a little too solitary for even her own liking.

SUSAN COLE-KING

I live my life in the shadow of this very famous, powerful man who was well known as a great figure in the Church, and I absolutely adored him. His name was Leonard Wilson and when I was about eight he became the Bishop of Singapore. He was very authoritarian. He was a stern, Victorian type of father, and I never questioned his authority. He was a passionate man. He had a tremendously deep spirituality and was fond of telling good dirty jokes. He also had quite a temper and could get very angry, so I was afraid of displeasing him.

My mother's father was tailor to King Faisal of Egypt and my mother was born in Cairo. She spoke fluent Arabic, and she lived there until my father went out as a missionary, and she met him when she was twenty-six. She was an intelligent woman, but she hadn't had much formal schooling, and it was my father who really educated her. As a result, she always felt rather inferior to him. She'd always felt that her family were rather inferior anyway; the expatriate society was a tremendously snobby one and her family weren't considered good enough because they were poor. Her father was just a tailor, just a shop-keeper, and shop-people didn't join the whites' club or the Pony Club. My mother's mother was Australian and she was a very strange woman, I hardly knew her at all, she was odd. Much more than that I can't tell you. Where my maternal grandfather came from we don't know.

My mother had an interesting life before she met my father. She'd worked for different people in Cairo, and for a spy during the First World War. She was very entertaining about her life then, and she used to sing Arab street songs to us, though her life rather changed once they moved back to England because she had to knuckle down and become a vicar's wife. I always think how exotic she must have been once.

I had an elder brother who died just ten days before I was born. He was two and a half, and died of meningitis. All my very early memories are of Christopher John, and how much he was loved, and how I couldn't ever compete with this dead brother. My father really adored him. I always thought that I was special to my father until my sister-in-law told me that twenty-one years later she heard him preach a sermon, and he started it by saying, 'Twenty-one years ago today I lost the great love of my life.' And Christopher John was what my parents remembered. They said that it was a special, wonderful gift that I had arrived so soon after he died, but there were photographs of Christopher John everywhere, they were always talking about Christopher John, Christopher John, this special beloved boy . . . I now know that it is very difficult to give to a child when you are mourning the loss of another. But I still worshipped the ground my father trod on.

Most of my early life was spent out in South-East Asia, in Hong Kong, then Singapore. There were three boys born after me, Tim, Martin and James, in that order. I really disliked Tim intensely when I was little, I was obviously very jealous of him, and when I was about three I pushed him into the swimming-pool on the boat going out to Hong Kong because I felt that he was better off out of the way. Martin, the middle brother, was always very special to my mother, the favourite, and we all knew it.

The relationship between my mother and father was not easy because my father's anger was so distressing. One of the reasons I've never really been able to play bridge is because they used to play and my father always made her cry over it. 'Why are you so stupid? Why on earth did you play that ace?' My mother used to cry a lot if she couldn't cope with things and he was very scornful of her. Mealtimes could be absolute misery. My father would say grace, and I got to hate grace because I associated it with rows. I still have difficulty with it. I remember once at supper there'd been a row about the housekeeping money and he'd made my mother cry and she'd left the room and gone upstairs, which she frequently did, and Tim suddenly confronted my father. My father couldn't stand criticism at all. He walked round to Tim and swiped out in rage and Tim ducked. Then my father swung round and lost his balance and we all burst out laughing, which I think shows how double-edged his anger was. Years later, when we talked about this, we agreed that Tim was the only one that could have done that. Martin would have had the courage to confront my father, but wouldn't have had the dexterity to duck. James would have had the dexterity to duck but not the courage to confront him. And I would have thought my father was right anyway. That rather sums up our relationships with him.

As I talk now, I realize that I've blocked out a lot because it was so painful. When I was still quite small my migraines began, and I used to get vomiting attacks. And obviously one doesn't reflect as a young child, but I think I felt I had to conform in order to be accepted, because of not being a boy; that somehow I had to compete with what boys did; that I had been a terrible mistake. The only way to cope with that was to show them that I could be as good as any boy, so I became very driven. I needed my father's approval and love, and perhaps I'm still competing with Christopher John even now. Later on in life I certainly felt a lot of paranoia; that everybody in the world hated me, and that I had to take the world on. I got tough.

Soon after we had gone to Singapore, war broke out and the Japanese started advancing on Singapore, and we had to leave. My father was interned by the Japanese for four years, and tortured. My mother took me and my brothers to Australia and my father chose to stay behind because Singapore was where his job was, and where the people were. I felt completely abandoned by him because I didn't get on terribly well with my mother. I don't have any early memories of my mother, my early memories are all of my father. She did the necessary things, I suppose, but when I was little she was grieving, and anyway she preferred boys, she didn't have much time for girls. Much later, after my father died, we became very great friends and I loved her dearly. But not then.

Everybody talked about England as home, but my life as a child was in bits. Hong Kong, Singapore, Australia, and my father in prison. It seemed like the war was always on. I remember thinking, 'Will there always, all my life, be a war? Will our family always be split up?' I particularly hated the time in Australia. I found the people very rough and unkind. There were quite a lot of refugee families there, and it must have been awful for my mother because she was very ill when we first arrived. It was perhaps the most miserable time of all.

I used to cry for my father all the time, to punish my mother. For those four years we didn't even know whether he was alive, so he became a kind of mythical figure for me. When the war ended we still didn't know whether he was alive or not. We'd heard nothing. My mother had had a couple of postcards but they were about a year old when she got them, and there'd been nothing in the last two years. Then my mother got this message. Listen to the radio. The Bishop of Singapore will be broadcasting.

Even now it still makes me weep, the incredible excitement of tuning into that recording and hearing his voice after all those years. He was preaching a commemoration service for the liberation of Singapore, and that was the first time we knew that he was alive. Just hearing him. When I actually saw him again he felt like a stranger to me. All my dreams of this father-figure were completely shattered by this man with a beard, and very thin. He'd always been so round. I was terrified of him.

My parents and two younger brothers went back to Singapore and my elder brother and I were left at boarding school in England. I was twelve. For the next two years we spent the holidays with our grandparents and never went out to Singapore, so I was separated from my mother and father totally.

It was when I was at boarding school that my own spiritual awakening really came about, and it came largely through my discovery of poetry, of Keats especially. I was absolutely blown over by it. I remember one summer night climbing out of the dormitory window in order to wander round the garden because I wanted to be at one with nature, but I was found by one of the mistresses and put in the sanatarium for a bit.

I loved nature. I was bemused by it. I just loved the countryside and going for long walks. I remember once walking through a wood and having this amazing experience of the absolute beauty of the place, and feeling that this was God's love speaking to me through the beauty of it all. When I came back to the school the only place I could think of to be alone – because I needed to be alone – was the loo, and I wrote a great long poem of praise to God on the loo paper, and that was my first mystical experience! And if I had to trace my sense of vocation back I would trace it to that day. I felt that God was giving me so much, and therefore something was required of me.

My headmistress, Betty Gibbins, was a very important person in my life at that time. Because I was away from my parents so much she took special care of me. When things were difficult she was somebody I could talk with, and I think I learned a lot about faith through her, whereas my father encouraged me to question the Christian faith. His experience of torture by the Japanese, and his experience of Christ throughout that, was very powerful, and I think it changed him. When I was in my late teens he would produce all kinds of books on Buddhism and Hinduism and Islam for me to read, and he'd say, 'Explore it.' He was very liberal in that sense. Truth was tremendously important to him.

I have no doubt that had I been a boy I would have got ordained, but because it was totally impossible I thought I'd be a nurse, because I'd always wanted to go and work in Africa, I'm not sure why. One of the great criticisms of the school is that they expected us just to be ladies and get married. You weren't supposed to be brainy and you were looked down on if you were. I didn't stay on to do A-levels, and by that time my father was Dean of Manchester, so I took a secretarial course there until I was nineteen and old enough to start nursing.

I still wished I was a boy. I deeply resented the fact that my brothers had the freedom that I hadn't to do things like travel round the world. I resented the fact that I was supposed to stay and help in the kitchen with my grandmother while the boys were out playing. When I was old enough, I started riding a motorbike and smoking a pipe to make up for it. My father smoked a pipe, and I suppose that's what that was all about. I didn't have a boyfriend for a long time, and I began to think there was something wrong with me until somebody told me that I wasn't kissable after I'd smoked a pipe. But because I'd not had anyone affirming my femininity I was pretty gauche. I didn't fall in love properly until I was twenty-one, and then it all happened very quickly: I had three boyfriends in the space of a year, and married the third one at the end of it.

I don't think my father ever forgave me for the way I told him I was going to get married. He never liked Paul. I knew that it was going to be difficult. Paul had insisted to me that I'd got to marry him, that I had to tell my parents and it had to be now. I'd met Paul in August, and I told my father we were getting married in September, and they'd never even met him. In the end, we delayed it until December so they had a chance to meet him. You see, in those days there wasn't any alternative to getting married: you didn't go and live with anybody; you didn't have a long courtship. When you were as passionately in love as we were the only thing to do was to get married.

Paul and I met at Butlins. He was doing a holiday job there and so was I, and he was the person who met me as I arrived – he was a Redcoat or something. By the end of my two weeks we were going to get married. There was never anything else. However, I did say I could only marry him on condition that he came to Africa with me, because in my heart I was committed to going there. My sense of vocation was such that nothing would deflect me from that. Not even being in love.

I think it was very hard on my father, and he never really

coped with it. Possibly it was the only way I could get away from him. Paul told me that I had to choose between him and my father; that if I really loved him I'd marry him. Looking back on it, I was very immature. But having agreed, I told my father. I said, 'I don't care what you say, I'm going to marry him. I'm twenty-one, I'm old enough, you can't stop me.' That was my one great defiance against my father. I'd always been so afraid of defying him, making him angry, losing him. He was always more important to me than anyone else. Defying him over Paul was a dreadful thing to do but I felt that I had to; I felt that I couldn't love another man without leaving him. You can see what a dominating person he was in my life. He died over twenty years ago now, yet I've really only begun to get loose from him in the last ten years.

I gave up nursing after a year and started doing A-levels in Biology, Physics and Chemistry. I decided what I really wanted to do was medicine, and I got into St Thomas's, where I'd been nursing, as a medical student. By that time I was married. Paul was reading History at Cambridge, so we lived there until he finished. Then we moved to London so I could do my medical training, and Paul became a teacher.

I told you that Africa grabbed me. My heroes were people like Trevor Huddleston and Desmond Tutu, people like that. I was also very influenced by Laurence Van der Post, he'd fired my imagination a lot. The country I felt really drawn to was Malawi, because I'd met the President of Malawi, Hastings Banda, when I was a teenager. He was a doctor and a very impressive man then. Malawi was also the poorest country in the world at that time, and that attracted me, the need that existed there. Once I'd made up my mind I was going to go I was absolutely determined, and then of course everybody else had to come too; husband, family, kids. It was either you come with me or we split up. I was obviously a very dogged individual.

My first two children were born while I was still a medical

student. I took a year off when Helen was born, and six months with Michael. The most difficult thing to do was the house jobs, because they were resident, but by that time my father was Bishop of Birmingham, so I came to Birmingham, because my parents were around, and that helped. We also had a live-in nanny who had her own son and looked after Helen and Michael during the daytime. I used to come back whenever I could. Even if I only had an hour off in the evenings I'd try to come back and put them to bed. People used to say to me, 'You'll give up your training now you've had kids. You'll give up the Africa idea.' And I'd say, 'No way.'

I finished my training and I wrote to Dr Banda. I said, 'I don't suppose you'd remember, but we met nine years ago . . .' and I told him that ever since then I'd wanted to come and work in Malawi. I told him that I'd got married in the meantime and I'd got kids, and I told him that I was a doctor, Paul was a teacher, and did Malawi need us?

In the end we spent nine years in Malawi. Our two younger children were born there and it was a very happy time, I think, for both of us. I was involved in setting up a national programme for children under five. I'd become very involved in preventive medicine and child health, and because there were practically no services outside the hospitals I campaigned for getting better maternal care and childcare into the villages.

Less than 0.5 per cent of the under-fives were getting any kind of health care on a regular basis, and that was mostly through the mission hospitals. Nine years later, 40 per cent of children were being reached by the Under-Fives Clinic programme, and some years later it was nearly 80 per cent, one of the most extensive in Africa. And I always felt, when I left Malawi, that if I never achieved anything else in my life, I'd actually achieved something worthwhile there. The sad thing is that it's been so undermined since then by all the refugees from the war in Mozambique, the drought, the famines, and worst of all the international debt. That alone has meant no money for transport, no money for salaries, no money for drugs, and eventually the things that we started over there have just fallen apart.

The international debt is still the thing I find myself most angry about. I think it's utterly disgraceful that countries in such poor situations are paying money back to the West at the rate they are. We talk about aid, yet they're paying back three times more in debt repayment than they are for their own health care. Now that I'm a member of General Synod, I find myself speaking very passionately on the subject. I feel very strongly that the Church should be speaking out much more strongly on these issues of international justice; and that means everybody, not just the bishops or the spokesmen. I've always felt that justice was a crucial part of what it means to be a Christian, that prayer and action are part and parcel of the same thing, which is why I wanted to work in Africa. And the deeper I get into a relationship with God, the more angry I get at the injustice of what's happening in the world. I can't tell you how frustrated I get with the Synod over these things. When we have a debate on international issues like Africa or the Third World debt the chamber half empties. It's simply not considered a priority.

People get far more hot about abortion and divorce than they do about international issues. I am Vice Chair of the National Board for Social Responsibility, but even there I haven't been able to get the Board or the International Affairs Committee to give them priority. The trouble with the International Affairs Committee is that it gives more time to international *affairs*, but not the kind of moral, ethical and development questions relating to issues of international *justice*, and there's a difference. The arms trade, GATT, the multi-nationals: those things never get discussed properly. Everybody knows that I'm a bit of a pain over the international debt question, and I tend to get shut up, and that makes me even angrier, because I cannot separate justice from my faith.

By the time we came to leave Malawi, things had got very difficult politically. My job had expanded so much that three people took it over after me. The Chief Medical Officer who'd been appointed to run the programme was intensely jealous of my influence, because I used to have access to the Malawian Permanent Secretary and clearly had a lot of respect from the aid agencies like UNICEF and Oxfam, who'd been funding us. I know I put people's backs up. I was European, I was white, I was a woman. Then this Malawian doctor came, a young man, as Chief Medical Officer. He didn't like the influence and power that I had, and the fact that we'd got such a successful programme going, and he was determined to get me out. I didn't want to put the programme at risk, so I resigned.

This was the first time I experienced real racial tension. Later, when I worked for the World Health Organization and UNICEF in a much more international context, I experienced the hatred of some nationalities against the British. People would just hear a British accent and flare up. I wasn't really surprised. When I thought about the history of oppression that they'd experienced from colonialism, I realized that I had to take some responsibility for that, or at least accept the consequences of it. Once at a conference in Addis Ababa, when I had been arguing for community involvement in decision-making in health care, I was accused of racism, and that hurt very deeply. I was accused of being colonialist, imperialist, and I just didn't think this was true. But I was a white in authority and that was enough, and I can understand the anger behind that.

In 1973 we came back to England. We'd already bought a house near Cambridge and we lived there. For the first six months it was actually quite difficult, because we didn't know what we were going to do, we didn't have any prospect of jobs. Then the first really terrible famine hit Ethiopia, and I got asked by Oxfam to go out there for three months.

It was quite frightening. I was totally on my own, and had very little experience of the country. Northern Ethiopia at that time was hardly known to the outside world. We had to go everywhere by Land Rover, and when I arrived I found that a French film team had pinched the Oxfam Land Rover; they were making some science-fiction film with Terence Stamp. So for the first few weeks I had to get around as best I could, hitching lifts with the old Luftwaffe helicopters belonging to the German relief team. Even later on one was begging, borrowing and stealing any sort of transport one could, in order to transport relief supplies to the villages, or visit the student teams I was supervising.

I was supposed to be setting up a child nutrition programme in remote areas, and I had an Ethiopian health officer to work with me, but I was often dropped on my own by helicopter in a remote mountain village and it was really alarming because you don't quite know whether they'll ever find you again, or come back for you. We visited these villages in attempts to set up bases where we could identify the malnourished children and distribute food to their families. We gave very basic medicines as well. But the whole thing was fraught with problems. Sometimes the local chief would threaten to kill our student workers because we were not giving the food to him. Sometimes we couldn't get any fuel or transport or drugs, and having to sort out those kinds of problems while trying to distribute food was incredibly difficult.

Meanwhile, Paul was happy to be at home, and the reversal of roles in the marriage became much more evident. Having had the freedom of Malawi, he actually couldn't face the idea of a nine-to-five job in England; the thought panicked him and he couldn't settle. It was tacitly accepted that I was going to be the breadwinner for a while, and I was for the rest of the time we were together.

Before I went to Ethiopia I was asked to apply for a job with the Department of Health in London. I was quite tempted by this, because they wanted somebody who could be trained to take over as the new Head of the Nutrition Department when the present Head retired. It was a very good job, but was this what I wanted to do? I wasn't sure. Then Oxfam asked me if I would go to Ethiopia, and that experience settled it. I remember thinking, 'This is what I'm meant to do. I could never settle to a

solid, respectable job in England. This is where my heart is.'
Ethiopia helped me realize what I was about.

After that trip I was contacted by the Institute of Development
Studies at Sussex, and offered the job with a new research
project on health planning and health aid in developing countries. That did seem to be right, and I accepted it. In addition to
the research work the job involved a number of consultancies
abroad with the World Bank and WHO, which meant I was
away a lot. The research on health aid involved interviewing aid
agencies like Save the Children, Oxfam, Christian Aid, to see
what they were doing, and I did that at Sussex until 1980. Then,
after twenty-five years, my marriage fell apart. Everything fell
apart.

The World Health Organization had been asking me to go and
work in Geneva for some time, and I had always said no,
because of the family. But when the marriage broke up, there
was no reason not to.

I worked for WHO in Geneva for just over a year. That was
a miserable time. I had been asked by the Director General to be
part of a small group developing a strategy called Health For All
by the year 2000. It was a typical example of UN 'globaloney'
but involved an awful lot of work. People don't realize what it's
like working in a United Nations setting, with the political
agendas going on all the time, but the politics of it are awful.
You are never playing straight, there are always underlying
things going on, power struggles, hierarchy, status, of a very
male-oriented kind. And despite my position, the secretaries
would refer to the male doctors as Dr this and Dr that and I was
just Susan Cole-King.

It was only later that I became aware of the discrimination
that was there. At the time I wasn't aware of feminism, really.
When I was put down by male colleagues, I just accepted that
that's how things were. The group that I worked with was
difficult. There was an Israeli Scot, who was very close to the
Director General, and had a lot of influence, there was a

Tanzanian doctor and a Peruvian ex-General, and of course they all hated each other's guts and wouldn't agree on anything. And I was supposed to serve this group, but because I could never get them to agree on anything I couldn't move forward and eventually – I'm rather embarrassed about this – I just burst into tears and said, 'You'll have to do it on your own.' This was a week before we were supposed to present the first draft plan to the Director General.

I realize now what a terrible crisis of my own I was going through. I had a complete breakdown. The two younger children, now teenagers, were at home with Paul, and I was sending money home for the family. We'd thought that it was the least disruptive thing for the children. But Paul would never get a job. I was earning quite a lot by that time and he used that, and the children, as an excuse not to do anything, and gradually we grew further and further apart. Looking back, it was the Malawi years that were good, and although it was never an easy relationship, it could have worked if we'd been in a situation where we both shared something, and he had a satisfying job that he enjoyed doing. But he had absolutely no ambition whatsoever, and I was so involved, and felt so needed and wanted in the world that I was in, that he became excluded from my life. He was actually quite proud of me to begin with, but it went sour: when I used to bring friends back to stay, he was so out of it. But we parted as friends. We still are friends. There was never any great bitterness, but there just didn't seem any point in going on: we were coming up to our twenty-fifth wedding anniversary and the marriage had ended long since.

I felt I had failed completely. I felt that I had failed personally and professionally. I hit rock-bottom and sank. I felt that there was no God, no anything, just emptiness, and I went into an acute clinical depression. I tried to deny to myself how bad things were but when two friends came to see me in Geneva, and said, 'Susan, you need treatment,' I broke down completely and had to recognize that I did. I had actually been contemplating suicide a few days before. One of these friends, Malcolm, said,

'The trouble is, you have completely bought into the sexism of our society, and you are always trying to prove that you are as good as a man. You don't have to do that, Sue. Why do you think you have to prove all the time that you can do it?' And I have never forgotten that, because he was actually dead right.

Shortly after my marriage broke up I did fall very deeply in love with somebody else. It was not something that could continue, and to be honest I know that part of my despair and depression was about the end of that relationship as well. There had been other people while I was married, the odd affair, and in some ways that was probably what made me feel that I couldn't continue with my marriage. But the person I really fell deeply in love with came afterwards, and that shook me. It was awful.

I went through a real spiritual crisis as well. The Church was always a major part of my life. My commitment to my faith and sense of God's presence had always been absolute, but the Church was something that I had a real love–hate relationship with. When my marriage broke up I thought that the Church condemned me. I felt a tremendous sense of failure and shame, because one doesn't break up marriages, marriages are there for life, and I couldn't see how my marriage break-up fitted with my idea of the moral way that I believed in. I had failed to live up to my own standards.

The marriage and the Church together had come to feel like a prison. I found the Church hypocritical, moralistic, pharisaical. It was a prison that was all about do's and don't's, and the first Easter that we had agreed to part I just had to cut myself off from the Church too. I remember Good Friday: it is the first and only Good Friday that I have not observed by going to church, and I went for a three-hour walk instead, and that was agony. I wept for most of it. But I had to get away from the Church in order to find God in an authentic way, and that was a very major step for me. Ending my marriage; disassociating myself from the Church; stopping being the kind of person that everyone thought I was, was a terribly important step in my finding God. I felt as though all my life I had been made to conform to a certain pattern and now I could be me.

I know what you're wondering. You're wondering about the children in all of this. I'm . . . I'm very sensitive about it. I think, actually, that I've had quite a good relationship with my children. They came and stayed in Geneva and later in New York. By the time I was in New York, the youngest had left school. Michael came and lived in the States for a bit, and Stephen got a whole lot of jobs in New York, so there *were* periods of time when they lived with me when I was away, and of course I provided an alternative home for them in another country which I think was actually quite exciting for them, quite an opportunity.

And yet. Yet I have a feeling that I was a bad mother because I chose to have a profession, and I've always had a lot of criticism for that. I've always been told I should have given up my job for my children. Perhaps I'm not a good mother. I'm certainly not a good mother by the traditional standards. I do have a lot of regrets over my daughter. She left home so early, when she was seventeen, long before the marriage broke up, so we never had a close relationship. With the boys it's different, I've always had an on and off friendship with them, but you don't get close to sons in the way that you can to a daughter. Now, with her being in France, we get on all right, but it's not what I would have wished. Though I think they're proud of me, my children. I think they think I've done something worthwhile. I think. Yes. Anyway.

My friend Malcolm went to the people in WHO and said, 'Sue's had it. She's not going to be able to continue working on this project,' and that was the end of my involvement with the Health For All project. They gave me other things to do in WHO and I stayed on for several months before leaving, having been offered a job with UNICEF in New York, as their Senior Health Adviser.

I found New York a very liberating experience. Because I

was advising on health policy all over the world, I travelled for about eight months a year, and that was difficult and unsettling. But the people in New York were so accepting, and I found the Church so alive, so thrilling, all that I'd dreamed the Church might be. In the end I was in America for seven years, which was one of the longest times I've been anywhere in my life. I quickly got involved with a parish and that provided a social life for me. New York is a much more open society for single people; you don't have to have a family to be accepted in the way that you do over here. I got to know a lot of people through the Church, and I also got to know convents that I could go and stay at, because I needed to get out of New York. There was one religious community about two hours out of the city that I used to go to quite a lot, and they became good friends. It was the first time in a long while that I began to feel accepted as an individual by a community and by the Church.

I should tell you about a key spiritual experience that happened years earlier. It was in Coventry Cathedral, on one of my leaves back from Malawi, before my father died. He was still Bishop of Birmingham, and he was doing a service there, and I had the most powerful experience in the Gethsemane Chapel in the Cathedral. I don't know if you know it, but it's an incredibly beautiful chapel. The service had ended, and I was sitting there alone, and it was as though I heard my name being called. I heard my name being called and I heard the words, 'Feed my lambs.' I interpreted it then as being the work I had to do with children in Malawi, and I do think that was what I was being called to do at that particular time. At that stage I wasn't even thinking of ordination. But the experience remained with me, and later I wondered whether it had anything to do with my vocation to the priesthood.

One of the things that always divided me and Paul was that he wasn't really committed to the Church, although he came to please me, and the moment we split up he stopped going to church. Prayer, for me, was terribly important, but it wasn't for him and we couldn't talk about it. When I was in New York the Church ceased to be the prison it had been, and I actually began to wonder if I was being called to the religious life, that perhaps God was calling me to be a nun. It was an odd sort of thing to think, but I'd felt for so long as though there were two sides of me that weren't together: my spiritual life, which was so important to me, somehow didn't connect with my other life, and I felt split in two.

I went off on retreat for a while, and it became clear that I wasn't being called to religious life, but out of the retreat itself came a shock: feelings about ordination. It took me a year until I could actually talk about it. At that stage all my instinct was still that women can't be priests. Once I'd actually mentioned it to somebody, I felt totally different. It was like I'd acknowledged who I was for the first time in my life, and there was a wonderful sense of everything coming together. It was scary, because I couldn't see how the future was going to work out at all, but for the first time I felt: at last, at last, at last I can get the pieces of me together.

To be able to speak of Christ, to speak of God, is the most wonderful thing, and what I think being ordained is all about. However, for a long time I thought it unnecessary to be ordained because surely you can do all that anyway as a lay person. But I realized that being ordained is about having the authority to do that. The Church confers authority to speak of God, of how God is not separate, and the spiritual not cut off from the material, and of how the two interweave. Being a priest is about helping people to make the connections.

The other thing I haven't mentioned, which is a bit difficult to explain because it's to do with dreams and things like that, has to do with the feminine, and my sense of my priesthood being a gift from the feminine. It was symbolized very clearly for me in a dream in which I was given a lamb to hold, and I could see a clear connection with the sacrament. The person who gave me the lamb in the dream was my mother, and the symbolism of that was really very powerful, because I've always had this feeling that somehow it's a feminine model of priesthood that I'm about. I don't really understand what it is, but I feel a real commitment to it now. I'd never called myself a feminist before, I didn't really know what it was, but I became a feminist at around that time. I became much more conscious of the oppression of women, and I began to see the poverty of the women I'd worked with in the Third World not just as something that *was*, but as something man-made, literally.

It was totally unconscious at the time, but I now began to question all the sexual and gender assumptions that I'd made previously. I know I was doing it as somebody needing to get out of the male way of identifying myself. I was actually having therapy at the time, because I wanted to understand Jung as part of the course I was doing on Spiritual Direction, and it was clear that what was coming out of therapy was the discovery of my own femininity, which had been so suppressed because I'd not allowed the feminine to be the dominating part of my life. It still is suppressed. I'm still in the process of trying to discover the feminine within myself.

I also did a course on feminist theology and I began to identify much more with the struggle of women. I realized I had bought into sexism to such an extent that I only made my way out of it by adopting the attitudes that I actually wanted to condemn. That was quite a discovery, and it was an exciting and challenging thing to try to bring the feminine back into my life again, and into myself, as part of my own vocation.

I didn't expect to get through the selection process. It was tough, far tougher than here. I found myself quite distressed by the two-day conference: they hauled you over the coals for what you believed, and I wondered whether perhaps my own views were too radical, or not radical enough. Then you had to have a test with a psychologist, to make sure that you were not in the mid-life crisis or something like that, and only then were you recommended. You also have to be more responsible for yourself financially because you have to pay for your training, whereas here they finance you. I paid for it out of my UNICEF pension, and after the first year I did three months of consultancy work for UNICEF in China and Yemen to earn enough money for the second year. I was used to earning $400 a day when I did consultancy work, so I could earn enough in three months to keep myself for the rest of the year *and* pay the tuition.

Giving up all the money wasn't as hard as you'd think. It's never been that important for me, probably because I've always had financial security in my life and lack of money's never been a threat. I felt like that even when I came back to England and was facing the prospect of no job. The waste of money in that international life was appalling anyway. The worst was the World Bank. I did a consultancy for them once, and I was terribly shocked because we had the most expensive hotels, the most expensive air fares, the most expensive restaurants, and it seemed such awful hypocrisy. I was sick of it.

Nevertheless, it took me a while to accept that ordination was really what I was being called to do, and I got myself into quite a state of depression over it before I finally accepted that it was what God was calling me to. I didn't want to leave the international world, in which I felt at home and known and near the top of my profession. I was fifty at that point. Why start again? I also had to look very carefully at whether I was still trying to prove myself to my father. It's an obvious thing to think, and lots of people did think that's what I was doing. But I think I laid that to rest a long time ago. I think that because I was in America and had rediscovered the Church there I came back to the Church in England free of him, no longer in his shadow. I was able to come back into what had been his world and make it my own. I'm sure there was an unconscious influence there, and I expect he'd be pleased if he were alive because he was very much in favour of the ordination of women. But I didn't do it for him.

He died over twenty years ago during one of my leaves from Malawi. It was shortly after he retired from Birmingham, and he and I went up to London where he was conducting a service at St Paul's Cathedral. We had a lovely time, I think because we were on our own together, and afterwards we were due to go home to Yorkshire where my mother was preparing this great big evening meal because it was their wedding anniversary.

As the train pulled out of Euston he had a stroke. It was relatively mild to begin with, but he was shocked. I managed to get him into a compartment so he could lie down, and he was frightened, really terrified. I was so glad to be with him. It calmed him down knowing I was a doctor and could cope. I think it was the first time in my life that our roles had been reversed and he was dependent on me.

The journey was long anyway, but it was even worse because there was a derailment along the way, and we were delayed for two hours. I knew the best thing I could do would be to get him home, and as soon as we arrived at the station I phoned my mother and told her to cancel the party and phone a doctor. The doctor confirmed what I suspected, that he'd had a mild stroke. We thought he would be okay, but he had another later that night and three weeks later he died. I was just so glad not to be abroad at the time.

My relationship with him never got much easier, not really. When I married Paul I had to throw in my lot with my father and he never came to terms with that. I remained frightened of his anger, of his rages, and I suppose I just swapped them for Paul's rages, because Paul could get so angry, he would lose his temper in the same way. Yet I always felt I could never live without my father. Even after I was married I had terrible nightmares about him dying and not being able to cope with it, and I did grieve very, very deeply for him when he died.

I can talk about it quite easily now. I couldn't for a long time, and I still find my mother's death hard to discuss. Losing her when I did was really traumatic, because she died just before I started seminary and it made it even harder to get settled into my new life. I was terribly disoriented. My job was over, my marriage was over, I was in a new home, and this time I was a nobody, a student again, unknown, having been somebody.

Although I missed my mother in a way that I couldn't quite sort out or understand, I loved that time at seminary. I'd always wanted to study theology, and it was really very exciting once I got settled. I just lapped it up! The reading that I could do! Not having any responsibilities, not having to chase around the world. I'd got so sick of travelling, and so sick of the superficiality of the sort of life where you think that you are doing good, you think you are changing the world, but actually you aren't at all. It was wonderful to stay still.

The theological training was divided into the theoretical and the practical. We were assigned to a parish as part of our student training, and we'd worship there on Sundays as well as getting pastoral experience by going with the Vicar to visit people, or attend meetings, all the sorts of things that one does as part of parish life.

I know it sounds rather arrogant but I think my American training is actually rather superior to most of the theological training that goes on here, particularly because one of the things we had to do, which I think is excellent, was three months of residential Clinical Pastoral Education. It's not done here in England, which is a great pity, because it was the most valuable bit of training that I had. It was compulsory hospital chaplaincy training. It was a very stripping experience, pretty painful, but in terms of training for pastoral *care* in ministry it was very valuable. We had to do a lot of what were called verbatims: interviews with patients where you write down, absolutely verbatim as far as you can remember, who said what. Then your tutor goes over it with you, and says, 'Why did you say that at that point? What were you thinking of there? Why didn't you follow that lead? Why did you feel aggressive towards this person?' It makes you much more conscious of what you're doing when you're talking with people – how sensitive you are to what's going on, or where you're blocking, or where your own problems are getting in the way – and I wish they did more of that kind of clergy training in England.

Unlike here, it's difficult to get jobs in the States because there are more people being trained than there are posts in the Church. I had done nothing about looking for a job when I finished my theological training, because I had spent the summer over here in England. All I knew was that I wanted to work in some way with the homeless. When I returned to the States, out of the blue I had a phone call from a church, All Angels Church. They were looking for a pastoral assistant to run a project with the homeless and had heard I might be interested. It was a two-year job and just exactly what I was looking for. It was ideal.

During those two years I was ordained as a deacon, and then as a priest. I was ordained priest by the suffragan Bishop of New York, but two English bishops came over for it. I asked the Bishop of Birmingham, Hugh Montefiore, if he would come over because I had this feeling that if I was going to come back to England, I wanted to have an English diocesan bishop involved in my ordination. I knew Hugh, and I think he responded because of my father having been a Bishop of Birmingham. It made a great difference to me him being there. I also had Donald Arden, who had been my Bishop in Malawi.

The ordination was just fantastic, *absolutely* amazing, a bit like a wedding. We had a blend of traditional music and folk music and Taizé chants. And the Bishop, who is black, he's lovely, Bishop Walter Dennis, he was absolutely on a high, walking on air. He said he was lit up by it, he said he hadn't had an ordination like that before, it was just marvellous. And lots of my family came over. Two of my sons were there, and they took part in the service and read lessons.

There was a certain amount of press coverage. The *Daily Telegraph* came out and took photographs, and we had a press conference beforehand. I wasn't the first Englishwoman to be ordained but there weren't that many of us who were being ordained as priests, and I think because of my father being known, and the fact that there were some fairly high-profile people participating in it, they thought it newsworthy.

When my job with the homeless came to an end in 1988, I

knew that I had to come back to England. I had had nearly eighteen months in a parish in New York, and I'd had a year there as a priest, so I knew what it was like to be a priest, but I hadn't become so identified with it that it would have been impossible to let go of in England.

I had to trust that one day women would be ordained as priests in this country. In fact, I was convinced it was only going to be a year or two before it happened. Two years before I came back there was a big celebration of Women in the Anglican Communion at Canterbury Cathedral, and I'd come over for that with a group of people from the seminary and found it profoundly moving. I felt caught up with the movement and realized that I needed to be here in England: I felt that part of why I was called to the priesthood was to be part of the struggle for women over here, so there was a sense of coming back as a missionary. But what I didn't realize when I came back was that I wouldn't be allowed to celebrate the Eucharist at all. I knew that I couldn't do it in church, but I didn't know that there would be a furore if I did it in a private house. I thought that I would be able to celebrate it in private homes so that people could have the experience of a woman priest. And when I did celebrate it privately I was totally unprepared for the reaction. It was an awful shock.

I'd done the Eucharist privately on one or two occasions and admitted that I did when I gave a press interview. There was an absolute furore! It was picked up by *The Times*, it was picked up by the *Telegraph*, it was picked up by the BBC, it was obsessive. I couldn't believe it! I mean, what I do privately, what the hell's it got to do with anybody else? A few people get together to pray and people get hysterical! It was quite bizarre. What was so painful, too, was that I'd celebrated on a retreat in Wales, and the Bishop who was running the retreat, who was a dear friend, had asked me if I'd like to celebrate and he asked the others if they would like it too. It was a small group of people: there was a Roman Catholic priest and a Roman Catholic nun, several Anglican priests, and an Anglican nun, and it was lovely, beautiful. It was early on our last morning together, and several of the people who were there had said how moving it was, and that they'd never had to think about the ordination of women before, and they just felt the rightness of it, that it all fell into place. It was a very moving experience.

Therefore, to suddenly get these phone calls from the papers and the BBC was really hurtful; that something as precious and special for those who participated in it was made to seem like a political act of some sort, an act of defiance. I was immediately labelled as challenging the Church. The words used about me in the media were all things like 'defiant'. 'Cole-King Defies Church Authority', and so on. Well, it hadn't been like that at all, that wasn't what I was doing. And later, when a group of women asked me to celebrate for them in Oxford, I did it privately in a house and I didn't have any problem with that.

Since then I've been labelled as a troublemaker. A lot of people have even accused me of coming back as some kind of a plot. People who know me say they don't recognize that description of me, but of course most people don't know me, so that's the reputation I live with. I've never seen myself that way. But all the press coverage actually meant that I couldn't get a job for quite a long time.

The other reason I came back to England was because this is where I feel at home culturally and this is where my family are. I know I said how good New York was, but I was lonely. I didn't have family there, and it wasn't my country, and I didn't have a vote. And after all the years I've spent in different countries where I didn't feel it was my country, and I didn't belong, it was profoundly significant being able to vote. I had a form and it had my name on it, and I could make a difference. Until I came back I hadn't realized quite how much I'd minded always being an outsider. I've always been a visitor with a visitor's permit. Always a foreigner. Never having a say in what happens. Suddenly to belong somewhere made a huge difference to me. I've spent most of my life not belonging.

*

When I first came to England I moved to Dorchester-on-Thames, because I had bought a house there knowing there were things in the area I could get involved in even if I didn't have a parish, and the Bishop of Oxford was very sympathetic to the ordination of women. I was licensed as Parish Deacon to the Dorchester team of clergy, but longed for my own parish because I felt I wasn't using my gifts properly. I was being asked to take the odd service, but I had no pastoral responsibility. I didn't have a single wedding to do in the whole of the three years that I was there. I occasionally did a funeral, when one of the priests was away, but other than that I had no funerals. It was intensely frustrating, and I knew that I couldn't stand much more of it.

I really wanted to have a parish. I wrote to the area bishop, the Bishop of Reading, asking if there was anything available. I'd heard that they might be looking for somebody for this parish, because the previous man was about to retire. Bishop John wrote back very encouragingly. He's a lovely, lovely man, really super, one of the best. And to my surprise, when I came here to meet the churchwardens and the Parochial Church Council, they were all very supportive. The previous vicars have not been keen on the ordination of women at all, so it was rather surprising to find many in the parish who were, and quite openly so. One or two were against it, but not so that it's been a problem for any of us. And that's one of the things that really amazes me about the media coverage of it: that at a parish level churches are not being divided and split up, but people are getting on with life as they always have. I just don't see the Church in crisis that everyone talks about, I really don't. I've no idea what the media think they're playing at, giving all this attention to the splits in the Church as a result of the vote to ordain women. It's so appallingly inaccurate and ignorant.

Because I've been conducting the services and preaching here, I'm already to all intents and purposes the Vicar. The only difference it's going to make when my orders are recognized here is that I will be able to celebrate the Eucharist, but in a way that's such a small part of my ministry, really. The main thing is that I'm the one who people come to if there is any problem. Funerals, baptisms, marriages, personal problems, all the things that vicars normally do, are my responsibility.

To begin with I felt quite a lot of anger at the injustice of it. You know, here I was as a priest, and just because I'm a woman I couldn't exercise my ministry. But I'm not good at being angry, I don't find anger very easy to deal with – I think because of my father, and being so frightened of his anger. I'm better at it now than I used to be. Some very hurtful things were said at the beginning of my first year here and I had to struggle a lot with that. It's one thing to know you're not going to be able to celebrate the Eucharist, but to actually experience the rejection is another.

What has always helped me is the feeling that experiencing rejection is to some extent a sharing in Christ's rejection, and therefore it is bearable. At times it's seemed almost a privilege to share rejection with Christ, and mine is such a minute amount compared with his rejection. I do think that when you link your own suffering with Christ's you can share your burden with him: 'Come unto me, all you who are heavy laden, and I will refresh you. Take my yoke upon you and learn from me.' Christianity's about sharing that yoke, about pulling together with Christ and sharing something of his rejection. Of course it isn't always like that. There are still painful things that one struggles with, but I feel that priesthood is about sacrifice and struggle. I know a number of English women in the States who had been ordained over there, who felt that they couldn't come back, that they found it too painful, too difficult, it made them too angry. To be absolutely honest, it hasn't been something that consumes me in the way that it clearly does them, but I think that that's a gift, it's not something I've achieved. I've always got angry about injustice on a greater scale. I get angry about homelessness and lack of housing. I get angry about Third World issues, and racism, of which there's a lot in the Church. It's when I see injustice being done to others that I get angry constructively, not when it's done to me. When it's done to me I just feel hurt, but perhaps that's another way of experiencing anger.

Most people accept that I am a priest anyway. My Bishop accepts that I am, and as a symbol of that I always wear my priest's stole. That is one thing I really have been tough about. It's my way of saying, 'I am a priest. I understand that I can't exercise that priesthood formally yet, but I *am* a priest and my stole is a symbol of my priesthood.' Even at formal functions where I participate with other clergy, I wear my priest's stole, and the Bishops here have had no problem with that.

The only thing that was a problem when I first came was the Maundy Thursday Eucharist, which is the service when the clergy renew their ordination vows. All the clergy in the diocese are invited to attend it, and in my first year I said I'd like to go but I would robe as a priest. This was the year when the issue was all up in the air, and the Bishop said he thought it would upset some people, and because of this they would expect me to robe as a deacon. So I didn't go. Because, contrary to my image, I actually don't like causing problems and doing things in a defiant way, and if it's going to cause problems I'd rather just not do it.

However, the Bishop of Oxford has already written to the Archbishop of Canterbury to ask him to get the paperwork ready so that I and Joyce Bennett, another priest in this diocese, can have the permission to work as priests right away when the thing is legal. That way, one Sunday I will be acting as a deacon and the next I will celebrate the Eucharist. We will probably have something special for my first Eucharist, as after nearly six years not having something special would be difficult. However, the thing that I would *really* love would be to take part in the ordination of the first women ordained in this country, to be one of the priests who lays hands on them. That will be a wonderful thing to do.

I've been thinking about what you said to me the other day:

that I seemed unsure of myself. I don't fit the image of the high-powered international executive. I realize that, yet I don't think I've changed that much since then. I've probably matured a bit. I mean, I'm nearly sixty now, and I know I've changed. But it made me think, you saying that, because I am unsure of myself, uncertain. I think when I was young I probably had a lot more passion and vision and came across a little more forcefully. But, you see, I've always felt I was better at being a mediator rather than a leader. In situations of international conflict I often found myself in the role of soothing people; people like that very volatile Peruvian General I mentioned, who was my counterpart in the WHO and who always wound up the Sri Lankans and shouted and lost his temper and stormed out of meetings. I always had to retrieve the situation and I think I was quite good at it.

It sounds as if I'm blowing my own trumpet. Perhaps I need to. Perhaps I need to because I don't have much personal confidence and I've always felt inadequate as a result. I mean, I find it very hard to see myself as others see me, as someone defiant or ambitious. I know people do find me a bit overpowering in the sense of what I have done, but I think when people get to know me it's different. Because I do feel really insecure about having to take leadership in this parish, and being a parish priest is the biggest challenge I have ever faced, as enormous as anything I have ever done in my life. I suppose by the world's standards it doesn't look like that, but I can tell you I found the Peruvian General much easier to deal with than the churchwardens.

My children often tease me about this. They say things like, 'How come you are so absolutely dumb about the basics of getting from A to B, and yet you have travelled all round the world by yourself? How come you have done all these things, and you can't somehow cope with ordinary life?' And I suppose that's rather true. I'm a walking contradiction, I realize that.

(*Susan Cole-King is now exercising her ministry as a priest in the Church of England.*)

GEORGE CAREY

Age: 58

Age at ordination: 28

ARCHBISHOP OF CANTERBURY

George Carey is the 103rd Archbishop of Canterbury. The first was
Augustine, who became Archbishop in 597, and the 102nd was Robert
Runcie, who held office from 1980 to 1991. As well as being Head of
the Church of England – a position which affords him the title Primate
of All England, which has always made me think of an episcopal
monkey swinging across the nation – George Carey is the principal
bishop of the Anglican communion, which has 70 million members and
450 dioceses worldwide. Although he does not rule the Anglican
communion and is not the equivalent of an Anglican Pope, he is
expected to maintain unity and exercise Christian influence within it.
The Archbishop of Canterbury is Chairman of the Church's parlia-
ment, General Synod, but although he can and does make his views
known within it, he does not dictate Church policy. As well as
preaching, speaking, consecrating bishops and buildings, and visiting
places both in Britain and overseas, the Archbishop of Canterbury also
has his own diocese to oversee, and he officiates at state occasions like
the opening of Parliament and coronations. In fact, the Archbishopric
of Canterbury predates the monarchy, and in strict order of national
precedence the Archbishop immediately follows the Queen.

Almost every hour of George Carey's days, and most evenings too,
are packed to the hilt with meetings, appointments, briefings, engage-
ments or services. Every day Lambeth Palace receives numerous requests
addressed to him from churches, schools, businesses, industries, academic
institutions, individuals, the press, radio and television. He is asked to
preach, make speeches, open buildings, visit people and places, and
comment on national and international religious, social and political
affairs.

Since his appointment in April 1991 George Carey has had to endure vindictive press coverage and clerical bitching of phenomenal proportions. Genuine and fair assessments of his leadership and style there have been, but more often than not George Carey has found himself on the receiving end of ill-disguised social, intellectual and ecclesiastical snobbery. He is not the first Archbishop to have met with such unrelenting intolerance. His predecessor, Robert Runcie, was persistently criticized for being too diplomatic, too ineffectual, too much of the old school. George Carey has been criticized for lacking subtlety, savoir-faire and the usual credentials. Both Archbishops have been accused by the press of surrendering to the Government and by the Government of interfering in matters beyond their domain. Robert Runcie was pilloried for refusing to budge from the Anglican fence. George Carey has been condemned for never having sat on it. His background, his education, his voice, his frankness, his family — everything about George Carey has been publicly dissected, scrutinized and judged.

I was surprised, therefore, that he agreed to speak to me. I wouldn't have blamed him if he hadn't wanted to. He offered me two two-hour interviews, but only after I'd been vetted by the Lambeth Palace staff. This was done in a very civilized fashion. Lambeth Palace staff host on-the-record and off-the-record events at which the Archbishop is present. On-the-record events are the ones designed to be reported in the papers. Off-the-record events are the ones which are not, so I will only say that the one I attended (in the form of lunch) was very nice but no less circumspect than the on-the-record events I attended later on. The vetting involved being asked the same questions in slightly differing ways by a coterie of quietly determined Press and Public Affairs Secretaries: it wasn't unlike being grilled by Customs Officers, except for the white wine and hors d'oeuvres.

I finally had George Carey (and his devoted spaniel) to myself for the best part of two sunny mornings. I liked him a lot. He is an affectionate and in many ways un-selfconscious man and I was greeted with cheery hellos and a hug on both occasions. He was clearly a little nervous to begin with, although he relaxed noticeably during the second interview. Anyone doing George Carey's job is bound to develop a means of self-protection, and if he has one it is his bonhomie: he has the determined bounce and joviality of a PE teacher on a bright cold day and once or twice this felt a touch impenetrable, although I don't think it was intended to be. He is a man of unapologetic and unflinching vision, which is exactly what his job demands but cannot always accommodate. He seemed unperturbed by my less diplomatic questions and genuinely undaunted by the many — some would say overwhelming — problems facing the Church of England. I wondered how realistic this was, but George Carey is the sort of man for whom the most exciting challenge lies in the greatest adversity. He is unfrivolous, tough and level-headed, with a rare and serious optimism.

GEORGE CAREY

Ah, Mary! Come in, come in, how nice to see you again. It is a lovely room, isn't it, I'm very lucky; haven't you seen it before? Have you met the Duke of Buccleuch? Yes, it is rather a mouthful, but we call him Buccleuch for short.

Now, where would you like us to sit? Tell you what, you have the sofa, I'll have this chair, is that okay? Is Lesley going to come and stop us when time's up or are we going to watch the clock? I'm very sorry we can't have more time, you know. That's the thing about this job; there's never enough time. It's a job of brief encounters.

I remember being taken by books at a very early age, and spending lots of time in books. I was a very *dreamy* child; so much so that my father used to call me 'Speedy Gonzales'. It's very funny, because I was on holiday in the States this year, and I met up with a man in Morgan Stanley and his nickname was 'Speedy' too. So I said, 'Why are you called Speedy?' and he said, 'Because I was so slow as a child, so dreamy,' and I said, 'Oh, snap!' So I was very dreamy, very reflective; thinking a *lot* about life and God.

I was also a very studious child. I was aware that in an East End environment I stood out a bit, because I did quite well at school and I enjoyed books, and as a result I was unlike a lot of my friends. But at the same time as being studious I was very involved in games. I enjoyed football and so on; I was *always* out on the street with my friends, or with my family. There are five of us altogether. I'm the eldest, and then there's my brother Dennis, who worked for the Ford Motor Company – he's just recently got early retirement. Then there are twins, Bob and Ruby, and Valerie is the youngest.

We were a close family, very close. Not particularly religious, although I'd say my parents would have fallen into the New Testament classification of being 'God-fearers'. They had a sense, an awareness, of God, and they had us baptized. They took their membership of the Church of England quite seriously, even if they didn't go to it, and I think there are a lot of people like that actually, in our society. It was important for them, even though it was only much later on that they came into a deep commitment to Christ. It certainly wasn't thrust on us as children. I mean, I was aware that my mother prayed, and she told me she prayed, but the main thing about home was that it was just very *affectionate*.

I was cheerful as a child, and I think quite well balanced. There's a lot of introversion in me, but I've found it very difficult to label myself either extrovert or introvert, because I was never terribly shy, and I quite enjoy public ministry. I've never found it difficult to speak in public, to perform, and probably a lot of East Enders are like that, quite happy to be public. I suppose in a way that's because I grew up in a very public family: what I mean by that is that we *did* things together, we sang songs, for instance. I remember when we used to travel to my Granny's, we would sing songs to each other, and everyone would join in. I remember going down to the pub too, to join in all the songs: 'My old man . . .' All those sorts of songs.

I had lots of close friends as a child, lots and lots. I was with a gang of people, and we played football together, you know, getting up to ordinary childish nonsense. There was one boy, Alec Harris, who was my close friend, and we got up to lots of mischief together. I remember one day his mother had sent him out to get the shopping, but he and I played truant and went to the cinema and spent his mother's shopping money having a good afternoon. We did this on a number of occasions. We'd go to the cinema and see a man there who was queueing up, and we'd say, 'Can we go in with you?' because it was usually an X certificate, and we must have been about eleven at the time. That particular day it was a horror film, and I remember it to this day: it was about a hand walking around and getting its revenge. I've forgotten the name of the film, but it gave me nightmares for a couple of years after that. And of course Alec got the biggest spanking of his life.

My primary school was called Monteagle School, and it was a wonderful school. Since becoming Archbishop of Canterbury I've actually had contact with some of the very old teachers from there, and one lady claims she taught me at Monteagle. I certainly remember the headmaster of Bifrons, my secondary modern school, he's well into his eighties now: a lovely man who always wrote in green ink, and he still writes in green ink. So they were two very good schools, both Monteagle and Bifrons.

I failed my eleven-plus, but late developers could retake the eleven-plus at thirteen, so I did. I passed it, and my parents, to my chagrin, apparently agreed with the headmaster that there was no point in my transferring to Barking Abbey grammar school, which I wanted to go to, because I was doing well at school and it would be unsettling for me. I suppose I must have given my agreement to it, but what happened was that I then left school at fifteen and a half without any qualifications, and I didn't have the opportunity to matriculate, which I would have done if I'd gone to the Abbey.

It was a pity at the time, but as you rightly point out, it hasn't exactly stopped me doing things, not at all, and more to the point, I often claim that it actually gave me a wonderful experience of life. If you have the experience of coming from a working-class background, you find that you are able to relate better to people in a job like this where you're meeting all sections of the community than if you come from the top down. I notice that some people who come from the upper classes find it incredibly difficult to relate to ordinary working-class people. I've never found it difficult. I mean, this weekend I was up at Coventry, and I was surrounded by lots of ordinary people, and I find if I have a weakness, it's very easy to lapse back into Cockney lingo. I find it very easy to relate to people because my links are there; it's very easy finding yourself going back to base. So I think it was good to start in that kind of way, and it taught me two things, really. The first was that it gave me a lot of determination: that I *will* succeed, in spite of what people think. The expectation that working-class people could never make the grade intellectually, well, I was determined to prove them wrong. Secondly, I realized quite early on that the only way you're going to succeed in life is by being disciplined, and you've *got* to be disciplined and work out your time and make use of it carefully, because you haven't got unlimited time at your disposal.

As a child I wasn't obsessed with pictures of God. I remember being interested quite early on in more philosophic questions to do with meaning and purpose in life, and I think I became quite convinced when I was still very young that if there was not an ultimate reference point to life, then life itself was not worth living; that if there are no absolutes in life, then nothing is ultimately worthwhile. I may not have put it in those terms at the age of thirteen or fourteen, but that was what my instinct told me.

I started to reflect and read a great deal at that time, and my brother Bob asked me to go along to the local church, which gave me even more of an impetus into thinking deeply. Out of that came a strong impression of God as Creator. I saw that we live in an ordered universe; that whatever chaos man makes of it, the fact of the matter is that life itself is intensely rational. There's a mathematical order about life, and that makes science possible. And I felt that if life is as rational as that, then maybe rationality is imposed on it from the very beginning, maybe it is encoded into the structure of reality. I felt that if that were the case then there were good grounds for believing in God. But if there is a God, is He good, is He knowable? Questions like that led me into the Christian way, and that led me to embrace the Christian concept of God as Father. There was no other rival to that concept, even less so then than there might be now in our multi-faith society, but the Christian concept made sense to me.

Later on, of course, I encountered other concepts of God, but that didn't rule out the deep impression that there must be a reality who reveals Himself to us through Christ.

I became a Christian in the May when I was eighteen. It was that specific. If you'd asked me on May 1st of that year, 'Are you a Christian?' I would have said, 'I believe I am. I'm searching, and I'm bewildered by the quest.' At the end of May I would have said with some degree of certainty, 'Yes.' In that month I travelled further into the Christian faith. It wasn't a kind of Saul of Damascus experience – I wasn't poleaxed – but I became aware that there is a God, that He is good, and that He's revealed Himself to me in the person of Jesus Christ. And my Christian pilgrimage started to accelerate from that moment on, even though in reality it started much earlier.

I'm not sure what the 'process' was: I find that quite difficult to answer, really. I think what happened in that month was simply that I made a step of faith, and I can't remember how it happened or anything like that, but *something* happened. I went into a tunnel, and I came out of a tunnel, sometime during that month. What sort of tunnel? Good question. I think it was two things. It was an intellectual tunnel, in which I found myself saying, 'Yes,' almost as Descartes did: 'Yes, I think therefore I am,' or in my case 'I believe, and therefore life is worth living.' It was also a commitment of the will. 'Okay, God, you're real. I give in, I'm going to live for you.' It was that kind of thing; a willingness to work out the Christian faith in my daily life. I think there was a sense in which I surrendered, surrendered to a quest. It was also a realization, a wonderful realization, that from the time of my birth to the age of eighteen, God was interested in me, as He is in everybody. He pursues us with His love, and He wants us to follow Him into Christian discipleship. So I saw baptism as a child and what I was doing at the age of eighteen as all of a piece, if you like; that even growing up in a generally uncommitted family wasn't irrelevant but was part of a process, and God had been involved in that process and was bringing me through to a personal faith. But it wasn't something

I could articulate, it was something which was essentially incho-
ate. And I had no thinking at the time of being ordained or
anything like that. I had no idea how I was going to spend the
rest of my life at all.

There were also other people involved in the process. For
example, there was the influence of the church I went to – a
lively, Anglican evangelical church, in the Prayer Book tradition.
In those days the only order of worship was Prayer Book, and it
was done very thoroughly, with a choir and very good music
and it was lovely, actually, I was quite entranced by it. I think
for a young person, coming into a church with an ordered
worship can be quite powerful. The church also had very strong
authoritative preaching, from a clergyman called Edward Porter
Conway Patterson: Pit-Pat, we called him. Actually, I have to
say I quarrelled with him a lot, because I couldn't take his
fundamentalism and his degree of certainty. He thumped at
people from the pulpit, and even at the age of eighteen, just
before going into the Forces, I wasn't going to have that. I
wanted him to make clear to me why he was so judgmental
against people and so on, because I couldn't accept it.

However, maybe the most influential figures of all were a
couple of young men slightly older than myself, twins, John and
David Harris, no relation of Alec. I still keep in contact with
them. They'd been to Barking Abbey which I'd never got to, and
they took me under their wings. I was very impressed by
them both, and the quality of their Christian lives, their thinking;
they were both very serious-minded, intellectual young men
with a great love of music. Now, I hadn't grown up in a family
which had a great *knowledge* of classical music, but my father
and my mother both *loved* music. My father had a *very* good
singing voice, very good indeed, and he wrote one or two pop
lyrics which were in fact published. I used to be entranced with
his singing – there really was a great love of music and singing
in my family. Anyway, David and John invited me along to
their home on Saturday afternoons, and I spent most Saturday
afternoons listening to classical music, and it was wonderful,

wonderful. I saw it as a kind of non-cerebral, visceral kind of experience running alongside the intellectual, making me aware of the wonder of creation and beauty and art, and that was very important indeed to me.

I started work as an office boy at the age of fifteen and a half, at the London Electricity Board office in East India Dock Road, near the Blackwall Tunnel. The person in charge of the office was a man called Mr Vincent, and he was a very austere person. I remember my first week, he sent me off to do a job for him as office boy, and I had to go out of the office with a pound note. And of course in those days, my first week's wages was something like £2 and 10s, and £1 was a lot of money. So he gave me this money, and I had to go to a shop and buy something, can't remember what it was, and bring it back to him. As I say, it was my very first week, and I put the pound note in my top pocket, and I went and sat at the top of the bus. I don't know what *possessed* me to do such a silly thing, but I took out the pound note. I had lots of bits of paper in my top pocket – I always have – and I went through my pockets tossing out and tearing up the bits of paper, and I tore up the pound note. Of course when I got to the shop and pulled out half a pound note to buy this thing, the shopkeeper refused to accept it. He said, 'I can't take *this*!' So I had to go back to Mr Vincent, who must have thought I was a real idiot, and he said, 'Right, learn your lesson. Go over to the Post Office and give them the record of the number on the remaining half of the note, and get another pound.' So I did. Then I had to go back to the shop and face the shopkeeper. But I learned a lesson not to dream so much, and that was an important lesson.

Mr Vincent was wonderful. He noticed that I read a lot, and he said, 'Have you read much of Charles Dickens?' and I said, 'No, not a great deal,' and he said, 'Oh, *wonderful*!' I thank God for Mr Vincent really, because I started reading all of Charles Dickens: I read every book of Charles Dickens by the time I was eighteen, before I went into the Forces. Mr Vincent was a great influence on me. He obviously realized that I wasn't destined to spend the rest of my life as an office boy, or as a clerk for the London Electricity Board. While I was there, though, I did actually join two unions. I joined NALGO and I joined the Engineering Union, and I used to go along to union meetings, which made me aware of another dimension of life. I mean, I didn't need to be introduced to the toughness of life, because I'd experienced that as a boy: I knew something about the suffering of my family during the war – of not having enough, and my father at times not bringing home a very good salary – but it was good to be made more politically aware.

My great ambition was to become a wireless operator. What I really, really wanted was to go into the Navy as a wireless operator, as a 'sparks'. That was my great dream. However, there were two problems. One was that the Royal Navy didn't take on National Conscriptsmen. You had to sign on for a longer period, and I didn't want to, I just wanted to do two years. The other problem was that I've always suffered from bad eyesight – myopia – and when I was young, out of pride and vanity, I didn't want anyone to see that I was short-sighted, so instead of wearing glasses I walked round half blind, bumping into things! I failed the medical on my eyesight, and they wouldn't take me. But I badly wanted to be a wireless operator, and I thought, where can I do that? Well, the obvious answer was the Air Force, because they would take people with glasses.

I joined the Air Force – wearing glasses – and I had a wonderful time. I think two years as a National Serviceman makes a man of a man. Certainly trying to work out your Christian faith in the Air Force was challenging, I can tell you that. My Vicar had said to me, 'When you go into a billet with the other people I want you on the first night to kneel down by the side of your bed and say your prayers,' so I did, and I did that through most of my service in the Air Force. I can tell you that two things happen as a result: the first is that you get things thrown at you across the room; the second is that people admire you for your courage. But my Vicar's advice was valuable advice, because it meant you were nailing your colours to the mast right from day one, and from then on everyone knows where you stand. First they'd say, 'Oh, Carey, he's *religious*,' and after a while they'd say, 'Well, he's a Christian, and he's working out his principles.' That meant that everything I did had to be a public affirmation of what I believed: this is where I stand, and I'm not going to deviate from it. It certainly never meant I lost friends – far from it.

Everyone has to do a particular trade in the Air Force, and when it came up to the time of choosing a trade, I chose to become a wireless operator, and went on the special course at Compton Bassett in Wiltshire, and did well enough there to be singled out to become a High Frequency Direction Finder, which was a special field of wireless communication. I still know Morse Code to this day, and if I'm bored I'll mutter it under my breath.

I was then sent abroad, and did three months in Egypt, and then fifteen months in Shaibah, in Iraq. Shaibah is near Basra, and very hot, very humid. I was still in the process of working out my faith, and I can remember going along to a weekly Christian group. In every place I went to there was always some Christian presence somewhere, and other people in the squadron found it quite easy to talk to me about matters of faith and religion and doubt in very explicit terms. And because I didn't cut myself off from the ordinary life of the billet, drinking and swimming and games and running, people found it very natural to see me as one of their mates.

One very interesting thing happened. Shaibah during the war had been a massive British airfield, and one day, walking around it, I came across a hut, which was locked. I looked through the keyhole, and there was an altar. There was no worship, no chaplain or anything like that in our squadron, so I went along to the Commanding Officer and I said, 'Is it possible to get the key to that hut?' and he said, 'What do you want it for?' I said, 'Well, actually, I wouldn't mind starting a service here on a

Sunday,' and he said, 'Fine,' and told me he thought the squadron doctor might be interested too. So I went along to the doctor and said, 'Would you be interested in helping?' and he said, 'Yes, I can play the piano.' So he became the pianist, and do you know – this is very interesting – we never had less than ten people who would come along for a service. I wouldn't want to say I was a reliable chaplain. I think I was probably very erratic, looking back on it, but I did take quite a few services. Now, I don't know whether God in His wisdom was testing me as to how good I'd end up being at this kind of job, and I think it may have given me a desire to consider ministry, but at that particular time I was not even thinking about ordination or any form of Christian ministry.

I ought to say that at this particular stage, at eighteen, I still didn't have an O-level to my name. I remember going along to the Education Officer in Shaibah and saying, 'When I get out, what do you advise me to do?' and he said, 'Well, you must start getting some O-levels.' Which I did. As soon as I got out, in February of 1956, I went along to see Pit-Pat, the Vicar at the church, and we talked a bit about vocation, and he said, 'What do you want to do?' I told him the two things that kept cropping up in my mind. One was teaching, and the other was ordination; and gradually it became more and more clear that I was being called to the ordained ministry.

At the same time, I met Eileen, my wife. I knew Eileen when I was seventeen and she was fourteen: we met when I started going to church, and she was already there. Her mother and father were Scots: they came down from Scotland looking for work, and she was born in Romford and grew up on the private side of the Dagenham estate. I was on the working-class estate, she was on the other side, and never the twain did meet. But we did meet in church, and the church is so often a great bridge. She was a bright girl, went to South-East Essex Tech. She wanted to go into medicine, and she became a nurse, but she could easily have become a doctor, I have no doubt about that. She is very, very able.

We met again when I got back from the Forces, when I was twenty and she was seventeen. I often tell people jokingly what happened. I'd just been demobbed that week, and my parents said there was a church party on and did I want to go? Well, I thought it'd be nice to go and see my old friends again, so I went. Now, Eileen's house was in this direction and mine in that direction, but the only way to get to the church was to go over a bridge, and it was a foggy February evening, and we quite literally bumped into one another as we were going to church. We fell in love and people have said I've been in a fog ever since!

While Eileen did her training at West London Hospital I went on to the London College of Divinity to start ordination training. Then, at the age of twenty, feeling called to the ordained ministry, I realized I had to get some O- and A-levels. I have to say, through the grace of God, and probably through some ability I had, I was able to achieve three A-levels and six O-levels in fifteen months. So I moved quickly. When Carey moves, he moves!

I went to the London College of Divinity at the age of twenty-two, and did a four-year course which combined theological training with studying for a degree in Divinity at King's College, London, all of which I enjoyed enormously. In fact, of all the Honorary Degrees I've received as Archbishop of Canterbury, and I've got about eight now, the one I later received from King's probably gave me the most pleasure of all.

I had a very clear sense of what I wanted to do. Because I knew so clearly what it was to come to a living faith, that was the thing I wanted to communicate to other people. I mean, to me Christianity is not just a religion, Christianity is a way of life; it is a way of looking at life; it is a way of Christian discipleship; it's a way of behaviour. *That's* what I wanted to communicate, and *still* want to communicate. I haven't lost that desire. Of course I've changed a lot over the years. My theological colouring has changed. I started out from a very definite, conservative, evangelical, Protestant, Anglican church, and I'm nowhere near that now. But I still find my roots there in the emphasis on the importance of a life-transforming encounter with the living and holy God. There's no question in my mind that that's what it's all about, and if it weren't I'd walk away from this job tomorrow, I really would.

However, since becoming Archbishop of Canterbury, people have put me into a box marked 'evangelical'. It's inevitable that people will box other people in, and if people call me an evangelical, fine, so be it, it's a proud word. I'm quite happy to be an evangelical, in the tradition of Max Warren of the CMS, Stephen Neill, of John Wesley and so on. But no one will ever hear me calling *myself* an evangelical, and they ought to note that. For me the most important thing is being a Christian, then being an Anglican, and those are the two most important words in my vocabulary. I don't box myself in. I've changed and I have learnt a lot from Catholic spirituality, the liberal tradition, the charismatic tradition, and no doubt there'll be other things I'll benefit from in the future. Now that I go rather more often into the Orthodox Churches I realize that one can learn a lot from them too, and I wouldn't have felt that when I was young. So I plead with people: don't allocate these terms as generously as that, because you may find they will boomerang on you. Don't box me in.

Now, of course my being an Anglican is an 'accident' of culture. I encountered God within the Anglican tradition, but later on, as I've made more of a journey, I find myself saying, 'I'm proud to be a member of this particular branch of the Christian family.' What I love about being an Anglican is its breadth. Wasn't it John Robinson who used to quote the Psalm:'O Lord, thou hast set my foot in a spacious room'? The Church of England is spacious, and our comprehensiveness is important. Not every Anglican affirms comprehensiveness, but for me it is a quality, and I can grow within it because it's much bigger than I am. I'm not a Roman Catholic, because at the Reformation the Church in this land, alongside other European Churches, believed Rome to have departed from the early traditions. I'm not a non-conformist because I believe that they stress too little some of the important traditions of the early Church. But I am the kind of Anglican who wants unity with both the Free Churches and Rome, and if in my brief period as Archbishop of Canterbury I can help the Churches to come closer together, then I will have achieved something important – however small it may be.

By unity I don't necessarily mean institutional unity, as some would understand it. I believe there's something quite important about all our own traditions, about being Anglican or evangelical or Orthodox or Roman Catholic; I believe there's something God-given about these traditions. I'm thinking instead of steps towards a unity that we cannot at the moment perceive clearly. I'm still content with the theme of organic unity, where you have in mind the idea of the human body with its unity and diversity. For me, diversity is a clear feature of the kind of unity that I seek, and I see unity as having three steps. Firstly, acceptance. The first steps towards unity must be an acceptance of one another's Churches as true Churches, and I think Vatican II gave an enormous impetus towards that because it did refer to the separated Churches as real Churches. Secondly, unity must be an *affirmation* of one another's ministries; and when the time comes when Anglicans, Baptists, Methodists, URC ministers and Roman Catholics are all able to say to one another, 'The ministry of your Church is a true, authentic ministry,' then that will be a second very significant step forward. The third step to unity will happen when we actually allow one another to receive Communion in one another's Churches, and when our Orders are interchangeable. We've got a long, long way to go before that happens.

Now, I know there are people who think that the prospect of unity with Rome has been ruled out by our decision to ordain women. I would say to anyone who claims that, that they would have a stronger case if the Vatican had accepted the final report of the ARCIC in the way that the Anglican Communion did. The ARCIC report is a series of documents which laid the foundations for unity between the Anglican and Roman Catholic Churches. In 1988, four years before the vote went through on the ordination of women in our Church, there was an overwhelming desire on the part of the Lambeth Bishops to take further steps towards unity on the basis of those documents. There was a different and more negative response from the Roman Catholics – the Vatican put further serious questions about the document out in late 1991. If they had received it with as great an enthusiasm as the Anglican Communion, that would no doubt have influenced the thinking concerning the ordination of women to the priesthood within the Church of England. As they didn't, it is hard to see the decision of November 1992 as the Anglican Church slamming the door in the face of the Roman Catholic Church on the issue of unity. There are many issues we are still struggling with theologically, which have got to be addressed. But ARCIC is still continuing its work. I know from my friends in the Roman Catholic Church that many of them are delighted by what the Church of England, and other sections of the Anglican Communion, have done with regard to women. So I do not see the ordination of women as a final and irrevocable barrier to unity – far from it.

I am absolutely *delighted* by our decision to ordain women, I really am. I didn't know what was going to happen that day we voted. I remember when I was thinking about this issue, I said to myself: I must set a very clear lead on this. There were people saying to me, 'Sit on the fence. Let Synod make up its mind, and then you can help the Church forward once Synod has made up its mind.' I discussed this with a number of people, including the Archbishop of York, with whom I get on extremely well – oh yes, we really do – we've got different gifts, different approaches, but there's an acceptance of one another. Anyway, I discussed this with him and I said, 'This is the way I want to do it, John.' I showed him what I wanted to say during the debate and he said, 'Fine. What I will do is not speak publicly because one of us must be in a position to be available for those who are opposed.' And that was wisdom.

So I decided to give it all I had, but I had no idea that it would go through that day, no idea at all. And when the note was handed to me by the teller on that occasion, I said to myself: I mustn't show *any* emotion or expression on my face, because I know that the television cameras will be keen to pick up a hint either way. But I can't *begin* to tell you how overwhelmed I was by that vote! I knew we were making history that day for the Anglican Communion, because although other parts of the Anglican Communion had ordained women, the Church of England is seen as the Mother Church, and from that moment on I knew it would be inevitable that other sections of the Anglican Communion would follow; and the ecumenical consequences of that would be very serious too. But it was a *wonderful* occasion. Wonderful.

However, not being a sitter on the fence as far as this issue and other issues are concerned has got me into trouble, and I would say in my defence . . . well, no, actually I'm not going to defend myself. Let me go back a bit, though. Look, I'd been two and a half years as a diocesan bishop and it's a whole universe away from being Archbishop of Canterbury: I mean, the distance is *so* enormous, and I wasn't prepared for the jump. Also, the Church of England — and I have to say it, and it *is* a criticism of the Church and the structures — the Church didn't give me the resources to help me to cope with the kind of transformation that was expected, and it's taken some time. I never chose this job. When I accepted it, I had to believe that God was calling me to do it. I believe in God, and His will, and I've never run away from any challenge in my life. So I took it on with a deep breath, saying, 'God must be putting me here and it must be certain qualities I have that the Church of England requires at this particular stage of its life.'

We're calling the nineties a Decade of Evangelism — and it's not a term that I invented — and if by that we mean we want the Church of England to be more outward-looking, to co-operate with society, to make a stronger contribution, then I, as Archbishop of Canterbury, have *got* to set a lead in such a way that people are not in any two minds about where I'm going, and where I want to take the Church. So that is what I try to do – and I will continue, don't worry!

I've had a lot of criticism for this approach and I think everybody is sensitive to criticism to some degree or another, and it would be foolish to say that if you read in print some nasty things about you, it's not going to sting. But it stung me more in the earlier days than it does now, because you gain confidence through what you're doing, and you gain confidence in your ability to express yourself and so on. You also see the way that God uses your ministry. I get tremendous affirmation abroad in the Anglican Communion, and I think I'm at my best with ordinary people, preaching and teaching. I also enjoy writing articles, and I enjoy going into the political world with a Christian message. My book, *Sharing a Vision*, expresses some of the things that I've been up to in the past two years. I am now quite confident that we're on the right lines, and I'm able to brush off the criticism and to treat it in some cases with the contempt it deserves, because I know who I listen to, and who I don't. But let me tell you how I deal with criticism. First of all I say to myself: if there are things here that I need to learn, then I will learn them. And I will talk with my colleagues, and if there's any truth in what they're saying about me, then let's find ways of learning from criticism. On the other hand, if there's nothing objective, if it's unfair, if it's malicious criticism, then I shouldn't actually lose one moment's sleep over it, and I don't normally. I'm developing extra layers of skin, and it's given by the Holy Spirit, I'm sure.

You can't win, of course. Take Robert Runcie: people have already forgotten that he had a terrible time. And his son, do you remember his son writing in the paper as Robert retired what it felt like as a family? Very painful indeed. But we've got a lot of support here. We've got a very, very good team, and we work well together. And I often remind people that if they think my leadership role is not appropriate, then they've got to account for the fact that this year, having talked about it for nearly twenty years, we've now taken women on board fully into the life of the Church. Furthermore, the House of Bishops is totally united, in spite of our differences, on how we're going to handle the thing, and this is tremendous. It is not a sign of weak leadership. Both John Habgood and I have shown the way, and that has been accepted by the Church, and for that I'm so thankful.

A number of people criticize the Church for not taking a moral lead. A lot of people say that the moral lead is being left to politicians and commentators and the media. I think that is incorrect. The Church is in the business of morality, but many people are mistaken in thinking that morality is only something very personal. Often the Church is expected to speak out on sexual ethics, and things like that – highly privatized morality – without realizing that issues of human nature, dignity, freedom, unemployment, exploitation of the earth's resources, are also moral questions. It's all very well for a government to want the Church to do something about moral change, but the Church's attitude is: we're not really in the business of being a moral guardian; we're in the business of calling people to a faith which has moral consequences. There's a difference, and you can't have one part of it without the other.

In my book, *Sharing a Vision*, so many of the themes are about what morality is, and how we recover the moral nerve as a nation. So I would repudiate the notion that the Church is not taking a lead, but having said that, we can do a lot better. I do think that from the sixties onwards the Church has been in a kind of tactical retreat. We've been too apologetic about the Christian faith, against increasing agnosticism. Instead of promoting the Christian faith in a vigorous and unapologetic way, we've retreated into a ghetto. Much of the preaching of recent years has been of a highly subjective nature. We have lost the epistemological basis for our preaching, and our sermons have not been the forthright proclamation of the Christian faith, asserting the verities of God. Instead, we have dwelt much more on people's own experience of God, on the subjective side, because that is regarded as more acceptable by our society. Now, subjective experience is important, but we need to emphasize both subjective and objective experience, and I believe that the task for the Church now is to be much more confident and up-front. I think the world needs it. And I think that the world will *respect* Christians who are bold and thoughtful and intelligent, and who are prepared to work with the rest of the society in building up the kind of community that we believe we all need.

Our society desperately needs the undergirding of spiritual values. I can think back to the war years when everyone seemed to pull together, and that's typically British: we are always at our best when we are fighting with our back to the wall. When we're cornered we always win. You say you find our country really depressing at the moment: I have to say as I look at our country that I'm full of admiration for our people. Wherever I travel in the world, I'm always thankful to return home. I love British freedom, I love British justice, I love British traditions. I think our sense of history is wonderful, and I wouldn't want to live anywhere else in the world, however warm the climate might be elsewhere. This is my home and I'm committed to it.

However, we are a much more fragmented nation than we used to be, and the class divisions are still pretty deep in society. There is a growing chasm between rich and poor: whatever people may say, that's the reality. The education system, which used to be second to none, no longer is. Also, and I have to say this, I think we all must take some responsibility for our moral decline. When you think that the average child watches twenty-five hours of television a week ... who is guiding that boy or girl in knowing what is right, or what is good, or what is bad: what is indifferent, what is excellent?

So how can we as a nation rise to heights of excellence in all that we do? If my career has anything to teach me on this, it is that I realized that having got off to a pretty rocky start academically, through no fault of my own, I had to make up for lost time, and that discipline was crucial to that. I'm still highly disciplined and conscious all the time that I've got to read avidly, and I love reading, so I put time aside for that. Now, if you have an inward motivation to do better, that's fine, but many children don't have that kind of incentive, and they may arrive at it far too late. Too late to do something about yourself; too late to better yourself. And I'm not trying to apportion blame, but I really do think that standards have declined at every level in our society. I think the most difficult profession now in our society is the teaching profession. We're not giving teachers the resources or the kind of salary that will motivate them to say, 'This is a job really worth doing,' and over the last fifteen years we've mucked about with education to such a degree that teachers are demoralized.

The kind of picture I'm describing is one of a fragmented, divided society which has lost its Empire. The Commonwealth doesn't really mean very much any more; we're not yet quite Europeans and committed to it. We're in a very big world and we're now very isolated. The Church is also a victim of this general decline. It's been in constant decline for the last 150 years, and I'm glad that we're bottoming out now. When I was Bishop of Bath and Wells I had 250 clergy, but only twenty-five years before that there were 500 clergy in the diocese; so within twenty-five years we'd lost *half* our workforce. Now, that is obviously going to have a real impact on the presence of the Church in Somerset, with too few clergy chasing around maintaining services in 597 churches – not to mention maintaining the buildings themselves. Eighty per cent of all Grade I listed buildings in this country are ecclesiastical, and nearly all of them are in the Church of England.

Now, I believe very much in the importance of buildings; and buildings and the maintenance of buildings are part of the mission of the Church. When I go to France, I thank God for the Church of England. So many churches in France which have been taken over by the State are in the most decrepit of conditions, I felt quite angry about that when I was last there. I think our Church buildings are well maintained and greatly cared for. Parishes have an amazing ability to find money for urgent repairs. I can tell you story after story of small churches with very few people in the congregation, raising terrific sums of money – £200,000 in a year or two years – to restore their buildings, and that will continue to happen, I'm sure.

The answer I want to give to your question about our future is that we need a much more entrepreneurial style. There can be no future for the Church unless we have collaborative styles of ministry, instead of the parish priest feeling that it all depends on him or her. That means taking lay people seriously; taking their leadership ability seriously. Let's imagine I'm vicar of a parish where I've got four or five churches and a combined membership of no more than 100 people. Let's imagine one church is in trouble because it's got eight regular members in the congregation and it needs lots of urgent repairs. You go back to square one. You call the people together and say, what are we going to do about this? You make an appeal to the wider community. You say, 'This building is valuable, and valuable for a number of reasons. Worshipping has been going on here for 800 years: do you care about it?' Then you start providing a ministry for the people. You start a Sunday School; you start a youth club; you start a football team – or whatever. You get *among* the people. You start having family services, to draw people in. You go along to the local pub and you walk in and advertise. You say, 'I'm George, I'm the local Vicar, I've just started. Here's the service we offer.'

What people will respect from the Church is integrity, enthusiasm and care for them. The Church is not in the business of maintaining buildings: we're in the job of promoting the values of Christ and the gospel. But if we're prepared to do that properly, then Church buildings can be seen as a wonderful plant for the glory of God, like a strawberry plant, around which you put out your runners into the homes of the district – things like house groups, discussion groups, prayer groups. When I was at Durham I ran a very successful thing called

Agnostics Anonymous for people who wanted to come along, no holds barred, no commitment, to have a drink, air their questions and their doubts, with no prayer, nothing religious at all, it was just a general free-for-all. It was highly successful: it never surprised me when people started to drift into the church and sit at the back and come and go. And what I *long* to see is a Church that is *open* to the community, so that people feel they *can* come on their own terms, and move away on their own terms too. That's how the Church ought to be. That's what I'd like to see.

All this means that the average clergyman now is under tremendous pressure: poorly paid compared to his or her contemporaries; having to work very long hours, then to still receive the complaint, 'We don't see you around.' This despite the fact that the majority of clergy are involved in community pursuits: clergy are usually chairmen or on the governing boards of schools, and we still have thousands of Church schools. The clergy are also often involved in Scouting, Guiding, or other youth activities, so it is an exaggeration to say they're never around, although, having said that, my plea to clergy would be to get out visiting more. I've always been a great believer in getting out into the community. You *must* be seen around the place. You *must* get involved. You *must* be there where people are in crisis – and there should be such a relationship between undertakers, doctors and clergy that the moment you hear of someone in trouble, you ought to be there before anybody else. The clergy have got a great advantage in this, because we are the only professional group which lives in the place where we're working. Doctors and nurses will come in from outside, while the clergyman or woman is there in the community.

People are usually very glad to have the clergy around, whatever they believe. Being told to get lost doesn't happen very much, although it happened to me once or twice when I worked in Islington, and what you *mustn't* do is to give up. Go back the following day. I always went back if that happened. One day I went to visit a lady and she slammed the door in my face. She said, 'I don't want to see the likes of you around here,' and slammed the door in my face. That hurt me, and I thought, what do I do? So I went back the following day and I took some flowers with me, and when she opened the door I smiled and said, 'Look, I may have caught you at a bad moment yesterday. I'm very, very sorry if I did. I've brought you a little gift to say sorry. I'm George Carey, I'm the curate of the local church, and if you ever want me . . .' and I explained that the purpose of my visit was to get to know people better. And the first thing she did, she said, 'Oh, I'm really sorry. I was in a bad mood yesterday, and when I saw a dog-collar that was the last thing I could face! Come on in.' And that was the start of a friendship. Now, I'd love to say that it ended in her coming to church regularly – it didn't. But it did end in a very deep friendship, and we used to pray on occasions in her home. And when I left, she was there at my farewell, and I still hear from her from time to time. So I would say: you don't give up as a clergyman, or as a Christian. You go back and make sure that if we, as representatives of the Church, have done something wrong, offended in some way, we try to put it right.

I did four years' curacy in Islington, and then, because they needed someone to teach Theology at Oak Hill theological college, I was unexpectedly asked to do some part-time teaching. I obviously got on well because the Principal invited me to do that permanently, and I joined the staff for four years. I then accepted an invitation to join St John's theological college, in Nottingham, and because it was anchored to the University of Nottingham, that seemed to me to offer more scope and openness. It's certainly true that the teaching there was quite different. At Oak Hill at that time, when you walked in and said, 'Good morning, gentlemen,' they wouldn't respond, but they would write: 'Good morning, gentlemen' down on their paper. At St John's, Nottingham, you would go in and you would say, 'Good morning, ladies and gentlemen,' and they would say, '*Is* it?' They were more relaxed, my five years there. I was very happy.

I've got a love–hate relationship with theological colleges, and theological teaching generally. On the positive side, I think training these days is very good. Compared to what it used to be, it's ten times better. When I think what it was like when I started out at Oak Hill in 1966, training today is far superior, because now we're making the connections between the academic life and the parish ministry. However, my complaints are these. I still don't think it's integrated enough. I would love to see theological training moving towards sandwich training so that we're giving men and women the experience of ministry. There's a danger that we're taking them into ivory towers, and they're doing their theology away from the real questions. It's all very well to talk about the existence of God when you're in a theological college; but how do you talk and feel about the existence of God when you see a woman dying of cancer in a hospice?

The second complaint is that a lot of our clergy who teach in theological college have very little experience of the real life of ministry. I did actually go back into theological college life once again. I became Principal of a theological college in Bristol in 1982, but at least it came out of seven years' ministry in Durham, where I had direct experience of the life of a parish, which I was able to bring with me. But after five years there I was already beginning to be rusty, because much as I tried to make the connections, I was five years away from the world I once lived in. And many theological tutors are very good theologians, but they're miles away from the kind of life they're sending their students to. So while the Church of England is quite excellent on ministerial information, it's not very good on ministerial formation. And formation means formation in prayer and in the *practice* of ministry, and I don't think we teach enough about the relationship between the two.

In short, what I'd like to see would be those people who at present are doing two years' theological training, doing three years' training. And those people who are presently doing three years' training doing four years' training. And I would like to see half of that time spent out in the world, where they would be given a fresh and rich experience of seeing God at work in parish ministry. Maybe the day is coming when we'll have fewer theological colleges and more Courses. I'm sure you're aware that we now have two forms of training in the Church of England. The Courses with a capital C are for men and women who for a variety of reasons cannot or do not want to move from their home situation into a theological residential situation, so their theological training is done at evening classes and at weekends. That's the cheapest form of training and it's now becoming more popular, and may lead to a further decline in residential training – which may not be a bad thing.

In 1975 I became a parish priest for the first time, at St Nicholas' Church in Durham. I loved being a parish priest, I really did. It was the people I loved. Just people. Have I said this before to you, that my ministry is now a ministry of brief encounters? Whereas in a parish ministry you're dealing with people from birth to death, and that's the richness of it, really: there's a tangible evidence of God at work in the lives of people. I also loved building up a congregation and all the challenges associated with that: putting up with tiresome people as well as exciting people; getting out into the community. You see, I wasn't just interested in church life: I was Chaplain to the prison; I was involved in the university; I was a Chaplain to the Royal Air Force Association Club, and used to go along there and play darts with them and that kind of thing – great fun. I went into old people's homes and schools; I ran a football team. Of course, all this is bearing in mind that I was a vicar at the age of thirty-five, so I was quite fit. I jogged and played squash and that kind of thing. So for me it was the encounter with people which was such terrific fun. Of course I still get that in my present job, but not in the same way.

But I still haven't answered your question about why do it in the first place? What can Christ mean for us today? The way I'd want to approach the question would be to ask: 'What do you already know? What do you know about this mysterious person who shaped the world?' I'd want to say that just as you can't talk sensibly about mathematics unless you know something about mathematics, so you cannot talk about Christ unless you know a bit about him. I'd say to someone who wanted to know something about Christ's relevance to us that they ought to read his history, and then we'd be able to talk properly on the basis of that. I'd hope to be able to show that he has an abiding significance, and that he still continues to shape the Church, because I believe he is *alive*, and I believe he does have an impact upon our lives. Those who are prepared to follow Jesus will find that he walks with them, and that he can change us from within. Interior conversion happened to me and continues to change my life, and that's why I can say, with confidence, to another person, 'Following Jesus Christ today *is* still really worthwhile.'

Interior conversion happens to more people than we realize, and it happens unexpectedly to people, and sometimes they realize it happened long after they're aware of it. But if someone's seeking conversion, I remind them of the verse and scripture which says, 'If you seek me with all your heart, you will find me,' because I think if people are serious about it, they will eventually find Christ; eventually the penny will drop. But it does mean that you mustn't play at it, that you've got to be prepared to follow Christ with all your heart. And if people are prepared to do that, it will happen. But they have to be prepared. At the very heart of faith or lack of faith is the fact that many people simply don't want to commit themselves because they know the consequences are going to be pretty radical; that a change of lifestyle is going to be required, or maybe the questioning of a relationship – and they don't want it. A lot of us want religion on our own terms.

I think one of the things that's happening in society these days is that no one now can avoid religion. Religion is not dying out.

We may be post-modern, post-capitalist, post-socialist, even post-Christian in the West, but no one can say we are post-religious; and the reason religion will never die out is because there's something about human nature which is deeply religious. Paul Tillich defined religion as things to do with 'ultimate concern'. We all reach beyond to something else. We all look forward in life. Therefore we ask: what is there *beyond* this life? Why are we here? People always ask the big questions. The second factor to bear in mind is that the challenge facing the Churches these days is that we're moving beyond denomination-alism. I really think that lay people are getting impatient with the quarrels between denominations which hold back our mis-sion. We are, after all, aware that we are baptized into the *one* faith. Now this area is a challenge to the Churches. Indeed, this is a problem to institutional Christianity, because we've always wanted our troops to be 'like us', to be Anglican or Roman Catholic or whatever. I'm not denying the value of being Anglican, Roman Catholic or anything else, but we've got to face the denominational questions, and I think that's exciting. I think it's going to present the Churches with a fundamental challenge in the days to come.

The other challenge facing the Anglican Church is how we, as clergy, view our role. The clergy are definitely not dying out as a breed: what is happening is that we're changing, and I think we've *got* to change. The 'one-man-band' ministry, the priest who goes around trying to fool himself and others that he is the only person that matters, the 'persona' in the parish – he is obsolete, and thank God for that. We need people now who are going to come from the congregation to serve the people that he or she represents. There will always be room for the ordained representative, but that representative must be *truly* representa-tive and allow others to exercise their own ministries. So in the next few years I think we can expect more and more changes in the ordained ministry. I hope an increasing number of people will be non-stipendiary, because we don't necessarily need more paid people: in fact it may actually be a genuine advantage to encourage more people to be ordained who also work outside the Church. The non-stipendiary minister has been a feature of our Church for at least fifteen years now, but there are still not enough of them.

Now you can say, who really cares, and it's true that relatively few people go to church, given the population as a whole, but then what are we actually talking about when we say, 'going to church'? What we see at the moment are changing patterns of churchgoing. There may be fewer who are committed to church-going on a regular basis, but you can say the same for so many other things in life. Life is so much more complex and competitive than it used to be. Where the Church used to be the only real social cohesion, now this is no longer the case. Nevertheless, more people go to church on a Sunday than go to Association Football, so there's still a healthy number of people who are committed to worship; and there's a larger number of people who go occasionally, once or twice a year, maybe more than that. There are all those who come for the occasional Offices like weddings and baptisms; those who encounter the Church in many different forms; through schools, for example. I sometimes go into schools where there will be assembly with maybe fifty or sixty parents entering into school worship, and I often tease them and say, 'You've been to church today,' and they don't realize that that's going to church. But there is a lot of room for growth, a lot of room for growth.

You mentioned the need to attract people of different ethnic backgrounds to the Church. That's a very important subject, actually, though it's not as bad as what you describe: there are some very *significant* black leaders in the Anglican Church, and there are a growing number of younger black Anglicans coming through. I mean, we have got one black bishop, and I would confidently expect that in the next few years we'll be seeing others moving into leadership.

The Committee for Black Anglican Concerns is also doing a wonderful job, and it's certainly true that when I travel the Anglican Communion, which is much larger than the Church of England itself, I'm meeting people like Desmond Tutu, who is just one among many black leaders in the Anglican Communion, and they're making the running now. I mean, I truly believe that as we go into the next century we'll be seeing – with the decline of Western Christianity – that the significant centres of Christianity are going to shift from Rome, Geneva and Canterbury to places in the Third World, to South America, the States, the Far East – certainly Africa.

However, it is true that I belong to a generation which can well remember the kind of Anglo-Saxon, Anglican Christianity of the fifties and sixties where there were no black people around to speak of; and when the West Indians came over in huge numbers in the fifties and sixties, many of them were practising and joyful Anglicans who wanted to join the Church of England, and they actually got a very cold welcome. Cold weather, cold worship, cold welcome. So they went off in discouragement and founded Pentecostal Churches. That's why black Christianity is booming in Churches like the New Testament Church of God, and other black churches, where gospel music is buoyant, and the message joyful. In fact one of the things I'm trying to do is to bring back an emphasis on black Anglicans and the nature of black music in the Church of England. That will come, I'm sure. It will.

How? Well, you see, the nature of the Church of England is such that while I and John Habgood may have plenty of influence, we have very little power. We do take practical measures, but we can't just deliver pronouncements. In the Church of England we have a democratic process of arriving at our decisions. Sometimes in frustration I would like to be able to say, 'I want so and so,' and click my fingers and change something. And maybe it's a very good thing that the Church is protected from the likes of me! But basically, the names of black clergy are coming through for the posts of bishops, and we make sure they're considered carefully, and we hope and pray that the right people will be chosen for the right job.

What we have to remember, and what is really good, is that we're no longer a monochrome nation and culture, and we've got a lot to gain from the richness of diversity. We've got a lot to gain from rubbing shoulders with people of different cultures and people with no beliefs, or strange beliefs, or bizarre beliefs, or orthodox beliefs. That's a real challenge, and that sort of contact will help to sharpen up the nature of the Christian faith, because challenge and collision have that effect. Secondly, it means that the kind of Christianity we promote is going to be more sharply honed by encounter, and therefore will be much more sensitive: evangelism will be less aggressive and less fundamentalist, because it will be shaped by real encounter with people. So I think the fact that our society is more pluralistic in every way than it has ever been is going to be very good for the Christian Church. When I go travelling around the world, I meet other Anglicans who have got greater experience of this kind of challenge and diversity than we have. We've got a lot to learn from them.

I said in Synod when we voted to ordain women to the priesthood, I said I really thought that that was going to be the most important element of my archiepiscopate, and the greatest hurdle for us to cross as a Church. As soon as I received the Coopers and Lybrand Report on the Church Commissioners earlier this year, I realized I was wrong. The Church Commissioners are spending more than they can properly afford. This is the most important challenge facing me and the Church in the nineties. How we face up to it is going to be very significant.

When we realized how much money we had lost – and even if it's not as much as the £800 million often quoted, it's still a lot of money – when we realized this, I started up an investigation into the loss. Now, it's quite clear that although there has most certainly been mismanagement by the Church Commissioners, there has been no criminal behaviour whatsover. So many businesses have collapsed through the recession. You can't point to any business which has not suffered, and the Church, because of its huge investments, was likely to take a pounding. There have been suggestions that there's been a cover-up and that someone is to blame for this, but that's not the case. It has not been covered up, it isn't a whitewash. It is very clear that no one in particular is to blame.

One has to remember, though, that for many years the Church Commissioners were doing very well and very few people were giving them credit for that. We're apt to forget the good years, when they were investing successfully, and there were good years. The eighties were good years for the Church, when you think of car loans for clergy, when you think of the amount of money spent on vicarages and the updating of them.

We're now having seven famine years, to use an illustration from the story of Joseph, and I actually think that this period will lead to a much healthier Church. We've relied too much on the past, and it's now time for the living Church to be responsible for its own life in a way that it has never been before. Giving of money from congregations has got to go up, and it's going to be a tremendous strain. But, you know, even if that hadn't happened, even if we hadn't lost that money, we would still be facing the same set of questions, in that we cannot go on indefinitely living off the past, because that money was getting less and less. And with more and more clergy living longer, we're spending out much more money on pensions – and you can't have it both ways. The money's coming from the same pot: wages for clergy, pensions for the retired.

So without excusing the problems, we have to say that this creates a *major* challenge for the Church of England, and it's one that we're going to face with confidence and hope. It's going to be rocky for the next few years, but I think that people will turn the corner in a few years' time. Maybe when I read your book in five years' time I'll flinch and say, 'Did I *really* say that?' but I think the Church *will* come through this. We all tend to be pessimistic actually, and we always fear the worst. So I think maybe we can say about our financial situation, 'Yes, it seems bad now,' but in five years' time we'll be looking back and saying, 'We're a healthier Church.'

In the meantime there's a lot to do. I don't know how long I'll be in this job but I'd like to see some of these problems through, and I'm sure I will. What I would hope to achieve before then – okay, now this is a big question – what I would hope is that as Archbishop of Canterbury I don't fail. I think in my retirement I'd most like to be able to look back and say to myself: under God we're a much more confident Church now. We're still the national Church; we're involved in every parish in the country. Now we have men and women working together in the ordained ministry and they're effective. We as a Church are growing, and we're much more accountable: priests are accountable to their Bishops, and everyone knows that they've got an incentive to have more people come into confirmation and baptism. We're more outward-looking, we're more integrated with our society. We got over those wretched problems to do with money in 1993 and 1994, and now we're much more self-sufficient. And isn't it marvellous that we now seem to be moving towards full unity with the Methodists and the Baptists and the Roman Catholics, that we're actually one Church of Jesus Christ in this land? Isn't it good the relationship we have still with the Government, which is of a critical, creative kind? And of course we still have questions about the establishment of the Church of England, but then that's been going on for 150 years. I'd also like to look back and see that we've got over our problems to do with the ordination of women, that all the fears surrounding the issue have disappeared, even though we'll be facing new ones, because the Church will never reach a position where it's complacent – it's always got new challenges to face.

As I look ahead, the challenges facing the Church of the future are going to be the AIDS pandemic, and global ecological problems, both of which are going to get even worse than they are now. There will be grinding poverty in the world communities. We're going to see an alarming increase of the world population: Bangladesh is likely to be 270 million people by the year 2020. The earth will be exhausted. I don't think anyone can be sanguine about the twenty-first century. An increasing number of very able people who know the world situation are beginning to fear that a third World War is a real possibility. So there's no doubt that the twenty-first century is going to be an unnerving period for, amongst others, the next Archbishop of Canterbury.

There's no question that I find the life of 'brief encounters' a frustration at times, no question about it. And yet at the same time, because I believe that this is the kind of work that God has called me to, I put up with it – and more than that, I enjoy it. I mean, it's great fun. But I do sometimes wish I could stay put in a place for a little longer and see what's going on, and get to know people. Of course it is exhilarating to travel the world and meet people and see clear evidence of the growth of the Christian Church, and to encounter genuinely good people who are doing wonderful jobs. Of course it's exciting to enter briefly into the political life of a country and see what's going on. But yes, it can be very superficial, and at times it's only the adrenalin that keeps you going.

I do recognize that there is a danger of becoming superficial myself as a result. Yes, I do. But for someone such as myself, well, I suppose people in the Church have got this great advantage in that for us the spiritual life is all-important, and therefore spending time in meditation and prayer is a priority. I work hard at that, and I think I've learnt more about the grace of God in the two and a half years I've been doing this job than in all the years before. I spend more time now in prayer than I used to because I realize I need the quietness and the meditation. The second thing is that my life in ministry actually does revolve around certain pillars. Evangelism and mission is one great pillar. Issues to do with human dignity, human nature, poverty, justice – that's another great pillar. That means that there's a commonality about so many of the things I'm doing or discussing wherever I travel in the world, like issues of justice for women, or freedom of the individual. There are great thrusts of commonality wherever I go, which means I actually avoid the kind of internal erosion you're talking about. At least, I haven't experienced it as yet. But I'm well aware of the danger, and I shall watch out for that. I shall.

Can I mention something on this? I get very alarmed when I talk to my political colleagues and some of them tell me they're not reading books – that they're too busy to read books. Now, I read fifty pages a day, every day, I commit myself to it; so in addition to all the reports I've got to read, I'm reading a biography of Harold Wilson, plus another couple of biographies too. I've got two or three books on the go, and every day whenever there's a spare five minutes – and you can read ten pages in five minutes, you know – I read. Unless you actually feed yourself that way, you are going to waste away inside.

I think that that's something the early years have instilled in me. I remember the moment in theological college very well when I realized everyone was drinking coffee all around me, and other things too, that people were wasting time. And I worked out that in fact I could save at least two hours a week by cutting short that time of coffee following the evening meal – so I did. I was able to spend it reading, and I was able to get ahead of the pack. But my love of reading is genuine: it arises from a great desire to do so. My thirst for knowledge doesn't arise from a fear of not having it: I just find life fascinating, and I've always had a genuine desire to learn – I love it. But I've always controlled my time, been disciplined about my learning, because I believe it's deeply important.

The discipline has stood me in good stead for this job, because it's so exhausting. We're doing a lot of work here on our timetable, because, as I'm sure you're aware, there's not enough space, there's too much going on, and the problem with too much going on is that you can end up cutting corners: and sometimes the corners are cut so tightly that there's the risk of turning over the vehicle. So I think that's something we've got to face up to here at Lambeth, but we've got a very good team here, so it's not a problem.

My relationship with John Habgood is also a very good one. He was my bishop in Durham when I was a vicar, and I must say there was some fear in me at becoming Archbishop of Canterbury when I was still a very new bishop. I wondered, how will John be able to cope with this? And when, as Bishop of Bath and Wells, I was asked who I would like to see as Archbishop of Canterbury, without any hesitation I said John Habgood. It wasn't to be, but he has given me tremendous affirmation, tremendous support, and because of that I'm never actually worried about working with someone of that ability, because he's very, very able indeed, isn't he? You'll have found that, I'm sure. So I say to myself, 'Well, it's all right because we're on the same side. I'm batting No. 1, and he's batting No. 2, but we're not batting against one another.' Despite what the papers might say, why should I be envious or reluctant about somebody who's able? Because as long as he's working with me that's great.

So all in all I love the job, I really do. Both Eileen and I enjoy the work enormously. She's very happy too, though she would make the complaint that there's not enough time for the family. Yesterday our daughter Lizzie gave birth to her first child. It so happened that we were able to get off the plane at five-thirty in the morning from Singapore, come here, have a shower, phone her to find out she was having the baby, jump into the car, go to Bristol, see her, and come back here for an evening engagement. Now, if it'd happened a few hours later, I would not have been able to get across there – not for days. So thank God for that.

Do you know, I think my background has equipped me very well for this job. One good thing about being brought up in the East End of London and Dagenham in Essex was that we were quite familiar with hardship. Most people from that situation have so many knocks right from a very early age. I mean, the war years scarred so many people: you had so many impressions of vulnerability and suffering. Now, I had the great advantage of having a very secure home life with a mother and father who were deeply caring indeed, and they secured us from any sort of damage that might have occurred to us. We were not allowed to grow up to be *hard* people – gentleness and compassion were very, very important in the family – but we were never inured from the real knocks of life, never inured from disappointment and failure. And all these things, all the disappointments in life, either end up equipping you, or they destroy you. And I like to think they've equipped me.

But of course constant reflection on what you're doing is important too, and you have to say, 'If there's basis for people's criticism of me, then I've got to learn from it.' And sometimes facing up to criticism is very painful, especially when it means confronting yourself. It's like listening to yourself for the first time on a tape-recorder: it's always awful, isn't it? But then you get used to it, and it's only if you're prepared to look at yourself on the television screen and see yourself as you are, warts and all, that you can say: okay, that's what I am. Can I do any better? If the criticism is unfair and unworthy, why should you allow it to burn a hole within you?

As far as I'm concerned, when the going gets tough I keep my sanity by saying, 'I'm accountable to God and His vision for me; and I'm also accountable to the Church. I must do my job to the best of my ability. I'm not accountable to the newspapers or to what other people think.' You have to hold on to that, hold on to belief in yourself. The moment that goes, you really are destroyed.

I've really enjoyed this. *Thank* you. Anything else you need to know, don't hesitate to get in touch, will you? I mean that. Anything at all. I'm only sorry we couldn't have more time.

CHARLES LAWRENCE

Age: 40
Age at ordination: 24

VICAR OF ASHTON–UNDER–LYNE, MANCHESTER

When I first met Charles Lawrence he was in a state. He was so late back to his house, following a visit to a parishioner, that I wondered whether I had got the week, let alone the time or the day, of our appointment wrong. When he finally returned to find me on his doorstep, inappropriately clad for the Manchester wind-chill, he seemed so distracted and ill at ease that I nearly offered to go straight home to London and return another time.

It took the length of time for Charles Lawrence to unlock his front door and get safely inside his house to find out what the matter was. He was in his last week as Vicar of Ashton-under-Lyne before moving to a parish a few miles away, and he was in turmoil. He felt bereft, sad, confused, neither here nor there. He showed me to my room, made some tea and took it through to the sitting-room. There the floodgates opened. He told me how much his present parish meant to him and how he didn't have a clue what sort of ministry he was going to have in the next one. He said he'd never thought he could mind so much about a place and its people, but he didn't think he'd felt this bad since his father had died. 'They never prepare you for the bereavement of it all,' he said. 'No one tells you how much you're going to mind when you leave a parish. It's awful. I can't describe it. But I feel like someone's died.'

Charles Lawrence is a rather beautiful man. He has large, mournful brown eyes and a very fit figure. His hair is short on top and at the sides, but he has grown a pony tail at the back, which sounds odd but looks good. He moves with extraordinary grace and his physical presence could be immensely powerful, but it is instead a little muted, as if he is trying to hide or deny something of himself. Simply dressed in jeans and a maroon sweatshirt, he sat very still throughout the

277

interviews, and nearly all expression and gesticulation were confined to his voice and eyes. He was very polite and seemed vulnerable, though by no means weak. He was quiet, firm and unassuming.

When his wife and children returned home in the evening, a lighter and more frivolous side of Charles Lawrence soon became apparent. He is a great raconteur and a good cook, with a love of alternative comedy, music and motorbikes. Before I left his home we paid brief homage to the motorbike in his garage, and he even offered to take me to the station on it, but by the time we got organized it was too late and too wet. As someone with a fondness for motorbikes, and my experience confined mainly to a bone-shaking trip across Bengal with my boyfriend on a battered old Enfield 350, having to turn down a smooth ride on a funky Suzuki 600 was almost impossible to bear. Fortunately, and very kindly, Charles Lawrence insisted that I return as soon as possible for a trip across the Pennine Way. I did not need much persuading.

CHARLES LAWRENCE

Daddy was born in Mauritius of Indian parents. It's quite a strange story, and some members of the family tell it differently, so I don't know whether this is totally accurate, but the story that Daddy told me was that his father was born in Hyderabad in India, to a Muslim family. Daddy would have been nearly eighty now, and his father was sixty when he was born, so we're talking about 130-odd years ago. My grandfather was kidnapped and taken from Hyderabad to Mauritius by an uncle who had had a feud with his father. He was then left in Mauritius, and the uncle returned to India without him, and Grandfather was brought up by Christian missionaries. He became a Christian, and took Lawrence as his Christian name: his name was Lawrence Saiboo.

Grandfather became a catechist, and the story that I've received is that he spoke twelve or thirteen languages, because his argument was that you couldn't speak to people about Jesus unless you spoke in their language, because the language held the culture, which held the philosophy, which held the thought patterns. He must have been years ahead of his time, because that sort of thought didn't occur to people until much, much later. His wife also was a catechist, and they were very, very poor.

Before the war Daddy was going to train as a priest, but when the war began he was conscripted, and he fought in the North African desert, where he was captured by the Germans and marched to Paris. He came to England after the war and went to the Continental Exchange at Blackfriars, which is where a lot of people who are from other parts of the world came to, because they had a language skill and could use it. Daddy's first language was French, and he learned English when he went to school, but he didn't have the facility that Grandfather had. That died with him.

In those days you couldn't put calls from continental Europe straight through, you had to go in stages, and hop across from one place to another; so when there were calls going through to Dublin, they would go through London, and from Dublin to wherever else it was that they wanted to connect to in Ireland. Daddy was utterly charming. He was utterly charming in the flesh, but he was also utterly charming over the phone, and as telephonists will, he would recognize people's voices. He recognized my mother's voice, who was also a telephonist in Dublin, and they began to correspond. I'm not sure how it happened, but he went to Dublin to meet her, and before he did, he wrote to her and said that she must realize that he was black, and he would quite understand if it was inconvenient, or something else had turned up, and she didn't want him to come.

They got married, and the story is awful. They were married in a church in Dublin, St George's Church. My grandmother, my mother's mother, was the only one of the family that attended the wedding. When they came home, my great-grandmother, who had a greengrocer business, supplied all the family with rotten fruit and vegetables to pelt them with, and cursed my mother as she left; which is a very powerful thing to do in Ireland, and we are talking about 1949. She said something like, 'Any sons she had would be thieves, if they were as good as that, and any daughters would be prostitutes, and worse.'

My parents left Ireland and came to England, which was almost as bad, because in the late forties black people and white people didn't marry. They lived in Brixton Hill, and it was a fairly difficult existence. Daddy really didn't want them to have children, because he knew what it had been like for him, and he didn't want his children to have to go through that, but they did. My sister Margaret was born in 1952, and I was born in 1953.

As a child I experienced a lot of nastiness, persecution, the inexplicable reactions of adults to me. At the time I just accepted it, because I was brought up to have respect for older people and to do what I was told. They were little things, but in our church primary school you either spent two years in the second to top class, or you spent two years in the top class. I spent two years in the top class, and I was the only person in the school called by their surname. I was never Charles, I was always Lawrence, and I was made to sit at a six-foot desk by myself, because I couldn't be trusted to sit next to somebody.

When I did the eleven-plus, instead of being congratulated on getting a good result, which I obviously did, the headmaster wanted me in his study to explain who I had cheated from, because my mark was so high I must have cheated. After that I never sat closer than ten feet to anybody, so that it was impossible for me to be accused of cheating. I never went to the toilet during the day at school because I dared not go into the boys' loo, because I would have been beaten up. I used to get beaten up in the playground, and if I was caught being beaten up I would be caned, because obviously I must have started it.

It was a peculiar existence, because Mummy was very middle-class, and so was Daddy, but most of the people at the school weren't, and Mummy was convinced that we were too good to play out with the children around, for fear of what we might pick up. But then the other children didn't want to play with any niggers anyway, so we lived a fairly weird, isolated life. I still really don't know very much about children. I mean, I've learnt a lot through being in this parish, particularly with the children in the school, and of course through having my own, but we didn't grow up with children.

There had been black people in England for hundreds of years, obviously, but the idea that Brixton was awash with black people then is absolute nonsense. I do remember a chap called Vivien Weathers, who came when I was about eight or nine, and he was the first boy from the Caribbean islands who had come to our school. Honey and Bunny Nerula were Indian, and came probably the year before that, but they had very rich parents, the father was a doctor or something, and they lived further up Streatham. So I wasn't surrounded by black people at all.

Daddy had this phrase, 'When you're a man, my son, then you will understand.' He used to tell me all sorts of things, and then the tag would be, 'And when you're a man, my son, then you will understand.' There are loads of things: like sitting on the end of your child's bed and almost weeping, because you love them so much. When parents say things like, 'I'm telling you off, but this hurts me more than it hurts you,' you think that it's a load of old cobblers, but then you have a child and you want only the best for them, and you can't stop them from getting into situations where they get hurt or make mistakes, and it does hurt you more than it hurts them.

As I've grown older, I have begun to understand, but I've also begun to say, 'No, that was unreasonable behaviour. There was no excuse for that.' I had a very, very retentive memory, and one day Mr Pamment, who was the teacher who called me Lawrence all the time, gave us this poem, which was a three-stanza poem and filled a foolscap side of paper. The first person to memorize the first verse would get a prize; the person to memorize the second verse would get a prize; and the same with the third verse. I read it through, and I thought, I could do that. So I waited about ten or fifteen minutes, because I thought, I'll only get into trouble if I say I can do it, and then I put my hand up.

'Yes?'

'Can I do the poem, please, sir?'

'Which verse, Lawrence?'

'Well, I wanted to do all three.'

'Get out!'

So I was sent into the corridor outside the room, which was also outside the head teacher's office, and I pretended that I was re-arranging books on the bookshelves, for fear that he would discover I had been sent out. I was called in again at the end of the lesson. 'I suppose Lawrence thinks he can remember one of the verses.' So I recited the whole thing and the teacher was furious, and I got one of the prizes, which I still have somewhere.

Now I went from that to failing my O-levels. For years I told myself it was because I didn't work, because I wasted time, or daydreamed. Now, as an adult, I think, 'How come you failed?' When I was at primary school I was desperate to come home for lunches, because I was literally a nervous wreck. I was jittering all the time, I couldn't keep still, it was just the pressure of being there. I couldn't take the pressure of being at school all day long with the amount of bombardment that was coming from the teachers, from the pupils; the names that I was called, being beaten up, the manifest unfairness of it. I tried to be good and it didn't work. So I tried to keep a low profile and that didn't work. It just kept on happening, and I thought, at least I'm going to secondary school now, and it's a new place, and they don't know me.

At secondary school I was put in the second stream to start with, but after the first term, when I got 90 per cent in all of the exams, I was put in the top stream. I then started coming across teachers who would ridicule me again for getting things right. We'd had a music exam, and I got 96 per cent. I ended up with 67 per cent. A chap in the class watched the music master changing the marks and said, 'Why have you changed Lawrence's marks?' He said, 'I'm not having *him* come first.' There was also a Latin master who used to ridicule me for getting 20 out of 20 for Latin tests, and eventually I learned that I would get into less trouble for getting things wrong than I got into trouble for getting things right. I mean, there's always more to a story than one person's version, but I now know that that was totally unreasonable; that there was no excuse for a teacher treating a child like that.

As I got older, it got worse. I perfected the art of getting things wrong, and I ended up with one O-level, an E in English, and I was very, very good at English before that. All the others I failed, some of them quite dramatically. Physics, Chemistry and Biology I flunked in a major way; but History, French and Divinity, there's no reason why I should have flunked those, especially as Daddy spoke French at home. I took them again and got some in the fifth year, and then I started A-levels. I wanted to read English at university, because I love English and I was quite good at it, but I thought there was no point in putting down English, because with my O-level results they'd not even entertain me. I put down Theology instead, because all my life I have known that I was going to be a priest. I had it all worked out. I thought I'd go to university, read English, and then perhaps tour the world in a rock group, because I played piano and wanted to have a band. Or at the worst I'd join the Civil Service and have enough money to go on holidays and do things, without too strenuous a life. Then when I was thirty I would get married, go to theological college, and at thirty-three, or whatever, I would be ordained, and that would be it!

So anyway, I filled in my university application form. The master who wrote my recommendation from the school said to me, 'Don't worry, Charles, because although your O-level results are pretty abysmal, when you get your interview you will shine in the interview, you will get a place.' Well, one day I happened to need to see a Maths master, who was the chap who collated all of the university application forms. I was waiting outside his room at the end of a lesson, and the pile of forms was on the floor outside; confidential forms, I shouldn't have touched them. Makowski's was the top one, and I knew that if Makowski's was on top, mine was the next one down. I picked it out and I read what that master had put. The first sentence was, 'Under no circumstance should Charles Lawrence be given a place at university, as he is totally incapable of sustained hard work.' And this was the man who had told me I would shine! I didn't even get an interview. So things like that have happened, and you can say, well, the guy was fed up with me – but there were a lot of other things going on.

I didn't know what racism was, intellectually. I only experienced it every day. Racism is something that people haven't talked about until fairly recently, although people like me have grown up with it. The thing that I say to so many black people is, 'You may be black, but at least you have a country that you belong to.' I have no country that I belong to, except here, and yet people here always want to know where I come from. When I say I was born in London, they say, 'Yes, but where do you *really* come from?' And that makes me feel as if I have no home, as if being black and English doesn't count. I can't walk into a room and have people think, 'There's another English person.' Now, I'm not black as the ace of spades, as they say, but my skin tone is not white, and people always think I'm not English. If I came from Barbados, or Antigua, or Bombay, I would have a culture, I would have a language, I would have family, I would have places that I knew, where I was the same as everybody else. Yet the only thing that I have ever experienced here – which *is* my home – is being an alien. Now, that doesn't account for all the people who have been lovely to me, the people who have been very close and very dear friends, but, as I say, racism is what I experienced but didn't recognize at the time.

I got into university. I was accepted to read Theology at King's College, London. I'm sure it was because the deputy headmaster of my school actually said something good about me. He put down that I was good at dramatics, that I played rugby for the school, that I was captain of athletics, and after all that he put, 'And Charles has for many years spoken of a desire to be ordained a priest in the Church of England.' That was picked up by the Dean of King's, Sidney Evans – Smooth Sid, we called him – and Smooth Sid interviewed me and went out of his way to make sure I got a place. He was a remarkable man.

I was accepted to study for a Bachelor of Divinity, and for something called the Associate of King's College – the one being a degree, the other being a diploma. You studied both for the first year, then at the end of the first year you either did one or the other, or both. The received wisdom was that the AKC is the eqivalent of a Bachelor of Theology, but the BD is actually a higher first degree. I just about scraped through to do the AKC, but I certainly didn't do well enough to do the BD, so I carried on with the AKC alone.

I passed my exams at King's and went to St Augustine's theological college in Canterbury for a fourth year of training before ordination. I was very distressed by it, because I wanted to be trained to be a priest. I didn't want to be trained to be a third-rate social worker, and they didn't seem to know what they were training us for. The other problem was that I've always found Western philosophy banal, and I didn't know why. I never bothered to get into it at any depth at college, because it just seemed facile to me. I couldn't understand people spending so much time putting up an argument, only for somebody else, a little bit later on, to counter their argument. I thought this was just a brain exercise, not actually geting to the root of things. What I now recognize is that I had imbibed far more Asian-ness through my father than I thought I had. I think I always thought of him as a European because he spoke French, and I didn't see him as being an Indian, because I didn't know his parents. But I now realize that he was much more Indian than I had ever thought, and that I had inherited that.

The man responsible for looking after me throughout my training, my Diocesan Director of Ordinands, was a wonderful, wonderful man called Canon Tasker. He was huge, six foot two or three, with a great big belly on him like Friar Tuck, and always had a hugely stained cassock; a lovely, lovely man. Just before I was due to be ordained, I had this very strange phone call from Derek Tasker. He rang me up and said, 'Charles, how are you?' I said, 'Fine. Why? Shouldn't I be?' He said, 'Has the Bishop phoned you?' so I said, 'No.' 'Has the Bishop written to you?' 'No.' 'Have you received your post?' 'Yes.' 'You're sure there isn't a letter from the Bishop?' 'No, there isn't a letter from the Bishop.' 'Right,' he said. 'You are to put the phone down and come and see me immediately. If the phone rings you are not to answer it, do you understand me? You are not to answer the phone, under any circumstances.' So I got on the number 37 bus, went to Richmond to see him, and he said, 'We've had a very disturbing report from the college at Canterbury.'

Now I knew some of the things that had been said about me at Canterbury, and they were lies, and they came out of the imagination of one or two people. Which is not to say that I wasn't a fairly bolshie member of college, because I was. I did things like ride a motorbike around the dovecote in the middle of the college courtyard: I used to smoke large cigars and not take a great deal of interest in what was going on. Part of that was the bravado of 'We're only going to be normal human beings for another few months, and then we're going to wear dog-collars and everything will change.' Yet no small part of it was that I just couldn't relate to what they were telling us as we were training to be priests. It didn't make sense to me.

So I said to Derek Tasker, 'Well, what's in this report?' He said, 'I can't tell you, it's confidential. Would you like a cup of coffee?' I thought, I can't cope with this conversation, it's leaping around all over the place. It later transpired that the reason I couldn't answer the phone was that Derek Tasker was terrified that the Bishop would phone me up and say, 'I'm not ordaining you,' and that once he'd said that, that would be it. Derek thought that if he could see me first, maybe there was something he could do, maybe it could be sorted out. So he said, 'I'm going into the kitchen to make some coffee, it will take me fifteen minutes. I won't come back until it's made. I'll just put this report down here.' Then he put it on the coffee table and just turned it towards me.

So I read it. And when I wasn't screwing all the girls in the next-door teacher training college, I was buggering all the men in my college; I was the leader of a small and very unpleasant coterie who were totally exclusive and disruptive in college, and various other things besides. I was a total waster, according to this report. If it had been sent to me I could have made a fortune out of it, suing the guy who wrote it.

When I was at Canterbury I had a couple of close friendships with girls in the teacher training college, but I also knew two-thirds of the students there by name, men and women, and I spent hours with loads of different people. There were a lot of lonely people at that college; young guys who would come and would desperately want to meet a girl, but they didn't know how to, and they were just getting more and more depressed; young men and women who had left a girlfriend or a boyfriend at home and were lonely. I used to sit with lots of these people for hours and hours, talking with them. I also played rugby for their Fifteen, and was voted player of the year. I was in a blues band. I was basically a regular guy, I really was.

And yet this – this *rubbish* – had been written about me. When Derek came back with the coffee I spoke to him about it, and he believed me. The priest that was going to take me as his assistant curate, a man called Colin Pritchard, had apparently seen this report too and his response was, 'I've met him, I stand by the interview I had with him. If he fouls up, it's down to me.' Now, that's an incredible thing for anybody to say, because I was his first curate, and he might never have got another one. So for all that there were people who were pretty awful to me, there were some who were quite wonderful.

I've said to myself that I will call that man from Canterbury a bastard to his face one day, but he probably doesn't even remember me. There were several people each year whose lives he would almost destroy. He had it in for different people every year, not just me; and there are plenty of reasons why he would have disliked me, and maybe I wasn't very easy – but maybe some of it was stereotyping as well, maybe some of it was sheer prejudice. It certainly meant that I almost wasn't ordained. I think it's only the hand of God that made sure that I was.

I met my wife when I was at King's. The Dean of women students, Dr Helen Hudson, told a friend of mine that she was having the first year ladies together for a weekend so they could get to know each other before term began. She thought they would be fairly bored by the end of the weekend, and could he find some 'safe' men to do an entertainment. My friend asked me if I would go over with Chris Bard – who was the guy I played blues with – and do some stuff. So Chris and I went and did a couple of sketches, and I played piano and he played harp. I'd just got this tail-suit in a jumble sale for 2s and 6d, with beautifully fitted trousers that were about ten yards wide in the leg, and I put those on over a pair of jeans, just for effect, and half-way through the set I took them off.

This caused quite a stir – as it had been intended to do. You see, Chris and I had a competition as to who would not only meet the most girls, but who would find out their names, and remember their names, and see how many of them would actually speak to us on the first day of term, which was the following Wednesday. So we were both of us going rapidly round all these young women, and I hadn't actually spoken to Prune at that stage, but after we had done our set we all went to the bar, and Prune was sitting there with a girl called Sue. So I sat down and started talking with them. Then I bumped into her on the first day of term; then the second day of term; then the third day of term, and the fourth day, and so it went on.

I had a very good figure when I was at King's and Canterbury because I was very fit. When I went to King's it was the first time in my life that I realized that women would find me attractive. I had grown up thinking that I was so ugly, and so unacceptable, that I would never get married. I wanted to, but I really believed that I would never get married, because who would ever want to be seen with me? When you have been called the names that I was called, and people had said the things that they had said to me, that's more or less understandable. And given that I had led a fairly sheltered life, and hadn't gone out, and didn't have friends, and didn't go to parties . . . well, it's not surprising. In fact it's only fairly recently that I thought, 'This has gone on too long. I'm not ugly. The face I've got is the face I've got.'

At King's and Canterbury I did a lot of flirting, and it really staggered me that women would actually respond to me. I was amazed. But when I met Prune I didn't even have the confidence to ask her out. We used to go to Twinings, for tea and coffee, at break-times and things like that, but I thought that was only coincidence, that she needed a cup of coffee. It didn't occur to me she actually fancied me too. Then one day, when Chris and I were arranging to go to a blues club, Prune said, 'Oh, I like blues. Could I come too?' And that was the first time we went out together. After that it just rolled along, and we got married.

She's called Prune because Chris Bard invited us to a meal at his flat in Vauxhall. There was hardly any furniture, just a couple of bits. He'd invited the two of us and someone else, and we were going to have a meal, but he hadn't actually got the food, so he and I went to the local supermarket. I've always been a reasonably frivolous person, and I saw this tin of prunes on the shelf, and I said, 'I'm going to buy those for Loraine' – which is her real name. They were 6½p, very cheap, very nice, and Chris and I agreed that they'd do just the job.

So I came back with this tin of prunes, and Prune – Loraine – was sitting in this winged armchair, which was the only armchair in the entire place. I leaned over and I said, 'Close your eyes and open your hands, I've got a present for you,' and dropped this tin of prunes into her hands. It was the first present I'd given her. Okay, it was a fairly bizarre present, but it was a present. She took them home and her father said, 'Has Charles been buying you presents, then?' and she said, 'Yes, I think he loves me.' After that she was always known as Prune.

I never wanted to be a priest. It's like saying you are going to be sixty one day. Most people, even at forty as I am now, don't want to be sixty tomorrow, but it's inevitable, and by the time you reach fifty-nine you are almost ready for it. It was like that with me: I just knew what God wanted me to do, that that's what I was born for, and that I would be a priest.

I have never not known the presence of God. I know that other people have known the absence of God, or just haven't believed in God at all, and I have to try and get inside that, otherwise I can't serve them. But God has sustained me all the way through my life. When I was about nine, we went to church on Good Friday, and we had a preached three hours –

which is an old tradition; the priest preaches for three hours like a sort of vigil – and I distinctly remember being desperately upset and saying to Mummy, 'I can't go, I can't bear it, I can't bear that God came, and we killed him.' I just couldn't bear to think about us killing God, because I knew Him and loved Him, and He was real and He talked to me. I now recognize that within me there is a deep experience of being persecuted for not having done anything, and an identification with that sort of suffering. I mean, I wasn't perfect by any means, I did loads of things that people should have been rightly upset about and annoyed about, but a lot of it was just the colour of my skin.

I always knew that when I was a priest I would do the preached three hours and the all-night vigil in Holy Week. I knew it would just be a drop in a million oceans, but that if there was any way that I could say to Jesus, 'We care about what you did,' then I would do it. And even if everybody fell asleep, at least I'd try to keep awake just a little bit longer. On Maundy Thursday we go into church at five and come out the following morning at eight, and then on Good Friday we always have a preached three hours. To preach for the better part of three hours takes a lot of concentration, but I do it for Jesus, I don't care if nobody comes. I said to the congregation one year, 'I could bore you rigid for three hours, and we would still not have the faintest notion of what it was like for Jesus.'

There have been a couple of years – there was one year in particular – when I have had spiritual experiences, when I have seen a purple light. It doesn't happen very often, but when it does it is as if God is right there. That particular year I had been struggling with Good Friday, and trying to think what the theme should be, and I had picked readings, but I couldn't get anything together. I thought, 'On Maundy Thursday I will meditate and it will come to me,' and nothing happened. It got to the point in the service where I had to preach, and I sat in the chair behind the altar, which is where I preach from, and suddenly the purple light was just there. And the effect it has on me . . . I shake, and the tears just stream down. It's like all the power in the world is just almost within hands' reach, and you can feel it. It almost makes me cry just to describe it to you. And I thought, 'Why do you worry? You're not supposed to be saying what you think: you're supposed to be speaking the word of God, and God is here, so open your mouth.' And I did.

It's that sort of awareness of the presence of God, and the power of God, that I've known always. I used to have terrible nightmares as a child. I used to wake up screaming and rigid with fear. We had an irregularly patterned wallpaper in the bedroom, and I used to see all sorts of horrible things in it. When I woke up from a nightmare I didn't want to close my eyes again because I would go into this terrible dream, and I couldn't keep my eyes open because I would see the wallpaper with the horrible shadowy forms looking at me. So I would say the Lord's Prayer, and then I could go to sleep. That happened over and over again. Nobody had told me to say the Lord's Prayer, I just knew that if I called on Jesus's name that he was there and I would be all right.

I was a very disturbed child. The nightmares went on for years. I said earlier on about feeling an alien, and as a Christian that can be a gift, because God has never promised that you won't have pain. He has promised that He will be with you when you are in pain, but he never promised that you would be without it. Millions of other people have experienced much, much worse things than I did, and not everybody treated me like shit, but plenty of people told me I was shit, and because of that I heard their voices. I didn't hear the other people telling me not to listen. When you are a small child and people call you names and adults treat you in a particular way, then you assume that that's because of who you *are*. And one of the things that it left me with was a desire to serve people: I knew that if I came across other people who had had similar experiences, or were being treated badly, that I wanted to do something about it; that I at least would not do that to them.

I did a little bit of teaching at a prep school up the road here. I taught Christianity and I was asked by the headmaster to set an exam. One particular boy, who was a Muslim, I put on his report something like, 'It was a delight to have him in the class.' He was a lovely, lovely boy. He worked so hard, and was so charming, if I could have given him 150 per cent I would have done. His mother stopped me outside the school and said she couldn't believe that a Christian priest would write that about a Muslim boy.

There was another little boy who happened to be Jewish, and was very, very quiet. Always had his head down; the sort of boy nobody would ever remember. I called him out to the front several times, to praise him for a piece of work, and mentioned his name to the form master and to the headmaster, and he grew, he stood up higher. Because he is exactly the kind of boy who would always be excellent but nobody would ever thank him or praise him. He's a very able boy, and it gives me joy and delight to be able to do that for someone like him. And I think, what was it with these men, with my teachers, that their delight was to destroy me? Why did they victimize me when the joy is to encourage someone to grow? I never wanted it to make me bitter, but it did. It did. I mean, there's still a lot of hurt, and it's interesting to me that only now, years later, I can talk about it and the pain is finally some distance away. If I had talked to you even a couple of years ago, the pain would still have been right here. Right here.

Now I no longer feel the pain of feeling inferior, but the pain of injustice. I was never rude, you know? I was never aggressive. I was brought up to be very polite; but even that was used against me because people thought that I was lampooning them. If I'd been white and had behaved like that, people would have said, 'What a beautifully behaved boy!' Now I know you can't dump everything at the door of racism, but I struggle to think of some other kind of explanation.

People still ask me where I'm from. I've decided that the next person who says, 'Where are you from?' and when I say, 'I was born in London' then says, 'Yes, but where are you *really* from?' – the next person who says that to me, I'm going to say, 'Fuck off! I'm going to be as rude to you, and as offensive to you, as you are to me. What right have you got to ask me those questions? I don't say to you, where are your parents from? I don't ask you intimate questions about your life. The answer is, "I was born in London, that's where I'm from, I'm English."' But we've got a long way to go before people accept that anybody who is black is English. A lot of talk goes on about being British Black, and I always stop it and say, 'No, I'm *English*.' British means the Commonwealth. Means I could have been born in Hong Kong, or Barbados, or Canada. I wasn't. I was born in England. I'm English.

People are very resistant to anything to do with racism awareness. It's just as bad in the Church as anywhere. They are no different from anybody else. We've had a lot of hassle here, much of it unintentional. It's only a few years ago that one of the members of the congregation, a good person, said, 'Father Charles, I wish you would stop saying that you're black,' which means that black is inferior, and we don't see you as being inferior. 'You're *not* black, you're like *us*.' One night at the PCC, something came up about racism – a paper had come down from Diocesan Synod for us to discuss – and one of the people on the PCC said, 'When I look at Father Charles, I don't see a black person,' and someone else said, 'Well, what do you see then? He is black. What are you trying to say? That you don't see him as a person?'

Eight years ago I joined the Association of Black Clergy and I had a watershed experience with that group. I went to a World Council of Churches conference with a group from the ABC, to Switzerland. It was just under a week, and it was the first time in my life that I have lived with black people and been the same, and I broke down. You don't realize the strains you're under until they're not there. Just to know that everybody who looked at me just saw me: they didn't see somebody who was different. I was exactly the same. Okay, we had different ethnic origins: some were African, or from the Caribbean, and I was the only English-born person there; but we were all the same, and I couldn't handle it. I completely broke down because I had lost my bearings, I didn't know who I was any more. I had never been the same as everybody else around me. That was the one and only time in my entire life.

We go to France a lot and every year I have traumas about coming back looking blacker than when I went. Every time we come back from France we get stopped at customs, and the *aggression* that we're met with, when I roll down the window! For what reason? 'Your address?' 'Holy Trinity Vicarage.' 'What's your job?' 'I'm a vicar.' Then they get flummoxed. 'Where were you staying?' So we'd say where we were. 'And did you have a good holiday, sir?' 'An excellent holiday, thank you.' 'Thanks very much, sir. Sorry about that. Off you go.' These are little things, but if I, as a clergyman, experience those things, what do the people in this parish experience? What do the people in Brixton or Southall experience?

Now, I'm fairly naïve on all sorts of levels, and I don't look for racism, but I've been called a fucking Paki in the street, wearing my clergyman's collar, and it's pretty hard not to identify that as racism. But I don't go looking for it, and I don't assume that every person who doesn't get on with me is like that because they're racist and there is nothing wrong with me.

Yet I remember a comment that another boy at school made to me once. He lived in the high-rises in Putney, in the days when they were 'Paki-bashing', in the late sixties, and he was talking about all these fucking Pakis and how they were going to do this and that to them, and then he turned to me and he said, 'I don't mean you, Charlie. You're one of us.' I remember then being very glad to be 'one of us'. Now I would say, 'No, I'm not one of you. And I don't want to be identified with the things you say, and the things that you think.' But I remember being embarrassed to walk down the street with Daddy, because however bad it was walking by myself, it was worse when Daddy was there.

I'm ashamed now that I could ever have been embarrassed by

my father. I remember thinking that he was such a fine person, such a lovely, lovely man, and being so embarrassed that I was embarrassed to be seen with him. I just thank God that before he died I grew to know who he really was. He really wasn't a child's father, he was a man's father. He used to talk for ages, he was a great philosopher, and I would listen to the things he said, and take them in. And I've said it to so many people, and I say it to you now: he was the finest man I've ever met, and one of the few 'men' I've ever met. I don't mean butch, macho, I mean a person, a real person. Most of the men that I meet are little boys in long trousers. A lot of the problems in this world are caused by men, who are just so stupid. He wasn't like that. He was a fine man.

When I was about fifteen or sixteen Mummy and Daddy divorced, and I was the only male in the house then. Even before then I was brought up among women; with Mummy and my sister and an aunt. For years I never went into a men's loo, because it was always with Mummy that we went out, and I would be taken into the women's loos. And I suppose I still don't find men's company very easy. I don't have the common experiences most men have. I didn't learn to belch or spit at school. I don't get drunk easily, but I get sick quickly. I don't mind going into pubs, and I have male friends and I go for a drink with them, but I don't find it easy. Maybe that's because of the sort of vibes that I have felt in pubs in the past, and therefore I don't want to be where there are loads of men, because I found men threatening. Perhaps I still do. I mean, these are awful generalizations, but women do seem to be much more in touch with reality. They can talk about how they feel, they can put their life in context. Men compartmentalize things. I suppose, as well, that because women have been kicked in the teeth far more than men, I can empathize better with them, especially in a parish like this. So many of the women here are very, very able, not just academically, but in all sorts of ways. None of them are the rubbish that half of them think they are, and it's because the education system has kept them in their place, and the men keep them in their place, and the welfare system keeps them in their place.

The Church has to take responsibility for the way that women are treated, because it goes back hundreds of years, to the original teachings of the Church: it goes back hundreds of years to social structures and strictures, which we haven't grown away from. That's why people in the Church latch on to issues like the ordination of women, or homosexuality, or the break-up of marriages. It's always sex, because we are preoccupied with sex. And not so very far below the surface of those issues are questions about one's own sexual security or insecurity. 'Am I sexually fulfilled or not? Are women a threat or not? What if some poofter comes along and touches me?' Or, 'Am I given any value because I am gay? Will people listen at all because I'm not married? Now that I'm divorced, have I lost all credibility? Do I have any place in society?' Now those things are important, but they are not what the gospel is about. The gospel is about God's relationship with all human beings, through Christ.

To me it is my understanding of God, and God's understanding of me, that is the constant thing, the important thing, and that is what the Church has to offer people. It doesn't have moral teaching to offer: that's the icing on the cake. What matters is that God loves you, and if you don't know, can I tell you? That's what Jesus said to people. He didn't say, 'This is what you've got to do. This is how you have to be.' I have a great vision of Jesus walking down the street, with Mary Magdalene, and him not being ashamed of her, because she was not a thing, not an object of desire, not somebody that 'nice' people would have nothing to do with, but a *person*. That is, for me, the thrust of Jesus's ministry. What he was saying to Mary was, 'If I love you, God loves you.' Her response was to love him back. I mean, that's such a liberating gospel, and when that is shared with people, they grow. All the theological ideas that are current at the moment should spring from that, but they don't. I fear that some of the reaction against the ordination of women to the priesthood has got nothing to do with the love of God, nothing to do with the gospel of Jesus Christ. It's pure gut reaction, and it's bloody women again, and there's no health in that, no healing in that.

I used to be very much against the ordination of women to the priesthood, maybe eight years ago or so, perhaps less. I thought through it and I couldn't think of a single argument that I had that wasn't based on prejudice, that wasn't absolute rubbish. In the end it came down to prejudice, that I didn't want to see a woman as a priest, because she'd do it just as well, and she might do it better! Given the calibre of the women that we've got, and the calibre of some of the men, she probably would do it better. That sort of prejudice was unworthy of me, so it's certainly unworthy of the Christian Church.

In recent years Anglo-Catholics have got such a negative image. Some of them have been very vociferously anti-women, and that means we are all seen as a bunch of conservative bigots. We're not, or at least most of us aren't. What I value about Anglo-Catholicism is the sacramental teaching of the Church, the 'otherness' that rituals and celebrations speak of. These very ordinary things – people joining hands together, or people pouring water on another person, or people taking a bit of bread and wine – speak volumes about eternity. The spiritual aspects of that are so wonderful and so rich, and they transcend us as humans, yet some people can't allow them to transcend the sexual level. One of the most obscure and most obscene things I think I ever heard was Graham Leonard saying that if he saw a woman in the sanctuary he would want to throw his arms around her. Now, that doesn't say anything about women, and it doesn't say anything about what a priest is supposed to be doing when he or she is in the sanctuary, but it says a lot about Graham Leonard.

The thing I really love about Anglo-Catholicism is that when I stand at the altar, I am just another priest. When I take part in those regular and rhythmic actions, like the elevation of the Host, and the blessing of the elements, I know that hundreds and thousands of priests have done that for generations and I could be any one of them. Who I am is not an important part of what I am doing. Sometimes when I'm celebrating mass I get a great sense that I'm standing there, where priest before priest before priest before priest has stood, and please God that there will be thousands after me.

Priesthood has no meaning if you don't remember that you have been a deacon, a servant, for longer: not to mention the fact that you have been a lay person for the whole of your life, and a priest is just a lay person in Holy Orders. The aspect of service is so important because you have a responsibility, under God, for the people that you serve. I celebrated the sixteenth anniversary of my priesthood last weekend, and I remembered my first mass, when I could feel something happen to me. I could feel that in some way I was a channel for the actions of God and God's people. That has never left me. Every single time that I celebrate the Eucharist; every time I bless people; every time I say the words of absolution; every time I consecrate the elements, it's different and it's special and it's wonderful. Now, I don't believe that the Eucharist is magic, and I don't believe that sacraments are magic, though they can sound precious close to it. I can't prove that God's there and I can't prove that what I feel is a real feeling. But I also can't preach about things I don't believe.

We've got at least thirteen ethnic groups in this parish, and I include English, Welsh, Scottish and Irish as being ethnic groups. We have African people, Afro-Caribbean people, Chinese people, Polish people, Italian people, Indian people, Pakistani people, Bangladeshi people, East African Asians. I mean, there are more than that, but that's quite a number of the ethnic groups. We've also had a massive demographic change in the parish, with half the available housing being bought by a housing association, and a lot of the families that have come into those houses are single-parent families. About 10 per cent of the families here are single-parent families. Unemployment is somewhere between 20 and 40 per cent. The main work here used to be the cotton mills, but now it's sweat-shops, small businesses, supermarkets, small-scale engineering workshops; there isn't anything big around here that employs people.

What's very peculiar about this parish is that it's not ghetto-ized; people live higgledy-piggledy. Another peculiarity is that it's surrounded by main roads, so people don't drive in here, by and large, and most of the people who live here don't have cars, so there's not a lot of traffic and it's almost like a village. The church, the school and the vicarage are on a central plot together, on an island, and architecturally they dominate the parish. In theory – and I hope now in practice – they are the focus for the activity of the people. We've converted the church and re-developed the west end of the building so that it's a community facility, used largely at the moment by the Pakistani, Bangladeshi and Indian communities, with a small amount of use by the church itself.

In our church school nearly 90 per cent of the children are either Hindu or Muslim. It could have been possible in the school, by force of personality, to encourage children to convert from Islam, or Hinduism, to Christianity. I would have looked like the great Charles Lawrence, who had gone in and converted tens of children to the faith. What I would also have done, effectively, would have been to destroy their family life, destroy the community, and destroy any possibility of working together for at least two generations. To me it is far more important that in the school, and in the community, I encourage people to be strong in their own faith because they believe in God. The challenge to Christianity in this country is not to convert people of other faiths: the challenge is to reach the people who don't know God, or say they don't know God. After all, there are plenty of people for whom their belief in God makes no difference to their lives, who are in church Sunday by Sunday, and dare I say it, I think some of them are clergy.

That means living where those people are. It means being on the spot. Now, I live in a massive house – goodness knows how many times the size of the people's houses who live around here it is — but at least I'm in the community. I shop at the local shops, I walk the streets, people know me and I know them. They welcome me into their homes, and that means that at some level, and obviously not a very deep level, I live part of their life with them. There is no point in me standing outside the city and lobbing rocks at it: I need to be in the city living the life with the people. Okay, I come from a different cultural background, I come from a different background in all sorts of ways coming from the South of England, but even so I am here and I can see what is happening with people, and what's being done to them.

What is being done to them is that they are being ignored or treated as second-rate. That of course hasn't stopped the Tory Government making sweeping statements about the unemployed and single parents, but then it's easy to say that sort of thing about people you don't know. Okay, they are backtracking now, and saying, 'Yes, we realize that a lot of single parents are single parents because they are widowed, or divorced, or whatever, and they're really nice people. It's just these horrible riffraff that we want to get. These cynical little schoolgirls who do this, this and this.' Well, they ought to see the way that some of these cynical little schoolgirls bring up their children, and how much they love them, and how much they go without so that their children can have as much as possible. They ought to see that when people do try to get council flats to live in it isn't just sheer callousness and use of the system, but *need*. And for goodness' sake, how many people who've got big cars and company expenses are fiddling the system? The Government would do a lot better to nobble *them*. Social Security frauds are infinitesimally small compared to tax fiddles. Yet we're taught to admire the person who fiddles their tax, and to despise the dole queue 'scrounger'. It's wicked.

In all of this the Church is massively out of touch with reality. All the fuss over the ordination of women to the priesthood shows how stupid we have become. It's not that it's a non-issue, but it is nowhere as important as these sorts of social issues, the issues that affect people's lives. It all comes back to what I was saying about living where people are, so that the voice of the Church comes out of our life and our experience, and that's something that I think that we in the Church have lost our nerve over.

I was trained by people who lost their nerve in the sixties. We were being partially trained as priests and partially trained as social workers, because they weren't sure that it was quite right to train people just as priests any more. The idea that you could exercise priestly ministry was deeply unfashionable, and so the prophetic voice of the Church became a pathetic voice, and now many clergy are depressed as a result because they feel under-valued. Yet all the evidence suggests that people *want* to hear what the Church has to say. They *want* to think that the Church is concerned about them, that it cares. There is this impression given that the Church is peripheral to the life of the people of England. It just isn't. In my own parish, okay, people don't come to church, but they would be devastated to think that there wouldn't be a priest to come to them. They want you there. And when I've had the nerve to say to somebody, 'Can I pray with you?', in my whole ministry I think only one person has said no.

It's not desperately obvious what you achieve as a parish priest. Yet someone said to me the other day, 'My life has changed. I'm happy. Things are going well, and when things go badly I know I can cope.' I'd spent a lot of time with this person and it was me they thanked, but it's God who does those things, and it is duplicated countless times throughout my ministry and the ministry of other clergy. Of course sometimes it's bloody difficult. The work in this parish has been incredibly hard, and often totally unrewarding. On the whole people don't say thank you, and you work and work and work and nothing seems to happen. But surely that was so for Jesus. I mean, there is no record of there being a massive conversion of the people who listened to him. Okay, they listened to him in their tens of thousands at times, but equally they shouted and screamed for his death. There is no real evidence that Jesus was a great success.

The clergy are not called to be successful. The Church is not called to be successful. We are called to be the body of Christ. We are not called to be a multi-national, with a turnover of x million: we are called to serve God's people. And if that means that somebody can spit at me, or kick me in the face, spiritually or metaphorically, didn't they do that to Jesus? If somebody can tell me to piss off, who has never been able to tell anybody in authority to piss off, but they can tell the Vicar, isn't that a good thing? And yet our diocese looks at my parish now and says, 'Not a successful parish. There is not work here for a full-time priest. It's a half-time appointment.' They say that because not many people come to church and the parish is not that big: there are only 2,000 souls all told, so as far as they're concerned I've got no work to do. The fact that there are parishes with 10,000, where the clergy are doing very little except keeping the place ticking over, escapes the hierarchy. The disposition of clergy is based on all sorts of things, but rarely on the work that is being done, or the work that needs to be done.

A very superficial response to the question of why that is, is that too many of the bishops have never been parish priests; and if they have been parish priests it hasn't been in parishes that have been representative of the Church of England. I mean, it is breaking down now, but the Old Boys' system, where you either went to Oxbridge or the right theological college, or you happen to know so-and-so, or you went to the right school in the first place, is still in operation. It's been said so many times, but I believe that there is a great deal of truth in the saying that you are marked out from ABM onwards. I was an ABM selector for a while and sometimes the other selectors would say, 'This is a high-flyer,' and when I said, 'Why?' they'd say, 'Because he's been a barrister, or a managing director.' I'd say, 'Why does that make him a high-flyer in the Church? What about this person who is a spiritual giant? Why isn't that person a high-flyer?' The crude answer is because they don't talk right and they didn't go to the right school. Now, what is that saying about the Church? It says that it's about class. It says that in order to get on, if you don't come from the 'right' background, you have to leap social hurdles, you have to leave your roots behind.

That is slowly changing. I think the biggest problem we now face in the Church – and it seems to me to be a massive problem – is that the average age of ordinands is so high. That really concerns me. This year I went to the ordination of deacons at our cathedral, and just looking at them, of seventeen people fourteen looked my age and older. The ones who were younger were not in their early twenties. Now, what does that say to young people? What does it say to the public in general? That the Church is for middle-aged people? That we're talking about a second-string Church? That we're talking about a Church that you offer yourself to when you have done other things? I think we are, and at its best, that's because those other things lead people to where they are now. But at its worst it means that the ministry is increasingly full of people who think, deep down, 'When I've done the things I want to do, then I might as well be a priest. When I go to the church every Sunday, it would be fun to be the Vicar, or act as if I'm the Vicar.' I resent the assumption that any bloody fool can be a priest. They can't.

The other side of that is that there are many people who because of constraints on their lives cannot offer themselves to full-time ministry, and they give of themselves over and above anything that could be reasonably expected of them. Because they are non-stipendiary and they have jobs, they give evenings up, they give weekends up, again and again and again. Yet why is the Church not producing full-time vocations? Why is it not reaching young people? Why is it that our vocations are coming from forty-year-olds? Because we are not reaching the ten-year-olds! Jack Nichols, the Bishop of Lancaster, who was in this diocese and made a huge impact here, was saying something about the death of Christianity in this country being because we have lost contact with two generations. That means that we've blown it. That's why it is so important to be in schools, to be in the community, to talk with children on the streets. And although that will show nothing for twenty years, maybe because you have been of use to a young person they will then come and trust the Church with *their* children, and will say, 'Well, we might not be getting married, but let's go along and take the kids to Sunday School.' Or they might think about having their children baptized.

It's obvious in parishes like this that the Church is breaking down. It's not so obvious in other parishes, because if you've got 10,000 people and 100 baptisms a year, it doesn't occur to you that that is only one per cent. You think you've got a lot. You haven't. I once heard somebody who ran a huge supermarket chain saying he couldn't understand the Church of England, when it had a branch in every conceivable part of the country, not maximizing its potential. We haven't maximized our potential, and I think that's because although there *is* something wonderful about having a church in every place, it leads too easily to a sense of apathy and torpor.

I don't think the Church can roll along merrily as it has done for years, because England has changed so much. We in the Church are still acting as though we are in village communities. We're still acting as if the Industrial Revolution, which has been and gone, is about to happen. Our strategies, our tactics, our vision, by and large, do not relate to the country that we serve. They're finished. The traditional points of contacts, the occasional Offices like baptisms and weddings and funerals, are gradually going to disappear. And unless the Church of England makes a conscious and deliberate step towards the people of England, then very shortly we will just be a tiny minority. We're a tiny minority now, for goodness' sake. So maybe what we need is disestablishment. Maybe we need to say, 'Who are we?' Maybe we need no longer to be able to say, 'We will be at every coronation, at every opening of Parliament, at every big State event.'

Something in me says that it is a very dangerous thing being too much hand-in-glove with the State. We need to regain a sense of prophetic vision, a sense that what we do now affects what will happen later. Most of the work that I have done in this parish was to set things up, or to get things moving towards something that will happen in twenty-five years, or fifty years from now. That means you need to have some sort of concept of where fifty years from now is, in order to work towards it, and that, I think, is where the Church falls down. It's lost its vision, it's lost its prophetic voice; and yet the prophetic role of the Church is so important because it is about interpreting our times in the light of *God*, and God's teaching. I think that Archbishop Runcie, for all that people slagged him off, was a prophet. He wasn't the weak-chinned, wobbly sort of individual that he was caricatured as in *Spitting Image*: a tiny man, compared to bigger puppets. That, maybe, was a very fair picture of the prophet. There's ample evidence in the scriptures that the prophet is not necessarily a very impressive person, and that they say things that nobody wants to listen to, and nobody hears. They're ridiculed or vilified. But later on, people say, 'If only we'd listened to them, we wouldn't be where we are now.'

It doesn't just need to be the figurehead people who are prophets for the Church, though people like the Archbishops of Canterbury and York do have a great prophetic responsibility. It needs to be the ordinary Christian in their place of work, or in the job centre, or in the supermarket, wherever they happen to be, feeling that they have got something that they can say, and that it doesn't always need to be strident. We all need to say that Jesus was God; that God walked on the face of this earth; that human beings talked to God, which hadn't happened since the Garden of Eden. I get so *excited* by these things! I think we have got so many good things to tell people, to share with people, to encourage people to realize what they know already. For a lot of clergy, that excitement is lost under the daily grind of administration, and a lack of vision of the Kingdom of God. But heaven is *here*. You only have to look about you.

For me our church school is a foretaste of the Kingdom, where people of different cultures and traditions and religions, and no religion, can sit down together and share in a common bond of love. When I first came here, the school was under threat of closure. We had huge public meetings about it, and we began the meetings with prayer. We were Christians, Hindus and Muslims praying together, and I tried to find common themes and didn't make it stridently Christian, because that would have been offensive to people. Anyway, there was one wonderful meeting when the councillors were telling me what they were going to do with the school, and a Muslim parent got up and said, 'It's all right if you close the school. But if you close it, you must provide us with another church school for our children to go to.' That just floored the councillors: that the parents weren't sending the children to the school because it was the nearest, and it was convenient, and the children didn't have to cross a main road. They were deliberately making a choice. They wanted their children to be educated in a place where God's name was held holy, and where God was respected. They clearly felt some real level of unity with us as Christians, as other people of God. Now, too often, you hear things about those awful Muslim people, and I'm sure those Muslim people hear an awful lot about those awful Christian people. We hear about the divisions. But here, in an ordinary little primary school, is a foretaste of the Kingdom of God, where the people of God are working together. That is the sort of thing that needs to be heard by people: that we can work together without compromising each other's integrity; that God gives us common purpose. There are many people who would knock it and say, 'You've not achieved anything, because you haven't converted anybody to Christianity.' But that's not the point. The point is that we've tasted the Kingdom and it tastes good.

That's where the Church has fallen down. Those people working with AIDS sufferers or the homeless: those people who are constantly going out to where people are, they're the ones who are regarded as weirdos and eccentrics. Because although from time to time in our ministry we go out to where people are, mostly we in the Church sit where we are and ask people to come to us. The Vicar is available at such and such a time, book your baptisms, weddings and so on then. Church services are at such and such a time: come to us.

We've blown the opportunity we had with people, and we have to start again. We've got to go out and assume nothing, assume that people will tell us to piss off. Because why should they bother listening to us? What's the Church ever done for them that they should bother talking to a representative of the Church? So I expect people to reject what I have to say. Like I said, that's what happened to Jesus. But I really want people to know that God loves them. I want people to know that God knows who they are and He still loves them, whoever they are, whatever they do.

Maybe people who have not known what it is like to be rejected, and rejected for no reason, don't feel like this, but I just knew I was born to do God's work. I grew up taking Him for granted, knowing that He loved me, and knowing that He always would. When I felt rejected by society I could always identify with Jesus because he had been rejected too. He has sustained me through my life and I want to share that. He has sustained me through the love of others, and his love, through them, has taught me that whatever people can do to me they cannot destroy my soul.

BILL KIRKPATRICK

Age: 66
Age at ordination: 42

NON-STIPENDIARY PRIEST, LONDON

Words are not Bill Kirkpatrick's medium. When he speaks it is in a deep bass voice and his native Canadian accent, and though he is perfectly willing to do so, he much prefers to listen. Still, tall, with broad shoulders, long limbs and heavy brows, he was wiry dark grey hair and a strong, gaunt face full of shadows. His life has been one of spiritual and philanthropic endeavour, but he looks as if it has involved hard and persistent physical labour.

The first time I went to meet him at his home, Bill Kirkpatrick was wearing a checked lumberjack-style shirt, jeans, socks but no shoes, and a large, smooth wooden cross around his neck. We drank tea and, concerned that I might not have had enough breakfast before I arrived, he made some toast. He said he was willing to be interviewed but wasn't sure he had anything worth saying. It was obvious to me that this was far from the truth: something I found hard to articulate made me aware from the outset that Bill Kirkpatrick was a very remarkable man.

Bill Kirkpatrick has chosen to exercise his ministry outside the mainstream Church. He is one of the 1,250 non-stipendiary clergy in the Anglican Church, and he exercises an unusual and eclectic ministry beyond the bounds of conventional parish life. As well as assisting at the local parish church and working at both the Terrence Higgins Trust and the London Lighthouse, he has made his home into a place where anyone who feels they need to can come and talk to him, about anything, at any time, on their own terms. He keeps an open house, an open mind and no written records.

Bill Kirkpatrick's home is a large basement flat in Earls Court from which he conducts his 'listening ministry'. The flat is fairly dark, with frosted windows well above head-height so that you can't see out at all.

Plainly decorated, with no more than the necessary amount of furniture, some of it covered with Latin American rugs, the environment is simple and unfettered. There are one or two pictures and photographs on the walls, and a large and very full bookcase by the front door, but no clutter. The entire place reflects Bill Kirkpatrick's own peaceful and monastic ascetism. Throughout the interviews I was dimly aware of noisy traffic outside and Radio 3 in the background, but the flat and our conversations felt strangely and pleasantly cut off from life outside.

At the end of our week together Bill Kirkpatrick took me to see the tiny chapel he has made in a shed behind the flat. It is directly beneath the pavement, and so low that he has to duck his head inside. It has a bench, a crucifix and an altar made from a roughly hewn log. The chapel is kindly and humble: it feels both used and loved. 'I'm very privileged to have this place,' he said. 'Very privileged indeed.' I felt privileged to have seen it.

Soon after our interviews were over Bill Kirkpatrick invited me to breakfast at an Italian café around the corner from his flat. On the way there, and in the café itself, he was greeted warmly by a number of men and women, some of them drunk, some of them homeless, all of them known to him. The café became a happy and long-term habit, and conversations with Bill Kirkpatrick became associated in my mind with garlic bread, hot chocolate and people stopping to pass the time of day with him and going away the better for it.

BILL KIRKPATRICK

My childhood's a bit of a mystery. I'm what you call a love-child. I eventually found out who my natural parents were. It seems my father was a fairly well-off Scotsman whose first wife died. Before marrying his second wife he had a housekeeper who I believe was a North American native, though I've not really been able to verify that part of the story. Sometimes I think I've got Indian blood, sometimes I'm not sure. Sometimes people say I look like one, but it's difficult to say and I can't prove it.

Within a month of being born I was shipped to a private orphanage. It was owned by a family whose name I took, Kirkpatrick. This was in Vancouver, Canada, at the height of the Depression, in the twenties, and the Depression closed the home. They had fifty babies there, and they took myself and another baby who was two years younger than myself, and she became my foster sister. I remember very little about it except being in a room full of small kids. That's all I remember of my early life.

The Kirkpatricks brought me up, but I was never legally adopted. I was fostered by default, if you like, and I always knew I didn't belong. It was no surprise to me when I was eventually told I wasn't theirs. I'd have been more surprised the other way. It's just something you know.

I started school at the age of six. Didn't get on too well, I don't think. I was dyslexic, and they didn't know about dyslexia then, and it was a bit rough; a bit rough. Then we moved out of Vancouver into a place called Burnaby, which is between Vancouver and New Westminster. It's now part of Greater Metropolitan Vancouver, but in those days it was all bush, and I went to school there until I was fifteen. By this time the parents had rented a huge house and turned it into an old people's home, and it became one of the models for Canada. That was where I had my early experience of attempting to care for others.

It was a very hard life. We had no time to play. We never knew what it was to play. Everything was timed, we did everything by the clock: going to school, coming back from school. It was a very old-fashioned Victorian upbringing, quite strict. We always worked before and after school, and we were known as the 'nick-of-time kids' because we always got to school in the nick of time. Then, when I was fifteen, my foster father died and I left school and took on his work, so in a sense I never had a teenage life.

I didn't really know my foster father much. He was a quiet man, nice man, but I didn't really know him. He died before I got a chance to, because in those days kids didn't talk to parents in the way people do nowadays, and even if you asked about their lives you weren't told. It was very much 'Speak when you are spoken to', and that was it. He was English. He was much older. I don't know what age he was when he died, but he seemed old to me.

My foster mother was a very forthright woman. A very domineering Yorkshirewoman. You knew when she was around. She was a wonderful carer of the people she cared for but like lots of caring people, if they have a family, they can care for those they are meant to care for but they don't seem to know how to care for their family, so I guess I felt neglected because we were second to work. And maybe that had to be, because they had to get the home going and I think we were around at a time when it was very difficult for them. But that still didn't make it any easier as a young person. It was quite — quite *heavy*.

I've always been a loner. I don't know if that's me or my upbringing. I guess if you've never been involved in things, you don't really miss them. We never had friends as children. It wasn't encouraged. I think I had my first friend at about the age of eighteen. My sister and I were close, but we were totally different. She was the rebellious one: I was the meek and mild one. She'd go against all the rules and regulations and I wouldn't. Though I used to read a lot, which was frowned upon, and I used to listen to music. I fancied myself being a conductor one day. Partly why I came over to England, but that's another story.

I worked at the home until I was about twenty-one, and I ended up literally putting the addition on the house for another thirty patients, but by that time I thought, I don't want to stay here, I've had enough. I wanted to go to England. It's something I'd always wanted to do, I don't know why.

In those days you were under your parents' control until you were twenty-one, and only then was I discharged by my mother. She was ambivalent about letting me go, because I had taken over from her husband. She used to become suddenly quite sick if I ever wanted to go out, you know, 'Here I am with all this work,' all that blackmail stuff. Then one day the Chaplain to the nursing home, Father Aelred Carlyle, said to me, 'You have to leave here. If you don't leave here, you'll end up in a mental hospital.' But I think my mother saw me taking over the home because I was the only one of four who had any real interest in how the home was run.

One of four, yeah. She'd been married before and had two of her own children, who were ten and twelve years older than me. All they seemed to be interested in was money, and money has never been my sort of thing. I saw what it was doing to people when I was young, people fighting over it, and I thought, I can't be doing with all that. I guess I didn't mention the others before because we didn't really get on; they thought I was a nuisance. My stepbrother, who's now dead, had his girlfriends and didn't want me hanging around, which was natural. My stepsister was married when I was fifteen or sixteen, so she wasn't around. There was really only Nancy and myself and the foster parents, and as far as my mother was concerned, I was the golden boy. Until I suggested something different. She wasn't really helping me as a person. I was caught up in her web in a way that wasn't healthy. Then along came her third husband and of course I couldn't stand him. Obviously there was jealousy there, but he was also a crook and she lost all her money to him. That gave me a chance to leave.

When I was eighteen I joined a local music and drama group, and it was there that I met my first partner, Jim, in 1948, and we were partners for over twenty years. Just clicked. Just clicked. People assumed we were good friends, which of course we were, but you didn't talk about being gay, and I don't think people thought we were. Neither one of us was obvious, and we weren't the picture of what people thought a gay person was. We just got on and quietly lived our lives.

In 1950 Jim's firm moved him to Chicago and I went with him as his assistant. We both wanted to come to England, so I left Chicago to earn the money to come over, which we finally did in 1952. I did two restaurant jobs in Vancouver before I left, and then I worked for a while on the Royal Mail Lines, as a cook. I also did some private auxiliary nursing, to a very wealthy person who was head of one of the big railways in America, and he was a real old battleaxe, he used to throw knives at people, though I got on with him okay. For some reason he never threw one at me.

When I got to England I went straight to London. Hadn't a clue what I was going to do. My first job was selling pots and pans in Selfridges. I didn't know one saucepan from another, and in those days I couldn't say alu-mini-um, I said it the Canadian way, aluminum, but I had the best stand, I took the most money. I thought the English were just so lazy, always having their cups of tea and nobody looking after their stands. My stand was always top-notch.

Selfridges decided they wanted to make me a buyer, but I said, no way, I'm not going to spend the rest of my life in a shop. At the same time I was friendly with Robert Farnon, a Canadian composer, and he wanted a copyist. Well, I'd been studying composition myself – I told you how I wanted to be a conductor – and I worked for him for a while. He'd give me the melody line of a piece and I'd write it out for all the other instruments. I couldn't do it now! After a while he got a contract in America and said he'd like to take me with him, so I talked to Jim and we decided we'd both go. However, when we were half-way over there we got a telegram saying it had all fallen through: so we stayed and worked in Montreal until we came back to England a year later, where I got a job in Foyle's bookshop, followed by one at Paxton's the music publisher until I thought, I can't be doing with this. We were living in Paddington with a few other Canadians, and BOAC, as British Airways was then, was advertising for recruits. I'd only been on a plane once before in my life, but my friends put an application in for me and I got a job as an air steward.

I was an air steward for about two and a half years, doing the Far East runs, which was a wonderful way of seeing the world at somebody else's expense. In those days, when you went to Tokyo you were away a month and you stayed at the best hotels: in those days BOAC was really highly thought of. You got passes to all the best clubs, but I've never been a clubby-type person so I'd go on my own to other places, or read and study music on the side. Wonderful experience, and after two years they wanted to promote me to Chief Steward, which normally happens after five.

One time I went to Calcutta on a trip and I was shattered by what I saw. The poverty. Here we were in the best hotel and you walked outside and saw all this poverty and beggars hounding you: and I guess I had a kind of 'experience', because I thought, I just cannot bear this, I've got to do something about this. I thought, 'What *can* I do? I've got no education. I suppose I could be a nurse.' That sounds bad on nurses, doesn't it, but in those days nursing was very basic.

When I got back I made inquiries about training as a nurse at St Charles' Hospital, Ladbroke Grove. In 1957 it was the only hospital that trained men as nurses, and by the end of an afternoon with the matron, Miss Titley, I'd signed on for the following September. She said there were going to be three other men, but when I arrived I was one among thirty women and ten years older than most of them, and they all stood up when I walked in.

It was a great three years: hard work and the pay was, oh God, unbelievable, less than £500 a year. Nurses have never been well paid. But I loved the training, and received the hospital medal – from Princess Margaret – and then specialized in psychiatric nursing. Guy's Hospital was in the process of taking its first male postgraduate nurses, and I became the first male to do the two-year training in psychiatric nursing. This time I got the hospital medal from the Queen Mother!

After I graduated I worked at St Luke's Hospital in Chelsea and I did night-duty, four nights on, four nights off. Before I went back on night-duty I always slept in the afternoons, and to help me sleep I would go for a walk in Hyde Park. One day, I was doing this, taking a walk with my dog in Hyde Park, and I had a kind of experience. I can't describe it. I was somewhere else. In another dimension. I don't remember how it happened, but I found myself in an antiques shop in Bond Street, looking at these two pieces of Salvador Dali jewellery. One was a heart, and one was a matchstick cross, and both just *did* something to me. I just can't describe it. I don't remember getting home. I remember having a snooze before I went to work, and feeling translated into the most wonderful, beautiful scene. All sunlight and a great feeling of being loved; tremendous feeling of being embraced in mystery.

The other three chaps I lived with, they all arrived home from their jobs and said, you've been on the booze. And I said, no, I haven't. I went to work that night and a nursing colleague said, hey, you been boozing? And I said, no, I haven't. It gradually wore off, but it lasted for three or four days, this fantastic thing.

I couldn't forget about it. I read *Time* magazine, and in it there was an ad, or an article, on the Taizé community in France, the first Protestant religious community in Europe since the Reformation. 'Young Men With Problems' it said, and I thought, well, I got a real problem! So I telephoned them and said can I come over, and I was there within the week, and stayed about three, and was quite convinced that this was where I was meant to be. The Novice Master was great. He thought it was all pure emotionalism. He said, if you feel like this in seven years' time then we might consider you. Which was sound advice.

I went back the following year and stayed a month. I was quite convinced on the day before I was due to leave that I would return for ever, but when I met the Prior and the Novice Master we all agreed 'No' at the same time. While I was there I'd gone to confession. I didn't believe in confession, but in deference to them I went. I thought hard and wrote stuff down and was as honest as I could be at the time, and we went to this little private chapel and I handed the confessor this script, and he laid it on the altar and said some prayers, then he handed it back to me and never even looked at it. He said, 'Now go and burn it.' And that had such an effect. He didn't read it. He didn't ask about it. Nothing. 'That's between you and God,' he said, 'it's got nothing to do with me.' I found that so moving, and I felt something too: I felt as if something had cleared.

All this was going on while I was training as a nurse. I hadn't been going to church but I'd been thinking about God, oh yes. God's always been in my life, you see. I've always believed in God. When God's dead, I am dead. God initiated me, created me. I'm in God and God's in me. You can't escape God. Sitting on the loo you're still with God. Having sex with somebody you're still with God. Everyday life. And we can't escape this mystery because we are caught up in it, I'm convinced of that.

I suppose from eighteen onwards I was always *looking* for something. I read about Buddhism, Hinduism, you name them, I looked at them. I've ended up saying yes to the Christian faith, and perhaps I hadn't any choice about saying yes because it's part of my culture, but for me the foundation of the Christian faith is about loving. We do it very badly, and the

Church has bastardized the word in many ways, but at its very core that's what it's about, and that's why I chose it.

Christianity demands that you love your neighbour as yourself, and learning to love yourself is the hardest thing of all. At least, it's the hardest thing I ever had to learn to do, to love myself as an individual, warts and all. It's taken years to do. Especially when as a child I was treated as though I was mentally subnormal. That's a form of mental abuse. It was cruel. I now know that I'm dyslexic, but they thought I was backward, they just couldn't see. I can survive it now, but when you're told for years on end that you're not normal, it takes just as many years to get through it, and that's probably why I've done the things that I have in my life, to prove to myself that I'm not what I was accused of being.

A couple of years after that strange experience in the Bond Street antiques shop I took a holiday in Sardinia. I stayed in a fisherman's cottage. The husband was away fishing, and his wife often let out the spare room they had, but when she saw how tall I was she said, 'The room's too small for you, the bed's too small, you have our bed.' So I had their bed, and, except for the wall facing me, all around me were statues, religious pictures, you name it, everything I didn't like. I went to sleep and in the wee hours of the morning I was awakened by the most beautiful woman I have ever seen in my life. She just stood at the end of the bed. Didn't say anything. Just stood there. And then faded away.

She wasn't ethereal. She was as solid as you are. She was six, seven feet away from me, but she was solid. And then she just seemed to fade. Oh, it was beautiful! She was a well-proportioned woman, nice-looking woman, wearing I think it was a white, or cream, plain dress, I dunno what period. I suppose it might have looked a bit like those pictures you see of angels, but I never really paid much attention to what she was wearing except that it was white. But her *own* colour. Beautiful! Beautiful! A beautiful well-tanned colour. She looked very healthy. But it was her presence that felt so good, there was something about her, an aura.

People I've told have assumed it was the Virgin Mary, but I just don't know. I don't want to label it. It might have been. I have never tried to put a name to it, but I know it wasn't a ghost. No way was that a ghost. She was too solid. Too real. It was a woman, like I haven't seen before or since, and it has always remained with me, for what, thirty years now. Gut level tells me it was not my imagination. All I know is that she was someone significant in the hierarchy of humankind: but who? I don't know because I wasn't told, I wasn't given a clue.

People are sceptical about these things, oh *sure*. Sure. But all things are possible with God. Obviously one has to discern whether something is of God or it's just a mental disturbance, but I believe we can tune in to other dimensions. People have done it all through history. Okay, so these two major episodes had a profound effect on my life, and would I have been any different without them? I haven't a clue. All I know is that they were real for me. They changed my life.

Anyway, after the second one I was *quite* convinced that I was bonkers, *quite* convinced. I was studying psychiatry, and I thought, 'I'm having a schizophrenic breakdown!' Quite convinced of it. So I rang Jim and said, 'Will you meet me at the airport, I think I'm mentally ill.' So he duly met me, and I thought, I *have* to see a psychiatrist. So I called this guy I knew, this psychiatrist, great big huge man, when he sat down he looked like Buddha: I rang Eric, that was his name, I rang him and said, 'Eric, I *have* to see you.' He said, 'Okay,' and he listened to me and said, 'Yeah. You need a priest.' I said to him, 'Eric, you *know* I've no time for priests. I don't wanna go to church. I have no time for the Church. I need a *psychiatrist*.' He said, 'Bill, you *don't* need a psychiatrist!' So we compromised. We found a psychiatrist *and* a priest!

The psychiatrist more or less confirmed my own diagnosis, that I was having a breakdown. The priest wasn't saying anything. I saw him for about three months, once every two weeks or something, and after a while I thought, well, I might as well sign on the dotted line. Be baptized. That's what I call it, you see: signing on the dotted line. So I was baptized in St Mary-Le-Bow, Cheapside, in the Chapel of the Holy Spirit, by a priest called Joseph McCulloch. He said to me afterwards, 'There's a confirmation by the Bishop at the end of May. We may as well book you in for it.' And I thought, well, okay, so what? But I didn't tell anybody.

I was confirmed in the Commonwealth Chapel in St Paul's Cathedral, and all this time I was working at Guy's, and the patients who were there kept coming back and kept coming back and I thought, 'There must be something missing in their lives. There must be.' There was a hospital chaplain there called Max Saint, and I mentioned this to him, and one day he said to me, 'Bill, I want you to meet a friend of mine.' His friend was Canon Stanley Evans, who was a remarkable Christian communist, wonderful man. I went to see him, and I spent three hours with him. He asked me all sorts of questions, and I didn't even twig what he was getting at, I was so naïve about how the Church operated. Finally he said, 'Well, what about it, Bill?' and the next thing I knew I started getting letters from the Bishop's chaplain responsible for training ordinands. I still didn't twig what was going on. Not until they started mentioning 'worker-priests'. Now they call them 'non-stipendiary' but in those days it was 'worker-priests'.

I just took it in my stride. I thought, oh well, two nights a week for the training, I suppose so, why not? So I went on the training for about three months, and they said, 'Now we have a weekend together.' So I thought, well, I guess we'll have a little party and that'll be it. A Saturday morning, I guess it was, and the Principal saw us all one by one. When he saw me he said, 'Where are your papers?' and I said, 'What papers?' so he said, 'Your ACCM papers.' I said, 'What's ACCM? I don't know anything about this.' He said, 'Well, how on earth did you *get* here then?' And I said, 'Well, I thought I was just attending classes on how to live as a Christian.' *Such* a naïve person! He just looked at me and I could tell he was thinking, my God, what *have* we got here?

The next day he made arrangements for me to go to an ACCM selection committee: they call it ABM now. I thought, well, they'll never accept me: I'll go just to humour everybody and then that'll be it, finished. I went to this selection thing and I wasn't impressed at all, it was so pious. All these pious young men flapping around as soon as they saw the Bishop's shadow, and I couldn't be doing with all that. I was quite convinced I would never be selected. I came home and said to Jim, 'Don't worry, Jim, I'm not going to be selected.' And sure enough, a letter arrived saying I had been.

I had two friends at the time who were really influential, and when this letter came I went to see them both. I showed it to Jim and he said, 'You'll be a priest. That doesn't surprise me.' The two others said the same thing. One of them was Geoffrey Watkins, who was a bookseller. I met him in his shop, because one day he told me not to buy a book: 'Don't buy that, it's no good. This one's much cheaper.' So after that, every time I went in we chatted and one day he said to me, 'I'd like you to meet a friend of mine. He has a little group called The Open Way, and they discuss subjects like psychiatry, philosophy and religion. I think you might like him.' And that was how I met Eric Howe, the psychiatrist who looked like Buddha. He was the man leading the group.

I completed my two years on the Southwark Ordination Course, which was great, because it was the first course of its kind in the country which trained you to be a worker-priest. But I wasn't very good at Biblical Studies, and because they thought I would possibly be a failure in this subject, and they didn't want any failures in the first course, they suggested that it might be good for me to go to theological college for a couple of years. I wasn't very keen, but I agreed to it provided I ended up a worker-priest. I never saw myself ever being a parish priest. There's nothing wrong with being a parish priest, I just never saw it as me. I felt I was being led, called, whatever word you want to use, to being a worker-priest.

When I'd finished my training the Principal of the college decided I should go into a parish. I said, 'But I can't go into a parish, that's not what we agreed.' He said, 'Well, you'll have to go or you'll never be ordained.' I said, 'Okay then, I won't be ordained. It's not the end of my life.'

I left college a week before I should have done, and of course that annoyed everybody, but this was always the plan, that I could be a nursing worker-priest, and it was they who broke the bargain. I felt I couldn't go against what I, at gut level, knew to be right. So they sent me to see the Bishop of Salisbury, Bishop Joe Fison, a lovely man, now dead, and he didn't try to make me change my mind. He just listened to my side of the story and said, 'Well, it's up to you, but if you wish to be a mini-Luther . . .' I said, 'I'm not trying to be a mini-anything. I'm just trying to do what I'm meant to be doing.'

I wasn't ordained. I was refused ordination by the different bishops who'd originally wanted me, saying they had no vacancies. They never told me why. I don't know to this day why I was refused. I suppose they probably saw me as somebody who was unstable, because I wasn't following the pattern. I think they thought it was my ego, that I wanted to be something different and a show-off and all that business; but I don't think I ever felt that, because I've always felt it was a tremendous privilege to be a priest, and I felt that judgement to be unfair. I was shattered really, because I suddenly realized that the Church is human and fallible, that it can make mistakes and misjudge a person's reasons.

At about the same time I was also involved in doing a book called *Sans Everything*, which was an exposé of the treatment of patients in mental hospitals, and of course that didn't endear me to the hospital world either, and this prevented me getting a hospital job when I left theological college. I didn't work for about a year, and I stayed with Jim, who was now married, and he and his wife supported me. They were furious at the way I was treated. They'd say, 'There's the Church for you.'

Jim met his future wife while I was at theological college and, I don't know, I used to go home at weekends and I just knew he was going to marry her. It's ironic. I find the Church and he finds a wife. In the same year. It's ironic. He said, 'Don't be silly,' and I said, 'You are. You're going to marry her.' Then he did.

I was devastated. But if you love somebody then you let them go if that's what they want. It does something to you, sure. It's like a death without a death . . . Ah well. He's still my oldest friend. He's my first love and always will be. We've always been good for each other, we've always helped each other to grow. He was the first person who ever made me feel I was a worthwhile person and *good*, and we've never lost touch. By 1998 if we're both still around we will have known each other fifty years.

I was one of the first men to join the Royal College of Nursing and I helped set up the Psychiatric Unit within the College, so I was fairly well known in the nursing world at that time. I used to write a bit, and one day I met a Miss Lunn, who was Matron of St Clement's Hospital in Bow. I ran into her on Oxford Street and she said, 'I've got to open a Drug Unit. Who do you think would work with drug addicts?' I said, 'I will. I need a job.' So I got the job, not at a rank like I'd had before, but I couldn't care two hoots whether I'd got a rank as long as I'd got some money, and I was there about a year. Then one day the hospital Chaplain said to me. 'Why aren't you ordained?' I said, 'I don't know. They won't tell me.' I told him a bit of the story as I knew it, and he said, 'Oh, that's wrong. You should be ordained.'

He and I found out much later that several people were battling behind the scenes to get me ordained, because they couldn't understand why I hadn't been. And eventually I got a phone call from the Bishop of Stepney, Bishop Francis Lunt, who said, 'The Bishop of London says you ought to spend the weekend with me and I have to decide whether we should make you a deacon.' So I said, 'Okay.' I spent the weekend with him and on the Saturday evening he said, 'Why don't you go to the local pub and have a drink?' So I did, and when I came back he said, 'Well, we've decided to ordain you as a deacon on Ascension Day,' which symbolically is a wonderful day to be ordained.

I didn't expect that. I expected to come away at the weekend and have them say the same thing, but I was pleased they were at least having another look. And the Bishop was great. I was the last man he ordained before he retired, and the only person ever ordained in Bow Church, and it was chock-a-block full: patients, doctors, nurses, people I knew, people I didn't know. There was a tremendous service, and when I came out they played the Bow Bells, and I said, 'This is like a wedding!' That was the first thing that came into my mind; this is like a blinking wedding!

In the hospital where I was working they put on a buffet, to which a goodly number of people turned up, and the Bishop came, and while he was there he said, 'Well, I hate to tell you this, but you'll never be priested. It's on your file that you're never to be priested.' I said, 'Okay, I don't mind. The Holy Spirit's got me this far. I'm not worried.' And I wasn't. I thought, well, so what? It's not the end of my life. I don't have to be ordained as a priest.

Bishop Lunt retired soon after that and Bishop Trevor Huddleston arrived in the East End, from Africa, to be the new Bishop of Stepney, and he sent for me. He said, 'Why aren't you a priest?' and I said, 'I don't know.' He said, 'Well, there's a file on you here. Can you tell me about your side of this?' So I told him my side of the story and he said, 'Hmm. What about Michaelmas for your ordination?' That was about three months later, in September; September 29th.

Being ordained authenticated me in a way that nothing else has ever done. I've always had a sense of God being here, and that I don't need to worry, and as time goes on I worry less and less. But with priesthood, something happened to me. There was something lifted. I mean, I marvel at times. When I came to England in '52 I was a meek and mild chap. I wouldn't have said boo to a goose. If anyone was two days older than me, I'd stand up and bow, practically. Thankfully I'm not like that now. But when hands were laid on me, I felt the tremendous weight of the Church, as though I was being ground into the earth; and in fact my first ordination, to the diaconate, had even more effect on me than the actual priesting.

The priesting made me feel that I was in some way acceptable, because for a lot of my life I lived as if I was a non-accepted person, a rejected person. Being born and being chucked out right away. Not being legally or formally fostered or adopted. Those kinds of things which really gave you nothing, no ground. Jim was the first person who gave me some sort of ground, but prior to that there was nothing, really. And here I was being accepted, if you like, in the Beloved. Accepted by God if nobody else.

So that was what ordination was for me. It's also a very humbling thing, and becomes even more so at times when people come to you. Lord knows what they expect from you. I don't know half the time. But they come to you and they tell you their most private things, their pain, which they may not show anyone else. And that's a privilege. They also think that you've got the answer to it and of course you haven't got the answer: but the answer to pain lies within ourselves and if you're alongside a person in the right way that person hears what's going on within themselves and can respond.

I don't see the priest as being any better than anyone else. I'm no different from any other man or woman. The idea of putting priests on pedestals and thinking they're better than you and they've got all the answers is nonsense. Priests have frailties and vulnerabilities just like anybody else, and the fact is, it's often the most wounded people who find themselves going towards ordination. Now, whether this is a calling of God or whether it is a way of compensating for weaknesses, who knows? Maybe it's a combination of both. But it certainly isn't, 'I'm the great guy and I'm going to save you' and all that nonsense. It's about loving. You read the Gospels and the thing that stands out about Jesus was that he was a lover, meaning that he cared for people: he cared for those that nobody else cared for. To me that's what priesthood is about.

Henri J. M. Nouwen wrote a book on ministry and he said there were four functions in ministry. Actually he wrote three and I've added the fourth. I hope he wouldn't mind. There's the priest, there's the pastor, there's the prophet; and there's the prayer. And a prayer is somebody who listens, because to me that's what prayer is all about. Listening. It's either listening to God, whatever God may be, or it's listening to another individual, or it's listening to oneself; and listening in such a way that you hear, because we don't often hear. We listen to people, but we don't always hear what they say.

Sharing God is being part of a sacred circle, a holy circle, a togetherness circle, and it's this circle that enables me to be involved in the HIV/AIDS field. If it was me who had to cure that person, I'd be lost. If it was me that had to help that person find a nice way to die, a meaningful way to die, I'd be lost. I'm just the channel to help that person settle into his Godness or her Godness, and let them find their own inner peace within it, so they can make the transition into the greater dimension. Therefore, it's my job to prepare myself as a person, to make sure when I'm alongside people that my own pains at that point in time aren't so large that I can't hear the people I'm concerned about. So before I go to be with people I clear the airways. I pray. And occasionally I help people not just by listening, but by reflecting back things they say, as you've done this morning. You probably don't realize, but you're doing with me what I do with other people a lot of the time because you are having to listen. The difference between you and me is that I'm also carrying a Christian symbol when I listen, and I'm carrying the priest's symbol when I put on my robes, which I do when I hear formal confessions. But whenever we listen to another person, whoever we are, we're just channels.

All thoughts of being a conductor had gone out the window by this time. I felt I hadn't got what it took to be a professional in the rat-race. You've got to be very good to stay in the rat-race, and I felt I hadn't got enough real background in music and there wasn't much point in trying to push it. I would also have had to take more studies and I couldn't afford to. I didn't have much confidence in those days anyway.

I worked at St Clement's Hospital in the Drug Unit, for about two and a half years. Then I went from there to the Regional Hospital Board, where I was Principal Nursing Officer, with responsibilities for psychiatric and mentally handicapped hospitals, and community nursing. While working there, it became clear that we should know more about the person's family and home situation, so we launched a pilot scheme of home visits from a psychiatric nursing team, and because that was a success it was suggested that I apply for a job as one of London's Principal Regional Nursing Officers, specializing in psychiatry, the mentally subnormal and community care.

In 1970 I left St Clement's Hospital and, partly at the request of the Bishop of London, Gerald Ellison, I went to work for a charity called Centrepoint, one of the first emergency night shelters for the young homeless in London. It was launched by Father Ken Leech, who was the curate at St Anne's Church in Soho and a remarkable young man. He's also a Christian socialist, as I am: I don't see how you can be a Christian without being a socialist, because it's all about social care, looking after people. Anyway, Ken left in 1970 because he got married and didn't think that it was the place to bring young children up. The Bishop knew that I'd worked with young people in the East End and he asked me to take on the chairmanship of the Centrepoint Management Committee; he thought that as it was a Church project there should be a priest chairing it.

My next five years were spent developing Centrepoint. It was during that time that Richie came into my life. Richie was my partner after Jim, and we too were together for twenty years. Anyway, Centrepoint is now one of *the* projects of the country as far as looking after the homeless is concerned, but we built it up slowly with a volunteer force of people. At its peak we had a large core of volunteers, and we used to invite young people off the streets, from whatever age up to twenty-one. The young people would come in and be offered a meal which we got from restaurants when they closed: all these posh restaurants would give us their left-over food, which a lot of the young people didn't like because they weren't used to that kind of food. We got beds eventually and turned the place into something quite nice. The money came through trusts and donations, and we never knew when our salary was going to be paid half the time. It's amazing the team stayed together, but we did.

Now it's a huge charity, and it's got several places. I suppose we gave it a firm basis, and that was our job, as well as getting paid staff, which they didn't have before. Volunteers are wonderful and they bring something that nobody else brings but I felt we needed a core of paid staff, because you can't demand everything of volunteers. Also, when you're getting money from funders they expect the place to be run by a small core of people who are responsible for certain aspects of the work, so you need to be able to pay people.

My salary came out of the donations we had. I've never been paid by the Church for any of the work I've done, and that's been my wish. I lived at Centrepoint in one room; one room and a toilet. In fact, the toilet and kitchen were divided: the partition in between was bookshelves. It would never have passed the health and safety standards! Never! But it was handy for reading books. So it was very primitive, but it was great. I loved it, it was one of my favourite places.

Nobody stayed permanently at Centrepoint. We were strictly a crisis centre, and the young people stayed three days to a week, depending. We felt we could do as much in three days as we could in a week, because we had a great antenna out everywhere as to where young people could go to after us. People only stayed in for the nights, not during the days. First we'd try to find out a bit about the person. We'd invite them in, find out what we could. They won't tell us very much the first night. The second night they'll probably tell us a lot more, because then they've found out they're with an accepting group of people, and they know the files are confidential. They would have meals, clothing if they needed it, medical attention. We were able to provide first aid, and most times we did find places for them to stay by working in conjunction with other agencies like the Soho Project and New Horizon: these were all agencies that were open during the day, so people had somewhere to go in the daytime. The short-term aim was to find help for the young homeless. The long-term aim was that through the various agencies they would get on their feet, be able to find a flat, find a job, and if it was right, to move back home.

With this kind of work you don't know how successful you are. Rarely does anybody come back to you and say, look, I've made it. It happened occasionally, sure. But of the ten lepers healed by Jesus only one turned back to say thanks. They probably know more about what happens to people now because they keep statistics and have a follow-up, which we didn't, because we hadn't the staff to do it. The saddest part of it was knowing that many people, after three nights with us, were just going back on the streets. We so often had to say, 'If we keep this person for another lot of three days, we're not seeing somebody else,' and that was not at all easy; but these things were always team decisions, and that eased the pain a bit.

Hopefully they received enough to enable them to do something for themselves, because that was part of it too, that they had to contribute as well. Otherwise you're doing everything for them and that limits people. But homeless people *are* very powerless, and people are homeless for all sorts of reasons. Some are made homeless by other people. For some, homelessness is the most positive move they can make from bad family situations, where it seems there's no way of getting out of it except by leaving. That group, if you can do something positive with them, will probably move on and make a go of something. They're prepared to take on all sorts of jobs just to make sure they're being responsible for themselves. Then you get the group who may be high-grade mentally subnormal, who can function if there's somebody around them but really can't function on their own. You get the group who may be illiterate, and they've probably never worked. Then you get the people who are perhaps depressive-type people, who may go into drugs and alcohol, and partly because they're depressed, and partly because it's escapism, they get caught up in drugs or prostitution and some of them may have been in long enough before they meet you that it's going to take a long time before they move out of it. So you just have to try to encourage them. That's all you can do.

The numbers of the homeless really have increased. That's to do with Thatcherism. Young people between the ages of sixteen and eighteen now receive no dole. Well, what are they going to do? Parents often can't afford to keep each member of the family, so it's, 'Johnny, you're sixteen: go and make your own living.' Whether Johnny's capable of making his own living is quite another thing. It's, 'Johnny, we can't afford you.' So out they go. Either that or they're creating a fuss at home and the family can't cope. Dad's not working. Mum's not working. They've lost a lot. So there are hassles at home. Dad nags. Mum does the same. The young people can't stand it and they leave. We probably all would. And they come down to London with such grandiose ideas, but it's not long before they realize they haven't got a hope, and get caught up in all sorts of things that are no good.

In three days there is very little you can do as an individual. Lots of people wanted to know, especially those who gave us money, what our success rate was. Natural thing to ask. I don't know what Centrepoint costs now, but it must cost at least a million pounds a year to run. That's a lot of money, and are you getting value for it? But I say, what's value when you're talking about individuals? If you've spent a million pounds on one individual and that individual's made a success of his life, or her life, then it's worth it.

Since before my time at Taizé I'd always wanted to try the religious life. I knew a lot of Franciscans, and I thought, if I'm ever going to do it, now is the time. So in 1975 I became an Anglican Friar with the Society of St Francis, taking the name Aelred William. I lived in Dorset, which was the main Franciscan centre, for about a year; then I went to live in Northumberland with Harold the hermit for a month. Harold lived as a hermit friar in a little caravan in a field, and that was my first experience of trying to live such a lifestyle. He was in this part of the field and I was in the other, and we met up for meals and services and that was it. Then from there they sent me to a monastery near Worcester, and I was there a year and liked it very much.

After that I was moved to a school at Hook for maladjusted boys from the ages of six to sixteen. I went there as the Chaplain and didn't fit in at all. Wasn't my cup of tea. I'd never worked with young children, I'd worked from sixteen up, not sixteen down, and they were highly disturbed, highly intelligent, and they walked circles around everybody, including me. I just didn't fit in, you know, it just wasn't right for me. But even before I went there I was beginning to think, I wonder if this is really me, whether I'm too much of a loner to be stuck in a community.

I joined it because it seemed right to join it. If I was exploring anything it probably was the contemplative side of myself, which has got stronger as I've got older, and certainly came to the fore then. At that time I was also seeing a nun called Mother Mary Clare, who became my soul-friend and my spiritual director, and she was quite convinced that it was the contemplative life that was evolving, and I did get on well at that monastery in Worcester and with Brother Harold. The only place I really felt awkward was at the school. I think it may have reminded me of my own early life, of feeling different, and maybe I hadn't totally come to terms with that.

Leaving the Franciscans seemed as right for me as it was to join them. It was a great experience of community life, and any fantasies about the religious life that one might have had beforehand – which I don't think I had, actually – they certainly disappeared. It took me from being someone who had been in authority one way or another to being someone with no authority. But I realized I was not where I should be as an individual, that I was very much a loner, and loners don't make communities; they sit on the edge of them but they don't make them. And I'm somebody who sits on the edge.

After a year living very quietly near Preston I came to Earls Court. I had come down to London to see someone I knew and came through Earls Court and just thought, 'I have got to come here.' It kept nagging me and nagging me, so I went to see Bishop Gerald Ellison and he said, 'Bill. You can do whatever you like in my diocese.'

I had to find a place, and I found this place. Then I had to find the money for it. I didn't tell the estate agent I was on the dole. I bluffed. I told him, 'The Trustees are all away until the end of the summer, and I won't be able to get any money until the middle of September, but if the people in the flat are willing to wait until then, I'll have all the money in cash.' Well, the next day I got a phone call saying they would wait, and for the next few days I went around laughing because I thought, this is stupid! Where am I going to get the money in six weeks' time?

After waiting for replies from various Trusts, and not hearing from them, I sought the advice of Sir Maurice Laing, of the Laing Trusts, whom I'd met during my early days at Centrepoint. This meeting came about as a result of Sir Maurice and Lady Laing waiting at Paddington station one day for their son John. While they were waiting they saw all these young people waking up and moving out of the station after spending the night there. They were concerned about this, and as Sir Maurice was quite busy, he asked his wife if she would find out if anybody was doing anything about the situation. A few days later Lady Laing was in St Paul's Church, Covent Garden, and she saw a notice about Centrepoint on the church noticeboard. She and Sir Maurice invited me to supper, which was followed by a lengthy discussion of the work of Centrepoint. They said they would like to support the work by contributing a full salary, which they did, and since I left Centrepoint they have continued to be very supportive of me and my various endeavours.

Anyway, after getting nowhere with the Trusts I had approached for money for the flat I sought the advice of Sir Maurice as to where I could borrow the money interest-free. He just smiled and said, 'Bill, *who* do you think is going to give you an interest-free loan?!' I told him what I wanted to do, that I wanted the flat to be a 'listening centre' available to anyone in the Earls Court area of London, and he said he'd come and look at it. On seeing it, he said he felt it was quite suitable, except that there needed to be a separate entrance 'if you're going to have all manner of people calling anytime day or night', and for that I needed planning permission. He then said that if this permission were granted he would approach his Trustees about funding.

Within a few days I managed to get the necessary permissions together, and I delivered the documents to Sir Maurice's offices. The Trustees met that evening, and I was invited along to discuss the proposal for the 'listening centre'. They certainly put me through the mill, and quite rightly so, but afterwards they informed me straight away that the Trust would buy the flat and they would continue to hold the property. So you see, things happen! It's what Carl Jung would call the 'synchronicity of timing'.

So that's how I got here. Hadn't a clue what I was supposed to do, except just wait, sit and wait, and for the first six months to a year hardly anybody turned up. I was beginning to think, I've lost it. I'd better go to the Laing family and tell them it's not working. I never advertised the fact that I was here. I call myself *Reaching Out*, but I keep no records, and I've always relied on word of mouth. You know, I started by going to the pubs and clubs and walking around the streets at three and four in the morning; getting some idea of what was happening at night. And then people started turning up, and I don't know how many people I ended up seeing in a year. Then out of that, from just being in the area and meeting a lot of rent-boys, I began to think, can anything be done about these young male prostitutes?

In 1985, seven years after moving to Earl's Court, I met with the Chairperson of the Rufford Foundation seeking advice and possible funding for a project to help these people. I wanted to set up a day centre for the young men involved in the sex industry at street level (because there are all sorts of different levels, and the street is the lowest). After much discussion, I was asked to present a proposal that could be put before the Trustees, and the Trustees, on examining it in detail, agreed to assist in the launching of the project.

The project was launched the same year, and became Street-wise Youth. I didn't want to run it, I didn't want to get back into the management fold. But I knew someone who had been a rent-boy and had also been raped, and the Trustees met him and agreed that he should launch the project. That someone was Richie.

For the first year we used this flat as a base for the project, but as it grew we needed somewhere else. Someone had to raise the money for a move, and as I had a name for raising money, the Trustees asked me to take it on. I said I'd take it on for two years, no more, and that's how it worked; with Richie doing the work and me raising the money behind the scenes. The actual meeting with the young people wasn't really my scene because I'd never been a rent-boy, I'd never been raped. But Richie knew all about that, and you couldn't pull the wool over his eyes. He had a wonderful way with young people, a tremendous way with young people. I'm being as unbiased as possible about that, but that really was one of his great gifts. He left the

334

project in 1987 because he was HIV-positive, and we had a new man take over from him, and then *that* chap had HIV and died, a year before Richie did. I then became the Director for two years, and I'm now an honorary consultant.

You see that photograph on the wall? His name was Jason Swift and he was murdered at the time Streetwise Youth was starting. We wanted to name the place after him, but the committee didn't. He was fourteen and a rent-boy, and it was his murder that inspired the need for a project like Streetwise Youth. People say, why didn't you start one for women, or a mixed one? Well, we tried a mixed one, but it didn't work. And the point is, there was already the odd project for women but at the time we started Streetwise Youth there was nothing for men of any description anywhere in the country, so we were a pioneer project in many ways.

The Outreach team would go down to the railway stations, the streets and the pubs where these young boys hang out, and they'd chat with them, give them a card with our telephone number and say, ring us when you're ready. Not all of the boys are homosexual. A lot of them are heterosexuals, and many of them are people who have been abused by a close member of their own family, which suggests to them that they're not worth anything. And you know, if you're not worth anything, you may as well sell yourself. We tried to break that psychological pattern, but you need time for that. You can't just do it overnight. Fortunately, the project is now getting funding from the Home Office, which is very hard to get. None through the Church. We didn't ask them. Though we've got about twenty-five individual sponsors, and many of them are Bishops, or people of that rank from other denominations.

I get lonely occasionally. I had a really dark time when Jim left, which was kind of a death. Going through all that and trying to understand what it was all about. Trying to work through it. And Richie dying. He died two years ago. Had HIV for about seven years. But he did a lot during that time; he wrote four

335

books. His last book, *Cry Love, Cry Hope*, he wanted to put together but he couldn't finish, so I finished it for him and it was good for me to do that. It helped.

I have my moments, of course. I have moments when I . . . I think of him every day. I know he was no angel either, I haven't got a halo stuck around his head; but see, part of Christian belief is that we move on to something greater, and it would be hypocritical of me to talk about believing that, and then when my own partner dies acting as though he hadn't gone somewhere worthwhile. Because I believe he has. I can't prove it, and I always say that at funerals, but something deep down tells me that it's all right. Sure, at times it's terrible and I cry and all the rest of it, but underneath it all he's okay, he just is, I know he is.

I still miss him. You walk down the streets that both of you walked down together and pictures come back, and a couple of times I think I've actually seen him. Somebody walked into a meeting the other day and I just stopped talking mid-sentence, the profile was so, so alike. God. I couldn't believe it. And I walked in here one day and I thought he was in the place. I thought he was here. Because he used to smoke a special type of tobacco that he mixed together, and it was a very special smell; and this flat was full of it. I went looking for him.

So we stay attached. In some way everyone who touches our lives does so for good and for ever. And the more that person touches your life, the more that person is part of the invisible fabric of your life. And that's what builds the bridge between this dimension and the next, this thing we call love.

Yet for whatever reasons, hopefully the right ones, maybe a few wrong ones too, I choose to live this way now: alone, from day to day. I might leave here tomorrow. I mean, I'm in Earls Court for as long as I should be here. I don't know how long that will be, and it doesn't matter. I don't really want to know too much about tomorrow. I suppose it's the freeflowing aspect of me. I live for today. You and I are having a good encounter, but if we never see each other again the important thing is that we've had a good encounter today. Working with the dying, with the bereaved, you realize it's *now* that's important. Now's the time to tell somebody you don't like why you don't like them. Now's the time to tell someone you love, I love you.

This is why I really want the freedom to *move* with the Holy Spirit. I'd probably not have been able to do it if I had any real commitments, because if you have emotional commitments they have to come first. Since I've been involved in the voluntary sector, life has never been ordinary, it's offered me a lot more freedom in a way. Why, sure, sometimes I think it'd be great to come home to a partner, but you can't have it all ways, you can't have the freedom to be available, which is my basic theme, I guess, and have a partner around. If you have a partner that partner should be the priority.

I haven't renounced anything. I mean, I wouldn't say no if somebody came along and it seemed right, okay? So I'm not saying no to a relationship as such. But there's no point in going round moaning because I want a relationship or I want sex or whatever, when in fact this may not happen. And in one sense it doesn't bother me the same way as it would have done maybe twenty-five years ago. I mean, I like people around and all the rest of it, but underneath it all or in the middle of it all there is a sense that it's right for me to be alone right now.

The Church has left me alone, which is fine, it's what I wanted, so I really can't complain. Ironically enough, it's the institution which I don't like that has let me function as I want. I saw somebody yesterday who was the first man I ever spoke to about the idea of being ordained, Canon Eric James, who's another odd bod in the Church of England, a tremendous guy. We were just chatting, and I don't know why we got on to it but he said, 'You really have been allowed to do so much.' Maybe I have. It's weird, really, because you'd expect someone like me to be shouting and screaming about the Church: and sure it's full of faults and all the rest of it, but as a person I can't complain. It's been all right for me. After deciding that I was safe enough to ordain; after that, they couldn't have been better.

I suspect that other clergy have mixed feelings about me, very mixed feelings. That I'm playing at it, and why did they bother ordaining me, and those sorts of silly comments. But it's up to God, isn't it? But then, I'm not in touch with many clergy. I sit on the edge of the Church. I don't have to go to Synods, I don't have to go to Church deanery things. I've been excused. So I can't complain.

Having said that, I'm sad that the Church is awkward about the whole gift of sexuality. I know I'm a bit biased here, but I'm terribly sad about it. I'm sad about the way they've treated women through the centuries. Those sorts of thing get me. I think it's wrong what they've done to women. Women are half of the human race. They have as much to contribute as any man. Yet women in the Church have been treated as second-class citizens and that's a load of . . . well, I don't see how *any* Christian or *any* institution that calls itself Christian can even *begin* to behave like that. But that all had to do with when the Church fitted in the political system of the day, when women were down there somewhere, when you were lucky if you were even looked at, because you were there to rear kids and keep the house clean or the equivalent. You weren't allowed to speak, you weren't allowed to recognize your own personal uniqueness. And that's cruel. That's certainly not what the faith is about.

I don't think there's one theological reason why women can't be ordained: you're just breaking the icon. And maybe some icons have to be broken. The North American Indians make a shell which consists of old pottery and new pottery, and they put a seed inside it. It's corn, to make sure they always have food. When they've finished, they break the shell and reconstitute it for the next year. The Church needs to do that. It needs to break its shell. We don't know whether Jesus would have ordained women or not. Had he lived longer he might very well have done, because he was a radical and women played a large part in his ministry. I think Jesus would have ordained women, because he was a rebel for respect and for truth in his fighting for the underdog, and that included women in those days; still does in many ways.

The thing that really gets me about the Church is how it hasn't picked up, in ways that it might have been able to pick up, some of the agonies of today. Sure, there are good things about the Church, sure. But in the HIV/AIDS field, say, which I've been in the last ten years, the Church has been very slow to get involved. When I started, I was the only priest requested by the Terrence Higgins Trust. Now there are many more, but it took ages of prodding for the Church to recognize that it should be here. The Church should be where there is pain, whatever that pain is, whatever its name, because that's its job. When it's not there, one says, well, why isn't it there? Partly because the clergy have all got individual hang-ups. Some bishops can cope with gay men, some can't. Some bishops are quite happy to have a gay pair into the house and invite them to a meal, but others wouldn't.

There's a lot of people who have difficulty with homosexuals, who don't know how to deal with you, how to cope with you. You see this at funerals of gay men who've died as a result of HIV infection. The parents don't know how to cope with the partner that's been left behind. They just don't know how. They say, 'I know he's my son's best friend but how do I introduce him to other people?' And the other relatives may know he's got a friend but never have any idea of what that entailed. And the Church mirrors that, not in the way it doesn't know, but in the way it refuses to know.

Now the House of Bishops have produced this thing called *Issues in Human Sexuality*. In it they suggest that lay gay men and lesbians can have sex with their partners, but priests can't. Well, that's a double standard. It's either right for everybody or it's right for nobody. People have said that I'm being too wishful, but I like to think that *Issues in Human Sexuality* is the first step; that next time they bring something out it will say that the same things apply to both gay and heterosexual relationships. The Church has got to come to terms with sexuality eventually. You know, it's saying: why aren't the churches full? But then you think how little there is to encourage gay men, because of the very nature of the Church and the services, and unless the Church says to gay people, 'Come and stay,' then it'll lose them. It's already losing all sorts of people because it's not offering what it's meant to be offering. The Church is meant to be meeting people from wherever they're coming from, not the other way around, but it doesn't because it's so full of fallible, vulnerable people who can't accept others because of their own hang-ups. And that's not me being judgmental, I'm just stating a fact. Perhaps the reason the Church is so unwelcoming is because underneath the pomp and circumstance it's the biggest body of vulnerable people you can find. Yet it's the Church's *job* to show its vulnerability. The Church *itself* has got HIV/AIDS – by the very fact that it has got baptized, practising Christians who have AIDS, or are HIV. The Church has got problems. The Church has got everything everybody else has got, because it's human.

A lot of people think that gay men are very promiscuous. They are, but so are heterosexual men. You see, for a man, a penis is the thing that says, 'I'm a man.' For a woman it's bearing a child, or at least being capable of bearing a child if she wants to. For a man, as long as his libido's there, he can say, 'I'm a man, I've still got libido. That's me.' There's a book out called *Intimacy*, by James B. Nelson, and he talks a great deal about this, and it's a fascinating discussion. He's a married man himself and he's got children, and he says that this is just a male thing, but that when a man can move beyond it and see that there's more to himself than just his penis or the sex activity, then it's easier. But most men are trained in the macho thing, and it's how much sex you can have, whether with women or with men. But now the men's movement is beginning to look at the more feminine aspects of a man, maybe things will change a bit.

In both my own relationships we never said, 'This is for life.' We just assumed it was. I have difficulty with the idea of gay marriage. Maybe I'm just being old-fashioned, but to me being married is a man and woman and bringing up children, and at this point in time it's not allowed for a gay or lesbian pair to adopt children, so there's a block in me somewhere about that. It's not a theological block because I think marriage is the school of friendship, and friendship is the same both ways because it's about love. I guess it's the icon for me. And I guess until the state recognizes it I'll have a problem with it because I know if I were to marry a gay couple it might be used as an excuse to strip me of my Orders. So there's some fear in there as well. And maybe I need to address that. Yeah, maybe I do.

But I see nothing wrong in blessing a partnership if the two people, whatever their sex, believe that it will help them. A lot of gay couples want a blessing of their partnership and I don't see anything wrong in that. I've been asked to do it several times, and I have. I look for signs of stableness in the relationship, but if I feel it's genuine, I don't have any difficulty with it. And I believe if we can bless battleships and instruments of war, why should we not bless something that may be an instrument of peace, an instrument of love, an instrument of growth? If you can bless battleships, you can bless friendships.

I have been alongside 1,250 people living with HIV/AIDS during the past ten years. And I've been alongside about 350 when they've died, and buried about half of them. And it's been a wonderful experience in a way, a wonderful experience. Humbling. Taught me a lot about spirituality. I've had great talks with many men on a spiritual level, talking about God in the way they wanted to talk about God, talking about death in the way that meant something to them, in the language that they wanted to use, not the language that I was used to. That kind of thing broadens you. And there's also the mutual caring. It's not just me caring for them, it's me allowing them to care for me as well. You know, the 'How are you? What have you been up to? I hear you've done so-and-so. Don't you think you're overdoing it?' That kind of thing.

I had a lovely little card from a chap the other day. He's been in hospital, what, three months, and I don't know whether he's going to leave it or not. But it just said, 'You are looking after yourself, aren't you? You don't have to visit me every other day, you know.' And that's important, that they're allowed to contribute as long as possible, that they're allowed to go on caring for others, that they're not just passive. It's terribly important. And sometimes you sit and discuss the daily news and what's going on, and sometimes you just talk. It depends on the mood they're in, and you have to be very sensitive to it, so that you either stop and talk or you just poke your head in the door and leave. But when people allow you into their souls, to their sacred centre, it's a tremendous privilege and a great responsibility.

I've also had to learn to be alongside people who don't want to talk. They like you there, but they don't want to talk. They may want you to hold their hand or give them a hug. Those things are still quite new in the caring world, because you're not supposed to get that close to people, you're not supposed to get emotional about people. Yet sometimes you can't help it. Some of these men I've known for years. And they're very open, they're very vulnerable, they talk in-depth about themselves and their beliefs, and that's all tremendous. And I find myself becoming more and more honest about who *I* am as a result. I would never be talking to you now the way I am if this were ten years ago. But being dishonest saves you from getting emotional, saves you a lot of pain. And a lot of people, a lot of priests, are afraid of that pain. You told me about the priest you knew, who said neither of you should get close to parishioners, that you should keep yourselves to yourselves. Well, that's rubbish. If you don't get close to people you can't love them.

But so many priests limit their own humanness, put themselves in a box because they're frightened. They label themselves 'the Priest', 'the Vicar'. But what is a priest? What is a straight person? What is a gay person? Those terrible labels that we've got. If you stick a label on somebody you don't have to go beyond the label, you just see what that label suggests to you and therefore you don't get the whole picture. You have to move beyond the label to begin to get the truth. And that means being open: it means recognizing your own weakness, your own woundedness, as well as your strengths.

I'm being taught how to be a priest all the time. And maybe I'm involved in the AIDS field because it's mostly gay men and I am a gay man, so I am looking after my brothers, if you like. Who knows? We never know all the reasons. Some of them are good, some of them are less good, I guess. I'd hate to say, 'I'm there because I'm a goodie and I'm doing good.' I'm there because I need to be there, for whatever reason. I just hope that my need to be there isn't greater than that of the person I'm meant to be alongside, because if it is I won't hear that person; all I'll hear is me, and that doesn't make for good relationships, good connections. And it's connections, it's listening, that lies behind what I try to do, because that's how I've been helped, through people listening to me in such a way that I can hear the real me. Now it's my responsibility to try to do the same for others. The main reason for telling this story to you is because if there are people reading it who are feeling, 'I got nothing. I can't get anywhere', it will show them that you *can* get there. That you *can* grow; you can grow through the hell of your youth.

Where I go from here I don't know. I'm sure that sometime in the not too distant future I will semi-retire; perhaps in the UK, perhaps to Canada, where I can live in a more solitary way. Forty years in the centre of London needs to be redressed with time in the country within view of the sea or the mountains. I feel I need that kind of nourishment now. Who knows. I've never really planned before, so maybe I should do now. After all, if you don't plan anything, you're not really taking risks, because you're just allowing things to happen: if you go with the wind you can always tell yourself that nothing's gone wrong with your life because you didn't plan it to go a certain way in the first place. Maybe the idea of changing so often is a need to make myself homeless every so often, a need to keep moving. Maybe I'm running away from something. But maybe I'm running towards something. Maybe both. Perhaps it's a tug both ways that makes what I do creative. I don't know. And I don't mind. The only thing that matters to me is that I continue to flow with the Holy Spirit.

RICHARD HARRIES

Age: 57
Age at ordination: 28

BISHOP OF OXFORD

The first thing I noticed about Richard Harries was his good looks. He is tall and handsome, in a military sort of way, slim bordering on thin, with regular features and good skin. In fact, he looks so permanently healthy that I once asked him if there was a sun-bed in his life. He denied it much more politely than I deserved, citing a recent trip to South Africa. His loyal and friendly chaplain, Martin, was more to the point: 'Mary, face it. You're just jealous.'

A vocal and fairly high-profile bishop, Richard Harries writes and broadcasts a lot. His intellectual ability and media exposure have earnt him a popular appeal that is resented by a number of people within the Church, largely because it is accessible to so many without. This is unsurprising given that one of the identifying features of the Anglican Church is not just its public tolerance of extremists but its private ambivalence about liberals. Yet despite being regarded as too smooth by some, and too spiky by others, Richard Harries's refusal to embrace cosy theology and easy answers has resulted in less criticism than admiration. That people undoubtedly find Richard Harries a little threatening may also be connected with the fact that in 1991 he, together with others, had the imagination to take the Church Commissioners to court over their 'ethical' investments policy. Some saw this as a move of una-shamed self-promotion: others as evidence of courage and integrity, and the end of any hopes of preferment that Richard Harries may have been harbouring.

I interviewed Richard Harries in his office at the headquarters of the Diocese of Oxford. Situated right on the edge of a quiet and pretty village just outside Oxford itself, Diocesan Church House is sandwiched between a beautiful Norman church and the A34, and consists of a hefty nineteenth-century vicarage on to which a large modern extension has been built. Functional though it is, the architectural result is a strange one: Victorian Gothic meets Lego in a car park.

I found Richard Harries unfailingly polite and friendly, but to begin with almost painfully shy and circumspect. On the first of our three afternoons together he sat in the slightly huddled fashion of someone waiting to see the dentist. However, once he'd ascertained that I was relatively safe, he emerged and relaxed, becoming noticeably warmer, wittier and more forthright by the hour. He was enormous fun to be with.

During the writing of this book I got to know him better and like him more and more, most of all for his readiness to laugh at himself. When I showed him the draft of his chapter he was horrified — not by what he had said, but by the way in which he had said it. 'Oh, no. Did I really say "one" thinks this and "one" thinks that?' I assured him that he did. 'Then I must stop immediately. It makes me sound like the Duke of Edinburgh.'

RICHARD HARRIES

I was sent away to boarding school at an age which most people these days would regard as too young, about eight. My parents went to Singapore, and in those days it wasn't so easy for children of my age to go too, so I was left behind. My father was a brigadier in the Army, and my mother was of the same social background. I was born in 1936, and I have a younger sister and brother. Being service people we were moved around from one part of the world to another, so I spent my childhood in different places: first the United States, then Huddersfield, then the south-east, then Catterick. Then boarding school.

I missed my parents a lot. My first prayer request, which got a resounding negative, was to pray long and hard that they wouldn't have to go abroad, so my experience of religion from the first is of religious disillusion, of God not giving us what we want. One missed one's parents, there's no doubt about it, but in those days you were taught to grit your teeth and not to show it. I can still remember my first day going away to prep school and my mother being in absolute floods of tears and me being in tears as well, but seeing that she was crying even more than I was it was my job as the man to comfort her. That's how it was: you simply gritted your teeth and bore it. So there was probably a great deal of suppressed emotion in one then, and perhaps afterwards. My parents being abroad also meant that I was farmed out to various friends and relatives in the holidays, which had its compensations, because everybody said, 'Oh, poor little boy. His parents are abroad. We must be sweet to him,' and one got thoroughly spoilt – but it wasn't the same.

My mother, who died about three or four years ago, was a very warm person, and I think that there is no greater gift to anybody than to be loved by their mother and basically affirmed as a person, and I'm always very deeply grateful that I had that experience, which seems to be denied to so many people. However irritating and aggravating my mother might have seemed to be in later years, I always felt that as a baby I was hugged and kissed and wanted, which gives one a certain emotional stability. And my father was very caring in his own way.

What was I *like* as a child? Gosh, I don't think it's a question that I've ever given much thought to. I don't think I've ever given any thought to it. Depends what you mean. I think that I've always been cheerful. I've been blessed with what you could call a 'sunny disposition'. I suppose for most of my life I've been fairly conformist, and that's probably one of the pre-conditions of being cheerful, that you don't kick against things too much. Obviously one can remember a certain number of childhood tantrums, particularly at birthday parties. You know, you build up this enormous expectation of your ninth or tenth birthday party and when the day begins something goes wrong, somebody's cross with you or you don't get the present you want, and everything ends in tears; but I think I was basically a happy child.

But then, you see, one was always conditioned to think one was happy. When people said, are you enjoying things at school, you always said yes because you were conditioned to say yes. Looking back, I wasn't as happy as I made out at the time, either at prep school or at Wellington. In those days schools were rather more barbarous institutions than they are now. I can remember some very fierce gang warfare going on, with some really quite fierce cruelties between the different gangs, and woe betide you if you became the butt of anything. It was very, very easy for those schools to turn on people, and when I was there, Wellington was a very tough, arrogant school which made few concessions to softness or feeling.

The other thing is that at my prep school, the kind of people who were teaching then were those people who weren't able to serve in the Forces, and they were a pretty rum bunch, quite frankly. I don't know whether you've read Evelyn Waugh's novel *Decline and Fall*, but the schoolteachers in that book were the kind of schoolteachers you had at prep schools in 1945: as I say, a slightly rum bunch. So I don't regard myself as having had a very good early education. I also lost quite a lot of time when I was in America. On my first day at school in England everybody else was writing away and I was still doing block capitals. That was a day for tears, I can tell you.

I was never interested in any particular subjects at school, though I was moderately sporty at Wellington, and I used to do quite a lot of running. However, what I *really* loved, and spent quite a lot of time doing, was reading novels. I can still remember my housemaster coming into my room at night, and he invariably made the same remark. He saw me having gone to bed early with a novel and he said, 'My boy, why aren't you *working*?' But novels let one into an imaginative world which feeds whole areas of one's life, and literature has remained a major interest of mine. It wasn't necessarily the classics that I read at that stage, but it wasn't rubbish either. I can remember reading Richard Llewellyn's book *How Green Was My Valley*. Have you ever read that? I read it three times straight through: once, twice, three times, I was so moved by that book. I also remember going through a great Daphne du Maurier phase, and being drawn into a very intense, imaginative world.

Perhaps I loved reading so much because I wasn't very extrovert. I've never gone in for a large number of friends. That's not been my style. Though I've always had three or four cronies that I did things with, at prep school, at Wellington, and later at Cambridge. Perhaps my not being extrovert has more to do with being at boarding school than I realized. Although my experience of school was not bad exactly, both my wife and I decided we didn't want our children to go away to boarding school, because it's such an unnatural life. As I say, I've never given it any thought before, but talking about it makes me wonder whether it's left its marks on me.

Partly because I never had a strong religious upbringing, it's always been a great puzzle to me about how anybody believes or doesn't believe. We practically never went to church as a family, and although in later years my father was a very devout churchgoer, for about twenty years he would never even go into church, not even on Christmas Day, my mother said. Wellington, like most public schools, had a very boring public-school kind of religion which I found totally uninteresting and it made no impact. Religious education made no impact, either. We all had to take School Certificate in Religion, and I think I scored seven per cent, because I just didn't take it at all seriously. Though funnily enough I can remember at about the age of fifteen one of my friends saying, 'Of course there isn't a God,' and me instinctively saying, 'There is,' which was my first confession of faith, and one that still puzzles me. Why did that answer come up rather than another? My own view is that faith gets in somewhere along the line without you knowing it, and looking back I think it must have gone in with my mother's milk. I really mean that seriously. I think that faith went in as part of the process of being loved. My mother taught me to say my prayers in a very simple way, and something elementary probably went in and stayed in as a result.

I left school slightly young, at seventeen, because my father wanted to save a term's school fees! I took my A-levels at home, and then I went to Sandhurst, which in retrospect I think was something of a mistake. I enjoyed Sandhurst, because their motto was 'Work hard, play hard' and I was young enough to take them on their terms, but I didn't really know that I wanted to go into the Army. But as Wellington is an Army school, it was expected that you would go straight into the Army when you left.

The Army had its advantages. You played a lot of sport, which I enjoyed; you earned money from day one. The Army also paid for you to go to university. Your parents didn't have to pay either for your training or your education, which was a very cushy deal. So I spent two years as a Second Lieutenant in the Royal Signals, after which I was due to go up to Cambridge to do Engineering, but it was during that time that a sense of vocation developed, and I resigned from the Army. You're officially meant to do five years in the Army after Sandhurst, and there can be great difficulty getting out, but if you want to be ordained they usually let you out without a fuss: though there were people who got out on that excuse who I believe were later found rubber-planting in Malaya! However, I didn't go rubber-planting in Malaya, I went to Cambridge and read Theology.

I really don't know how my sense of vocation developed. When I was in the Army, I used to go to church occasionally. I'd been confirmed at school, and I can remember thinking: if Christianity is true, it must be at the centre of my life: if it's not true, then I should drop it altogether. Either way, I didn't like it being on the periphery of my life, so I decided to look into it more thoroughly, and one day, when I was in a library, instead of picking up the usual Hardy or something, I picked up, by chance or providence, a book of essays by Roman Catholic priests entitled, *Why I Was Ordained*. I read it, and for some strange reason I said to myself, 'Wouldn't it be funny if one day I were ordained.' A few months later the thought reappeared in a different form: 'One day you *will* be ordained,' and I thought, that's very nice. What better way to end one's life after a successful military career than to become a country parson? Then suddenly I realized that if I was meant to be doing it I must do it now. I should give it the best years of my life. Once that thought got in, it wouldn't let go. It took hold of me *totally*, it was like falling in love, and I knew I had to act on it.

I applied to the relevant authorities to go for selection and I got through. I'm sure I wouldn't now. I'd never been a member of an ordinary parish congregation. I knew nothing about the Church. I can still remember the Bishop at the selection conference looking me in the eye and saying, 'Do you feel you're truly called?' and because I'd been brought up to look people in the eye and say yes, I looked back at him and said, 'Yes.' I mean, supposing I'd wavered or lacked confidence or something!

My parents didn't know anything about all this, and they were amazed and horrified when I suddenly told them that I was leaving the Army to be ordained. I'd been rather naughty not to mention it, but you get in a turmoil with these things and you don't always do things correctly. I know they thought I was just mucking up my life, just being very foolish, and they weren't keen to pay for me because they still had my brother to educate and I think they felt they'd done their bit. So instead of going up to Cambridge on the Army, where you not only get your fees and allowances, but also a salary, I went up with no money at all, not even a local authority grant. The local authority gave grants according to your parents' income, which meant that I got about £20 a year, which was ridiculous.

In the end I took up the matter with my local Member of Parliament, a man whose political views I could never have agreed with, but I must say he did me very well on that occasion. He managed to persuade the Authority to treat me as independent of my parents, and in the end I got a full grant and managed perfectly well on it. But I always had real faith that things would work out, I felt so bowled along. I mean, I doubt I'd take that sort of risk now. When you're young you're capable of things you'd never do in middle age. It was worth it, though. I loved Cambridge.

After that I went to Cuddesdon Theological College in Oxford when Bob Runcie was the Principal, and I was among his first students. It was a pleasant enough experience, but I didn't make best use of my time there, quite honestly. I think the most valuable thing that I did was a six-month course at the Littlemore Mental Hospital in Oxford, because in a parish you meet a lot of people who are mentally disturbed, and having had practical experience with disturbed people you can recognize mental illness when you see it. More importantly, you know what you can cope with and what you can't. You recognize what is beyond your province. And that was invaluable, because it's important to know your own limitations as a parish priest.

Cuddesdon had been a very strict and austere college. No

women at all were allowed in the college in those days. I'd got engaged at Cambridge, and my wife, who was a medical student then, was finishing off her medical training in London, and she used to come down at weekends to visit, but women were only allowed in the college for half an hour after the Eucharist on Sunday mornings. It was the only time when it was assumed that the grace of the sacrament would keep the lust of the young men down. The lust of the young women hadn't been thought of then!

Things did begin to loosen up a bit under Bob Runcie, but he did it very, very gradually. The emphasis in training was still upon a regular rhythm of the Church Offices like Matins, Evensong, Compline; the Eucharist; personal prayer; community living, and that's not a bad recipe. It certainly gave one stability and discipline. There were also lectures and pastoral placements, but it was mostly assumed that the job of the priest was to say his prayers, to celebrate the Eucharist, and to help people grow in the Christian life. The great agonizing about what a priest was didn't really come in until the end of the sixties. I was at theological college in the early sixties, and at that point it was only just beginning to happen. One of my friends trained as a psychiatric social worker as well as a priest. Two or three people dropped out with a crisis. The tremor in the Church was beginning, but the explosion didn't come until a few years later.

I was ordained in 1963 and was a curate in Hampstead. I was married that year too, and we had two children while I was in Hampstead. I was blissfully happy there, I really loved it, and I stayed there for six years, which is much longer than normal, because it was such a stimulating place and the Vicar let me do what I wanted. Partly as a result of my experience at Littlemore, I started a Samaritan befriending group, and I was chairman of an organization called Arrowline, which was started by teenagers in Hampstead to do social service, like visiting old people and generally making themselves useful. There was so much religious idealism around in the sixties. A lot of people were interested in

Eastern religions and Buddhism and meditation and things like that, so religion was very much on the agenda for people. I even ran a group called Out Of Doubt for agnostic teenagers, the ones who never came to church.

The parish church in Hampstead also had a very strong tradition of good preaching. Every Sunday a man called Joseph McCulloch used to preach. You probably haven't heard of him but he was rector of St Mary-le-Bow in the City, and although he never achieved any major career in the Church of England he was a very brilliant and articulate man, and he used to preach every Sunday with us because he didn't have to do things in the City on Sundays. Whatever he said from the pulpit was always interesting and important, and it was from sitting at his feet for six years that I really learned that sermons can be interesting. I'm not the best preacher, though, I'm very mixed. Now as a bishop I might have ten or twelve speaking engagements in one week, which is too many, and I'm often conscious of lurching half-prepared from one engagement to another, so I'm good only on occasions, which is a pity really.

Perhaps I've got less good as I've got older anyway. I had so much energy as a curate. I've still got lots of energy, but as a curate I was so idealistic, as all curates are. They have to be, otherwise they'd never go into the job in the first place. Being ordained was so fulfilling for me, and I know I keep mentioning the sixties, but things really were beginning to bubble then and it was an exciting time to join the Church. Harold Wilson had taken power. There really was a feeling of the brave new world and the Kingdom of God being just around the corner. You know, it was a very, very *hopeful* time. People now look back on the sixties as a time when all moral standards collapsed, and I think in a way they did, but things were changing for the better as well as for the worse.

After Hampstead I went to Wells to lecture in Doctrine and Ethics, which wasn't something that I'd previously thought of doing. To be honest, I didn't want to to do it. I knew what I wanted to do, and that was to be the Vicar of a church near the middle of London. I didn't want to be right in the centre with an eclectic congregation; nor did I want to go out to the edge and worship what E. M. Forster called 'the great suburban Jehovah'. I wanted a mixed London parish, but there wasn't anything available at the time, and the one or two jobs I wanted, I wasn't offered. So when I saw this advertisement for Wells I applied because I thought I should, because I had to do something, and I got it. The churchy world of a theological college really didn't appeal to me, because I'm much better operating on the borderlands, but I'm so glad that I went there because it set the foundation for all kinds of things.

It was only when I began teaching that I really began to learn. Having to produce lectures week after week forced me to get my own thoughts on God, on the Church, on society, in order. The sort of work that I've done since then, and particularly the books that I've written, have in some sense been built upon the foundation of the work that I did at Wells. I've always been interested in ethics. Understandably, most people prefer theology because it deals with the more fundamental questions about God and Christ and so on. But Christian ethics – *how* we apply theology – is important and has been a very neglected field in the latter half of this century.

I hadn't been at Wells terribly long when I got an offer from the Bishop of London saying would I like to be Vicar of All Saints, Fulham, which was just exactly what I was looking for. He knew that, and it was very sweet of him to remember. It was a very mixed community. Although it was getting gentrified it still had every socio-economic group and quite a flourishing church with plenty of potential, and two church schools.

In some ways my life as a priest has been very different from what I imagined. I had a very strong conviction that this was what God was calling me to do, that this was my appointed lot and destiny, but if I ever envisaged what I thought I would do, I saw myself knocking on the doors of some depressed northern industrial town in the rain and bringing light and comfort to the inhabitants. That's how I envisaged my role as a parish priest. A very paternalistic image, and a very, very conventional image too, very conventional. And of course the reality was very different. But I'm sure my early notion of it was clearly linked to my strong sense, which I had then and I have now, about the truth of a Christian view of existence, which was that people would be a great deal *happier* – in the proper, profound sense of that word – if they believed in God and made God a part of their life. And this wasn't simply about going to have tea with people: it was about trying to help people to discover what I believe is the meaning and the purpose of all our lives.

I just knew that this was what God wanted me to do, though I'm certainly very willing to admit that there are all sorts of other reasons why I've ended up doing what I have done. It's always possible to find psychological, sociological and no doubt biological explanations for everything we believe and do, and I believe that the 'religious' explanation for things works in conjunction with these other explanations, and not as alternatives to them. But as you pointed out, I've probably not considered my own motives very deeply because I'm not a very introspective person – which is actually quite a shrewd comment, if I might say so. Because I'm not. And it doesn't worry me at all, because I'd much rather leave you to speculate as to what has motivated me than try to work it out myself!

In the same way that there are psychological explanations for people's religious beliefs and choices, there are also explanations for people's atheism and agnosticism. My own faith has been put to the test at times, not just intellectually, but emotionally and spiritually. I have always believed that the one really serious stumbling-block to a belief in God is the existence of so much evil and pain and suffering in the world, for all the philosophical arguments leave the matter open. You can neither prove nor disprove the existence of God. So while I believe that faith is natural to human beings, I can quite see why so many people don't believe in God, because the character of life is often so awful that it seems inconceivable that it could have been created by a wise and loving power. I wrestle time and again with evil and suffering not only in their extreme forms, but also in the sheer banality and boredom and littleness of a lot of people's lives. I found it very difficult when I was a parish priest, seeing the lives of so many people, and how difficult they were. You know: did God create this amazing universe just for *this*? You think of people who lead very petty and frustrated existences: is this all there is for them? Is this all that millions and millions of years of evolution amounts to? Does it all lead up to this? And if so, *what for*?

I'm a great admirer of the playwright Samuel Beckett, but after seeing some of his plays, like *Waiting for Godot*, you start to see life as he sees life, and it's very, very bleak. And the point is, Beckett is being truthful. That *is* what life is like from one aspect. It's not the only aspect, but it is possibly the dominant one for many people: a universe from which God has fled. Do you know that play he wrote with the woman stuck in a pile of sand up to her neck? *Happy Days*. That is so utterly bleak. It's utterly spine-chilling as a metaphor for our life and yet there's so much truth in it. So I do think it's very important to try to deal theologically with the bleakness of life. I don't think there are any definitive answers, but it is something I've written on. I've probably written on far too many things, but this is one of the things I've tried to think through very, very carefully, because I think we need enough of an answer at least to help us live with the problems.

Yet the question-marks remain. Evil is the one serious, huge problem, and the Christian approach to it contains a number of strands, of which God sharing the suffering is one, and the fact that the world has been given a genuine autonomy is another. There's the big question as to why God doesn't interfere more, and overrule human freedom, and I think that needs to be faced: but if God *did* do that, we would live in a topsy-turvy, Alice in Wonderland world, which would be impossible for rational human beings to exist in. If every time there was a calamity God slowed up or diverted the ordinary course of events, we wouldn't know whether we were coming or going. The basis of rationality is that you're able to predict the future more or less on the basis of the past, and if God interfered, then we couldn't do that and we wouldn't survive as a species.

I don't actually think any of these problems can be addressed without the Christian hope that in the end 'all shall be well, and all manner of things will be well'. I think those Christians who try to give an answer to the problem of evil and suffering without bringing in the prospect of eternal life are doomed to failure, but the extent of belief in an afterlife is not very high in our society at the moment. Even among churchpeople it's surprisingly low. Yet for me the Christian faith stands or falls as a whole. There certainly huge question-marks against a belief in God, but if I am going to believe in God then I will take the whole package, and that includes a belief in eternal existence. If God has created this universe with all its anguish and struggle, in which so many millions of people die with their lives stunted or unfulfilled, there must be some possibility of further development beyond this life. The view I take is that the real me, whoever I am, and the real you, whoever you are, is known to God, and although when we die our knowledge of things may seem to come to an end, God's knowledge of us will not. St Paul talks about a body of glory or a spiritual body, but as we have no idea what that is I don't really think there's much point in speculating. I accept it. I take it for granted.

I take my faith for granted. Faith to me feels like a constant undergirding of my life, like breathing. It's part of the rhythm of my life, and I hope it informs all that I do. I don't worry when it goes through emotional or empty phases, because I think one needs to sit fairly light to religious feelings. Feelings are very important, don't get me wrong, but I don't think they should be taken as a sure guide to what is real. I believe that I have a relationship with God, and I live my life on that basis, but it's not a relationship like any other kind of relationship, and it doesn't always feel very real. But I take the view that the intensity of one's relationship with anyone, including God, is very dependent upon one's biochemistry, and I tend to conduct all my relationships, including my relationship with my Creator, on a fairly even keel. If one has a manic-depressive temperament, or tendencies – as many very great figures in religious history have had – one will go through phases of feeling extraordinarily ecstatic and over the moon about life and God, and then one will swing into great depths and feel suicidal, feel cut off. That never happens to me. Because I'm not made that way, my relationship with God does not have that kind of intensity.

I've always thought that faith in God works quite simply. It's necessary to have a predisposition to trust other people for any kind of human contact to take place. You do come to mistrust certain people but unless there's a basic assumption of trust you preclude yourself from human experience. I would say that an attitude of trust towards God is a perfectly proper assumption to make. As a result of all the anguish and evil in the world you may come to doubt or totally disbelieve in God, but I would say it is rational to work on the assumption that God exists until such time as one is disabused. I don't mean that you can prove the existence or non-existence of God, because you can't. But if you assume that there is a trustworthy power behind the universe, that opens one up to the possibility of faith.

Faith in God is one thing, but for me, *Christian* faith is not possible without some kind of belief in the Resurrection of Christ. I do not believe that Christ was resuscitated in the same kind of body that he had before, but I do believe that the tomb was empty. I do believe that he was raised in what St Paul calls a spiritual body, whatever that might be. Perhaps the only parallel with the Resurrection is the Creation of the world in the first place *ex nihilo*, or the winding-up of the universe at the end, where presumably matter dissolves again into nothingness or is transfigured into the stuff of glory and eternity. If the universe has a beginning, a middle and an end, then we have some clue as to what the Resurrection is: both a new Creation and the beginning of the end.

That is quite an orthodox view. Where my view is not quite so orthodox is over the question of Christ's Resurrection appearances. When Christ was raised, he was raised to the right hand of the Father, i.e., to a universal contemporaneity. What the disciples had afterwards was an experience of the risen ascended glorified Christ, but because this experience had to be described in the gospel it was described in terms of an encounter with a risen person. That I do find hard to believe. I'm sure that, rather like some of the miracles, what the disciples actually experienced was beyond words or pictures. I don't think their experience was necessarily physical, nor do I think it was explicable or rational, just as I don't think one ever comes to faith by a rational process. Yet I do believe that the Christian faith does justice to the heights and depths of human experience. The image of the Cross as a sign of God sharing in human anguish seems to me to be the fundamental feature of Christianity which enables one to live with evil and suffering and, most importantly, to believe that in the end all things will work out for good and not ill.

That doesn't mean I think that Christianity is the only way to God, because I don't. I don't regard my grasp of religion to be such as to exclude other people having valid, truthful insights. Basically, I have always believed in religious dialogue. I know that's an over-worked word, but by 'dialogue' I mean seeing other faiths in their terms, rather than through the spectacles of one's own religion. However, I'm totally opposed to a watering-down of religions or a putting-aside of one's own convictions as a pre-condition of entering into dialogue. I think integrity demands that you bring to other religions what you believe most fully about your own faith.

This is admittedly a safe approach, but that's because it's an approach which is based upon relationship. I don't think that hard-line evangelism, say, is a logical approach to the multi-faith question. I think that if there is one Creator of the universe, and this Creator seeks to disclose something of His or Her mind or purpose for humanity, it would be very odd indeed if only one section of the human race had any glimmering of understanding of what this was. It's fundamental to my belief in God that He or She discloses Him or Herself to all people in all cultures at all times, because all human beings are capable of having an apprehension of God. But just as you can really only know another human being when there are moments of special disclosure, I think that while God discloses Himself to humanity through every culture, He does so *specifically* through the Judaeo–Christian tradition.

I actually have a special role and responsibility in relation to Judaism. I'm Chairman of the Council for Christian Jews and was until recently the Archbishops' Adviser on Jewish–Christian relations, which means I have to do a lot of speaking up and down the country to audiences of Jews and Christians. One of my greatest concerns is to re-educate the Christian constituency to have a more positive attitude towards Judaism. I think that so often we are blinkered by stereotypes. We teach the Christian faith as the good guy against Judaism as the bad guy, and this unconscious anti-Judaism is really destructive.

I do think that the relationship between Christianity and Judaism is a very special relationship, and is not the same as the relationship between, say, Christianity and Islam or Hinduism. The relationship with Judaism is a unique one, and we need to affirm that before we even start to say things about Christianity's relationship with other religions, for the simple reason that the religions are clearly saying mutually incompatible things. I mean, to take one obvious and rather extreme example, there are certain forms of Buddhism which in Christian terms are atheistic: therefore it's incompatible to say that Zen Buddhism and Islam and Christianity are equal ways to the truth. Intellectual integrity demands that one faces the fact that they are not.

Now, you can argue that they're not attempting to move in the same direction, but don't you think we all hanker after the idea that in the end truth is unified? That there is an ultimate truth? I think we do. I mean, to continue using Buddhism as just an example, it may very well be that Buddhist insights are a valid apprehension of some aspect of the ultimate truth: they have a lot to say about achieving internal serenity and not being too attached to the things of this world. But in terms of a metaphysical system there's clearly a big difference between, say, Allah or Jehovah, and the non-being, the Nirvana, which Buddhism sets as its goal. They are simply not all on a par.

On the other hand, the more common ground one can affirm, the better. There has been so much traditional religious animosity, and it's been so destructive. It still is. People say religion starts wars, and sadly that's often true. I know my emphasis on the need for dialogue might make me sound like a weedy liberal, but somebody once said that we are always most zealous about trying to convert other people to those truths that we feel least sure about ourselves. That's why I very much regret the demise of the old-fashioned atheist. Where have they all gone?! As one priest said to me recently: it's so difficult to operate in a culture of benign indifference. So soggy.

Being a parish priest is immensely demanding, and it was a relief to move on to another job after Fulham. It felt as if for nine years we hadn't sat down to a meal without the telephone going or somebody at the door, and one wouldn't have minded that if somebody had died, or somebody was worried about their soul, but most often someone would just want the key to the church hall. Also, the dynamics of running a congregation, of holding warring parties together, of trying to stop people getting upset all the time, was demanding and wearing.

This makes it sound as if the experience was all hard, and it wasn't, not really. The congregation was a very committed bunch, and very committed to the Church, and I learned a great deal from the people there. But vicarage life is a great strain on family life because there is no clear distinction between work and home. The particular strain is on the wife, because she's usually got her own career, plus the family, plus parish expectations, which means one more set of expectations on top of the normal two which most women find difficult enough to manage. I'm not sure that the clergy divorce any more than any other group, but there are certainly more clerical separations than there were, and it's not surprising. You've also got the particularly constraining situation of the vicarage itself, and the difficulty of getting time off when you're in it. You particularly notice it when you go away for a lovely holiday and the minute you walk in the front door you're back at work. The doorbell's going and the telephone's ringing because you're living over the shop.

Some clergy are also quite straitened for cash. We've always been all right because apart from anything else my wife has been working, but in some clergy households there is not a lot of money around, to say the least, and that can create real tensions. You actually have to take positive steps to be able to manage work and marriage, and you have to believe that it's worth spending time with your family rather than time on Church meetings and parish business. You actually have to believe that that's important and want to do it. Some clergy really are able to do that and I admire them. Most clergy overwork and find it difficult to manage that side of things.

Me? I think I've found it difficult. I would say that I have a tendency to overwork. I really admire those clergy who are able to be that much more unpopular with their parishes because they give more time to their children or spouse or whatever, but I've found that difficult. I've found that side of things not at all easy.

Anyway.

I went on to become Dean of King's College, at the University of London. That was a relief, it really was. I mean, I love parish life, because you have privileged access to people's lives at moments of great happiness and unhappiness, which is wonderfully satisfying, but being able to sit down to a meal with the family without the telephone going was an enormous relief. For the first time we had our own house, and we separated work and home.

The other interesting feature of the job was to be a colleague with other colleagues in a moderately ordinary nine-to-five job. In a parish, you might go visiting in the afternoons, and you don't exactly see a representative section of the population at that time. You see those housewives at home who are not working, or old people, and for that reason one's ministry is directed towards women a lot of the time, because it tends to be mostly women who are around when you are. However, at King's there were more men than women and that I found very refreshing, it was a change for me – apart from the fact that being Dean of King's College is one of the best jobs in the Church of England because you have the freedom to do almost exactly what you want.

Every dean's job is different. There are deans of cathedrals, deans of faculties, deans of colleges. As Dean of King's College you're overally responsible for ensuring that the religious purposes of the College are carried out, but because the College has a team of chaplains to do that, the Dean, as well as being number two or three in the College hierarchy, has the minimum of responsibilities and the maximum freedom. Your only required job is to run a course called the Associate of King's College Theological Lectures. It's an extra-curricular option, and when I was there an amazing number of students did that course, about eight or nine hundred of them, so that was really fun.

King's was also anxious for me to do outside things, and I continued to do quite a lot of regular broadcasting. In fact, my broadcasting career began in a rather funny kind of way. When I was at Wells there was a right-wing coup of the Colonels in Greece, and they claimed that this was a right-wing revolution in the name of Christianity, which was totally spurious. It so angered me that I wrote an article which was published in a magazine called *New Christian*, and it wasn't long afterwards that I was asked to do something for the BBC. In those days they had a programme called 'Prayer for the Day', which was at six forty-five in the morning, and was like 'Thought for the Day', except that you always ended with one very short prayer, and I ended up doing it every Friday for eleven years. I enjoyed it because one could build quite a following: one year I was number ten in the BBC Man of the Year competition on the

'Today' programme. I do 'Thought for the Day' now, which has a much bigger audience, about four million, but they're not as receptive as the audience an hour earlier.

I've enjoyed broadcasting a lot because one does need a creative outlet, but you can become dependent on the attention it brings, and that can be dangerous. I mean, there must be a strong impulse within me to be known. There must be, or else I wouldn't do it. Some people are much more interested in power, and I'm basically not interested in power, although as a bishop one has quite a lot of power in the sense that the buck stops with you in terms of decisions and appointments. Power's certainly not a drug for me as it is for some people, nor, I hope, is broadcasting, but the fact that I do so much of it certainly says something about me. I suppose I do need to be known, recognized, respected, appreciated. Who doesn't?

I was also pretty involved in the nuclear debate during my time at King's. That was in the early eighties, at the height of the nuclear question, and I wrote various articles and a book on it and did a lot of stomping up and down the countryside. On marches? No, not marches! I was on the other side! I used to do a lot of arguing on Town Hall platforms up and down the country against Bruce Kent and Paul Oestreicher. I was a defender of nuclear deterrence, in a qualified way, because I thought then and I think now that it's the balance of terror which actually prevented the kind of horrible situation which we've got at the moment, where the world is open to one war after the other, whereas you could never have had a conventional war between the United States and the Soviet Union because it would never have been in the interests of either side to do so. For the first time in human history, the human cost of going to war outweighed any conceivable advantage. There was a stalemate, and that seemed to me preferable to war.

I think I've been one of the few Christians actually prepared to defend a policy of nuclear deterrence from a Christian point of view. Everyone associates Christianity entirely with idealism and people's potential for good, and hard-nosed realism doesn't go down well with people because they think you've sold out. But Christian realism can be traced to St Augustine, to Luther, to one of my great heroes, Reinhold Niebuhr, an American theologian. We live in a pretty brutal world and you have to make the best of it. That means taking into account the reality of human sin as well as human beings' potential for good.

I get a lot of flak for holding that sort of view, and people have always found me difficult to place politically because on some issues I'm rather left-wing and on others people assume that I'm right-wing, which I'm not. I argue that I'm consistent and everybody else is inconsistent, because I argue from a moral consistency and most other people buy a political package. On things like sanctions against South Africa and development issues I'm much further to the left than many churchmen. I've always been an admirer of Denis Healey, and my standpoint is close to his on most things. In other words, I believe in the controlled use of force in international relationships but I'm very committed to social justice in terms of the world economic order.

As we all know, the Church has been criticized for being too involved in politics in recent years. I don't think the Church can escape having a political dimension, for the simple reason that so many decisions which affect human well-being today are political decisions. It's difficult for the Church to avoid making statements on things like housing and poverty without becoming party-political, but I do think it should try to avoid party politics, and concentrate instead on being some kind of reconciling force. For most of Christian history it's been possible for the Church to do good at an individual level, like founding hospitals or schools, but now, because the State has taken over so much of our life, if you're seriously concerned about human well-being you have to be concerned about politics.

The most recent criticism of the Church has been from the Tory Party, who say that it has become too involved in the life of the nation. I don't agree. I think the Church's job is to try to keep neglected issues on the agenda. During the last general election I, together with a lot of other people, tried to keep the question of aid, development and the Third World debt on the political agenda, and it was very, very difficult to do because the Government just wasn't interested. Perhaps the Church could do more, but my own feeling is that we are getting our involvement with the State about right at the moment, against very great opposition.

I became Bishop of Oxford in 1987. I was very, very sad to leave King's, because I loved the job, I loved the College, it was very stimulating: I loved having quite a bit of time to think and reflect and write. As a bishop you're much more tied into the Church as an institution than you ever are as a parish priest or college dean, and it's your responsibility to make the institution work. Perhaps it's odd that I became the Bishop here, because I like to be on the borderlands of Christianity, outside mainstream things. But then this job is not the kind of thing you can really turn down because it is an honour: you can't help but be flattered by being offered a job like this one. So although I had doubts about it, I suppose I didn't turn it down partly because I felt it would be foolish to do so, and of course it gives me an opportunity to exercise and develop aspects of myself that were not needed at King's. Now I actually have to give a definite lead. I have to bring a sense of cohesion and strategy to this unwieldy diocese, and that's something I've found challenging because I'm not sure I'm a very natural leader.

I can tell you're suspicious of my motives, and I think that's very healthy, that's absolutely right and fair. Perhaps I have been motivated by a need to conform, and by flattery, when making professional choices. Perhaps I have. My professional path looks a fairly conventional one, I admit. There's a rather nice story told by Harry Williams, who's a well-known monk: 'A bishop came and knocked on the door of a vicar offering him promotion. The vicar said, "Well, Bishop, I'll have to go away and pray about it if you don't mind." Meanwhile his wife went upstairs to pack.' Harry Williams's point is that the wife is much closer to God than the husband because she was being honest about her feelings. But perhaps it *might* have been better for me not to accept this job if it was something I felt so mixed about, and I do often ask myself the question: is one actually doing what is most *useful*? The world is in a terrible state, and sometimes I think to myself, well, wouldn't I be better involved in some kind of development project or working for Christian Aid or Oxfam? Shouldn't I be exactly where the obvious need is?

I'm a great believer in the fact that whether you like it or not you take on the attitudes and outlook and assumptions of your environment, and an episcopal environment is such a privileged environment it's unreal: it's not where a Christian priest should be, or at least not for too long. Since becoming a bishop I've had the increasing sense that where it's really at for Christians is in rundown parishes; trying to create community where there is no community, where there is much more tension and violence; trying to do something at the grass roots. So if I have fantasies about myself in alternative lifestyles, alternative situations, that's what they are. But I don't feel guilty about being a bishop, because I feel it utilizes such talent as I have.

It's a lonely job in many ways. I don't really work with people in the personal way that I did as a parish priest, and I miss that, I miss it quite a lot. That's probably why one of the first things I did when I was made Bishop was to form an episcopal cell: I found half a dozen other bishops who were consecrated at about the same time as I was, and we meet together twice a year for twenty-four hours at a time. It provides a little support group, a little network, where we can really let our hair down and be totally scurrilous and outrageous without worrying about it. Because the trouble is, people start to treat you differently as soon as you become a bishop. I like to tease a bit, and when I first became bishop and found myself doing that in a jokey kind of way, I suddenly realized people were taking one seriously. I suddenly had to watch what I was saying all the time. Similarly, it became totally counter-productive for me to make my point of view known at the beginning of a meeting, because people would then shrug their shoulders and say, oh well, if that's what the Bishop says it's going to go through anyway, so what's the point discussing anything? I had to learn to exercise a certain discipline about not making my own contribution strongly, and as a result there's always a kind of barrier now, with me, and to some extent it's a barrier I've put up to protect myself.

However, I have to say that in terms of hassle it's a great deal easier being a bishop than being a vicar because you're protected by so many other people. There are huge demands, but I have two secretaries and a chaplain, and people have to get through them before they can get to me. I hardly ever speak to people on the telephone these days, whereas a vicar's at everybody's beck and call. As a vicar you suffer enormous emotional wear and tear, because in a parish the vicar's the focus for tension, and unless you're careful you can be everybody's sort of hated father-figure. I mean, you may love your father dearly but a lot of people don't, and you'd be amazed how many people love to find a father-figure they can take their frustrations out on. As a bishop you're spared that. To put it most bluntly: people are not as unpleasant to their bishop as they feel they have a right to be to their vicar.

I wouldn't want to do this job for ever, but I've always wanted to help make the Church an effective Christian witness in the world, and that is an aspect of being a bishop that I love. There are so many things I feel strongly about that I try to achieve on a diocesan level. For example, we are one of the dioceses that are really trying to encourage women in ministry. We have got at least two in this diocese who are in charge of parishes, and so far we've had no objections from anyone. Some parishes are not opposed to the ordination of women in principle, but they're not used to the idea of a woman vicar, and they take a little bit of persuading that this is a possibility. Once they do have a woman in charge they're always very pleased, particularly because the women we've appointed are so good. So despite what the press will have people think, I can honestly say I've not received any opposition to the appointment of women in this diocese. There's only been one case where I very much wanted to appoint a woman to a particular parish, and although the majority were in favour, the minority who were against made up the congregational hard-core. They clearly felt it would be wrong to impose something which was divisive, so I didn't appoint her. I've always tried to achieve a very big consensus before imposing anything.

I have deliberately not made it a major issue for myself. I've always been totally in favour of the ordination of women. I made my views public before I became Bishop of Oxford, in particular in a pamphlet I wrote together with two Roman Catholic priests, showing the utter fallacy of the arguments of the last Bishop of London, Graham Leonard, and how wrong he was on theological grounds. I've not actively campaigned on the issue, partly because as a diocesan bishop you are meant to act as a symbol for unity, but I've always made it quite clear where I stood, and where I voted.

We also have some divorced and remarried clergy in this diocese, and the Church now is much more accepting of this than it was even five years ago. Not long ago I appointed one to a parish, and when I spoke to the PCC and the churchwardens about it their only answer was to shrug their shoulders and say, 'Oh well, that'll go down well here. Everybody on this estate is divorced and remarried.'

The most recent legislation does allow ordinands who are divorced and remarried, or married to somebody who's been divorced before, to go forward for ordination, but there have been a lot of problems with remarriage and the Church, with some clergy refusing to remarry divorcees, and others doing it at their discretion. There has always been division over this, and there still is. The Church's position on it is illogical, inconsistent, maybe even hypocritical, there's no doubt about it. The difficulty is that the Church still holds to the ideal of the lifelong union and it's a question of trying to do justice both to the ideal and to people who fail to meet it. It's a real tightrope.

The other tightrope which relates to this is homosexuality. I was one of the bishops who wrote a booklet called *Issues in Human Sexuality*, and you may be aware of how that treads a thin line between wanting to welcome homosexual people into congregations and being unwilling to set up homosexual clergy partnerships as role models. I know I helped to write it, but I do tend to go along with what it has to say because I don't think that same-sex relationships are the ideal. I think that there are a lot of people, for instance, who in their teenage years go through a homosexual or lesbian phase, and I think the Church ought to provide role models to encourage people into lifelong heterosexual unions for those who are able. As the clergy still act to some extent as role models, that means having heterosexual relationships.

However, there are some powerful arguments in favour of homosexual and lesbian clergy. Geoffrey John, who was Dean of Magdalen College here in Oxford, has written a very, very powerful pamphlet, the best that I've read, arguing that the Church ought fully to accept clergy homosexual relationships, and there's an awful lot of truth in what he has to say although I'm not yet totally convinced by it myself. Yet I do think it is a great pity that the Church makes it so difficult for people to be open about their sexuality, and I very much admire people who are able to say that they are gay. I know clergy who are gay or lesbian, and I know ordinands who are gay, but as a bishop I don't inquire into a person's private life. Most gay clergy will tell their Bishop that they accept an ideal of celibacy, but whether or not they live up to it one's not in a position to know – and frankly one doesn't want to inquire.

My mind is not totally closed on this issue, and it could be that this is an area where the Church will move. Certainly I'm very keen to encourage people of a homosexual orientation to be ordained if they feel that that is their calling. But if a homosexual or a lesbian came to me and said that they were in a permanent relationship with somebody and they intended to live together in the vicarage, frankly I would find that very,

very difficult. I just don't think the Church as a whole is ready to accept homosexuality openly; not in that kind of way.

I'm lucky, blessed, or unusual, having always had a very strong sense of vocation and of doing the right job at the right time. I've had very difficult patches in my ministry and done things I didn't necessarily want to do at the time, but on the whole I've got precisely what I wanted, and that's partly drive and partly altruism, which I don't think is the same thing as ambition. I've never been ambitious. All right, I'll correct that: I've never been ambitious in an *ecclesiastical* sense, for appointments and promotion. Perhaps that's because, like I said before, I'm a conformist person who doesn't kick against things.

I'm sure that being conformist has helped me. I'm sure it has helped me when I've questioned, as I occasionally have, the things I am doing with my own life as a Christian. You asked me whether I thought that the clergy were in danger of becoming obsolete, and I think they are, oh definitely. Definitely. They have become seriously marginalized. This hasn't been enough to make me consider doing anything else, but it is a great problem. The Church has been pushed to the edges and is now largely associated with people's pastimes and leisure activities. People go to church in the same way they might play bowls or skittles or go to the pub, and the parson's there to cater for that, and it's all regarded as a little bit obscurantist and fuddy-duddy. I think that a lot of clergy feel that, and I think they hate it.

What has really undermined the clergy's role in society is not so much the pressure of work as the lack of validation by society as a whole. In the nineteenth century it was fully accepted that a clergyman was a respectable professional doing a valuable job. Now the clergy don't command that kind of confidence. People will go instead to see their psychiatrist or their GP or their social worker. And what does the clergyman think he's doing catering for these people who have a strange thing called spiritual needs?

Apart from the professional aspect, there is also the inescapable fact that we in Western Europe are now in a post-Christian society. In England, we've become a pagan society again. And why? I think it's only partly to do with belief. I think a lot of it has to do with the fact that people can find fulfilment in all kinds of non-religious ways. The English have never been a very religiously observant people. We're nearly unique in the world in being so little concerned with religion. My father was Welsh, and perhaps I have always felt closer to my Welsh roots than my English roots because the Welsh, the Irish and the Scots are all more naturally religious than the English.

Religious indifference is not simply associated with modernism either, because if you go to places like Singapore, Taiwan and South Korea you'll find that religion is absolutely booming, and happily allied to the electronic revolution and technological whizzkiddery. And look at countries like Poland or Russia or the United States, where the percentage of churchgoers is still extraordinarily high: in the United States it's over fifty per cent of the population.

I do think our religious indifference has got something to do with imperialism, actually: there's a sort of arrogance about it that is peculiarly English. It was one of Queen Victoria's Prime Ministers who said, 'We must have a religion that is cool and indifferent and such a one as we have got,' and that description still applies to the Church of England. What was it you called me last time we met? 'Measured and careful.' Well, I am. That is the very *nature* of being an Anglican. It is the nature of the Anglican Church. Perhaps it is all tied up with English understatement, about which there is something quintessentially Christian, in that you're not placarding your goods in public. There's a wonderful poem by W. H. Auden called 'The truest poetry is the most feigning', and it ends with the wonderful line, 'Truth, like orthodoxy, is a reticence'. I think that's true. Truth is about the mysteries of the faith, not its certainties, of which there are so few. Perhaps Anglicanism at its best is really an acquired taste, like the best wines.

Joking apart, I do regard the Church of England as part of the universal Catholic Church and I do think that it has particular strengths to offer. It's a cliché, I know, but I do think the Church's strengths lie in its willingness to draw on tradition at the same time as trying to respond to the modern world, in its attempts to be sane and truthful. These things I think are good. These things I think are right.

Let me read you something that puts it rather better than I can. When you are ordained as a deacon or priest, or consecrated as a bishop, something called the Preface to the Declaration of Assent has to be read, and I think that Declaration is a very accurate statement of what the Church of England is and what it believes.

> The Church of England is part of the one Holy Catholic and Apostolic Church, worshipping the one true God, Father, Son and Holy Spirit. It professes the faith uniquely revealed in the Holy Scriptures and set forth in the Catholic creeds, which faith the Church is called upon to proclaim afresh in each generation. Led by the Holy Spirit, it has borne witness to Christian truth and its historic formularies, the Thirty-nine Articles of Religion, the Book of Common Prayer and the ordering of bishops, priests and deacons. In the Declaration you are about to make, will you affirm your loyalty to this inheritance of faith, as your inspiration and guidance under God, in bringing the grace and truth of Christ to this generation and making him known to those in your care?

I think that achieves a wonderful balance between a sense of the past and a sense of duty to the present, and that, for me, is what the Church of England stands for. But there's no doubt about it, the Church is walking a tightrope. The clergy are walking a tightrope. And as we near the end of this century, I sometimes wonder how we will keep our balance.

CHARLES ROYDEN

Age: 33
Age at ordination: 28

VICAR AND ASSOCIATE METHODIST MINISTER, BEDFORD

Charles Royden never stops talking.

'Hi, Mary, how d'you do, great to meet you in person, you look pretty different from what I expected. Let me take that for you, how was the train? Ever been to Bedford? It's boring, isn't it? I mean, look at it, there's nothing going on, no fun, no decent nightclubs. Give me Merseyside any day. You all right there? What do you mean I'm driving fast! This isn't fast, hey, Mary, if you want fast . . .'

Charles Royden's wife, Corinne, knows what he's like.

'Hi! How lovely to see you, have some coffee. He talks non-stop. It's best to just ignore him. Did he drive okay? He doesn't usually.'

Charles and Corinne Royden live in a medium-sized, modern vicarage on a private housing estate in Brickhill, Bedford, with their two small children. The house is light, comfortable and welcoming, which has as much to do with its laid-back inhabitants as anything else. Each time I visited them, Corinne Royden would cook a vast lunch, Charles Royden would crack open a couple of bottles of wine, and the afternoon following an interview would be entirely given over to epicurean pleasures. Whenever I started to make vague noises about train times, they'd simply refill my glass: 'Get away! Take your time. Have some more wine.' Rarely have I been made to feel so welcome by people who up until that week were almost total strangers.

Charles Royden clearly enjoyed the interviews. After much standing around in the kitchen gossiping with Corinne we'd go into his study, and Corinne would follow with a tray laden with tea, coffee, homemade cakes and biscuits. Charles Royden would pour himself coffee, light a cigar, and settle happily into the sofa as if he had every intention of staying there for ever. Indeed he claimed he would have been quite happy to do so as long as Corinne, the television, and a good bottle of claret were within reach.

Charles Royden was to the audio-tape what a fidgety model would be to a life-drawing class. His voice and Scouse accent were so full of modulations that my tape-recorder, which is a relatively swanky model, couldn't cope with it: the needles kept swinging from left to right across the dials, constantly jamming in the red reverberation zone. After half an hour spent fiddling with it, I gave up and resigned myself to a recording full of light and shade. Not only that, but Charles Royden managed to pack almost twice as many words on to C90 tapes as anyone else, which made him mighty good value but hell to transcribe.

Of all twelve contributors, Charles Royden was the most overtly gregarious, though by no means the easiest to interview. He is a man of undeniable commitment, drive and vision. He is hugely entertaining and utterly exhausting, and getting a straight answer out of him meant keeping up with his thought processes, which required a phenomenal amount of energy. I could see why Corinne had provided so much caffeine and cake. Quick wits also make for good defence, and Charles Royden was not without his barriers, although fortunately he was well aware of them, and would hoot with laughter at my attempts to break through them. 'Oh, go on then,' he'd say. 'You've rumbled me. Twist my arm a bit harder and I'll tell you.'

Charles Royden also left the best messages on my answering-machine. 'Hi, Mary, Charlie here. Sorry I didn't get back to you. We went away to see Blondie in concert, and now you're out on the town. Scandalous! I blame the Church for not taking a moral lead.' 'Hi, Mary, Charlie here, you wanted to know about that bit I quoted. It's Mark's Gospel. You'll find it in the New Testament: that's the bit at the back of the book.'

CHARLES ROYDEN

You know your last book? Right, those chapters: how long an interview went into getting a chapter? A week each?! What, for those little tiny chapters! I enjoyed it, yeah, not bad, don't get me wrong, but I don't generally read that sort of thing. I read gardening books and fishing books, but I don't have time for story books, to be honest. No, I do have time to read story books, that's not true, but I prefer to watch television. We've got a satellite dish on the outside of the house, and I find that if I come in late, like about ten o'clock, I'll sit down and watch a movie, lots of people getting shot and a bit of escapism and everything.

I read theological books, but I find that theological books date so quickly. If you buy the thoughts of somebody, then in a year's time you read the thoughts of the same person and they've all changed, so I prefer commentaries. Dad gave me the set of Calvin's commentaries, and they're hundreds of years old but they're still valid, even if they do have a go at the Pope, so you can use them *and* you're not wasting your money!

Generally speaking, I'll do what I did with your book, and that's get it out the library and have a look at it, and say, 'Do I want to keep this? Has it got something enduring?' And if not I'll just read through it, get the bits out that I think are useful, put it on computer, and it's all there then. For example, if you said to me, 'Charlie, I want to know about slavery,' then I can whack up 'slavery' on the computer, and it's all there; whereas if I'd bought the books and they were on the shelves, I'd have to sit here and pull them all out and start *reading*. So I prefer the computer, because it's all there at your finger-tips. It's brilliant. You see, I like things in their place. A place for everything, and everything in its place, that's what I say. I like things tidy, I like to know where things are. I like order.

*

I grew up in Merseyside. Mother, father, two brothers. Dad did thirty years in the police force, and then he took retirement and went into the Church full-time. He started as a local preacher in the Methodist Church, went part-time in the Church of England, and when he went full-time Anglican there was a piece in the *Daily Mirror* which said, 'Top Cop Swaps Baton For Bible'. And at about the same time, my elder brother Ross went into the Anglican Church too.

I valued my upbringing, because it was good and strict. We weren't allowed to answer back to our parents. We were brought up to think that was a bad thing to do. We had order in our lives, and it was stable and secure, and I hope that that's the kind of family that I have got. My children are given a certain amount of freedom, but they know what's wrong and they know what's right. And I think children like that, they appreciate that security. I think policemen do bring their children up strictly, probably because they see so much chaos. We were quite churchy too – no, that's the wrong word, because it probably makes you think we sat holding hands saying grace together, and there was none of that, nothing heavy, but we did go to church. Church was important.

I was a normal kid. Happy, enthusiastic, worked reasonably hard, wasn't particularly bright at school. I started off in just normal little county primary schools in Liverpool, then took the eleven-plus and went to a grammar school on the Wirral and did O- and A-levels there. By that stage I was quite active in the Church. I started getting active in the Church from my early teens, did lots of youth work, and even then I was thinking about ordination myself. I certainly stood out at the grammar school because I went to church and that was something that you didn't do. Oh, I admitted it, absolutely – I was Head of the Christian Union, for heaven's sake, and it was a very active group. We put this huge mission on in the school, with films and talks, and the hall was full, people loved it and went away thinking it was fantastic. And it did the job. Got people talking about God. So although I got loads of flak, the advantage was that when I was in the Sixth Form at school, I was always regarded as a good boy, and wasn't kept a watch on. So on Wednesday afternoons, which were for sports, I used to say I was going fishing, which they accepted as part of the sports curriculum, and instead we used to nip off to my house and play Monopoly, or somebody else's house and have a glass of cider. Whereas other guys, who perhaps had a bit of a reputation, wouldn't get away with that sort of behaviour. I got away with an awful lot because I was capable of playing the system. A right creep!

A lot of Christianity made sense to me then. People ridicule Billy Graham, but he made sense to me, and it was partly because of the kind of message he preached that I decided there was something meaningful in Christianity for me, and I became much more involved in the youth work in the church. We had eighty kids in the youth group, and at one stage it went to over a hundred. We weren't particularly involved in the life of the church as a whole, because it was pretty exclusive really; children weren't allowed a look-in and in the Church you're a child until you're about thirty-five. So the youth group was more like an agitating force in the church, and resented almost. I remember having arguments with older people in the church, and feeling, 'You're wrong! You are definitely wrong.' The church was dull, it was lifeless. We used to go on Sunday evenings, and we would say this antiquated service that meant nothing to us, sing hymns that were completely out of touch with where we were, in this boring, cold, dusty building.

Some of the youth group left and went over to other Churches, Baptist Churches, House Churches, Pentecostal Churches, and it was always a question for me: shall I stay in the Church of England, or shall I leave? So for a while I didn't go to the services, until the Vicar called me into church and said, 'Listen, Charlie, I've had a complaint,' and I said, 'What's that, Geoff?' and he said, 'Well, you're a youth leader in the church, and a couple of the folks have noticed that you don't actually come to the church services.' I said, 'Well, to be honest with

you, Geoff, they're dull: they really do not scratch where I itch.'
So he said, 'I appreciate that, but you should come.' And that
was decision-time for me. My decision was that I would stick
with the church and try to make some kind of difference to
what goes on.

I stayed with it through continuing boring years, and slowly
changes began taking place. The Vicar there was brilliant. He
probably didn't want to go to church on Sundays either, he
probably went along thinking, 'This is dull and boring'; but
when he left the church was the way I would have wanted it to
be in my teenage years. It was lively, it was expressive, people
were allowed to take part. They got rid of some of the old
traditions which kept people back from expressing their worship.
I mean, you used to go in before and there was some grouchy
old fuddy-duddy on the door saying, 'Hello, how are you, have
a book and sit down.' So you sat down, and you couldn't touch
anything, everything in the church had to remain exactly the
way that it was, even the cobwebs were sacrosanct! I remember
once someone shaking a tambourine during a hymn, and the
organist stopped playing!

When I eventually went back there as an adult, they had
moved the pews! I mean, that would not have been allowed
before. There was a music group, and women were preaching.
Before, we weren't even allowed to have women entering the
pulpit. If a woman came along and she was a missionary, and
she wanted to give a talk about something she had done in the
missionary field, she had to do it from the lectern. You had a
PCC which was dominated by older people who had been
there for donkey's years: it was death to the church, and lots of
people went off to form their own Churches. There was a
mushrooming of involvement in other Churches, and when I go
to visit those Churches now, I see in them a reaction against the
Church of England as it used to be, which makes me really sad,
because if you go round the Church of England and see what's
going on, you find that there's a lot of life, a lot of vitality and a
lot of excitement, which people perhaps don't expect. Anglican

Churches are growing now: the Church scene is actually very exciting right now. All the stuff you hear about the Church dying, it's just out of touch, it's not right.

When you're a kid, if you think you might fancy ordination, you can go off on one of these lovely little courses that the Church lays on, to think about things. So when I was eighteen, some of us from the youth group went off to York on a course. It was pretty good actually, because I came back with a girl-friend, but the *important* bit about that weekend was that there was this nun there, and I remember her sitting in this pub with a pint of Boddingtons, and she said, 'If there's anything you can do to prevent going into ministry, then do it!' And I thought to myself, 'Well, I haven't got to go into ministry. I'd rather be a policeman.' So that's what I did.

That nun, you know, it was sound advice she gave me. I suppose guidance is the kind of thing where there are no flashing lights in the sky, but God opens doors and God closes doors, depending of course on whether or not you believe in God. By the time I left school I was still thinking about doing theology, and I went on interviews to different universities. I was quite interested in Durham but I didn't like it, it was a bit snooty. I went on holiday there with a girlfriend, and I kissed her in the Cathedral and got shouted at. Isn't that amazing? Some boring old fart in a cassock came up and shouted at us. I wish it was now: now I'd go off like a double barrelled-shotgun! Anyway, that put me off Durham. Put me off the Church a bit too.

I think I was partly considering theology because I was a bit too small for the police force, and it had always been a choice between the two. You had to be five foot eight for the police, and at that stage I was less than that, and my eyes were a bit dodgy, you couldn't go in if you wore glasses. All the same, I went along for the medical, with this strange doctor telling you to take all your clothes off and do physical exercises. It was a hoot. He says, 'Take your clothes off,' and you take your clothes off. Then he gives you an inspection, and he says, 'Do thirty press-ups,' so I do my thirty press-ups, and jump up, and he says, 'No, do thirty press-ups,' so I say, 'I've just done thirty, I'm not doing another thirty!' They're really tough on you. Anyway, when they came to measure me I must have grown a bit, so I thought, 'Right, that's it then. I'll go into the police force.'

I got a lot of stick when I was training, because Dad had been a Superintendent. Some of the guys who he'd sorted out were a bit miffed and thought they'd have a go at me. I remember once standing in a line against a wall, and this instructor who thought he was God's gift walked down and banged my head against it. I remember my head kind of like shaking inside: it was very brutal, some of the training. There was also some guy who'd been a dog handler, and Dad had had him done or something, and when we were on parade once he came and stood behind me, saying, 'You bloody little toe-rag: do you know you're a toe-rag?' So I got a load of stick, a lot of aggro, but I had a great time really. The aggro made me acceptable to my colleagues.

The training was only eight weeks, although it's longer now. Then I had three weeks in the Force, which is when you get your uniform and you're sworn in and you take your oaths and promises and all that business. Then you go away for eight weeks, and when you come back you're pretty much on the job. I mean, imagine! I'm eighteen and a half, and I've done all my training, and I'm in the Merseyside police. And I don't look old now, so imagine me at eighteen and a half with a big hat on, walking round the streets. It was criminal, really.

I was in the police for five years. Great. Smashing. Loved it. It was very exciting and loads of fun, *loads* of fun. I'd always enjoyed action and excitement and adventure, and to go into the police force and be given the ability to lock up baddies and get involved in all sorts of exciting situations and to exceed the speed limit and drive fast, all that kind of stuff, it was *great*; you know, it got the old adrenalin going, and that's good for a young man.

Any good for justice? Yeah. Yeah, I think it was, because if you really do enjoy the chase – I'm not talking about speeding down the road and running people over – but if you enjoy the excitement of catching someone who has done something wrong; if you enjoy the pursuit, the hard work going through paperwork, house-to-house inquiries, finding out what's happened, and eventually going round to somebody's house and locking them up for something really bad; if you enjoy that and you're keen, and you put the hours in and work hard, then that's what the country needs. And I worked with a group of men and women who gave absolutely everything they had to defend law and order.

When I went into the police force I had to make a promise to uphold justice, and to serve God and the Queen, and the vows and promises that I made then were very, very similar to statements made in Isaiah, when he talks about defending the fathers and pleading for the widow, all this kind of stuff. And if you have a strong sense of right and wrong; if you believe that people shouldn't be able to beat up other people; that people shouldn't be able to raid old ladies' homes and leave them on the floor for dead; if you get angry about all that and you enjoy bringing people to justice, that's brilliant.

What you don't want is people going into the police saying, 'This is a good career, and if I keep my nose clean for four years I'll be an Inspector.' You don't want that. You want people who go into the job because they really do want to see law and order upheld. I remember one night, this little girl was crying her eyes out at the sports centre because some guy had indecently assulted her, and I was called out to see her, and I said to the girl, 'Okay, come on, we'll go for a walk and we'll see if we can find him.' So we wandered along the roads, and all of a sudden the girl stood there absolutely petrified, petrified, and she pointed to this guy up the road and said, 'That's him.' And her face: I was in no doubt that this was the guy who had done it. I chased up the road after him, and as I got near to him he turned round and gave me such a good hiding, he really did hit me. I picked myself up, ran after him again, jumped up on top of him and whacked him on the head with my torch. He was a big guy, he must have been about six foot three, and he was built like the back end of a bus. And I remember screaming at the top of my voice, 'You do that again and I'll bloody kill you.' And we locked him up. He'd had loads of convictions for indecently assaulting children, and I remember going to court with this guy and feeling really pleased because he was an offender who deserved to be punished for his crime.

Whenever I went to court in that sort of situation and stood in the witness box, I'd take a bible and promise under oath to tell the truth, the whole truth and nothing but the truth, and that meant something to me. So when you get some barrister who's paid to defend a guy like this one, who is on legal aid, who's lying through his teeth, who's got previous convictions, and has lied through his teeth on those, what happens? I go to court as a policeman and I'm called a liar and looked on with suspicion. And the guy, when he is eventually convicted, gets some minor sentence. I think that's *scandalous*.

Now, think what that does to the policeman. In my time in the police force I had one broken leg, two broken noses. I had a terrible boot in the groin which laid me up for about three weeks. Loads of injuries all the time. But you take those injuries because you believe in what you are doing. You believe that these people should be stopped. So when you're called a liar and you're hauled over the coals, what does that do to police morale? It destroys it. Therefore, I think that we get the police force we deserve, and if the police are ever less than keen to get involved, we've only got ourselves to blame.

Take the Toxteth riots in 1981. I was in plain-clothes at the time, at our little Vice Squad on the Wirral, and the Wirral was full of vice! We were having a great time doing brothels and porn and all kinds of stuff. I used to have long hair and go round in civvies into pubs to lock people up for dealing drugs, and it was really, really exciting work. I worked with a girl who looked just like you, with the kind of long hair, and the –

well, she was very attractive, very attractive; and she and I used to go into pubs and have a few drinks and look like a couple on a night out, and then we'd lock people up who were pushing drugs.

Then one night we were on duty and this call came in that things had started off in Toxteth, and I had to go back into uniform. I'd been out of it for a year, but I got into uniform, tucked my hair up under my helmet, and we went over to Toxteth. And oh my God. Police cars were getting overturned. Bobbies were getting battered. I remember being on the lines and people throwing bricks at us, and bobbies having bricks embedded in their hats, because we never had crash hats then. And I don't know whether you've had a good look at a police helmet, but they're no protection to anyone because they just come off. Anyway, these poor old bobbies had these bricks in their heads, and the crowd were lobbing railings at us with spikes on the end, spears, and the bobbies were down at the hospital being bandaged up and coming back with bloody bandages and standing on the lines again.

Folks were saying to us, 'Please don't retreat, because if you go the mob will get us.' It was that bad. The place looked like a bomb site: burglar alarms going off everywhere, flames piling out the houses. It was a right bloody mess, really awful. And here's these bobbies, giving it everything they've got, working on and on and on into the night, for days, because it went on for days, Toxteth. And *then* what happened? *Then* what? You get the Anglican Bishop of Liverpool and the Roman Catholic Bishop getting together pronouncing an *amnesty* on the rioters, saying, 'Bring all the loot and drop it off at the churches as an amnesty.' Bloody hell!

What I wanted to hear from society, from the Church, was what Martin Luther said: he got in the pulpit and condemned the mob, condemned the rioters. I wanted that. I wanted the Church to say, 'This is *wrong*.' We knew, as police officers, that the riots were being co-ordinated on walkie-talkies by drug dealers. After the riots there were no drugs raids allowed for ages because they feared that we would incite a further riot, so the drug dealers had an open season. All right, there was unrest about unemployment: yes, there were a whole load of social factors involved, I know all that – and yet that does not excuse people beating up other poor people.

We got so much flak after the riots. I just wanted to see justice and order and people being protected, so that women can go on the streets at night and not get raped; so that little girls are not going to get molested just because they walk down the road; so that old people can sleep easy at night. That's all. I wanted the Bishops in Toxteth to go visit the poor bobbies who were in hospital with blood pouring out of their heads, and I wanted them to say to the media, 'This is what rioting does,' instead of bloody pandering to the rioters. We sleep safely in our beds at night because young lads like I was, and women, wander round the streets on their own in the dark protecting us. Without them we'd have chaos.

I think the legal system is as responsible for the fiasco as anyone. I think that the legal system is totally corrupt. I mean, take an incident where I go to court and I've got a broken nose. I was in Pizzaland one night with a mate, and we're having a nice meal and these squaddies come in who have just got back from the Falklands and they decide that they're going to sort the waitress out. There's four or five of them, and we say, 'No, fellers, this is naughty,' so they start on us. Now there's only two of us, and these other guys are squaddies, they're working out all day, they're heavy lads, and we took a fair good hiding. I got a broken nose out of it. And we go to court, and what are we told in the court? 'My client will plead to a Section 47,' which is ABH, Actual Bodily Harm. I said, 'This isn't an ABH, this is a GBH! He deliberately broke my nose!' But it's all about pleading cases down; bargaining; everyone knowing that some- one's guilty, but solicitors going to court and getting people off, and I think it's *wrong*. People come in to the station and tell you, yes, they're guilty, but then they go and see the solicitor and he gives them a good excuse . . . oh, I was sick of it by the end. I couldn't stand it. That's not real justice. And it's justice that I care about.

During the five years that I was in the police, I was still very involved in the Church. I had a dis-ease, a feeling that what I should be thinking about, ultimately, was ordination. And ordination was something that became more and more compulsive. I had felt from the moment that I went into the police force that I wanted to be there, and that I might stay in for thirty years, like my father, but after those five years I felt that I had to leave – and very reluctantly, because I really did enjoy it. I loved the people that I worked with; great folks, great guys. But I knew I had to move on.

I went to Wycliffe Hall in Oxford. I did the three-year degree, and then I had to do my ministry training on top of that, so that was four years altogether, which was far too long. Ridiculous, really. The selection committee said they would only accept me provided that I did a degree in a university setting, and I have mixed feelings about that, about our affiliation in the Church of England with universities and college systems, because you've got tutors who've got half the year off, you've got students who've got half the year off. We can't afford that any more in the Church of England. I think we should be saying, 'Right, you're going to train for two years, and if you don't have all the big holidays and you work properly, you'll get it all done in two years.' I mean, I went out of a full-time job where I was working three shifts, some of them twelve hours, for forty-eight weeks of the year, all of a sudden into an environment where everything slowed down.

At the end of the day what made it worthwhile was doing theology, because if as Christians we believe that we have some kind of God-given book, then it's important that we try to understand that God-given book. The majority of the Bible was written about 2,000 years ago, in a country the size of Wales, where *in vitro* fertilization wasn't even thought of. So how are we going to make sense of the things that are in there? The only way that we are going to bring it into today's society is understanding what it meant when it was written in the first place. Which means we've got to look at the documents; we've got to do Greek; we've got to do the languages to help us understand the original texts; we've got to gain some insight from the people who've provided thoughts on the stuff, which means reading Calvin and Luther and people like that. It means looking at the early Church Fathers, and finding out what they said and why they were wrong about some things. Because if you just get a bible off the shelf, and stick a pin in it and ask, 'What's it got to say to me today?' you're going to get the wrong passage and end up with a whole load of rubbish, not proper theology.

The rest of the training, the pastoral stuff, was a bit of a waste of time. I mean, let's talk about doing the job. You can go to college and learn all about funerals. But you don't actually learn about funerals until you actually go and sit with a family that have lost someone that they love, and find that you don't have to say anything at all, you just have to be there and feel their pain with them. And the best way to understand doing a funeral service is to go to one with a clergyman who does it, and see how he responds, and how he acts. That's what curacies are all about. You work with a man who's supposed to be a good mentor, and you are also put into small groups of other curates who get together to discuss what they're learning. That was the way I learned to do the job – practically, not in college.

When I was in the police force they taught you aikido, and all these weird and wonderful things like how to twist people's fingers, and how to control them when they're fighting and all that stuff. Yet when you get into the police station, they just say, 'If someone's hitting you, just hit them back as hard as you bloody well can, and make sure that they're not going to hit you again.' It's the same with theological training. When you go to college they teach you all kinds of ways of dealing with people, and then you get into the parish and you just have to get on with it. I know that some clergy are confused about their own roles, and you can talk all day out of books, but at the end of the day it's far better to just get on the ground and do the job.

In the ministry you're paid a stipend, and that's not a wage for doing the job, it's a stipend so that you are released and given freedom for what ministry you *may* have to do; and that means you can choose areas of ministry that you want to specialize in. As a minister you can't do everything. I look around my parish and I could do youth work, I could do children's work, I could do old people's work, I could organize community centres, I could do a whole range of things. But I'm not omnicompetent, and in the areas that I can't tackle I try to delegate to lay people. Now that's a problem for some clergy, because they haven't got a check-list to say, 'I've done that, that and that today, and now I can go to bed.' And because you could work twenty-four hours a day, every day of the year and still have loads of work to do, you have to resolve in your own mind that you're not expected to do that. I have to tell myself that God isn't dependent on how hard I work because God is bigger than me. There's always the danger of thinking that God only values me in the ministry if I *do* lots of things.

I did my curacy in Bidston, Birkenhead, an area which is covered by the Merseyside police, so I was actually a curate in the place where I had been a policeman, which was weird but great. As a curate, I tended to have not so much to do with the drug dealers and pushers, and more to do with the victims, but I did have to stand at the door of the church and shake hands with people I had locked up, and that's interesting. It raises the whole question about your honour as a policeman as well as your honour as a minister. Because they could have turned to me and said, 'How can you stand there, when you behaved the way you did?' and they never did. My certificate from the police force said my conduct was exemplary, and I like to think it was.

The church was a very old building which was really not going many places. It was a bit of a mess, old, very cold, lots of pews, poor toilets, no phones. You know, your typical old parish church. Lovely outside building, no one inside. We had a parish of about 16,000 and the congregation was very small, and we had to think how on earth we were going to make this church mean something to all the people who lived around it on the council estates. There was very high deprivation, eighty per cent unemployment on the estate and massive drug problems, loads of single-parent families. Society broken down, at its lowest ebb. What were we going to do about it as a church? Because in that situation you can get into the pulpit every Sunday and speak to your heart's content, and there's no one there to listen to you.

There was a dire, dire health problem. The children, when you took them from the schools to play with other teams, you found that they were smaller, they weren't as developed. So we opened a Baby Clinic inside the church. We used to have girls coming and booking their weddings when they were fifteen, for when they were sixteen. Then they wouldn't get to the altar because they'd be pregnant already, and they'd have gone off and got a Registry Office marriage quick. So we put a Family Planning Clinic inside the church and we got doctors in, inside the church. We also employed a community worker with a grant from the Church Urban Fund, and with her hard work we got a lot done.

There were old people, isolated, with no care. What's the Church going to say about that? So we set up a lunch club, and got the old folk in and gave them meals, and company, which was important to them. There were people who were being really trodden underfoot in terms of not understanding the system that they were in, with benefits and that kind of thing. So we got a Welfare Rights adviser in, inside the church, and a community worker.

Young people were getting involved in drugs and crime, so we set up a youth group inside the church. We put a satellite dish on the roof of the church, and pumped in MTV, so that the kids could come in and watch it in a safe environment after school. We had clubs operating at night, so that those who couldn't go straight home after school weren't getting into trouble but were in the church with people from the community running it and looking after them.

We also had one of these old organs. Organs are the bane of the Church's life. Churches used to have lovely orchestras, and then organs came in, orchestras were sacked, and one man played the organ and became God in the church. Anyway, our old organ used to take up a massive part of the church, so we pulled it out, put a little electronic job in, which actually sounded 100 per cent better, and where the old organ was we put toilets and kitchens and offices and counselling rooms. We took all the pews out and put comfortable chairs in, so that on Sunday you'd got nice comfy chairs to sit on. They were movable, and on Sunday nights we stacked them at the front of the church, drew some doors, so the little holy bit was left at the top, and we were left with this great expanse we could put play groups in, and a whole range of different things.

We called it an Act of Repentance, the church: going back to people and saying, 'We *do* care,' and showing that in practical terms. As a minister you believe that life is a whole. God hasn't created a holy bit and a secular bit. You know the words in Genesis, 'God looked at all He had made, and it was good.' It's *all* of our lives that God is concerned about, not just the holy bit on Sundays. And if that's true, then the Church must have something to say, for example, about unemployment. If I've got eighty per cent unemployment in my parish, I've got to say something about it. I've got to tell the Government that it's wrong. If they shut down bits of the steel mill, as they did, and ship it off to China and ruin our industrial base and make all those people redundant, I've got to say, 'That's *wrong*. You shouldn't do that.' If they shut down Cammell Laird and all our shipbuilding industries, leaving people without work, then as a minister I've got to *say* that's bad.

As a Church you have got to get involved in all those issues, and it's no good just talking about it, you've actually got to *do* something. If I believe that people are being exploited by loan-sharks, then I've got to do something about that; so we set up a Credit Union inside the church which allowed people to save and borrow from one another so they weren't being exploited and they didn't have to pay interest. You'd be surprised how many people don't understand what interest is. They say, 'Charlie, I've got a bailiff on the door, because I haven't paid this debt back.' So I say, 'What was the interest you were paying?' and they say, 'What's interest?' and suddenly you realize just how much people are falling foul of the terrible system.

And it's not just the loan-sharks, let's be honest about it, let's be honest: loan-sharks are bad, but what about Barclaycard? Access? They're more worrying than loan-sharks, because they can put bits of paper through your door; they can give you credit limits that you can never, never afford. So you get a single parent with four children going and buying her shopping on a credit card every week and then not being able even to keep track of the interest, and eventually she has debts of thousands and thousands and thousands of pounds that she'll never be able to pay, and she's getting bailiffs round at her house.

I got involved with the Citizens' Advice Bureau in Birkenhead, because I believed that they were doing a very important spiritual job. I regarded them as angels, the women who worked in Debt Advice, because they were taking burdens that people had and doing something about them. They were helping people to deal with the likes of Barclaycard and Access, and the banks who were exploiting people. I mean, the Bible has a lot to say about usury, and we don't listen to that very much because it has become part of our society. But the Church must be prophetic about these kinds of things. It must say, 'Well, it might be part and parcel of our society, but that doesn't mean to say that it's right. It's *wrong*.'

Therefore I felt that it was right, as a minister, with my dog-collar on, to go along to the County Court when people were having tremendous debts and burdens, and say, 'The credit card company's gone wrong here, Your Honour. This person shouldn't have to pay off all this debt because they'll never ever be able to pay it. We don't want this person to be a slave to interest rates for the rest of his or her life.' I counted doing things like that as an important part of my ministry.

I know there are people who say that the Church shouldn't be political, but the Church has got to be political. Look at the Magnificat. Look at the Sermon on the Mount. You put the Sermon on the Mount into practice, and that's politics! You say something about slavery, and that's politics! You say something about women, that's politics! The Church has been important in things like child labour. Think of Shaftesbury and Wilberforce and people like that. The Church is a prophetic voice and that prophetic voice must always be there, challenging the accepted norms of society.

Then people say, 'Okay, you can be into politics, but you shouldn't be into *party* politics.' But as soon as you make a political statement, you are going to upset one of the political parties. I adhered to that policy of not being party-political for quite a number of years, but I don't any more because I think there's nothing wrong with being involved in party politics and giving a lead, if you believe that that is the right lead to give. Sure, if you keep your mouth shut you can be friends with everybody, but I actually believe that it's right to upset folks, and to challenge people who have views which you think are wrong, and for them to challenge you. I regard that as being part and parcel of my job. I don't want to alienate people from the spiritual message that I'm bringing, but I'm afraid the spiritual message also has a political content.

The trouble with the Church is that we're very concerned about some things and not very concerned about others. I mean, we're very concerned about all the sexual issues, aren't we? We're very wrapped up in all that. But we're not very concerned about law and order. We're not very concerned about injustice. We're not very concerned about exploitation, in terms of people being given debts. I don't hear the Church shouting about those things very often, and we should be. We're not there to help the powerful, but the powerless. That's what the Magnificat's about; about God looking on those people who haven't got a lot of power and authority and actually favouring them. The Magnificat is a charter for revolution, isn't it, when you look at it? 'He hath put down the mighty from their seat, and hath exalted the humble and the meek.' I mean, that is absolutely *fabulous*, isn't it?

The education system is a disgrace in this country. The health situation in this country is a disgrace as well. The Church should be shouting about that. I do. I put it in my sermons all the time. I think that we should close down private medicine. I think that we should close down private education. Because if you have the leaders of our country being able to send their children to schools which are outside the education system which they are meant to be providing, then you're going to get a less than perfect system, because they don't use it. The same goes for private medicine and the NHS. My God, private education, private health, I want to shout about those as a minister. They're so wrong.

In my last parish we had a fence around the council estate, and everyone inside the fence had worse services than those people on the outside of the fence, and it's wrong, wrong. Everybody is worth the best, because they are created by a God who loves them all equally. The ground is level at the foot of the Cross. Nobody is going to take their role or their riches to heaven with them. Thank God. And we have a very good gospel to remind us of that, a very good gospel. You can twist the Bible to make it mean anything that you want, but it is actually a tremendous charter for human rights and human dignity. Yes, you can justify something like apartheid with some obscure text in the Old Testament, but we as a Church have got to challenge all that, and *that's* why theology is so important, so that you can do that effectively. It's no good me debating with somebody about the wrongs of apartheid if I've got someone who is better at the book than I am. You have got to be able to argue really well as a Christian. It's important.

*

I saw real poverty in my previous parish. There are some people in my present parish who are as poor, but most of the folk here are fairly affluent. We are doing Christian Aid at the moment, and you say to people, 'Will you give to Christian Aid?' and they say, oh no, I haven't got enough – as they put their 2p in the envelope. But when you look at the real poverty of the people that that money is going to, people in the Third World, people who are being exploited by us, you realize that even the very poor in my parish are affluent in comparison.

Yet those poor people in the Third World are unique. They have fingerprints. They are important to God too. Therefore it's no good to say, 'Well, we live in England and we'll look after England. As Christian prophets we've got to look after all of God's Creation and that's why the Church must make people aware of poverty and where it is. Yet even when we've got this terrible financial crisis going on in the Church of England, and I say to people, 'Please give more,' they say, 'We're already giving a lot,' and I say, 'Do you realize how much you're giving, out of your tremendous wealth? You are giving peanuts, a pittance!' We were asking people to give over £3 a week, and some people were having heart failure at the thought of giving over £3 a week. Now, if God is the all-important thing in your life, and you believe that some of His Creation is starving to death, then it isn't actually a tremendous commitment to help the Church to help others, is it? I don't think so.

All this talking, and my cigar keeps going out! But you see, the way we're set up as a Church doesn't lend us to political action, because we're too involved with the status quo. We've got bishops in the House of Lords; we've got a monarch who is Head of the Church. I never used to be into disestablishment until recently, because the glorious thing about the Church of England is that anyone who lives in any part of the country has a vicar they can call upon and call their own. They don't have to come and put their bums on my seats on Sunday to be a part of the church here. People can always have a ministry from me, and I don't want to lose that, I really don't.

However, I do now think that we can disestablish and still retain that contact. I think what we have to do in the Church is become far more democratic in our structures and our government. All this business of power and privilege, and people wearing the right ties and doing the right jobs: it's wrong. You've got to have some kind of system where if a post becomes vacant, then that post should be advertised, and *everyone* in the Church should be given their elective rights. It's all very well my going out there saying to folk, 'Pay up, everyone. Contribute. We need you to take an active part in the Church.' But then what? They're not allowed to be involved in the most important decisions. It's scandalous. So we need to have some good discussions in the Church as to how we are going to elect our leaders and move honourably into the future.

The trouble with the Church is that it's about power structures and privileges which are totally unaccountable. I mean, you should *never* give power to anybody unless that person is *answerable* for that power. Power is a very dangerous thing, and it shouldn't just be given out under a cloak of darkness, for life. It should be given by the people, and the people should be able to remove it. But this hasn't been the case in the Church of England, and it's time things like clergy appointments changed. You shouldn't have this business where a clergyman is suddenly appointed to a parish without the parishioners getting a look-in. This business of nods and winks, and people suddenly appearing in a position as if they are sent by God like Elijah, it's just ridiculous!

Now, the lovely thing about my job, it being an ecumenical job with both the Anglican and Methodist Churches, is that it was advertised in the paper and I applied for it. The parishioners got our CVs, and they were able to go through them and short-list and interview and appoint the person they thought was right for the job at that particular time. That's got to be a good thing. Yet how many jobs in the Church of England does that happen with? A tiny, tiny percentage, and the rest are all held in patronage. It's a disgrace, a disgrace. The merit of the individual in those circumstances doesn't come into it. It's all about who you know. And when we have a system that is fair, which is honest, which works on merit, then I think that God's people will be served a lot better.

Let's talk about the Methodist Church, okay? In the Methodist Church we elect people to jobs, we elect Presidents. The Head of the Methodist Church is the President of Conference, who holds the term of office for a period of one year and then may be re-elected or not, as is usually the case. It's very different from the Anglican Church. When the Bishop of Bedford retires I won't have any say in who is appointed to be my bishop, and I would like to have a say. I don't want my bishop appointed for life either. Why not a maximum of seven years like a Methodist District Chairman? But we have all these paths of authority in the Church: churchwardens, Church Councils, Deanery Synods, Diocesan Synods. What it actually means is that nobody can do anything.

And what is it that gives the Anglican Church the right to have so much authority in this largely un-Christian country? Just history. The Roman Catholics aren't established. The Church of Scotland isn't established. The Methodists and the Baptists aren't established. Because I'm an ecumenical vicar we have multi-faith services in our church here. Obviously, I want to stress the uniqueness of Christ, but I don't want to have another Crusade, which is what you end up having if you don't have dialogue. The fact is, we've got a multi-faith society and we've got to live in it, and we're only going to have growing resentments if we continue with the present form of establishment.

I'm not going to say to my Methodist colleagues, 'Your Church isn't as important as mine.' Yet although I preside in the Methodist Church, the Anglican Church doesn't recognize the fact that my Methodist colleague is ordained, so if he ever wanted to join the Anglican Church he'd have to be re-ordained. Try and explain that to your average person and they'll say the Church is mad. It's so hypocritical when you think how angry the Anglican Church gets about Rome not recognizing *our* Orders, and shocking when you realize how much richness there is in Methodism. It's back to what I said before: the sheer arrogance of Anglicanism.

Anglicans have this incredible reluctance to share, and yet what is really important about the Last Supper? The sharing. If you look at the Gospels, it's the cup that we share that's significant, important, vital. It's a very powerful image of the way we are meant to be as Christians. The real scandal of it is that here's this meal which is meant to unite us, and it's actually dividing us. My brother Ross always says that churches get closer to the real meaning of Communion when they have coffee and biscuits after the service than they ever do when they're taking a chalice of wine. Sure, you make your Communion with God at that point, but that's a very vertical kind of thing, isn't it? Me and God. We've made it into a very private affair, and yet Jesus's ministry was, *par excellence*, about sharing.

Look at the origins of Christianity: look at what Jesus expected, and what the early disciples did when they broke bread together. They were all meeting in one another's houses, breaking bread, having a meal, sharing. The Greek word *ecclesia*, the Church; all it means is a meeting. In Acts there is a reference to an *ecclesia* of silversmiths, and it was just a group, like the modelling club or something, there was nothing holy about it.

And yet what have we done? We've made the Church into something where you have to have the badge of Confirmation before you are able to share in the Communion meal, and I think that is absolutely and utterly scandalous – that we should prevent children and unconfirmed adults from taking Holy Communion. We want children to become part of the Church, and to live their life in the Church, and yet we deny them the one thing that Christ gave us which creates our unity. Absolutely ridiculous! All this rubbish about having to have a level of understanding before you can take Communion, it's crazy. Christ gave Communion to the disciples who very shortly were to desert him, to leave him, to deny him three times: their understanding of him was so fickle, so weak, so poor, and yet he gives them this Communion, he allows them to share in it. And we say, 'Ah, but you can't have it, because you don't *know* enough yet. You haven't been confirmed. You haven't been through our little *procedures*.'

I would give Communion to anybody. Wesley called Communion a 'converting ordinance'. It was something that *enabled* you to believe. You didn't have Communion when you were able to understand and believe, you had Communion so that you were *helped* to believe. Somebody once said to me, 'Charlie, do you realize you just gave Communion to a Buddhist?' and I said, 'Hallelujah! That's great!' Because I'm an arrogant Christian, I believe that I've got something that people should try and grasp hold of. So giving Communion to a Buddhist might help him to believe, and I think that's fantastic.

I once heard a minister say, 'All who love the Lord Jesus are welcome to come forward.' That's an evangelical way of saying, 'Come up if you're in the club.' I'd want to turn that around and say, 'All whom the Lord Jesus loves can come forward to Communion.' And that's everybody, I'm not into barrier Christianity. Yet did you know that we used to refuse Communion to people who were divorced? I had a lady who came up to the Communion rail once, and when I got to her she looked up and said, 'I'm divorced,' and put her head down again. And I turned to her, and I said, 'Would you like to take the bread and the wine?' and she said 'Yes,' and she hadn't had it for over *twenty* years.

What this Church does to people. It makes your heart bleed.

Do you know, this is just like personal therapy. Do a lot of people say that to you? 'What are we going to talk about today, then, Mary?' 'Well, what do *you* feel like talking about, Charlie?' 'Well, Mary, you see it's like this: I'm a vicar and nobody takes me *seriously*.' I went into a pub yesterday, we were having lunch with some of the local curates, and you go in with a dog-collar and they treat you like you're an idiot, you know, 'Here you are, dear, do you want your knife and fork?' Honestly, put a collar on and people think you've had your brain removed, it's incredible, it really is.

Having said that, I went to play squash last night, and to cut a long story short they'd double-booked us and we went to this private club; and when we got there the girl on reception said, 'I know you from somewhere. You're the Vicar, aren't you?' And it transpires that she comes to one of our groups at the church, so she said, 'Look, just go on for free.' So the vicar treatment is not always that bad.

I remember what I wanted to talk about today. You were asking about my relationship with God. A relationship with God, obviously, is like a relationship with anybody, in that it obviously grows and changes, and hopefully becomes better. We have ups and downs, of course, but I'd like to think that my relationship with Corinne now is different from the way it was five years ago: I'd like to think that it's deeper now, and better, and it's the same with God.

All right, now let's talk about what it means for me to be a Christian, okay? For me to be a Christian involves two things. It involves things that I do with my head and things that I do with my heart. And those two things make up who I am, and what I am. With my head I would say I am specifically a Christian, rather than just a person who believes in God. With my head I believe in the humanity of Christ, the deity of Christ, and I believe in the divinity of the Holy Spirit, that God can be experienced and known now.

Now, there are a whole load of other things around that: baptism; Communion; what are the sacraments? How is Christ present in the sacraments? You can talk about Creation: is Creation good? Is it bad? What do we believe about Creation as Christians? What I believe about all these kinds of things, over the period of my relationship with God, has changed. I would still want to see the central core of my faith – of Christ being God made man – as being important, and I would hope that wouldn't change, because I would cease to be a Christian if that was the case. I might have a relationship with God, but I wouldn't be a Christian.

The heart aspect is something I'd want to describe in terms of a commitment; in terms of believing that if those things are really true about God – and I believe that they are – then with my being I want to respond to them and make a commitment of myself to God, which I would express by constantly searching out what He wants me to do with my life.

Okay: now people will want to know what God is, who He is. I'd want to say to people who ask that question: who are we? Where do we come from? Who made us? Why is it that people feel lonely? Why is it that people feel guilty? What do we do when we feel sorry about something? I'd want to try to address some of the questions that even kiddies ask about life. 'What happened to my hamster?' 'Do we matter to God?' 'What happens to Granny when she's dead?' I talk to Alexandra, and she's three, about funerals. She says, 'Where are you going today, Daddy?' and I say, 'I'm going to do a funeral.' 'Oh dear, has somebody died?' I say, 'Yes.' She says, 'What happens when we die?' and I say, 'Well, God loves us, and God made us the way we are, and when we die we go to meet with God. He's like our father in heaven, and He cares for us.'

Jesus said, 'In my Father's house there are many mansions,' i.e. many rooms, and I always say to folk: imagine that someone is coming to stay with you in the next few days and you get the place ready for them; you put a clean towel on the bed and you hoover round and tidy up and you make the place nice. Well, God is preparing a place just now for whoever has died, and He is preparing that place for them in His house because when we die we go to stay with God for ever – and because those are the words of Christ I feel justified in using them. I think that's a fairly simple way of describing who God is, and that we're important to Him, and that He loves us. And if you want to take that deeper, if someone says, 'Well, *how* do we know that God loves us?' I say, 'Well, we wouldn't know that God loved us except for the fact that God became man in Christ, and when we look at Christ we see God.' Christ is like a window on to God. Not all of God is encapsulated in Jesus, but through him we can see what God is like: someone who cares for us, who loves us, who trudges a very lonely road to a Cross, and dies for us. And because we see a God who is prepared to do that, we can have confidence in Him.

Now, of course the whole thing's a matter of faith. And belief in Christ wouldn't be faith if we knew it for certain, if we had proof. I always say to people who don't believe in God, 'Well, do you believe in anything?' And if they say, 'I'm an atheist, I don't believe in God,' then I always say, 'Well, do you believe that we are an accident?' And actually, when you talk to them, most people do not feel like an accident. We're all unique. We each have different fingerprints, and most people do feel as if their life counts and matters, and don't want to just evaporate when they die. There is something deeper to life, and I think that when people explore that, that journey of understanding can often lead to a morsel of faith.

I don't want people to feel they must come to church as card-carrying Anglicans. I'd like to think the Church can encompass people who have little morsels of faith too, because a small faith doesn't mean an insignificant faith. You don't have to assert the Thirty-nine Articles before God loves you. You say that some people have intellectual problems with Christianity: all right, but I'm not quite sure how valid that is. You might have difficulty with who Christ is, you might have doubt, but doubt is an important part of belief. In the past we have pounced on doubts, and said, 'Oh no, Christians can't doubt that.' But doubt is to be encouraged because it's something that helps us grow. A muscle gets stronger by stretching, and so our faith gets stronger by testing. The worst thing that you can do is accept a faith which someone else has given you, and never question anything. And one of the great things about theological training is that when you go into theological college, you start exploring and whacking your Bible apart and doing all kinds of textual analysis, and your faith is suddenly, wow! It's exploding! The hope is that you come out of all that with a faith that is ten times stronger. Otherwise, when something really catastrophic happens in your life which tests you, it will fail.

The Church may have done some very courageous things in its time, but on the whole it's not what you'd call a fast mover. Take the issue of women: we should talk about that. It's only recently that we've begun to understand the contribution that women can make in the Church, and that worries me, that worries me a great deal, because it means that for 2,000 years the Church has been blind. Now we're going to allow the ordination of women. Fantastic! Yet we must keep in mind the terrible legacy we have inherited. As a Church, instead of all this recrimination, instead of wondering what we're going to say to the poor chaps who don't actually want to ordain women, all those prats who are throwing tantrums, instead we should be saying, 'How can we say sorry to all these women for all the oppression we have caused?' *Where* is the apology? The Church just cannot bring itself to say sorry, it just cannot. And why? Because it's so bloody arrogant.

One has to ask why, for 2,000 years, we have kept women out of the Church. Remember I was saying how important I think theology is? If we look at the history of the Church we get some very conflicting pictures. For instance, in the Bible, Paul, who's regarded as the great misogynist of all time, starts giving women important roles in the Church. And think of the tremendous liberation that women got out of the ministry of Jesus, where he actually taught women, which is something they hadn't had before. Jesus started a good movement for women, and Paul actually went further, by allowing them to take active roles in the Church.

Then something goes drastically wrong. We suddenly see people like Tertullian coming in and calling women 'the devil's gateway'. We suddenly see women being really downtrodden and oppressed, and I think a lot of that stemmed from a male antagonism towards women and sex – men blaming women for their own sexual desires – and it goes right the way through the group of men we call the Church Fathers. Look at people like Jerome, for example. His attitude to women was disgraceful. In that book by Karen Armstrong, *The Gospel According to Woman*, she makes you really aware of the kinds of voyeuristic hang-ups that men like Jerome had about women. And now, that disdain of women and sex has become incorporated into the thinking of the Church, and stayed there. You can't even say that the Reformation did anything particularly marvellous for women, when you look at their treatment by people like Luther and Calvin.

Now I find this really worrying because for hundreds and hundreds of years the Church thought that slavery was okay, and we justified it from scripture. For hundreds and hundreds of years we've been oppressing women, and we've justified it from scripture, and I think that should ring alarm bells in all of our minds. We certainly shouldn't be paying people to leave because we've finally got round to ordaining women. We should be *celebrating!* I mean, isn't that a bloody disgrace? If someone's conscience means they have to leave the Church, then off they should go. Conscience does have a cost, but it's *your* cost, and no one else should be paying you for it. If someone isn't able to accept others democratically recognized by the Church, then they shouldn't be in the Church in the first place. The truth is, the Church has done its sums and worked out that it can afford to do this because it will end up saving on pensions, but that's not the point. If a principle is worth fighting for, you fight for it. If a principle has to be paid for, it's not worth it. It's that simple.

It's also really hypocritical when you consider that we've been ordaining homosexual clergy folk for years and years. Okay, the attitude has been that homosexuality was all right provided it was kept under wraps, but we've been doing it, no problem. Yet lots of homosexuals are now challenging the way the Church keeps them hidden, and the Church is going to find this a very, very difficult issue because it's going to have to make its mind up. Are we saying that homosexuality is wrong and sinful, and you shouldn't be ordained as a homosexual? If that's what we are saying, then obviously there are a lot of clergy who are not going to find it possible to remain in the Church any more. Or are we saying that homosexuality is fine? If we say that, then that's going to create real shock waves, and a lot of homophobia. All I would say is this: if we were having this conversation a hundred years ago, it would probably have been unthinkable to talk about the ordination of women. Therefore we have all got to be very careful indeed about running to our Bibles and getting texts out of Leviticus saying that homosexuals should be stoned to death.

Personally – look, I've got to be honest with you. When I was in the Vice Squad I used to have to lock homosexuals up all the time. I used to have to go into toilets and catch people for importuning, and it has produced a prejudice in me. I mean, I'm heterosexual, and I can't understand how a guy could possibly want to have sex with another man, I find it incomprehensible, inconceivable. In the past, I would have run to my Bible and dragged out some oblique verse. I might have even found some verses in the New Testament which are more overt in their criticism of homosexuals, because the New Testament talks about how homosexuals shall never enter the Kingdom of Heaven, but it also talks about thieves not getting in either, so running to the Bible produces problems. This is coupled with the fact that when I go to the Bible a) I see it endorsing slavery and b) ordination's not mentioned anywhere at all.

So there's a big problem here, a dilemma. I have a theological dilemma and I have a personal dilemma in that I'm heterosexual, and it's very easy to criticize people of a different sexual orientation than your own. You know, what is good sexuality? Oh right, well, good sexuality is what I do. And what is bad sexuality? Well, it's everything that I *don't* do. So I have to be very careful about my own hang-ups.

If I'm really, really honest, and I don't want to be but you will twist my arm, I'm not ready to say, 'Go ahead. Ordain homosexuals openly.' Neither am I ready to say, 'We should not ordain homosexuals.' I think the Church ought to debate it and get it into the open, and at the moment I don't know which way I would jump. That's being truthful. Just honest. And if I have a couple come to me, who are homosexuals, and they say to me, 'Will you bless our union?' what am I going to say to them? What am I going to say to them? Bloody big problem here! Am I going to say, 'Go away, I don't want to know, you're homosexuals, you're living in sin. Homosexuals will not inherit the Kingdom of Heaven. You're wallowing in a cesspit of your own making'? Which I could say, quoting the Romans passage. Well, of *course* I'm not, but my police background has had an effect on me, and your background obviously affects your reasoning and your judgment. That doesn't mean I think I'm in a position to sit in judgment upon homosexuals, because I don't. We've had homosexuals in the Church for 2,000 years, and it seems a bit worrying – and a bit pointless – to suddenly sit in judgment now.

The History of Mistakes, that's really what the Church is, and we should admit it. Slaves, black people, women, homosexuals and divorced people: divorce and remarriage is a *real* million-dollar question. The Church has been pussy-footing around with remarriage for ages. It says, 'We will bless a remarriage, but we won't do it.' But I won't say that to people. It's down to my discretion as a minister what I do, and I will not say to somebody, 'I will bless your remarriage, but I won't do it for you,' because I think that's wrong. The Church likes to have it both ways, likes to sit on the glorious fence, but I do marriages for divorced people, because I believe that it is absolutely the only position of integrity.

This is a very difficult one for me because it involves talking to you about something very painful that I would rather leave in the past. In fact I was going to ask you to just slip it into your introduction: Charles Royden, thirty-three, can't drive, nice wife, two kids, bit of a prat – oh, and divorced. But if I'm meant to be honest, that's not really good enough, is it? And if things aren't mentioned they just become dark secrets. Moreover, if I try to imply that I don't have these difficulties, I'm just contributing to the myth about the clergy being different. Somebody once said that the definition of a saint was someone who hadn't been researched well enough, and I'm convinced that's true.

Well, it happened. I've been married before and divorced, and it had a tremendous impact on me and has obviously contributed to the person that I am. I was married at twenty and remained so until I was in theological college, in what I regarded as a perfectly happy marriage. My wife was fully involved in the plans for my transition from policeman to priest, but she decided to pursue another relationship. That was her choice and I was unable to do anything about it. This now seems very easy to reflect upon, but at the time it was an unmitigated bloody disaster. I would never have imagined such pain to be possible. The fools who speak of the ease of divorce are fortunate never to have lived the nightmare.

Divorce is not something which qualifies a person particularly well for Anglican ordination. Many people in the Church made their disapproval extremely apparent and were horrified that I wanted to continue my training for ordination. My family and friends were really supportive, and I also had a fabulous response from those who actually had to make decisions concerning my future: my college Principal and Bishop supported me, so I finished my course. And I know it sounds daft, but Mindy my dog was a real comfort. Dogs are so faithful.

However, the problem was that three years after my divorce I met Corinne. She for whom the stars shine! I met her when she was in Bedford, doing teacher-training there. I was about to graduate from Wycliffe Hall and I came over to see my brother, Ross, who was a chaplain in Bedford at the time, bumped into Corinne in Ross's kitchen, and said, 'Hey, Corinne, how do you fancy coming over to graduation?' *Terrible* pick-up line, isn't it! Terrible pick-up line! So she came over to Oxford, sat through this boring service, in Latin, incredible, and of course any girl who can sit through that can cope with anything in ministry, can't she? Anyway, we had a really great day, and a week later I sent her a letter, and in the letter were two tickets to see *King Lear*. I said to her, 'Hey, Corinne, come over to Oxford, and we'll go and see Shakespeare. PS. If you don't want to come, please could I have the tickets back and I'll take somebody else.' Awful, isn't it, really bad taste! Perhaps she should have sent the tickets back: sod off and go on your own! But she didn't, she accepted!

Within a matter of weeks I asked her to marry me, and that's when the problems started. Church law says that a man can be divorced and ordained, but he cannot be divorced, *remarried* and ordained, or at least not without special permission from the Archbishops. The result was that we had to wait until after I'd been ordained deacon and priest until we got married, nearly two years, and that felt like a long time.

Unfortunately that wasn't the end of it. I remember after ordination going to look at a parish in the Chester diocese, just outside Manchester, that needed a curate. The Vicar spent a long time showing me round until finally saying that it wouldn't be right for me to work there because people would find out I was divorced, and they had standards, you know. Well, Anglican training had obviously worked wonders, because four years earlier I'd have told him what he could do with his bloody standards. That kind of self-righteous hypocrisy was one of the things that Jesus got really mad about: he said some really offensive things about people like that. 'There but for the grace of God go I' is a very humbling phrase and we do well to remember that we all fall short.

I guess from this experience I have been able to be a little more accepting than I might otherwise have been of those who don't fit into the Church mould. And my hope is that we as a Church will be more tolerant of those who through no fault of their own, or even if it *is* their fault, find themselves in difficulties such as divorce. We still have a tendency to treat divorced

people badly. We are still made to feel like lepers, untouchables
– and we forget that those were the very people Jesus touched.

All these issues. Don't you think it's a crying shame that that's
what the Church seems to be all about? I mean, I want to talk
about the Cross, basically. I want to talk about the fact that if
my faith means anything, it means that there *is* a God, and that
that God actually bothers to get to know us. When I speak to
folk in this bloody awful world, where they are lonely and upset
and guilty and worried and fearful, I want to be able to give
them a message that God cares and God loves them, because I
think that that message is timeless and important and means an
awful lot to people. I don't want to be diverted into side issues.
The one thing I got ordained for was to preach the message of
the Cross. I don't care if I change my mind on homosexuals,
change my mind on disestablishment, change my mind on a
multitude of things throughout my ministry, provided I'm still
able to say, 'Isn't it marvellous that God still loves us, in the
midst of all our confusion?'

If we can talk about God's love, then I think that all the
things which divide us, the things which make Churches behave
like football teams playing in the same league, all that will cease
to matter. And that's the message of evangelism, which I'm
passionately concerned about. Evangelism is done through showing God's love. It's not done by clever courses and learning how
to talk about your faith, or doing what those Jehovah's Witnesses
were doing at the front door this morning, trying to argue my
next-door neighbour into heaven. People don't get argued into
heaven. You don't have a debate with someone for an hour, and
all of a sudden they say, 'Do you know what, Charlie? You're
absolutely right. I think I'll become a Christian.' People don't
become Christians like that. They become Christians through
slowly beginning to be wrapped up in the love of Christians,
one for another, and the message of love which that brings from
God. That's how it works. And when people say – understandably – that Christianity's ridiculous, because you're all fighting
amongst yourselves, because homosexuals are throwing bricks at

the heterosexuals, men are throwing bricks at women, women are throwing bricks at men, whites at blacks, evangelicals at Anglo-Catholics, I want to say, '*Forget* all that. There is something that binds us all together. The love of God.'

I think as a clergyman you've always got to be aware of your own weaknesses. You look at great religious men and see what they have done as a result of just being ordinary human beings. I'm a very pessimistic sort of person, because I do think that generally speaking we are depraved. Listen, I won enough bets on the last election to buy my satellite dish simply because I acknowledged the fact that we are all depraved, we all look to our own selves, and we vote very, very selfishly. When you acknowledge that kind of inbuilt mechanism inside us, it gives you a very realistic approach to the kind of person you are yourself, and clergy and Church people aren't immune from that. There's just as much sin in your average Parochial Church Council meeting as there is in the betting shop or the pub. Just as much.

I get really angry when I read some biographies of religious people. The kind that say they rose at five o'clock and spent two hours in prayer, did Bible study, and then went out visiting around the parish and all this kind of stuff, and you think, yeah, but where's the sin? And of course it's there, because the truth is that we're all sinful. Look at Augustine and all his dalliances with women! He had a woman and got her pregnant and then left her, yet he's a great guru of the Church, a foundation stone of the Reformation. He wasn't a saint, or at least if he was, he was the same kind of saint that I am, and that's a mucky one.

So you've always got to be so careful. Clergymen are constantly tempted, just like anyone else. I mean, I know I'm a sexual creature, and for me to say I wouldn't be tempted just because a) I'm very happily married and b) I'm a clergyman, is just ridiculous: it would be denying my own weaknesses and denying my own sexuality, as well as denying the other person's.

So if a woman comes to me and wants any more than just a one-off meeting I always direct her to another woman for the counselling to take place. And I'm always very, very careful about getting into one-to-ones with women, because of the kinds of relationship which can take place. You only need to look at the number of clergy who get involved in – how can I put it? – unfortunate relationships, things which perhaps just *happened*, to see what I mean.

So as far as sin is concerned, I think we all live in glass-houses and the clergy have to be very careful not to play with people by threatening them and saying, 'If you do not do as I say, you're going to hell.' I don't find Christ doing that. I find him really attacking and scathing of the religious people. I find him telling the religious leaders that they're hypocrites, that they're all shiny bright on the outside, and smelly bodies inside, that they're just as sinful. And yet his approach to the sinful was always, always forgiveness.

You can't deny that you do come across real evil sometimes. I can look back and think of people I dealt with when I was a policeman. I remember this guy, a convicted rapist who'd reoffended and was proud of it, proud of his convictions for rape. That is evil. That is really horrible, and I don't honestly think that talking to someone like that in terms of saying that they should feel sorry, or they should feel afraid of burning in hell, is going to do them any good. But I don't know how God deals with that, I really don't. I'm much more concerned with dealing with those people who are trying to make sense of God's forgiveness *despite* the evil they have done.

I'm not really into dealing with evil in the religious sense, because you just end up going round in circles, but I'm quite into talking about crime and punishment in the here and now. I mean, take multiple rapists: I'd castrate them. No problem. I just don't think that there's any justification for locking people up for life instead, just to make society feel as if it's not taking some kind of illiberal stance. I must also confess that I would have no problem over certain capital punishment sentences. So many people have committed murder, and have gone on to do it again, and again, and again, and society keeps giving them another chance, and another chance, and another chance. And if I were to catch the guys who plant bombs and blow up kids and innocent people, I wouldn't just say, 'Oh well, let's hope that they repent!' No way! But I think society goes on appeasing murderers simply so that it can say, 'Ah, but we're *enlightened*.' We're not enlightened. We live in a grubby world, a fallen world.

Now, I know it's not ideal, but you show me what an ideal is, and I'll go for it. I don't find it easy to say this, because people will think I'm one of the hang 'em and flog 'em brigade, and I'm not into that. But when you see real evil, sometimes the only thing you can do is rid society of the menace. We're never going to grow to some eventual stage where humanity comes of age; never. Evil will always be with us and we'll always have to deal with it. I don't see any other way of dealing with it than saying, 'Those who live by the sword die by the sword.' I used to be much more right-wing and aggressive over it than I am now. When I was in the police force, people used to ask, 'Would you slip the catch on the hatch and hang these fellows?' and all the guys I worked with would have said yes – including me. I mean, what do you do with people when they chop other people to bits? You know, it's very nice to sit in a study surrounded by books and talk about our liberal attitudes and how we want to reform these characters: when you're actually con- fronted with the blood and the mess, you have to do some- thing.

If you speak to many of the old-time evangelicals about sin, they will want you to talk about hell, but I won't, and as a result I'm regarded by them as being wishy-washy. What I do say is that God made us, God loves us, God cares for us, and when we die we have to trust the words of that verse in Genesis where it says, 'Will not the judge of all the earth do right?' I say that God knows better than I do about judgment. I might have some strong views about the here and now but when it comes to heavenly judgment I haven't got a clue.

We were talking about doubt before, and it's a very important part of it. If I sat here and pretended that I had an answer for everything, I'd be wrong, because I don't, and as a Christian teacher I have to say, 'I cannot give you the answer to sin and evil.' I always think that sin is a little bit like my computer, you know, occasionally in the early days of using it I'd put a load of stuff on the hard disc and press a button and it would be gone, disappeared. And it makes me think about the Psalm in the Bible when God says, 'As far as the East is from the West, I put your sin away.' It's beautiful, that. It's really beautiful. As far as the east is from the west: that's how far God puts our sin from Himself. It's only us who keep dredging it back up again.

You sometimes hear people talk about going into the Church as a career, and when you look in *Crockford's Clerical Directory* at people in senior positions, you can see what they mean. These people start their career off in a good public school; they go to college, a decent college, preferably after Oxford or Cambridge; then they'll go and do a curacy somewhere; then perhaps they'll go into a theological college and do a bit of lecturing; then they'll maybe make rural dean or go straight on to becoming a bishop.

Now I've always found it hard to look at the Church as a career. I have no career objective. I really don't know what each year is going to bring, to be honest with you. Will I still be a minister in ten years' time, even? Or will God call me to something else? I don't know, but I'm open to that. When I was ordained priest, they said, 'You're now getting something no one can ever take away from you: you're a priest for ever – even after death!' I wonder about that whole idea, really. It's not for me. Yes, I was ordained, and we prayed for God's holy spirit to enable me to do that task which He had called me to do: but does that mean I can say to God, 'I'm not going to change, because you've made me a priest'? Why could I not leave and do something else? Lots of men have been ordained as priests and have done other things in the Church and outside the Church, so I'm open to whatever might come along. God willing I'll hit the right button. I mean, we were talking about guidance, weren't we, yesterday, and it's hit and miss. You pray that God opens the right doors and closes the wrong ones. But Corinne and I have talked about this, and we really don't know what will be in store for us – and it would be pretty boring if we did. If all I had to look forward to was going from this step to that step to the other step, eventually reaching a level of achievement in the Church, then – oh, my goodness – I think I'd give up tomorrow. That would drive me over the edge.

Just before I actually got ordained I went through a lot of difficulty with the whole idea of being a priest. It was stupid, really, but the thing is, I had to go off on a silent retreat before I was ordained as a priest. Well, I'd already been on one when I was ordained as a deacon, and that was quite enough for me, but no, we had to go away *again* on another weekend where we couldn't talk to one another.

Well, can you imagine me in a place where I can't talk to anyone! Can you imagine it? You're stuck there all weekend, and even at mealtimes you can't talk, and you're sitting there and you want the salt and it's down the bottom end of the table, and you've got some prat playing Bach or something in the background, and you think, 'How am I going to get the salt up here without *talking* to anyone?' And I'm sitting there, and I'm really having trouble with this, I really am. Big, big crisis! It was bad as well because the women I was ordained deacon with weren't allowed to come and I had a problem with that: I was having another ordination because I was a man, and they weren't because they were women, and I thought, hey, what am I *doing*?

Anyway, I remember getting quite hung-up about the whole bloody thing that weekend, and I remember ringing a guy up, a friend of mine who lived not too far away, it was kind of like a 999 call, and I rang him up and said, 'Brian, I'm going out of my tiny mind in this place, I can't even ask people to pass the salt! What the hell am I doing?' And he came and waited for me outside, and I sneaked out of this place, and we went to the pub. When we got back, I said, 'Come in, I'll give you a coffee.' He said, 'But I can't come in there. You're not allowed visitors.' So I said, 'Oh, come on,' and we sneaked over the wall, because they'd locked the gates, and we were wandering through the gardens and there's this row of stairs leading down to my room, and I'd left the window open. Anyway, you know those old stone pillars with a ball at the top, that they have by the gates in big houses: well, there were these pillars and I put my hand on one of these balls, you see, and the bloody thing rolled off. So it starts rolling down this slope, and I have to chase after it, and I'd had a couple of pints of lager and I'm rolling around with this enormous great big stone ball, and Brian's going, 'Ssshhhh!' And I go, 'It's all right for *you*, mate, it's me who's getting ordained.'

You'll get me bloody shot, you will, if you put this in. But you know, I'm serious about it. It was a real farce that weekend. I mean, listen, if I'd gone in to those non-speaking meals and played a *Right Said Fred* album, people would have said, 'That's disgusting! This is a silent retreat, and you're playing *Right Said Fred*?!' But if I was to put on *Mozart*, right? That's *okay*, that's the *done thing*. *Mozart*! Mozart was a real bender, wasn't he! Well, he was. Have you seen the film about him? There you are, then. I mean, I like some of Mozart, Mozart's great. Magnificent. But to somehow think that Mozart is morally superior to other kinds of music is ridiculous, and that kind of attitude is so endemic in the Church; it's cultural imperialism, isn't it? Got to fit into our mould, you see. Got to appreciate our architecture, got to listen to our music, got to speak our language. Otherwise it's: sorry, but you just don't fit.

I find that kind of attitude so sad, such a waste. It puts so many people off, and within the Church itself there are so many people falling out with one another. You've got the very High Church folk on the one side; you've got those on the evangelical side of things; then in the middle you have got ecumenical folk saying, 'Let's not put up barriers, let's just get on with life together.' I've even written to other denominations round here and said, 'Let's do things together,' and they've written back and said, 'No way.' I think that that's very sad, because it's great to have diversity, great to put away the things we think are sacrosanct. After all, it's not the distinctions that are important, it's the things that we share.

In terms of other faiths, if I start saying anything other than Christ is God, I'm being dishonest, aren't I? If I believe that Christ was God, the Messiah, then the Jews have missed him, Islam has missed him, the Buddhists have missed him. And this isn't something that we can negotiate as Christians. Take away Christ as God and I cease to be a Christian. I might be a God-fearer, but that's not the same thing. That's not to say that those people who are not on that path are all going to burn in hell. That's not what I'm saying at all. But I am saying that there is something special in Christianity that needs to be communicated, and that's why I believe in the importance of mission, of preaching and teaching who Christ was, and doing it now. Today.

Isn't it funny: we live in this world, and I suppose it gives us tremendous security to think that Christ isn't coming again. Because that way we can just get on with all our paraphernalia, and our rules and regulations and the things that occupy us. But when you start talking in terms of this world having a shelf-life, then things take on different priorities. I think if we could recapture the fact that Christ is returning, that Christ is coming back and expects us to be waiting for him, things would be very different, because the return of Christ imposes upon us an urgency about what we are doing.

There was a guy at church, when I was fourteen, called Arthur Blessed. Arthur was a bit of a radical, a bit of a way-out, and he always used to say that if you went down a road and saw a house on fire, you wouldn't go to the door in a very timid way and ring the bell and say, 'Excuse me, I believe your house is on fire.' You'd ring the bell and if nobody answered the door the first time, you'd bash it down to help the people trapped inside. And in a sense the return of Christ places upon the Church an importance about its mission, an importance about what's going on, because the important thing is that Christ is coming back, and let's tell people about that, let's get ready, let's break the door down.

But you do have to be careful as a Church. I could go round and do what the Jehovah's Witnesses do, but that just puts people off. I've said to you, nobody's argued into the Kingdom of Heaven. That's not the way. I think the way is to make an impact, and I would seek to make an impact in this parish by doing very ordinary sorts of things: dealing with people when their babies are ill; visiting them in hospital when they're poorly; baptizing their babies; presiding at funerals; meeting people when they are upset or want to talk about God and who He is; just getting involved in the *stuff* of life.

That's why I'm here, you know? That's why I'm here. People often say to me, 'Charlie, which is better: the Church or the police?' And I say, 'Get *away*! The police every time!' But Christ gives us a challenge to reassess our priorities, and that's what I did. And you ask me if I *honestly* think Christ will come again! Hey! Listen! Do you really think I'd have given up a job I loved if I didn't? Do you really think I'd be stuck in this job, working in this Church, having to put up with its pettiness and prejudice and in-fighting, and endure the kind of ridicule I endure when I walk down the road in a dog-collar if I didn't believe passionately that there was something else? I can tell you I wouldn't. Absolutely no way. I would not be doing this unless I believed passionately that Christ is coming again and that there is life after death in God's presence.